# PageMaker 3
## by Example

PC Version

M&T BOOKS

# PageMaker 3
## by Example

PC Version

**David Webster
Tony Webster**

M&T Publishing, Inc.
Redwood City, California

**M&T Books**
A Division of M&T Publishing, Inc.
501 Galveston Drive
Redwood City, CA 94063

**M&T Books**
*General Manager,* Ellen Ablow
*Editorial Project Manager,* Michelle Hudun
*Project Editor,* David Rosenthal
*Editorial Assistant,* Kurt Rosenthal
*Cover Designer,* Michael Hollister
*Cover Photographer,* Michael Carr

© 1989 by M&T Publishing, Inc.
Printed in the United States of America
First Edition published 1988. Reprinted 1989
Originally published by Webster & Associates.

All rights reserved. No part of this book may be reproduced or transmitted in any form or by any means, electronic or mechanical, including photocopying, recording, or by any information storage and retrieval system, without prior written permission from the Publisher. Contact the Publisher for information on foreign rights.

Library of Congress Cataloging in Publication Data
Webster, David.
   PageMaker 3 by Example / David Webster and Tony Webster.
      p.   cm.
   Includes index
   1. Desktop publishing.
   2. PageMaker (Computer program).
   3. IBM PC (Computer) -- Programming.
    I. Webster, Tony, 1940- .   II. Title.

LCN  89-061855

ISBN 1-55851-050-8 : $22.95

93   92   91   90        5   4   3

Adobe Illustrator and PostScript are trademarks of Adobe Systems, Inc.
Arts & Letters is a trademark of Computer Support Corp.
AutoCAD is a trademark of Autodesk, Inc.
Headline is a trademark of Corel Systems Corp.
IBM is a registered trademark of IBM Corp.
LaserWriter is a trademark of Apple Computer, Inc.
Macintosh is a trademark of McIntosh Laboratories, Inc.
Microsoft Word, Microsoft Windows, Microsoft Windows Write,
and Microsoft Windows Paint are trademarks of Microsoft Corp.
1-2-3 is a registered trademark of Lotus Development Corp.
PageMaker is a trademark of Aldus Corp.
Personal System/2 is a trademark of IBM Corp.
Publisher's Paintbrush is a trademark of ZSoft Corp.
Windows Draw and In-a-Vision are trademarks of Micrografx, Inc.

# Preface

This book has been written to make PageMaker 3 as easy to understand and use as possible.

Its contents and approach are based on over 1000 hours of classroom training with a variety of desktop publishing packages. It can be used as a self-paced training book for individual teaching, or it can be used as the workbook for classroom training.

The book is broken up into modules where each progressive module covers more detailed operation of PageMaker. Each module includes an information section as well as a detailed exercise (except for Module 1).

## Self-Paced Operation

For those PageMaker users who purchase this book to help them learn the many new concepts of version 3, the approach outlined in the following paragraphs is suggested.

As indicated above, each module contains an information section which is designed to introduce and outline the associated concepts. This part of each module should be read first. This information section complements the PageMaker manuals by providing many examples of how different concepts are utilized. Extensive use of screen illustrations helps to reinforce the learning process.

Following on from the information section is an exercise for each module (except the first). These exercises are summarized on one page at the front, so that people of all levels of experience with PageMaker can use them to gain maximum benefit. Those people, for example, who are feeling confident, can attempt the exercises without further assistance. For those who need further prompting, the detailed steps for each exercise are also included. Again, extensive screen illustrations are included with each exercise solution, making them as simple as possible to understand.

These exercises use sample files that are included with the PageMaker system. Depending upon your geographical location, publications or templates that you open with Pagemaker may be designed for A4 or Letter pages. In some cases, your sample files may differ slightly from those contained in our exercises. This should not make any difference to the thrust of these exercises, however.

## Classroom Operation

In classroom use, the attendees work through each module in conjunction with the course instructor. Instead of the user reading the information section of each module, the instructor would explain the concepts in front of the class. The attendees are strongly recommended to keep this information on hand for future reference.

The exercise sections are then attempted by the attendees on their own as part of the classroom tuition. As for the self-paced approach, these exercises may be attempted without assistance, or worked through by following the detailed steps that are included.

There are thirteen modules contained within this book. Each one covers a separate section of PageMaker and can be considered individually. Later modules, however, require knowledge which is explained in earlier sections.

Good luck in learning PageMaker. We hope this book contibutes to your success with this package.

## Acknowledgments

We would like to acknowledge the assistance of the following organizations and people who helped in the production of this book:

- Aldus Corporation, including John O'Halloran, Ben A. Rotholtz, and Bernie Bowers.
- InfoMagic, the Australian Distributor for Aldus.
- Barbara Larter, who assisted in proofreading.
- IBM Australia, including Paul Walker, for assistance in taking screen shots.

## Limits of Liability and Disclaimer of Warranty

The Authors and Publisher of this book have used their best efforts in preparing the book and the examples contained in it. These efforts include the development, research, and testing of the theories and programs to determine their effectiveness.

The Authors and Publisher make no warranty of any kind, expressed or implied, with regard to these programs or the documentation contained in this book. The Authors and Publisher shall not be liable in any event for incidental or consequential damages in connection with, or arising out of, the furnishing, performance, or use of these examples.

# Contents

## Module 1—Starting up PageMaker    13

Menus...15
Starting a PageMaker document...20
Title bar...23
The Toolbox...24
Style and Color palettes...26
Page number icons...28
The page...29
The pasteboard...29
The rulers...30
The scroll bars...31
Page views...34
The Preferences command...37
Undo command...38
Close (File menu) command...38
The Close (System menu) and Exit (File menu) command...39
Using PageMaker with Windows...40
Full Windows...41
Run-time Windows...43
The Windows menu...47

## Module 2—Loading Files into PageMaker    49

Treatment of files...51
Loading files...52
Options for importing text...63

**Module 2 Exercise    65**


## Module 3—Manipulating PageMaker Text Blocks    77

Moving text...79
Resizing text blocks...80
Resizing vertically...81
Resizing horizontally...83
Column guides...84
Margin guides...87
Warning about guides...90
Reflowing and following on text...91
Automatic text flow...94
Semi-automatic text flow...95
Temporarily changing text flow modes...96
Resizing multiple text blocks...97
Removing text blocks...98

**Module 3 Exercise    101**

## Module 4—PageMaker Text Editing    115

Correcting errors...116
Deleting letters...117
Adding text...118
Moving the flashing cursor...119
Deleting more than one character at a time...121
Changing text attributes...125
Type specs command...127
Some font, size, and style examples...132
Paragraph command...133
Indents/tabs command...138
Spacing...142
Define styles command...145
Creating new text files...146
Exporting text...151

**Module 4 Exercise    155**


## Module 5—PageMaker Internal Graphics    175

Altering graphics...179
Changing borders and fills...179
Moving...182
Resizing...183
Editing...184
Changing the printing order of graphics...186
Transparent and solid graphics...188
Rounded-corner drawing tool...189
Line drawing tools...189
Rulers...190
Multiple selections...195
Setting the graphic default...196
Maintaining aspect ratio...197
Wraparounds...197

**Module 5 Exercise    199**

## Module 6—Introduction to Imported Graphics   219

Importing graphics...222
Moving graphics...226
Simple wraparounds...227
Graphic resizing...230
Proportional resizing...232
Graphics cropping...233

**Module 6 Exercise   237**

## Module 7—PageMaker Advanced Picture Formatting   251

Introduction...252
Irregular wraparounds...252
Altering the appearance of graphics...259

**Module 7 Exercise   267**

## Module 8—PageMaker Master Pages   277

Theory...278
Master page icons...278
Document changes and guides...279
Text and graphics additions...280
Headers, footers, and page numbers...281
Removing master items...284

**Module 8 Exercise   287**

## Module 9—PageMaker Templates   303

Creating templates...304
Text and graphic placeholders...310

Graphic placeholders..310
Text placeholders...312
Heading placeholders...314

**Module 9 Exercise        317**

## Module 10—PageMaker Printing    331

The Control Panel...332
Errors...342
Creating print files...344

**Module 10 Exercise       347**

## Module 11—PageMaker Style Sheets    353

Adding new styles to a style sheet...355
No style...356
Body text and other default styles...357
Defining styles from scratch...357
Applying styles...362
Editing styles...364
Removing styles...367
Basing a new style's definition on one of the current publication's existing styles...368
Renaming styles...371
Copy an existing style sheet from another publication...371
Importing styles with the imported word-processed document...373
Overriding styles...374

**Module 11 Exercise       375**

## Module 12—Setting PageMaker Defaults   395

Introduction...396
Application defaults...397
Publication defaults...398
Protecting defaults...400

**Module 12 Exercise   401**

## Module 13—PageMaker Color   411

Using color...413
Paper...413
Black...414
Registration...414
Other default colors...414
Creating new colors...415
RGB...417
HLS...418
CMYK...418
Editing colors...420
Removing colors...420
Copying colors...421
Applying colors...421

**Module 13 Exercise   423**

## Appendix A—Keyboard Shortcuts   437

## About the Authors   439

## Index   441

# Module 1

# Starting Up PageMaker

# Starting Up PageMaker

In this first module we are going to look at PageMaker basics, including the screen, menus, palettes, and other tools, and see how these are used together to create, modify, close, and open your publications.

This training material is not designed to teach you how to use a PC. Although it is not necessary to know how to use the operating system of your machine (MS-DOS or Microsoft Windows, for example), a little knowledge in this area would certainly help.

PageMaker 3 is designed to run under an operating environment known as *Windows* (version 2.03 and above). It can be run two ways—either with a Windows *run-time* version, or the *full* version (run-time is provided with PageMaker). In this module we look at running PageMaker with a run-time version—basically the only difference apart from the multitasking capabilites of Windows is the way PageMaker is opened. See the Full Windows and Run-time Windows sections towards the end of this module for more details on operating PageMaker with Windows.

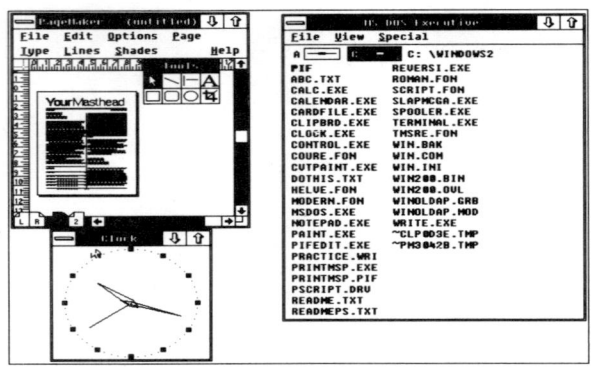

*Figure 1.* The full version of Microsoft Windows allows several programs to be run together, as well as allowing DOS operations to be performed.

To start PageMaker, assuming that it is installed correctly on your machine, is simply a matter of typing PM<Return>.

After performing the operation as listed above, your screen will appear as shown in Figure 2. This is the PageMaker *desktop*—at this stage we have not yet created a new publication or opened a current one. This requires additional steps.

*Module 1 - Starting Up PageMaker*

*Figure 2.* Upon opening PageMaker, you will be greeted with a screen similar to this.

## Menus

For the moment, let's look at PageMaker's *menus* (Figure 3).

The menus are the names at the top of the screen—names that include: **File, Edit, Options, Page, Type, Lines, Shades,** and **Help**. Each one of these menus contains several *commands* that are used to help put a publication together.

To see the contents of these *drop-down* menus, move the mouse over any of the menu names and click the mouse button. The list of commands relevant to that menu will drop down (Figure 4). To get rid of the menu invoked, move the mouse away from that menu, and click the mouse button again. The menu will then disappear.

Alternatively, a menu can be temporarily invoked by moving the mouse to a particular menu and holding down the mouse button. Moving the mouse away from the menu and releasing the mouse button causes the menu to disappear.

*Figure 3. The menu bar.*

*Module 1 - Starting Up PageMaker*

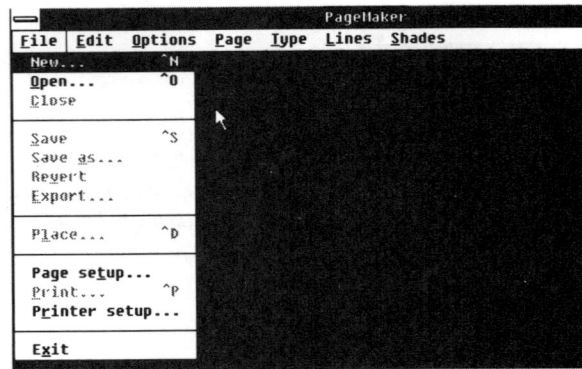

**Figure 4.** *A menu is activated by moving the mouse so that the cursor is on top of one of the menu names, and then clicking the mouse button.*

In any particular menu, there are a number of commands listed. Some of these commands appear in black, while others are listed in gray. If a command is listed in gray, it cannot be selected at the current time. Some other function must be performed before the command can be selected.

Commands listed in black are selected by moving the mouse over them and clicking. The command you clicked on has now been selected.

A command can also be selected by holding down the mouse button on a menu name, running the mouse down the menu, highlighting the command in reverse video, and then releasing the button.

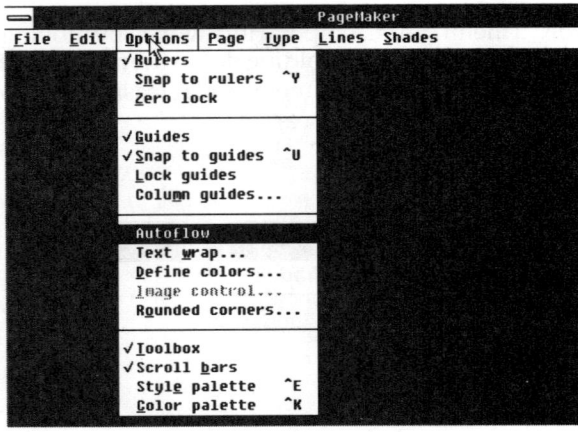

**Figure 5.** *A command is activated by clicking the mouse button on a menu to invoke it, and then clicking on the command you would like to use—here we invoke the Autoflow command from the* **Options** *menu.*

*Module 1 - Starting Up PageMaker*

An alternative to selecting a command in the above fashion is to select the command using the *shortcut key method*. Every menu name and command has one letter that is underlined that can be used to invoke this command. However, menus and commands are selected slightly differently from one another.

All *menus* can be selected by holding down the Alt key and pressing a letter—either F, E, O, P, T, L, S, or H (the first letter in each menu name). After doing this, the relevant menu will drop.

After a menu has been dropped, any *command* in that menu can be selected by pressing, on the keyboard, the letter underlined in that command name (*without* holding the Alt key). That command will then be selected.

In this way, commands can be selected far more quickly than with the mouse alone—although the shortcut key method can be used in conjunction with the mouse if need be.

*Figure 6*. A menu can be invoked by holding down the Alt key in conjunction with the underlined letter in the menu name.

*Figure 7*. Once the menu has been invoked, any command can be selected from that menu by clicking on the keyboard the underlined letter in that command name.

Other menus have function keys or control keys to invoke certain commands. The **Type** menu, for example, allows you to use its commands by hitting function keys—bypassing menus altogether. It also allows you to hold down the Ctrl key with some letters to use commands (Ctrl-T for *Type Specs*, Ctrl-M for *Paragraph*, etc.).

*Module 1 - Starting Up PageMaker*

Other commands within different menus have ellipsis marks following them; for example, the *New, Open, Save as, Export, Place, Page setup,* and *Print* commands from the **File** menu as shown in Figure 8. All these commands (and they occur in a number of different menus) open a *dialog box.* The **Type** menu in Figure 9 gives other examples.

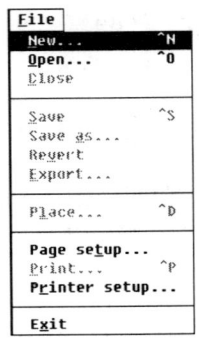

*Figure 8. The different commands within the **File** menu that include the ellipsis are clearly seen.*

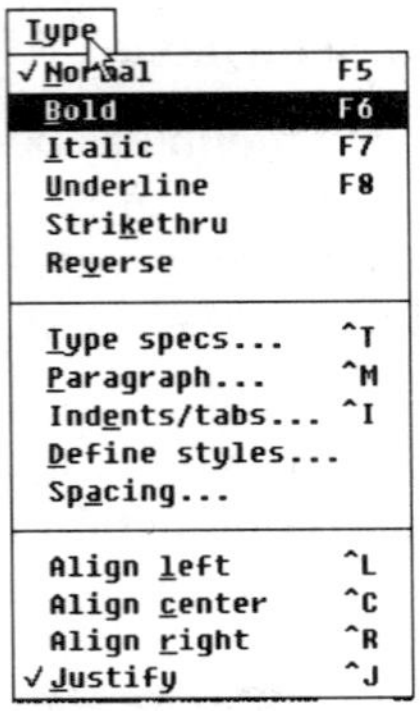

*Figure 9. The **Type** menu also includes commands with ellipsis marks for opening dialog boxes.*

A dialog box (Figures 10 and 11) is basically a selection of features presented when certain commands are invoked. A dialog box appears as a rectangular window sitting in the middle of the page, a list of several choices within. Many commands use dialog boxes, and most are vastly different from one another.

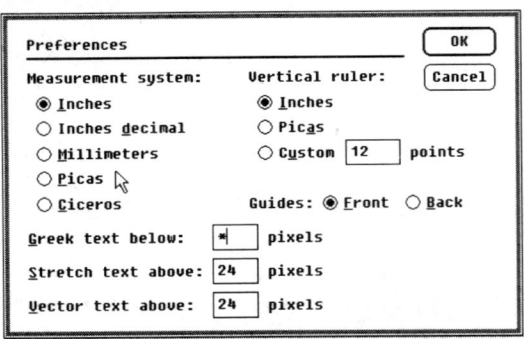

*Figure 10. Dialog boxes appear after invoking many commands in the PageMaker menus. A dialog box simply gives you more control over the execution of the command. This dialog box represents the Preferences command from the **Edit** menu.*

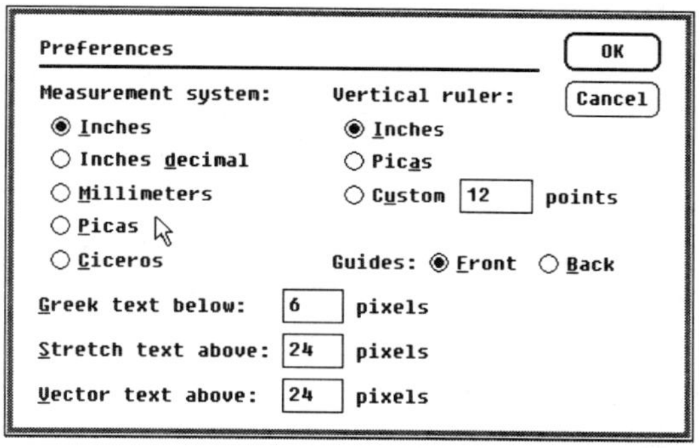

*Module 1 - Starting Up PageMaker*

*Figure 11.* Choices can be made from the dialog box by clicking the mouse button in the circles, boxes, or text areas.

Although circles and boxes within a dialog box represent options to be selected, a group of circles usually means that only one of this group can be selected at any one time. Small squares usually represent several options which can be invoked together. A filled circle or a checked box is a selected option.

Text squares, the larger rectangles, require you to click in the squares with the mouse, and use the Backspace or Delete key to erase the current words or numbers (if there are any), then use the keyboard to insert the new values. Upon opening a dialog box, some of these larger text squares often show a number in reverse video. To replace the particular number, you type in directly without deleting anything that may have already been there.

For example, see Figure 13; under Page size, only one group of circles can be selected (in our case it is Letter). Under Options are the small squares, and in our case we have checked both. The larger text squares include the different Margin dimensions. We have typed our own values into these. After selecting all the choices you like within a dialog box, either select OK by clicking on it, or press the Return key.

If you invoke a dialog box by accident, or you select the wrong options within a dialog box, press the Cancel button.

Three things may happen after selecting a command in a menu. First, it may appear as though absolutely nothing has happened. In this case, you may simply have activated a command that does not become apparent until a certain task is performed. Second, you may be confronted with a dialog box. Third, a visible change may take place on the screen.

19

*Module 1 - Starting Up PageMaker*

## Starting a PageMaker document

A PageMaker document is referred to as a *publication*. We can create new publications, or edit existing publications. By opening a publication we bring it into the computer's memory and onto the screen.

As you open PageMaker you are not immediately thrust into a new publication. As we indicated above, it is up to you to decide whether you want to open up a new or an existing publication.

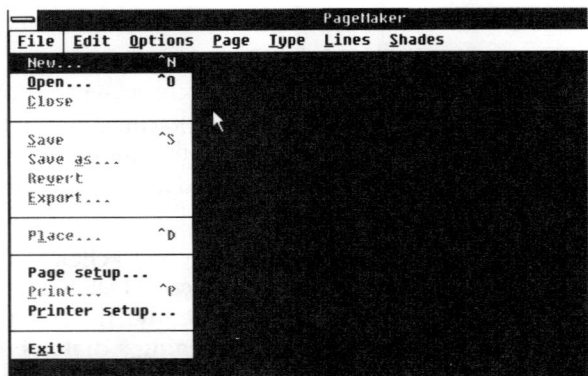

*Figure 12.* A new PageMaker publication is opened by selecting the New command from the **File** menu. Alternatively, you could have chosen an existing publication by selecting Open.

To open up a new publication you must select the *New* command from the **File** menu (Figure 12). Upon doing so, you will be presented with the dialog box of Figure 13. This is the dialog box you will be confronted with every time you wish to create a new publication.

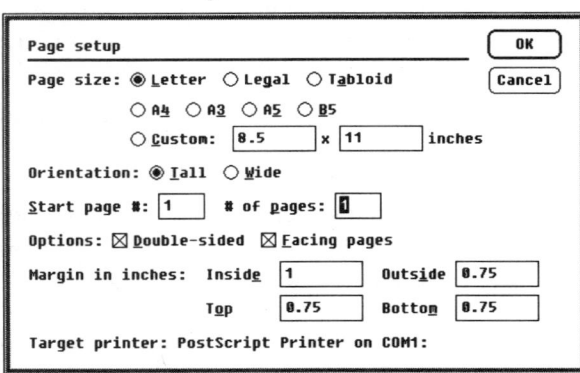

*Figure 13.* Every time the New command is opened, this dialog box appears. Basically, it askes you to specify what kind of page (and how many) you want to use for this new document.

Your first choice is what page size to use (Figure 14). All the traditional sizes are included, but if they are not, you can create your own special page. Every time a page size is selected, its actual size is listed in the two boxes next to the word Custom. If you want to create a special page, click in the circle that says Custom, and insert whatever page size you like in the two boxes to the right.

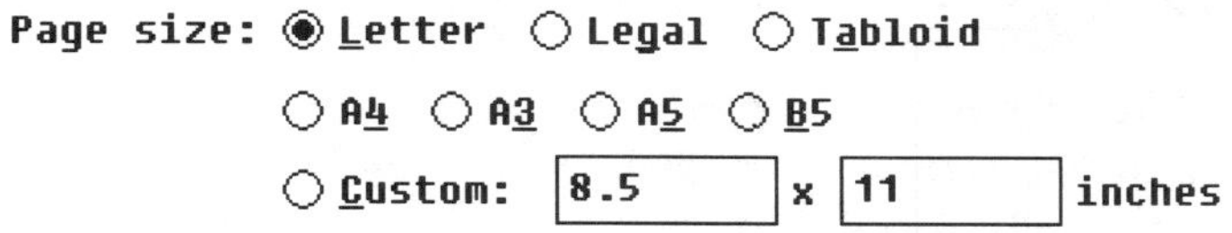

```
Page size: ⦿ Letter   ○ Legal   ○ Tabloid
           ○ A4  ○ A3  ○ A5  ○ B5
           ○ Custom:  [8.5]  x  [11]       inches
```

*Figure 14. The Page size options.*

Your next choice is whether to use a *portrait* (vertical or tall) or a *landscape* (horizontal or wide) page (Figure 15). These two types of pages cannot be mixed in the same document.

```
Orientation: ⦿ Tall   ○ Wide
```

*Figure 15. The page orientation options.*

The next line asks you what page number you would like to start on, and how many pages you would like to use in this publication (Figure 16). Keep in mind that any of the choices made in this dialog box can be altered after the publication has been opened, except for the number of pages. (This is changed differently as we will see later.)

```
Start page #: [1]    # of pages: [1]
```

*Figure 16. The Start page and number of pages options.*

Your other options are whether to use *Double-sided* pages, and whether or not to use *Facing pages* (Figure 17). You will find that publications are much easier to work with if both of these commands are selected (they are selected if a cross appears in the little box next to each command). When these two choices are selected, it is possible to view and work with two pages at a time.

Obviously you would not choose Double-sided if you are working with a publication that only prints on one side of the page. Generally, this type of publication is rare.

```
Options: ☒ Double-sided   ☒ Facing pages
```

*Figure 17. The Double-sided and Facing pages options.*

## Module 1 - Starting Up PageMaker

Your final choice is the margins for your particular page (Figure 18). These will cause guides to appear on the page—guides that will not print, but will display on the screen to make sure text and graphics are in the right position on the page.

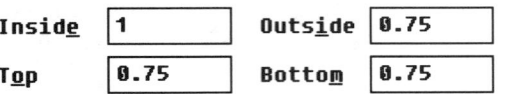

*Figure 18. The page Margin options.*

After choosing the correct page setup details as shown in Figures 13 to 18, you then click on OK (or press the Return or Enter key), to bring you into the initial publication window. This is shown in Figure 19.

The target printer is also displayed along the bottom of the dialog box—make sure that this is the printer you intend to use before you start the publication. (To change the target printer, see Module 10—PageMaker Printing.)

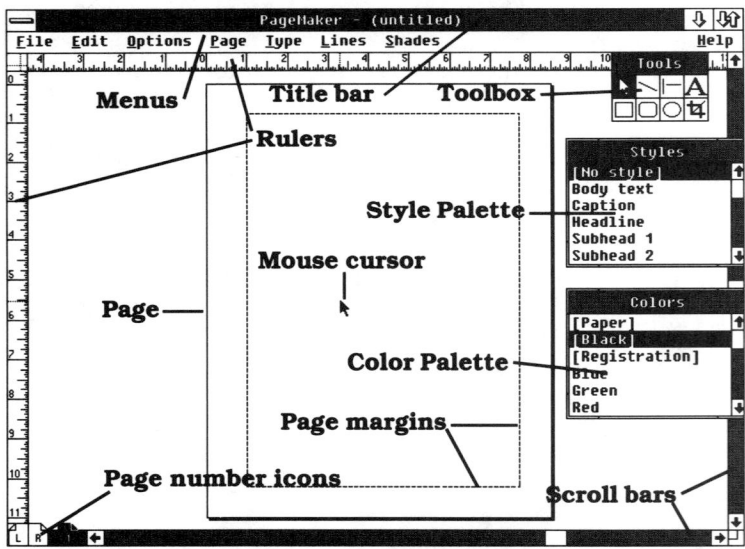

*Figure 19.* The initial publication window. Not everything in this window will necessarily appear on your screen at first, so there is no need to panic.

We will now look at the different components highlighted in Figure 19 in more detail.

*Module 1 - Starting Up PageMaker*

Before we look at the page itself, note that the *Page setup* command in the **File** menu, once invoked, uses a dialog box similar to that of *New* (Figure 13). The majority of the options selected when you choose *New* can be altered using this *Page setup* command, while inside the publication.

## Title bar

The title bar is the shaded strip just above the menu names. At this stage, the name in the middle of this bar of Figure 19 reads PageMaker - (untitled). This means that a new publication has just been opened, and has not yet been saved. After a publication has been saved, its name replaces the word *untitled*.

The title bar also contains, right in the top left-hand corner of the screen, the **System** menu icon. This menu, once invoked, allows you to Move, Size, Minimize, or Maximize the window, and use the Clipboard, Notepad, and Spooler. (To use these commands, see the Windows section of this module.)

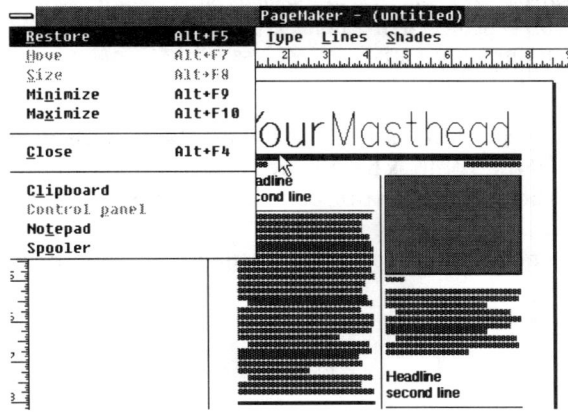

*Figure 20. The PageMaker* **System** *menu (common to all Windows applications).*

In the top right-hand corner of the title bar are two arrows—one pointing up, and the other down. Clicking on the right-hand arrow maximizes screen area. For this reason, always make sure you click on this right-hand arrow when you start PageMaker—it makes it much easier to use. The use of these arrows is also described in more detail in the Windows section of this module.

*Module 1 - Starting Up PageMaker*

## The Toolbox

The *Toolbox* is a feature of PageMaker that is used very heavily. It is, literally, the box from which we select a tool to perform a certain task. To select a tool, simply click the mouse on that tool. The title of your Toolbox may read *Toolbox* rather then *Tools* (as in Figure 21)—this changes with different screen types.

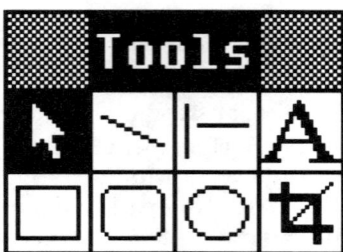

*Figure 21. A blown-up picture of the Toolbox—usually situated near the top right-hand corner of the screen—although it can be moved around at will. Currently, the pointer tool is selected.*

Before we actually look at each of the available tools in more detail, note that the Toolbox has its own title bar, one with similar properties to the publication title bar. The Toolbox can be moved around by holding down the mouse button on its title. It can also be hidden or shown by selecting the *Toolbox* command from the **Options** menu.

*Figure 22. The selector or pointer tool.*

The first tool in the Toolbox is the selector or pointer tool. This tool is used most of the time, as it is the one that must be used to select most elements on the page. Its use will become much more apparent as you work with PageMaker more and more.

24

*Module 1 - Starting Up PageMaker*

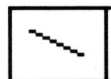

*Figure 23.* The diagonal-line drawing tool.

The second tool is the diagonal-line drawing tool—this creates only straight lines, but in any direction. Freehand drawings cannot be created within PageMaker. Holding down the Shift key allows this tool to become identical to the perpendicular-line drawing tool (below).

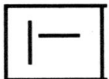

*Figure 24.* The perpendicular-line drawing tool.

The third tool is the perpendicular-line drawing tool. This tool allows only straight lines at 45-degree angles to be created. This is especially useful for creating forms, intercolumnn rules, and for any lines that must be either horizontal or vertical.

*Figure 25.* The text tool.

Following the perpendicular line drawing tool is the text tool. This tool is the one to select to edit text in PageMaker, to create text, or to change the properties of existing text.

25

*Module 1 - Starting Up PageMaker*

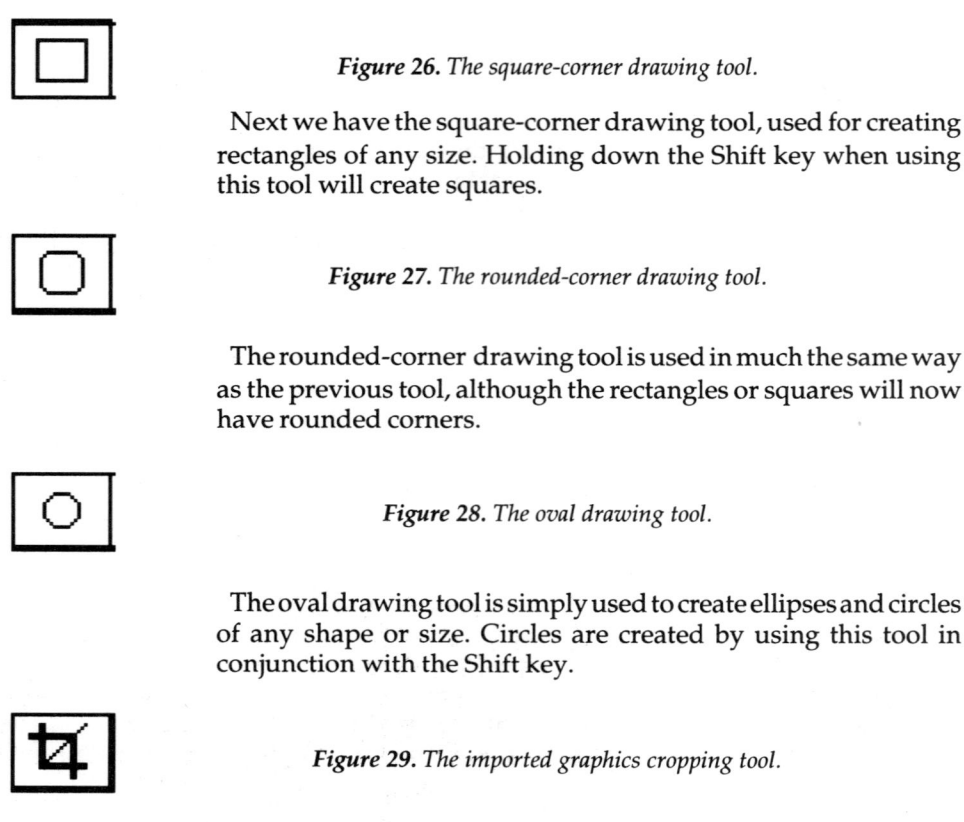

*Figure 26. The square-corner drawing tool.*

Next we have the square-corner drawing tool, used for creating rectangles of any size. Holding down the Shift key when using this tool will create squares.

*Figure 27. The rounded-corner drawing tool.*

The rounded-corner drawing tool is used in much the same way as the previous tool, although the rectangles or squares will now have rounded corners.

*Figure 28. The oval drawing tool.*

The oval drawing tool is simply used to create ellipses and circles of any shape or size. Circles are created by using this tool in conjunction with the Shift key.

*Figure 29. The imported graphics cropping tool.*

Finally on the Toolbox is the graphics cropping tool. This tool is used to remove portions of imported graphics—much like a knife.

## Style and Color palettes

Figures 30 and 31 indicate the *Style* and *Color palettes* offered with PageMaker.

The Style palette allows you to select text and change its style according to a preset style type. For example, you may decide that your normal text within a publication is to be set at 10 point Palatino with 12 point line spacing, 2 point spacing after each paragraph, justified, a first line indent, and two tabs set at particular intervals. This can all be preset and named as a *style type*. Any text brought into the publication can be selected and applied this style type.

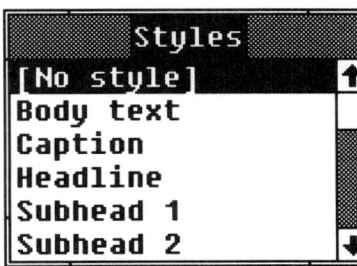 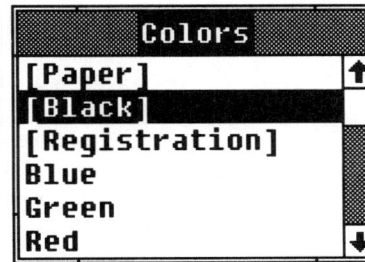

*Figure 30. Style palette.*  *Figure 31. Color palette.*

Similarly, subheadings can be, say, 12 point bold Palatino with certain spacing above and below, with or without indenting. Again this can be preset, given a name, and applied to all relevant subheadings. This approach to document assembly leads to increased productivity and a more consistent publication layout. A style's specifications may be revised at any time. PageMaker will then apply those new specifications to any paragraphs that have had that style applied.

The Style palette of Figure 30 contains several default styles. These can be added to at any time.

The Color palette allows color to be added to selected text or graphics. Again, any number of color types can be named, specified, and added to the Figure 31 palette. If you have a color monitor, the results will be immediately apparent. The color approach still works with black and white monitors—in this case the resulting printout on a color printer will indicate the results.

Don't try and use too many of these tools or palettes yet—all are covered in great detail in following modules. If you are still unsure as to the function of these tools, don't worry—you are not yet meant to understand them completely.

The Style and Color palettes can be hidden or shown using the last two commands in the **Options** menu.

Module 1 - Starting Up PageMaker

## Page number icons

Down in the bottom left-hand corner of the page are the *page number icons*. Depending on how your document is set up, you may see just a few, or many icons in this area. Quite probably, you will see an L, an R, and a 1. The highlighted 1 tells you this is page 1 of the current document. As we start creating larger documents, the 1 icon will be accompanied by a 2, a 3, a 4, and any number of icons up to 128. The icon currently highlighted in reverse video is the page currently being viewed on the screen. In this way, you can move to a specific page in your document simply by clicking on its page number icon.

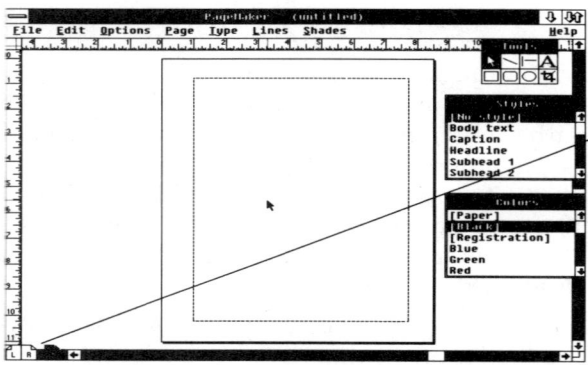

*Figure 32.* The page number icons, situated near the bottom-left of the screen, tell us what page we are currently looking at, while also giving us quick access to other pages.

*Figure 33.* A blown-up look at the page number icons—in this case indicating that we are on page 1 of 1. The L and the R refer to the master page icons—covered in a later module.

The L and the R represent the master pages. The use of these master pages is covered in detail in later modules.

28

## The page

The first thing you will probably notice when working with a PageMaker document is the representation of the page on the screen. This representation is based on the choices you selected upon opening up the new document. The outline of the page itself should be visible, as should the dotted margins defined for that page. If we had columns defined for this page, column guides would also be visible.

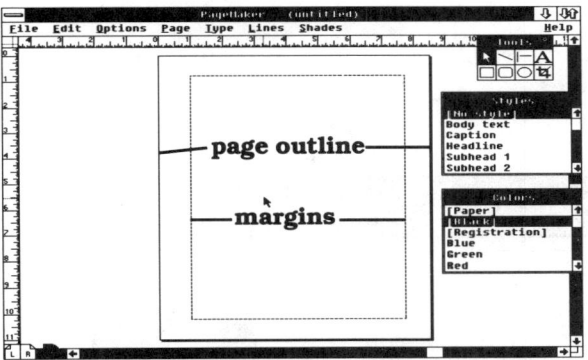

*Figure 34.* The outline of the page itself is very easy to spot. The dotted lines on the inside of the page indicate the page margins as described in the Page setup dialog box of Figure 13 (the dialog box that appears after selecting New from the **File** menu).

## The pasteboard

The *pasteboard* is the area around the page and can be used to store any imported or created text and graphics. If we look at the page as an actual page, then the pasteboard should be viewed as the desk around the page. It can be used to great effect—it is a kind of visual computer memory. We can place all kinds of articles and pictures in this pasteboard area and choose visually between them. This pasteboard area remains constant no matter what page you are looking at in the publication. Nothing in the pasteboard area will print, and the pasteboard is always saved with the publication.

Module 1 - Starting Up PageMaker

# The rulers

Through the *Rulers* command in the **Options** menu, it is possible to choose to display or not display horizontal and vertical rulers on the screen. Figures 19 and 35 show the rulers displaying. These rulers can be of considerable assistance in placing text and graphics on the page, and can be used in conjunction with special horizontal and vertical ruler guides.

Figure 35 shows the top left-hand corner of the page. Normally, for a single page viewed on screen, the ruler's zero position will begin at this point. For Facing pages view, this is not necessarily true. In either case, it is possible to change the zero position, both horizontally and vertically.

The use and flexibility of rulers are explained in more detail in later modules.

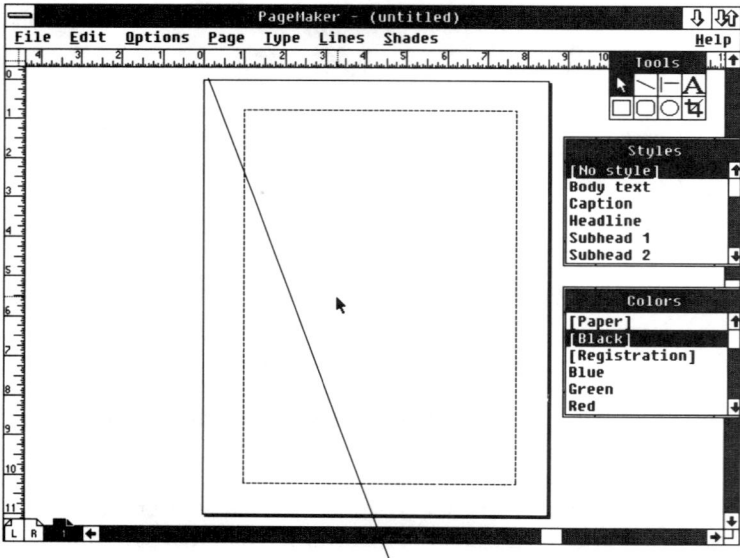

*Figure 35. The ruler zero point can be seen at the top left-hand corner of the page.*

*Module 1 - Starting Up PageMaker*

## The scroll bars

Along the bottom and the right-hand side of the page are the *scroll bars*. These are the bars that allow you to move around the page to view different sections of the page in certain views.

On large, high-resolution screens, scroll bars are used very little. When the whole page can be viewed and read at the same time, there is no real need to use the scroll bars. However, on the average PC screen (including Hercules, EGA, CGA, and VGA), there is no way you can view a whole page of text and be able to read it at the same time—the screen is just too small. To read the text, you will find that you will only be able to see about one third of the page at a time. Consequently, the scroll bars must be used to move yourself around the page. They can be manipulated in a variety of ways, as described below.

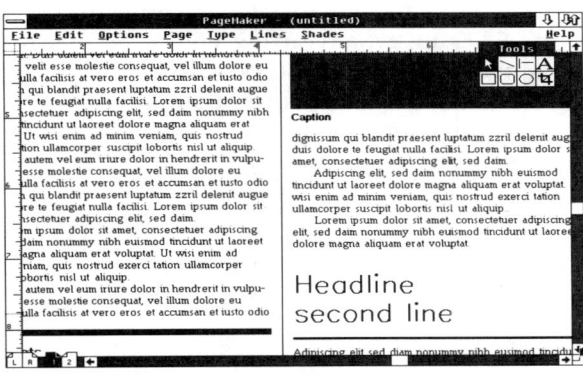

*Figure 36. Scroll bars help to move the page around in order to edit different sections of that page. Compare this figure with the one below...*

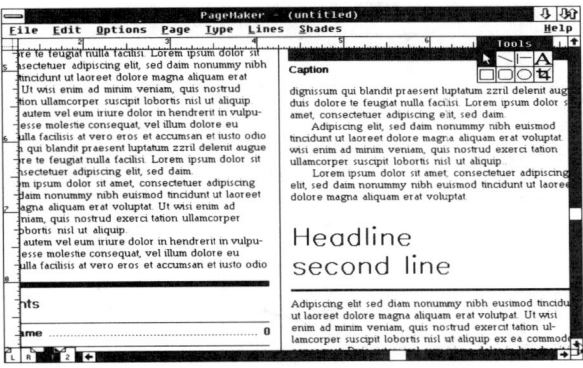

*Figure 37. ...and you will notice that a little more text is visible at the bottom of the page. Note also where the mouse cursor was clicked to achieve this page movement.*

*Module 1 - Starting Up PageMaker*

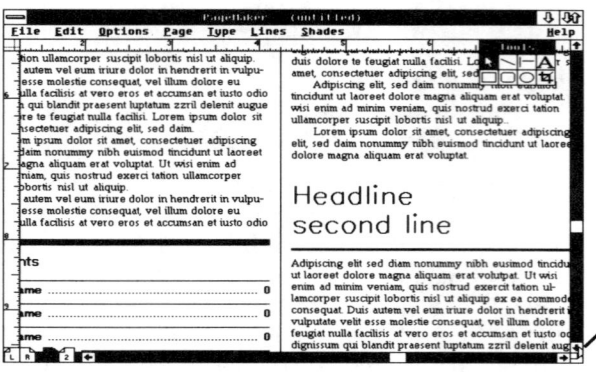

***Figure 38.*** *Here even more text is visible at the bottom of the page after clicking on the scroll bar arrow yet again.*

Both sets of scroll bars have an arrow in each corner (top, bottom, left, and right). Clicking on any arrow will move you in that direction in relation to the page. Many people get a little confused here—they tend to think that clicking on a certain arrow is going to take them in one direction, when in fact it takes them in another. Experiment to see which way your page is going to move when clicking on a certain arrow.

Without having text on the screen it can be a little tricky following exactly which way the scroll bars are moving.

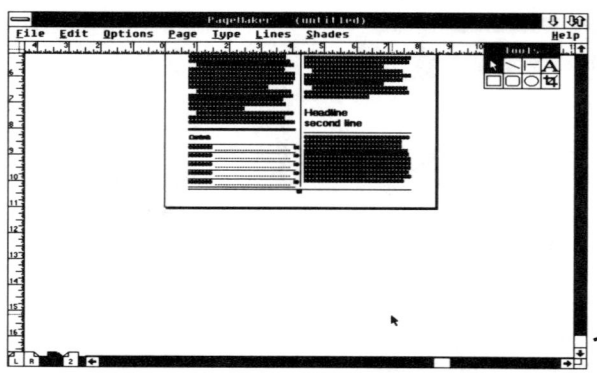

***Figure 39.*** *Even in reduced (Fit in window) view (described in the next section) the screen can be scrolled. When we are looking at the bottom of the page, note where the white square is situated in the right-hand scroll bar—also at the bottom.*

*Module 1 - Starting Up PageMaker*

Clicking on these arrows is the slow way to move around the page. If you click on the gray areas in the scroll bars, you will move around much more quickly—on the smaller screens about a screen at a time. Before you try this, however, note one thing about the scroll bars. They both have a little white square in them. This white square represents what part of the page you are looking at in relation to the total screen area. For example, if this white square is situated near the bottom of the right-hand scroll bar, it means that you are looking at an area near the bottom of the page. If the square is near the top of the scroll bar, you are looking at an area near the top of the page. When you click in the gray area of the scroll bar, whichever side of the white square you click on is the direction you are going to move. As you scroll, watch the white squares change position in the scroll bars.

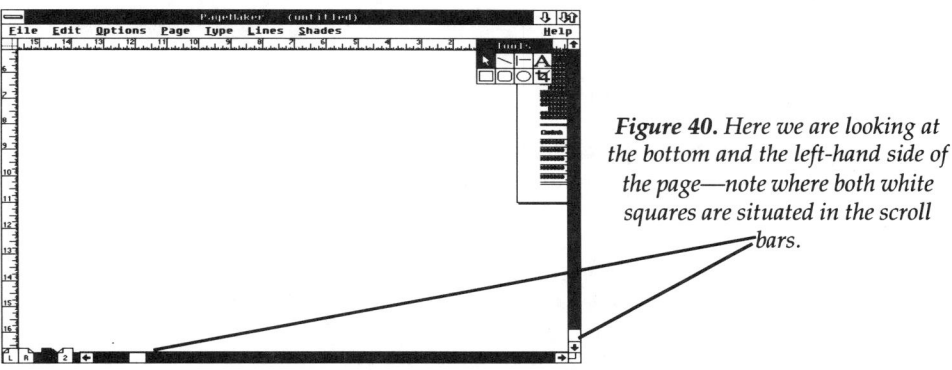

*Figure 40.* Here we are looking at the bottom and the left-hand side of the page—note where both white squares are situated in the scroll bars.

Another way to scroll around the screen, and perhaps the easiest way, is to hold the mouse button down on one of the white squares, and move it up or down (or left or right). Release it when it appears that the white square is going to be situated where you want the page to be. For example, if you are looking at the top of a page and would like to look at the bottom, hold the mouse button down on the right-hand side white square, move the mouse down the page until the white square is situated near the bottom of the scroll bar, and release the mouse button. The whole PageMaker screen will reformat so that you are looking at the bottom of your page.

*Module 1 - Starting Up PageMaker*

The final way to move around the PageMaker screen is to use the *grabber hand*. By holding down the Alt key and the mouse button, the pointer turns into a hand. The screen then moves in the direction that the mouse is moved. Holding down the Shift key restrains the movement, horizontally or vertically.

# Page views

Before we go any further we must look at the different ways we can view the PageMaker publication currently open. In Figure 41 we are viewing the full page of a document. This is generally the default way to view the page and is called the *Fit in window* view.

To view the overall layout of your page, *Fit in window* is generally the best choice. When *Fit in window* is selected (**Page** menu), the page appears as big as is possible given the current screen size. However, many screens are of a size that makes it impossible to do any editing when a page is at *Fit in window* size. There are other choices, however.

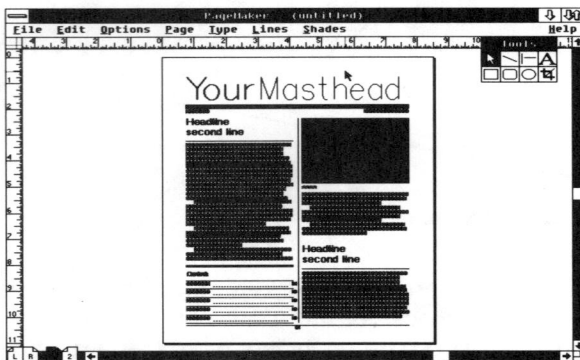

*Figure 41. Here we see a chapter opened in reduced or Fit in window view.*

Listed in the **Page** menu are all the possible page sizes that can be selected to view the page (Figure 42). Experiment by selecting different page views to see how a certain page size can be used for editing, another for viewing layout, another for precisely aligning graphics, and so on. PageMaker has a great variety of ways to view the currently open publication.

*Module 1 - Starting Up PageMaker*

See Figure 42 for the five different ways illustrated at the top of the **Page** menu. These include *Actual size, 75% size, 50% size, Fit in window,* and *200% size.*

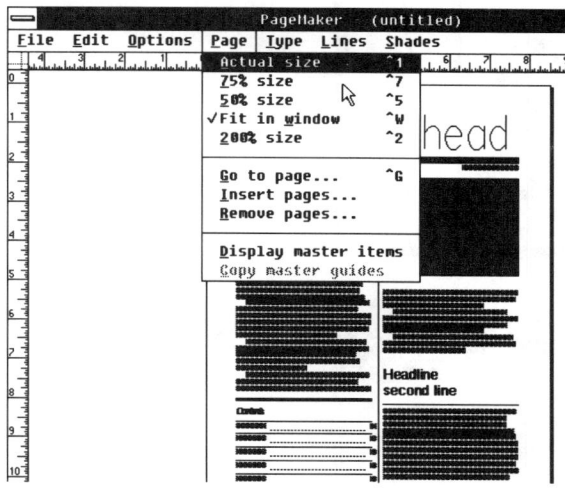

*Figure 42. The **Page** menu gives you a wide range of choices to view your PageMaker publications.*

One additional page view is possible. This is achieved by holding down the Shift key while selecting *Fit in window* from the **Page** menu. What you get in this case is shown in Figure 43—the whole pasteboard area as well as the page or pages. This is useful when you wish to view the whole Pasteboard area.

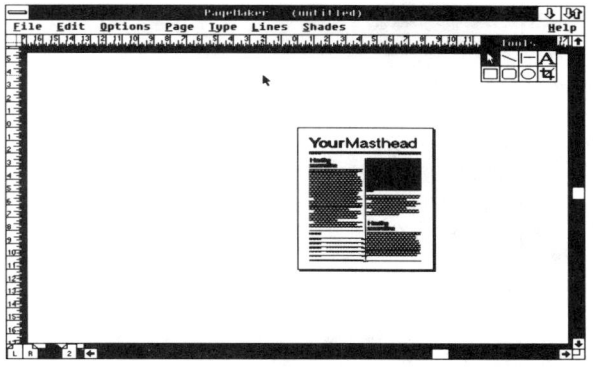

*Figured 43. This view shows you the total pasteboard area around the page or pages and is achieved by using the Shift key while selecting Fit in window view.*

35

*Module 1 - Starting Up PageMaker*

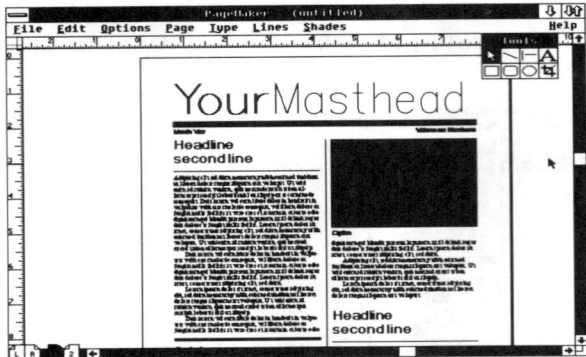

***Figure 44.*** *Here we see the same page as Figure 43 at 50% size...*

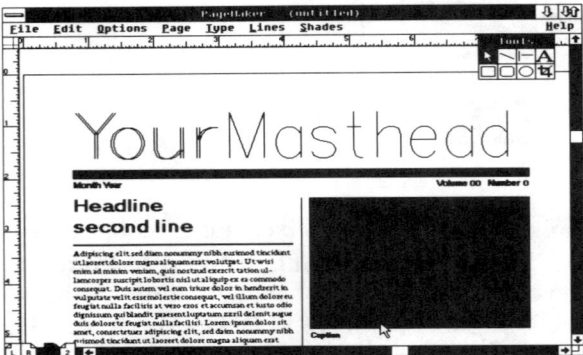

***Figure 45.*** *... and again at 75% size...*

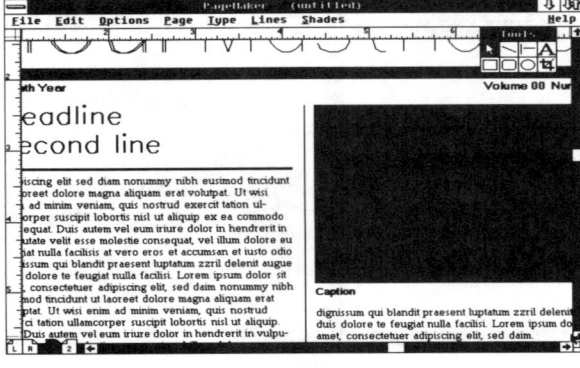

***Figure 46.*** *... and again at actual size...*

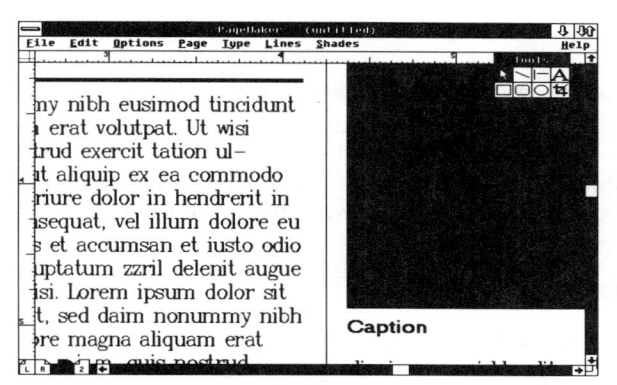

*Figure 47.* ... *and finally at 200% size.*

## The Preferences command

It is a good idea to look at the *Preferences* command before we go any further, as it helps you customize PageMaker to your own liking. Invoke the *Preferences* command in the **Edit** menu (Figure 48).

From this command there is a major choice to be made—that of which measurement units should be used. There are several units to choose from so choose wisely—measurement units turn up everywhere in PageMaker. Whichever measurement unit is chosen is the one that appears in all future dialog boxes. This may be overridden at any time as we will see later.

It is also possible to set different measurements for the horizontal and vertical rulers in the dialog box of Figure 48. Again, this will be discussed in a future module.

*Figure 48.* The choices in the *Preferences* dialog box, accessed through the Preferences command in the **Edit** menu, help to customize PageMaker to your special preferences.

Module 1 - Starting Up PageMaker

## Undo command

Located at the top of the **Edit** menu is the *Undo* command. This is a safety factor that allows you to undo virtually all PageMaker functions—including moves, deletes, copies, pastes, and so on. Always remember this command is here—however, remember it cannot undo everything, and it will only undo the very last step you took.

## Close (File menu) command

The *Close* command in the **File** menu (Figure 49) is used to close the currently open publication. As you choose *Close*, you will be prompted to save the changes you have made to this publication (unless you have just saved those changes). You can choose *Yes*, *No*, or *Cancel* (Figure 50). *No* closes the publication saving no changes—everything you changed since you last saved has been lost. *Cancel* takes you back to the PageMaker page. *Yes* will save all changes to the publication. The saving process is discussed in more detail later.

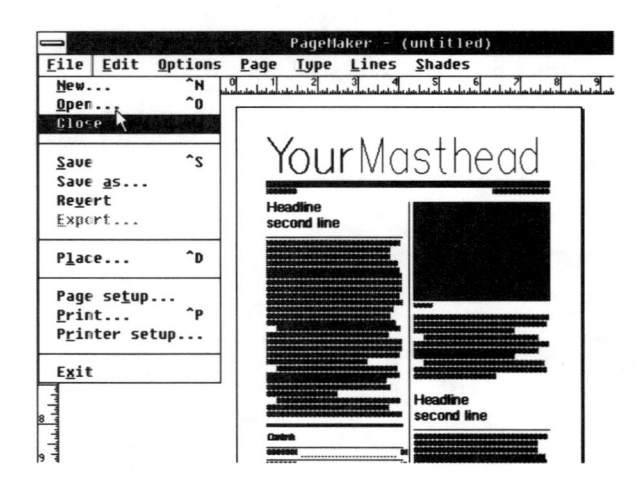

*Figure 49. The Close command will remove the currently open publication from the screen—regardless of whether it was a new or existing publication.*

*Module 1 - Starting Up PageMaker*

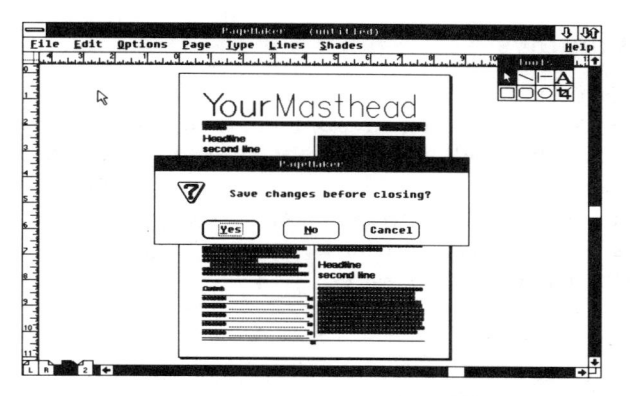

*Figure 50. This warning will appear if you have not saved your work before closing. As we will be discussing saving in a later module, at this stage if you are confronted with this warning click on Cancel.*

After closing you must choose *New* or *Open* to get back into PageMaker—or *Exit* to leave it.

## The Close (System menu) and Exit (File menu) command

The command *Close* from the **System** menu (Figure 51) works in the same way as the *Exit* command from the **File** menu, and in both cases the PageMaker program is quit and left. You will be prompted to save the changes of the current document if you made any changes since last saving.

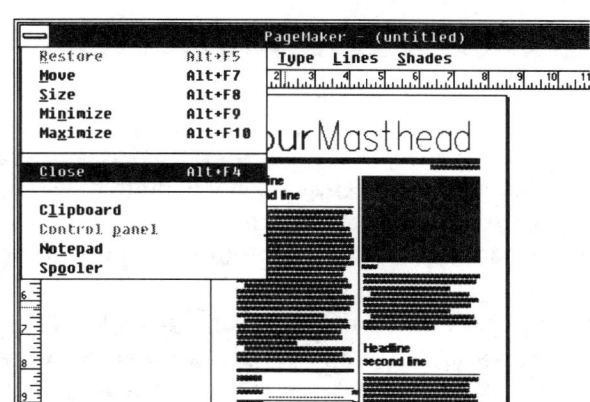

*Figure 51. The Close command, from the **System** menu, or the Exit command from the **File** menu, will return you to either the Windows desktop or the DOS prompt.*

At the conclusion of every information section and exercise (where applicable) in this book, you should close the current publication and *not* save the changes. Use the *Close* command from the **File** menu to do this.

39

Module 1 - Starting Up PageMaker

## Using PageMaker with Windows

As has been mentioned earlier in this module, PageMaker on the PC runs under an operating environment called Microsoft Windows. Microsoft Windows is a graphics environment that is available separately to run on your PC—this is the full Windows we refer to. Several other programs are available to run under Windows—including spreadsheets, graphics, word processing, and desktop publishing software.

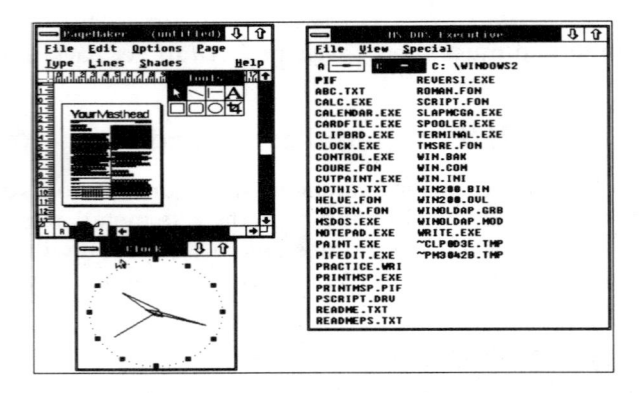

*Figure 52.* Windows provides a graphic interface for many programs to run simultaneously. PageMaker is one of these programs.

For those people who do not possess a copy of Microsoft Windows (version 2.03 or above), PageMaker is provided with a run-time version. This run-time version is only enough to let PageMaker run—you never have access to the file handling capabilities of Windows, nor can you run other programs simultaneously.

In this case, the run-time version of Windows provides the graphic interface PageMaker needs to run. However, because PageMaker does run under Windows, whether it be run-time or full, there are several features incorporated in its use which are actually a part of Windows.

In this section we will look at these features as well as some of the features found in the full version of Windows—although this is not intended as a guide on how to use Windows as a separate product.

## Full Windows

The full version of Windows (2.03 and above) allows you to open several windows of information at once—and run different programs in each (not all programs are supported by Windows). Several handy utility programs are also provided with Windows, which for many people replaces DOS as the operating system. It allows virtually all DOS functions to be carried out in its graphics shell.

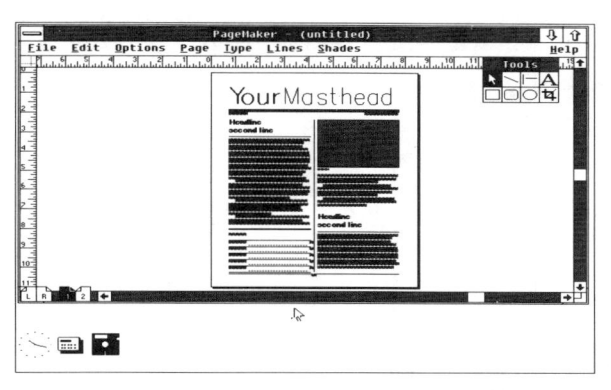

*Figure 53.* Here PageMaker runs in the major window, with other programs lined along the bottom of the screen.

To open PageMaker from within Windows, you must first of all change to the directory that contains the PageMaker program. This can be achieved through the *Change Directory* command in the **Special** menu. (PageMaker 3 will normally be installed in a directory on your hard disk called PM.)

*Figure 54.* The operating system of Windows. Here we see a DOS directory—from here programs can be run, or DOS operations performed.

*Module 1 - Starting Up PageMaker*

After changing to the correct directory, you should see a file called PM.EXE (Figure 54). Double-clicking on this file will start the PageMaker program. A new large window will open up, overlapping the Windows desktop, and PageMaker will be running in this window.

When looking at a directory listing in the Windows desktop, PageMaker can be started by double-clicking on a publication or template name (Figure 55). In this case, PageMaker will start directly into this publication or template—saving a little time. (These are the files with either the PM3 or PT3 file extensions.)

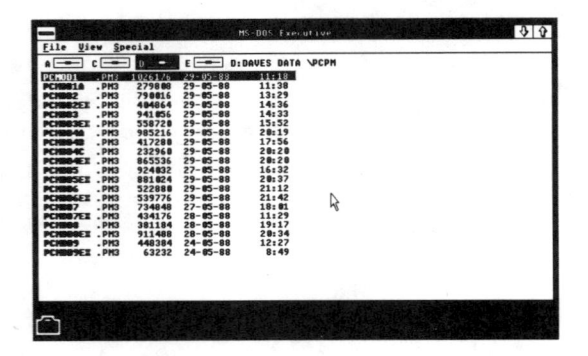

*Figure 55. Here we see a listing of PageMaker files— double-clicking on any of these file names will launch PageMaker 3 automatically.*

It is quite possible to open up PageMaker in one window, a graphics program in another, and a word processing package in another. Graphics and/or text can be cut or copied from the other program's windows directly into PageMaker's—once again saving a bit of time by reducing steps.

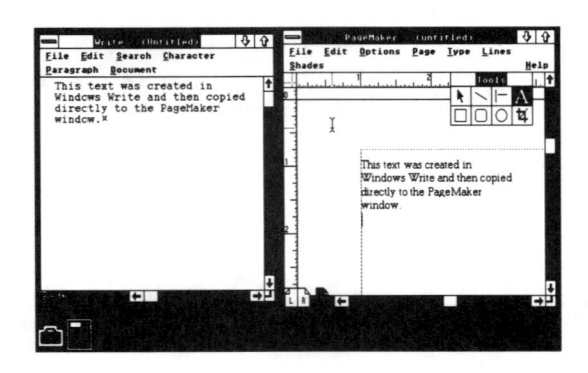

*Figure 56. If a WP and PageMaker were opened together, text typed into the WP can be copied from the WP window directly to PageMaker.*

42

## Run-time Windows

Apart from the features discussed in the last section, whatever form of Windows you use with PageMaker, it will operate the same way. In this section we will look at a few of the features of windowing—how we can move, resize, close, and use windows with PageMaker. All of the things discussed from here are relevant whichever form of Windows you use.

When PageMaker is opened, it sits on the screen in an area known as a *window*. This window, as you may have noticed, does not fill the entire screen—there is a little bit of room all around the window (normally, not necessarily). We are going to look first at how we can change the size of the window in which PageMaker sits.

Move the mouse very close and very slowly to near the edge of the window. You will notice that as the mouse passes over the very edge of the window it changes shape—usually to a two-sided arrow (Figure 57). When the mouse is a two-sided arrow, hold the left button down, and move the mouse in the direction of either arrow. When you release the mouse button, you will find that the window is a new size. This can be achieved from any side of the window—including all the corners. It can be a little tricky when the side of the window is close to the side of the screen.

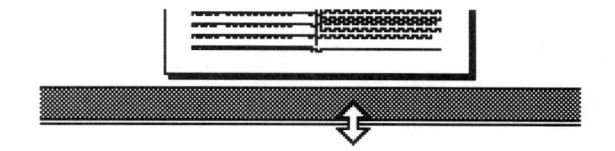

*Figure 57. Note how when the mouse is moved very close to the edge of a window, it changes shape to a two-sided arrow.*

*Module 1 - Starting Up PageMaker*

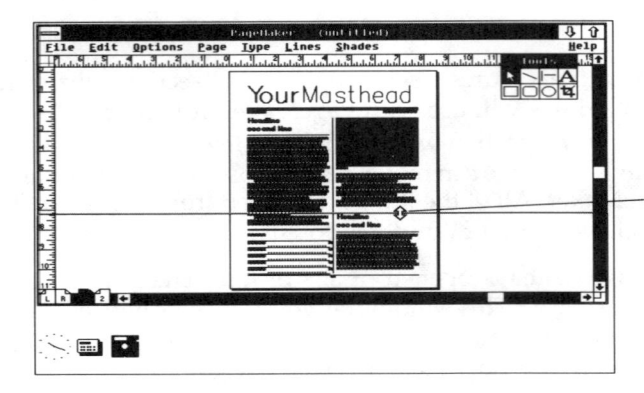

*Figure 58.* After the operation of Figure 57, if the mouse button is held down when the mouse has changed to this arrow, the mouse can be moved up or down (keeping the left mouse button held down)...

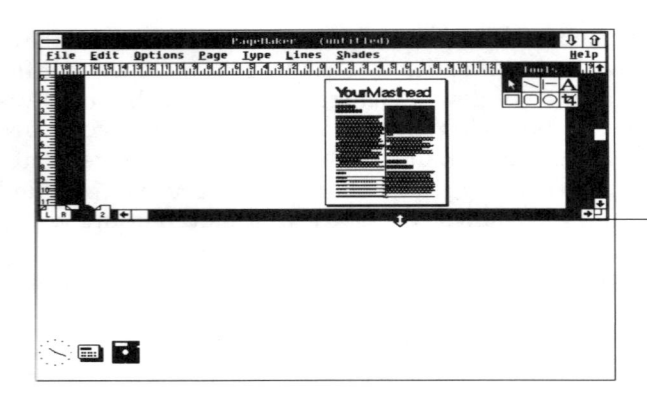

*Figure 59.* ...and if released, the window changes size to reflect the movement of the mouse.

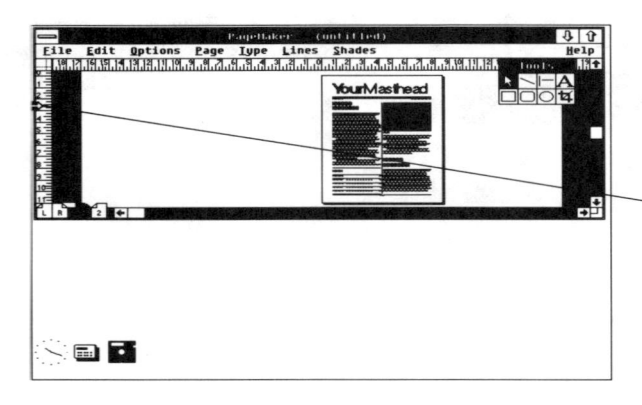

*Figure 60.* Here the same steps will be taken to resize the window from one side. Move the mouse near the edge of the window. It will again change to a two-sided arrow.

*Module 1 - Starting Up PageMaker*

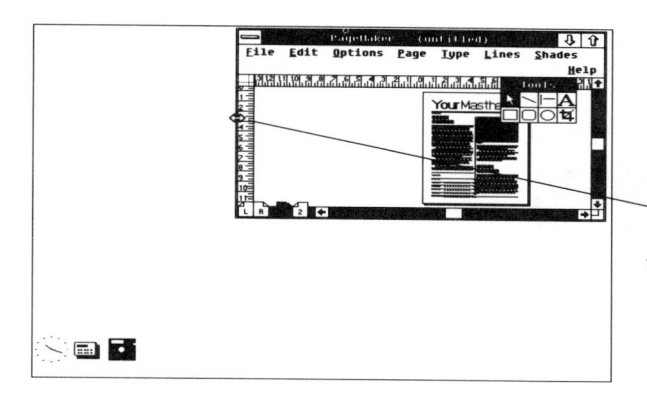

***Figure 61.*** *Once again, after the Figure 60 operation, hold down the mouse button and drag the mouse across the screen. When released, the window reflects the movement of the mouse.*

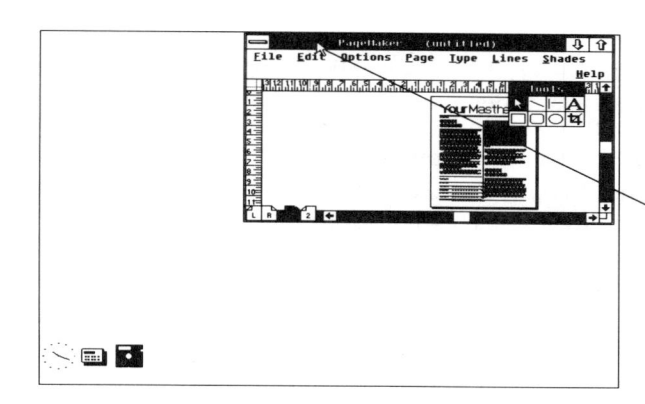

***Figure 62.*** *To move the entire window, hold the mouse button down in the title bar and move the mouse around.*

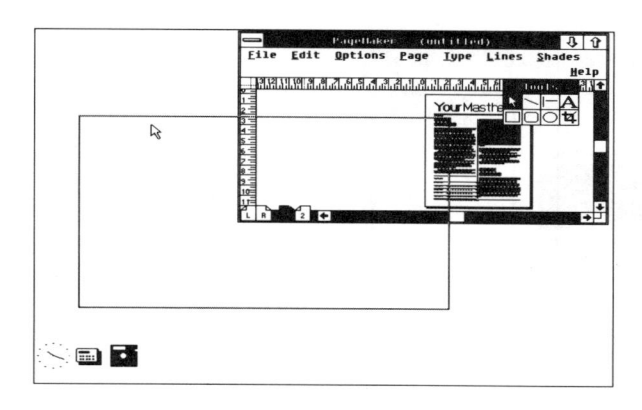

***Figure 63.*** *As the window is dragged across the screen, a rectangle represents where the new window will appear.*

*Module 1 - Starting Up PageMaker*

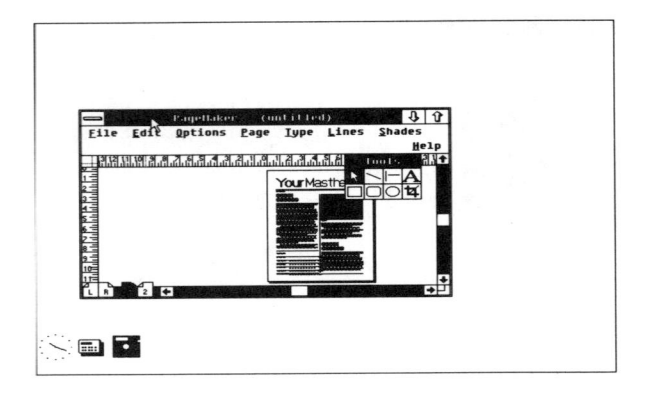

**Figure 64.** *As the mouse is released, the window reformats in its new position.*

Let's say, however, that we want the window to snap to the full size of the screen. When we are working with a program such as PageMaker, this is one of the first steps we should take. Instead of stretching the window from all sides, click on the right-hand arrow in the top right-hand corner of the window—the arrow that is pointing upwards. This will cause the arrow to double, but more importantly, it causes the window to snap to the full size of the screen (Figure 65). Once the window has snapped to the full size of the screen, it cannot be resized. Clicking on this arrow again (which has now turned into a two-sided arrow) will return the window to the size it was prior to the first click.

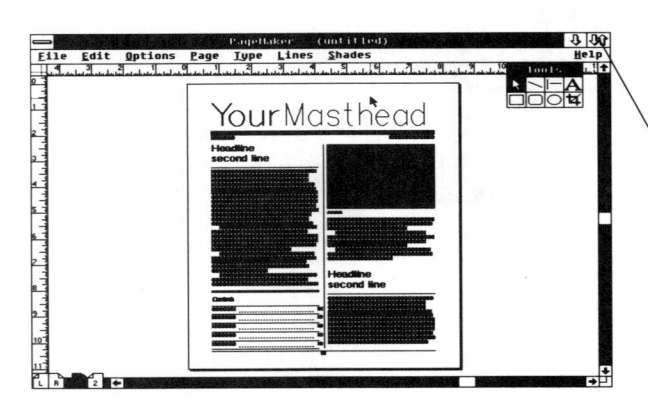

**Figure 65.** *Clicking in this arrow (when it is a single arrow) causes the window to snap to the full screen size. If this arrow is double, it means the window is already at full size.*

*Module 1 - Starting Up PageMaker*

Clicking on the left arrow will *minimize* the window—it turns the window into a small icon in the left-hand corner of the screen. Double-clicking on this icon will return it to the size it was before the window was minimized. With full Windows, several program icons can be aligned along the bottom of the screen, and a quick double-click will launch you into any program.

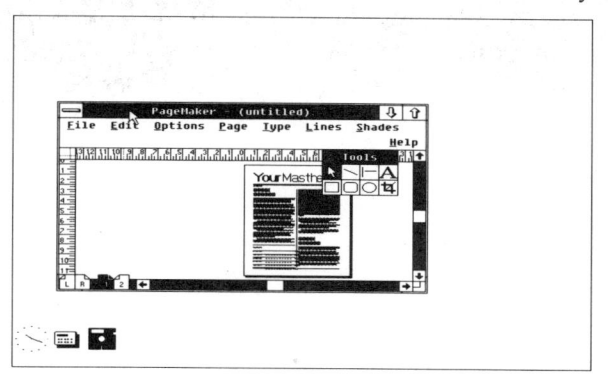

*Figure 66. A minimized window appears in the bottom left-hand corner. Here three windows have been minimized.*

## The Windows menu

Every single Windows application has what is known as a **System** menu or a Windows menu (Figure 67). (This is the menu just above the **File** menu—it is signified by a small disk drive-type icon). Within this menu are commands that allow you to resize, move, minimize, and maximize the window—simply a way to resize without a mouse. The easiest way to achieve all of these steps is as described in the previous paragraphs.

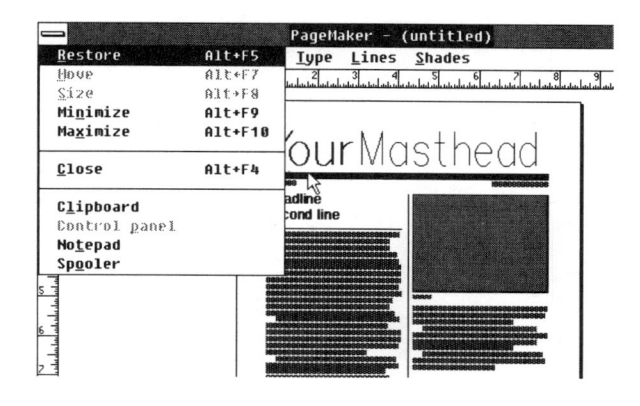

*Figure 67. The Windows **System** menu. This menu allows certain operations to be performed as an alternative to the mouse.*

47

*Module 1 - Starting Up PageMaker*

The **System** menu will also contain some information on PageMaker, access to the PageMaker *Spooler* (which will tell you what is currently printing—the Spooler will open a window just as PageMaker did), access to the Control panel (which helps to set up printers—see Module 10) and also allows you to change screen colors and or shades, as well as a few other minor settings. It also contains the *Close* command—one of the ways to close the window and remove it from memory.

## Module 2

# Loading Files into PageMaker

# Loading Files into PageMaker

PageMaker is a tool that allows us to manipulate and put together files that are generally, and most easily, created using other computer applications. Although we can create many publications using PageMaker alone, its real strength lies in the fact that it can accept formatted files from virtually all other major MS-DOS and Macintosh applications. Text files are best created in dedicated word processor packages, like Microsoft Word; while far more effective and professional graphics can be created in packages such as Corel Headline, Arts and Letters, and Windows Draw. Files created in these and other applications can be slotted directly into PageMaker.

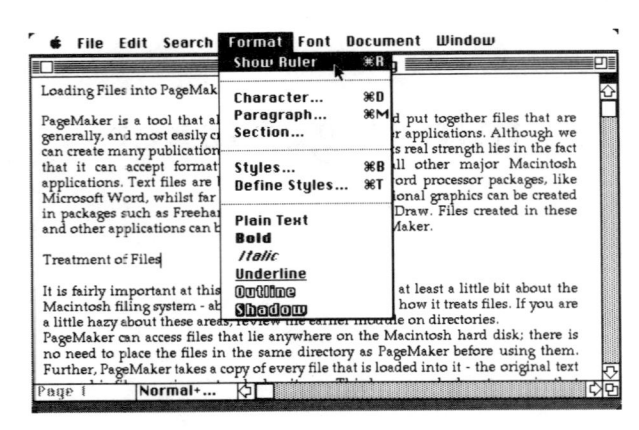

*Figure 1.* Microsoft Word version 3 (on the Macintosh) was used to create the text for this book.

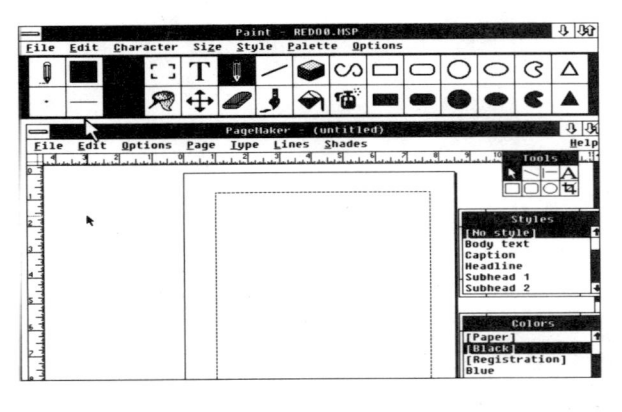

*Figure 2.* All the screen shots used in this book are in Windows Paint format, and could have been edited in this program before importation into PageMaker.

50

## Treatment of files

It is fairly important at this stage that you understand at least a little bit about the MS-DOS filing system—about how it uses directories and treats files.

PageMaker can access files that lie anywhere on hard or floppy disk; there is no need to place the files in the same directory as PageMaker before using them. Further, PageMaker takes a copy of every file that's loaded into it—the original text or graphic file remains untouched as it was. This has several advantages, in that the original file can now be used in other applications as well, and that the PageMaker publication is treated as one file rather than a mixture of several. It also has the disadvantage that any editing done in PageMaker is not reflected in the original file, and vice versa. The *Export* command discussed in Module 4—PageMaker Editing, does solve most of these problems, for text at least.

Most of the time files can be accessed in their original form. Occasionally, you may have to do something a little different to a file to allow it to be used in PageMaker. For example, PageMaker cannot accept Headline files in the Headline format—the default format for such files. PageMaker can, however, accept Headline files in their EPSF format. Other packages have similar options for saving their graphics in a compatible format.

*Figure 3.* Corel Headline could have been used to create fancy text and graphics for this book.

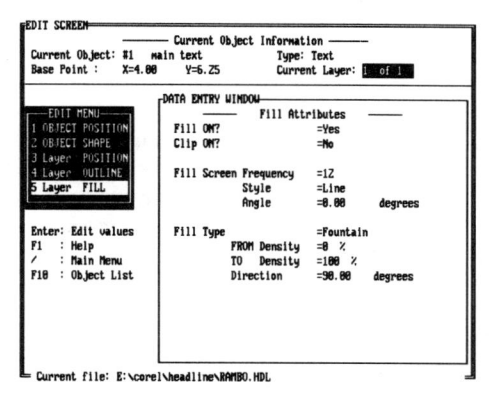

*Figure 3a.* A Corel Headline created graphic.

*Module 2 - Loading Files*

# Loading files

All types of files, whether they be text or graphics, are accessed through the *Place* command (Figure 4) in the **File** menu. After selecting this command, you will be presented with the dialog box of Figure 5. To help you understand the concepts of this module, you may find it useful to follow our discussion by working along with PageMaker as you read our comments.

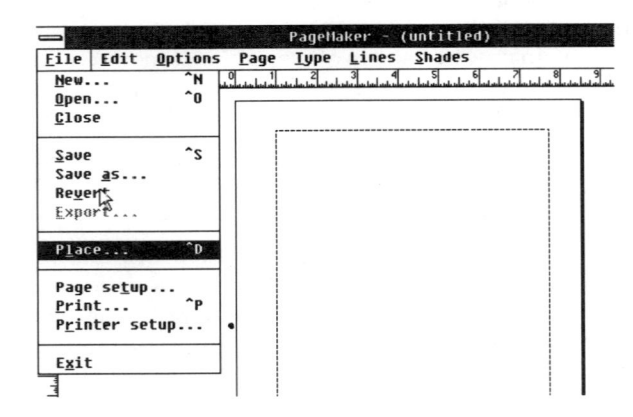

*Figure 4.* The Place command is used to gain access to the files on the hard disk, and/or floppy disks.

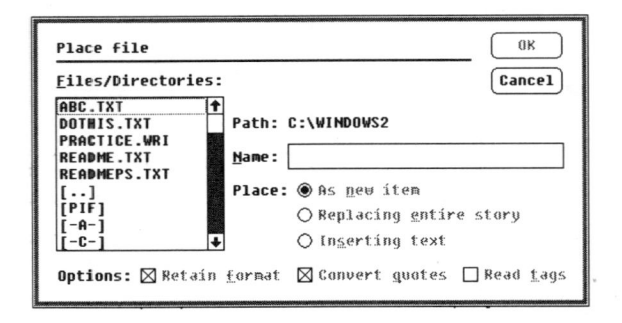

*Figure 5.* This is an example of the dialog box that appears upon selecting the Place command. Yours may look a little different—it depends on where you opened PageMaker from, and how it was loaded on your machine.

This is where the idea of *directories* becomes so important. In order for you to change directories to access different files, it is vital to understand what exactly you are doing.

In Figure 5, we are looking at the files and directories from within the directory that PageMaker was started from—in our case the directory C:\WINDOWS2.

*Module 2 - Loading Files*

Within the list of names on the left, directory names are listed in brackets, while all compatible files are listed as they are. Incompatible files are not listed at all. If you wish to list all files (compatible or incompatible) insert *.* in the Name rectangle to the right and hit the Enter key (Figure 6). This you may need to do from time to time, as PageMaker will decide what files are compatible and which are not by looking at the file extension - which can really be anything. Depending on your file naming specifications, compatible files may not be listed until the steps described above are taken. Upon selecting a file that uses a non-standard extension, although it may be compatible, PageMaker may ask you exactly what type of file it is by presenting you with a list.

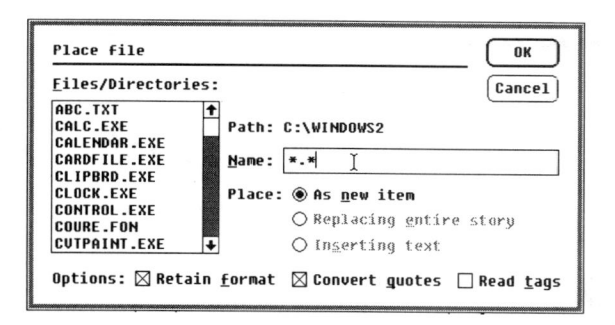

*Figure 6*. Inserting *.* in the Name rectangle (and hitting the Enter key) shows all files in the current directory—compatible or not.

The name of the current directory is listed after the word *Path*.

Much of the time you will find that the file you are after is not resident in the current directory at all, so we must change directories. There are two possibilities here, depending on whether the new directory exists within or outside of the current directory.

To change to other directories not contained within the current one, which is often the most common first move, follow these steps. You must first move the mouse over the double-dots in brackets (if they exist). They will not exist if you are already at the root directory—but be sure to check by scrolling down the list of file names (see Figure 7). If you double-click in these double-dots, you will move up a directory level. If you keep doing this until there are no more double-dots in the list, you will have reached the *root* directory (see Figure 8). The directory name above the selection rectangle will be C:\.

53

## Module 2 - Loading Files

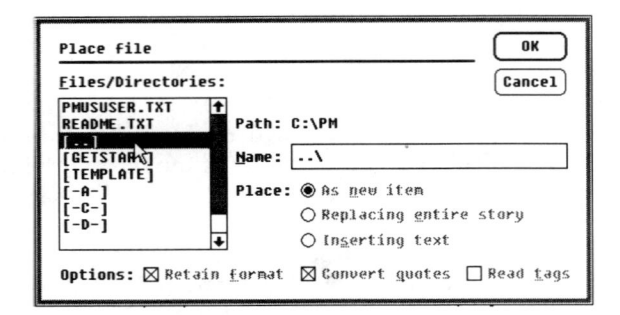

*Figure 7.* Locate the double-dots in brackets and double-click on them. If nothing appears to have happened, you may need to double-click a bit faster.

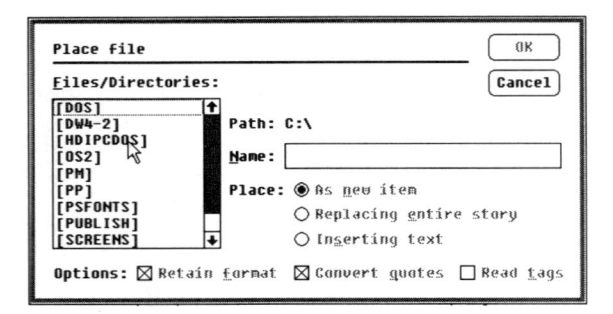

*Figure 8.* Here we are at the root directory—called C:\ (see above the Name rectangle). Once here, we can see the major directories on the disk, and no double-dots.

To change to a different disk, whether it be hard disk or floppy, click on the letter identifying the disk drive you are after in the brackets. Note the A, C, and D entries in the list of Figure 7.

From the root directory (Figure 8), you should see a larger list of directory names—double-click on the directory you want to move into. From within that directory, you may either select the file you are after, or move down another directory level by double-clicking on that directory.

The concept of directories and files on a hard disk may at first be a little confusing—a little knowledge in this area would certainly help a lot. Imagine your hard disk to be a filing cabinet, where directories are merely different folders in the cabinet, and files different elements within folders. Each folder can be further subdivided into other folders.

*Module 2 - Loading Files*

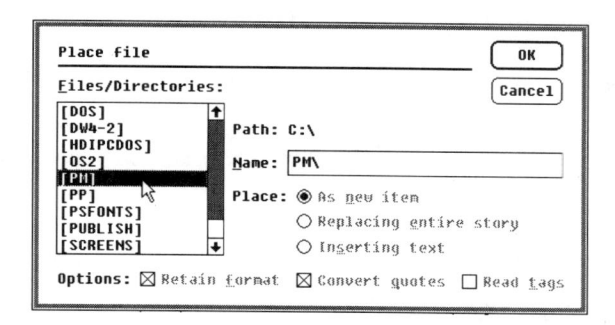

*Figure 9.* This is the same dialog box as Figure 7. To move into the PM directory to access its files, double-click on the directory name PM.

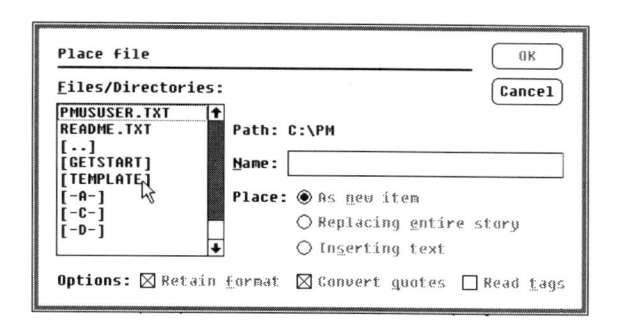

*Figure 10.* Here we are inside the PM directory (note the name above the Name rectangle). We could now either select one of the two listed files, or move into other directories listed here (in brackets).

If you are sure a file exists in a directory but is not listed in the window, it may well exist in a format incompatible with Page-Maker. Return to the program in which the file was created to make sure it is saved in the current format. It is also possible that the file has been named in a non-standard manner—use the method described earlier to remedy this.

Figures 11 to 15 on the following pages show how to load the BROCHURE.DOC file from within the GETSTART subdirectory, which is in the PM directory.

## Module 2 - Loading Files

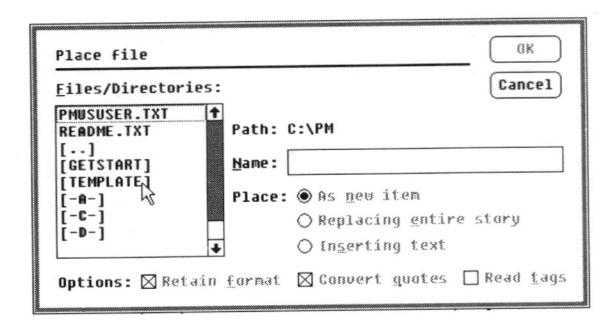

*Figure 11.* Let's say we decide to move into the GETSTART subdirectory from here. We are currently inside the PM directory.

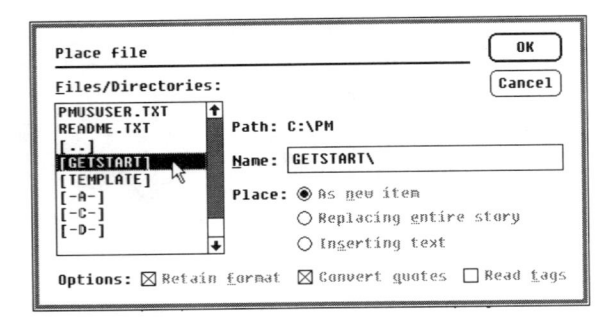

*Figure 12.* Double-click on the subdirectory name GETSTART.

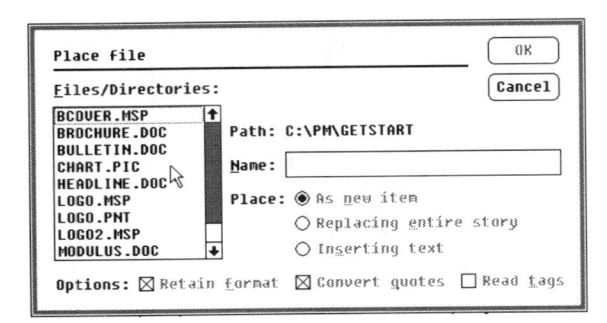

*Figure 13.* We are now in the GETSTART subdirectory within the PM directory. Many compatible files will now be listed, from which we can choose which one to load.

*Module 2 - Loading Files*

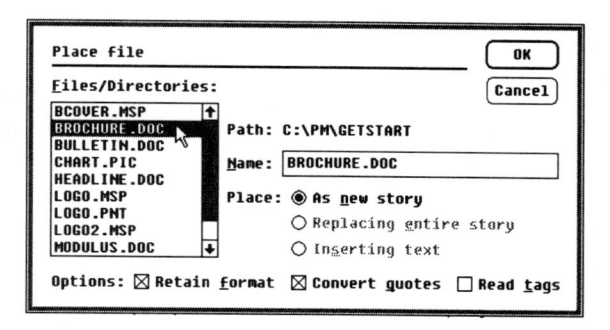

*Figure 14.* To select a file to load, double-click on the file name quickly, or once on the file name and once on OK. We are selecting BROCHURE.DOC. Note that after clicking on it once, its name appears in the Name rectangle, as well as being highlighted.

We are going to now load the BROCHURE.DOC file, located by following the steps outlined in Figures 9 to 14 captions, into PageMaker. When at the Figure 14 position, you are now ready to load your selected file onto the PageMaker page. To do this, you can choose any one of two methods. First, you may click on the name of the file and then click OK. Alternatively, you may double-click on the file, the same way as you would to move down a directory. Additional options required in selecting your file are described at the end of this module.

After a few seconds (depending upon the format and the size of the file being loaded), you will be returned back to the PageMaker page (Figure 15), with very little apparently having happened. However, the mouse cursor will have changed its appearance, once again depending on the type of file that is being loaded.

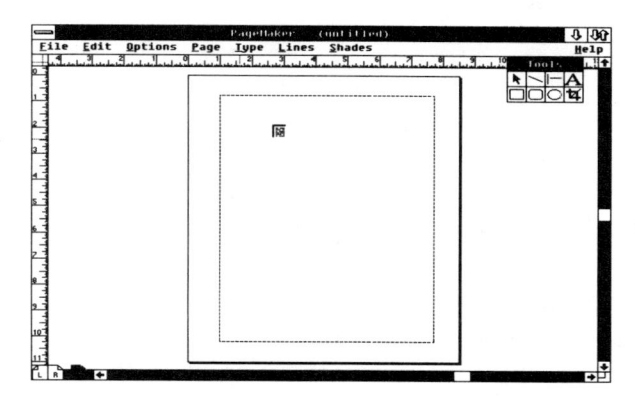

*Figure 15.* After selecting a file to load, the mouse cursor will change shape once you have returned to the PageMaker screen.

57

*Module 2 - Loading Files*

Text files loaded in will cause the mouse cursor to change its appearance to any one of the three options shown in Figures 16, 17, and 18. Graphics files, however, will cause the mouse cursor to take on a variety of different forms depending on their format. These are shown in Figures 19 to 22. The different text and graphics possibilities are briefly discussed below. The detailed operations of these different place methods are described in future modules.

*Figure 16.* When text has been selected to load into PageMaker using the Place command, the mouse cursor may change appearance to look like this. This is called manual text flow and is the PageMaker default mode.

*Figure 17.* This is the semi-automatic text flow cursor appearance.

*Figure 18.* This is the automatic text flow mode.

*Figure 19.* The EPS or PostScript mouse cursor.

EPS graphic files will cause the mouse cursor to look like Figure 19. Files from programs such as Corel Headline, Designer, and Arts & Letters could well be imported in this format.

58

*Figure 20. The draw-type cursor.*

Draw-type files will cause the mouse cursor to take on this appearance. Files from Windows Draw, and other similar applications, will cause the mouse cursor to look like this.

*Figure 21. The TIFF or scanned image cursor*

TIFF files, which are usually scanned files, will cause the mouse cursor to take on this appearance.

*Figure 22. The paint-type mouse cursor.*

Paint files, such as those from PC Paintbrush, Publisher's Paintbrush, and Windows Paint, cause the mouse cursor to take on the appearance of a paintbrush.

Once you have loaded a file through the *Place* command (changing the mouse cursor) you must get the file from memory to the page. Quite simply, to do this, you just click the mouse button. (Don't do that yet.) In Figure 23, we are about to load the file BROCHURE.DOC, after the process shown earlier in Figures 9 to 15.

Before you click the mouse button, you must locate the mouse cursor where you would like the text or graphic to start flowing. If it is a text file you are loading (as in our case), make sure that the mouse cursor is flush with the left margin of the page. It should snap to this margin (see Figure 23). If you click the mouse cursor now, the text will flow, from where the mouse is located, across and down the page (Figure 24). This text file is now loaded. Such an operation may take a few seconds.

*Module 2 - Loading Files*

Before clicking the mouse, ensure that the mouse cursor looks the same as in Figure 23 (which is the manual flow mode as illustrated also in Figure 16). If not, go to the **Options** menu and choose the *Autoflow* command. (The reasons for doing this are explained in the next module.)

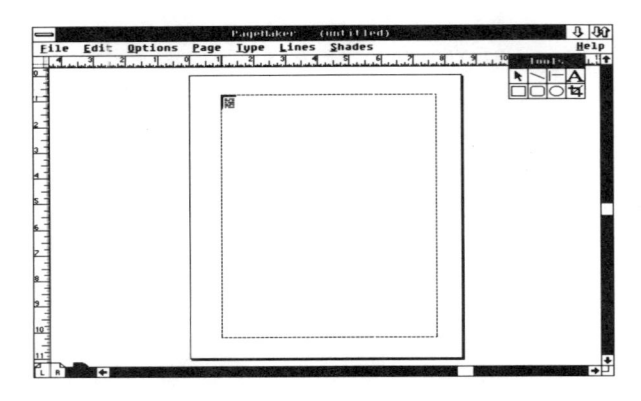

*Figure 23.* To flow text onto the page, locate the text cursor flush against the left margin, as far down the page as you wish.

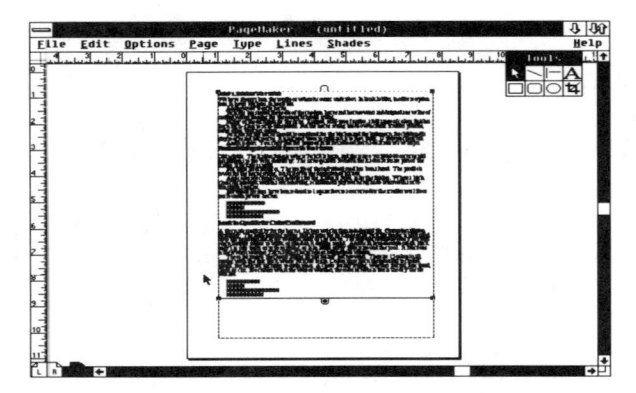

*Figure 24.* Here we located the text cursor in the top left-hand corner of the margin before we clicked the mouse button.
The text flows within the bounds of the left, right, top, and bottom margins.

60

There is a second method that can be used to flow text and/or graphics onto the page (this is the method that should always be used with graphics). Position the mouse where you would like the top left-hand corner of the file to be, and hold down the mouse button. Now move the mouse down and to the right of the page, keeping the mouse button held down. A box will be drawn indicating the area in which the text or graphics is going to flow. Once the mouse button is released, the text or graphics will flow into the area bounded by the box. See the example shown in Figures 25 and 26.

If you have already flowed your text, go back to Figures 9 to 15 and repeat the steps to load BROCHURE.DOC. Use the second method of flowing text as outlined in Figures 25 and 26, and in this case, flow the text in the pasteboard area to the left of the page.

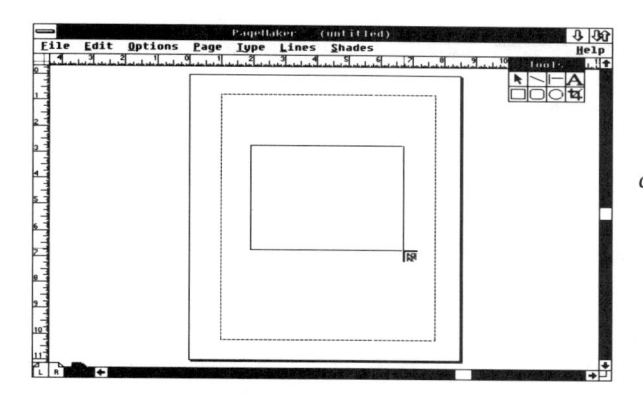

*Figure 25.* After the cursor has changed appearance, hold down the mouse button and drag the mouse diagonally to the right and down the page.

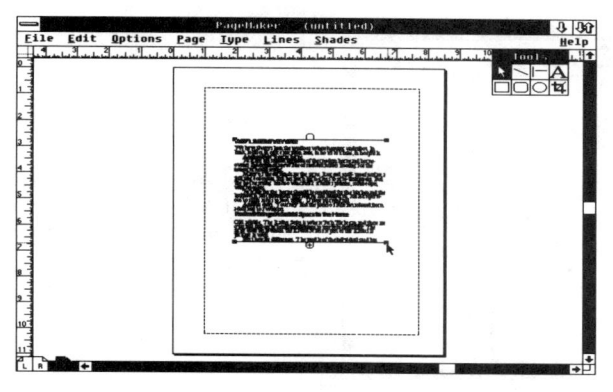

*Figure 26.* Release the mouse button when the box is the size you wish it to be. The text now flows to fill this box.

*Module 2 - Loading Files*

In Figures 27, 28, and 29, we are shown loading the PHOTO.TIF file from within the GETSTART subdirectory using the *Place* command. This is being loaded using the method described in Figures 25 and 26—i.e., loading a file into a designated box area. You may note that it is possible with this approach to upset the correct proportions of a graphic. Don't worry, this is easily fixed and is described in Module 6.

If you wish to follow this approach and still have text in your page, place the picture in the pasteboard area to the right of the page.

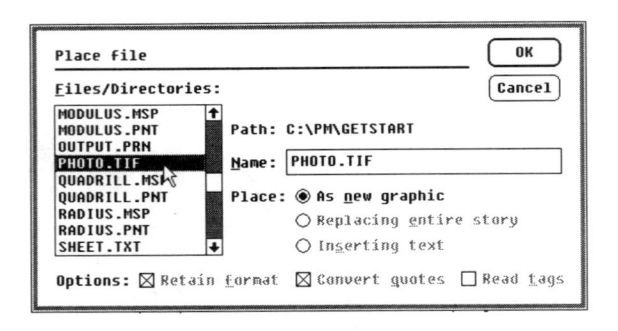

*Figure 27.* Here we have selected the file PHOTO.TIF to load onto the PageMaker page.

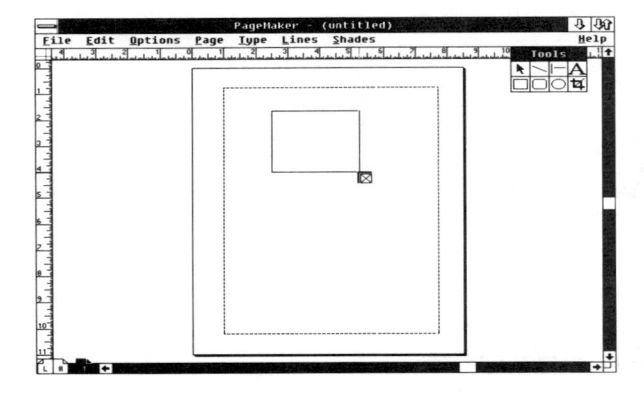

*Figure 28.* We hold the mouse button down and once again draw a box the size that we would like our picture to come out at. If your page is filled with text from the previous examples, use the area to the right of the page.

62

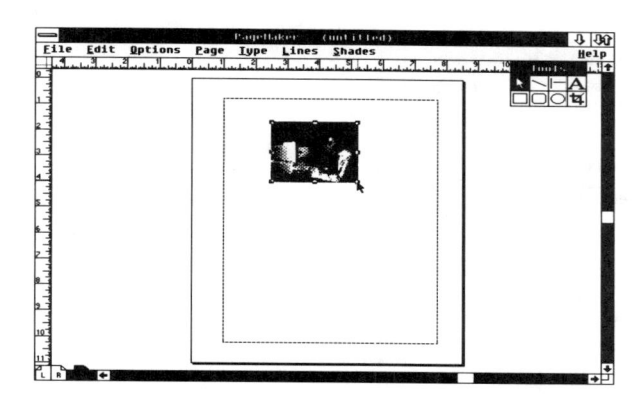

*Figure 29. When we release the mouse button, the image fills the box we created for it.*

Very simply, this is the way to load files into PageMaker—choose the *Place* command, select your file, and flow it onto the page. The following modules will look at ways in which these files can be manipulated, once imported, including both text and graphics.

If you wish to clear your screen of text and/or graphics, select the pointer tool from the toolbox, and click on each text block or graphic. As you click on each item, press the Delete key.

## Options for importing text

You may have noticed several choices that can be made when importing text files—the choices that appear along the bottom of the Place dialog box. These include *Retain format, Convert quotes,* and *Read tags* (see Figure 30).

*Retain format* will, if selected, make sure that any formatting applied to text at the word processor level still applies in PageMaker. If it is not selected, the text will not come through with any of the formatting applied in the word processor.

*Convert quotes* will convert the " and ' quotes often used by word processors to the more professional ", ", ', and '.

*Read Tags* (which is discussed in more detail in Module 11—PageMaker Style Sheets) will read formatting codes imbedded in the text at the word processor level.

The other options, located to the right of the window include: *As new story, Replacing entire story,* and *Inserting text.* These are discussed in Module 9—PageMaker Templates.

## Module 2 - Loading Files

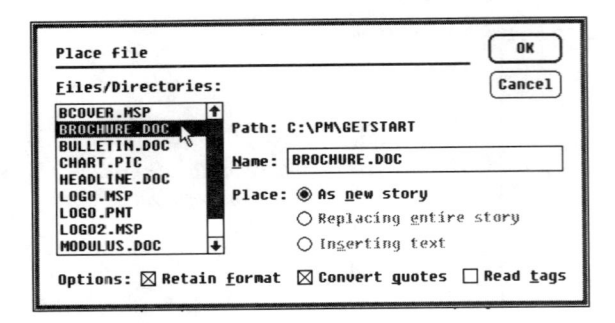

*Figure 30.* Several options can be selected when importing text. These options are located at the bottom of the Place file dialog box.

# Module 2 Exercise

# Loading Files

# Module 2 Exercise—Loading Files into PageMaker

In this exercise we are going to load files into PageMaker, both graphics and text. We will also go through the process of locating these files on the hard disk from the PageMaker *Place* command dialog box.

This training material is structured so that people of all levels of expertise with PageMaker can use it to gain maximum benefit. In order to do this, we have structured this material so that the bare exercise is listed below this paragraph on just one page, with no hints. The following pages contain the steps needed to complete this exercise for those that need additional prompting. The **Loading Files into PageMaker** module should be referenced if you need further help or explanations.

## Module 2 exercise steps

1. *Start PageMaker.*
2. *Create a new PageMaker document, using these parameters:*

    *A4 page*

    *20 mm margins all around the page*

    *Double-sided, Facing pages*

    *One page long*

    *Orientation tall (portrait)*
3. *Set the measurement preferences to use millimeters.*
4. *Load in a text file from the GETSTART subdirectory called BROCHURE.DOC. Flow this text onto the first page using the manual flow method.*
5. *Load in the graphic PHOTO.TIF from the GETSTART subdirectory and place it in the pasteboard area.*
6. *Change the page view to Actual size and scroll to the top right-hand corner of the page.*

The detailed steps to complete this exercise are located on the following pages.

*Module 2 Exercise - Loading Files*

# The steps in detail

*1. Start PageMaker.*

This first step is achieved by either locating the PM.EXE file from Windows (if full Windows is loaded in your machine), or by typing PM at the DOS prompt. If your machine has some sort of menu system loaded, it will be totally different. Figures 1 and 2 refer to starting PageMaker from Windows.

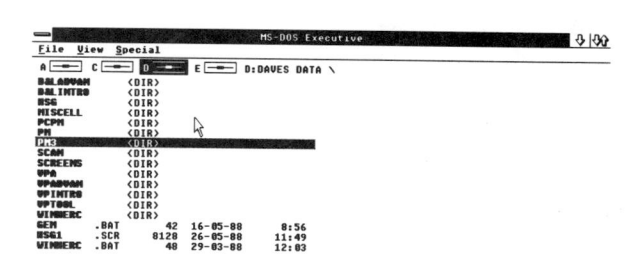

*Figure 1.* Through Windows you must locate the PM.EXE file, most probably located in a directory called PM.

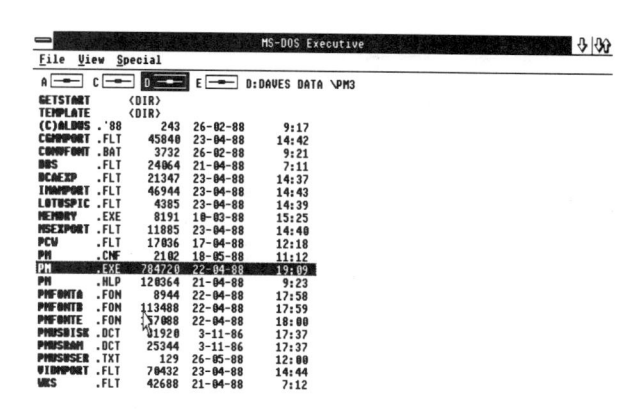

*Figure 2.* Within the PM directory should be files similar to these — although not necessarily the same. Locate the file named PM.EXE and double-click on it to open it.

Module 2 Exercise - Loading Files

2. Create a new PageMaker document, using these parameters:

    A4 page

    20 mm margins all around the page

    Double-sided, Facing pages

    One page long

    Orientation tall (portrait)

After starting PageMaker, a new document is created by selecting the *New* command (Figure 3) from the **File** menu. From this command comes the dialog box of Figure 4.

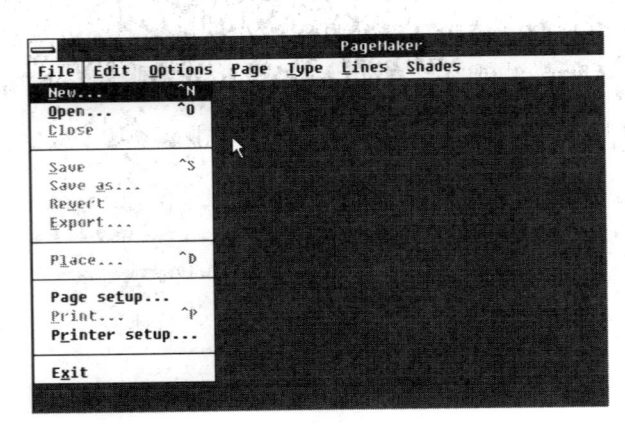

*Figure 3*. *The New command from the **File** menu must be used to create a new PageMaker publication.*

*Figure 4*. *The New dialog box contains all the options we need to create the page described in step 2 of this exercise. This figure shows current default values. Figure 5 shows the new values required for this exercise.*

*Module 2 Exercise - Loading Files*

In this dialog box you set up all the parameters listed in step 2. The page size is set to A4, the margins altered to 20 mm each, Double-sided and Facing pages is set, and the Orientation is set to portrait (tall). The # of pages is set at 1. The dialog box will end up as shown in Figure 5. Make sure that you have not specified 20 inches as the margins. To ensure that 20 mm is the margin measurement (even if you are working in inches) put 20m in each margin rectangle. This will ensure margins are set exactly to 20 mm. Click OK when your dialog box matches Figure 5.

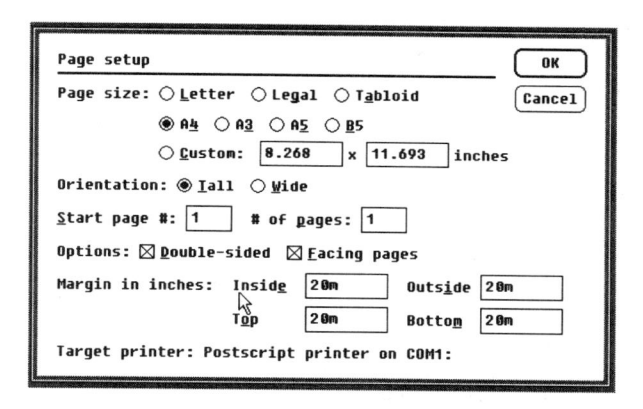

*Figure 5. Your dialog box should be set up exactly as is this one.*

3. *Set the measurement preferences to use millimeters.*

These preferences are set using the *Preferences* command in the **Edit** menu. Invoke this command (Figure 6), and set up the dialog box as shown in Figure 7.

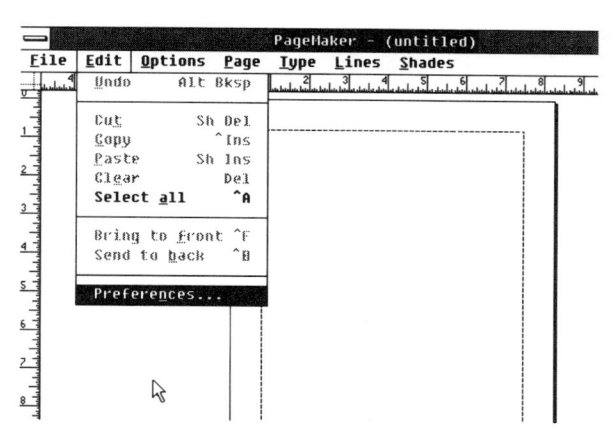

*Figure 6. Use the Preferences command to set measurement units.*

69

*Module 2 Exercise - Loading Files*

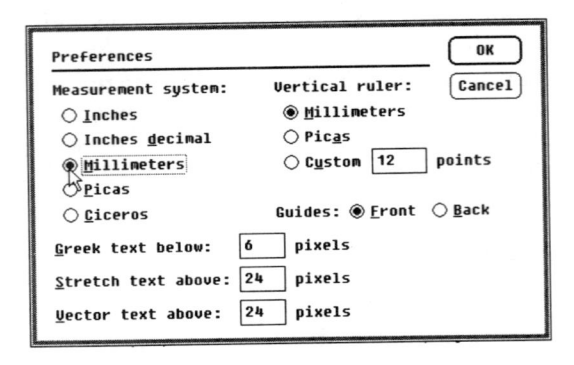

*Figure 7. Select the correct measurement unit and click on OK.*

As this is only an example of using the *Preferences* command, you may prefer to set the measurement units to something more suitable to you—perhaps inches. Remember, this unit of measure can always be overridden by inserting m for millimeters, p for picas, and i for inches in any dialog box.

*4. Load in a text file from the GETSTART subdirectory called BROCHURE.DOC. Flow this text onto the first page using the manual flow method.*

The first step here is to use the *Place* command from the **File** menu (Figure 8). From there, you will be presented with the dialog box of Figure 9.

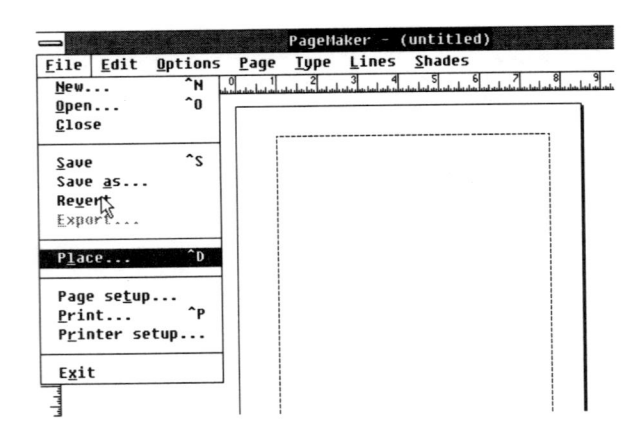

*Figure 8. The Place command is the one used to import all files into PageMaker.*

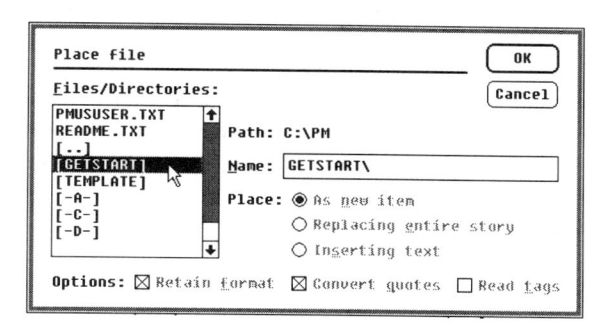

*Figure 9.* If you opened PageMaker from the PM directory, you will be presented with a list that contains the subdirectory GETSTART—this subdirectory exists within the PM directory.

If you opened up PageMaker from the PM directory (either through Windows or not), you will be looking at something similar to what we are looking at in Figure 9—the subdirectory GETSTART should be listed. If it is, double-click on its name. If it's not, double-click on the double-dots until you reach the root directory. Now search for the PM directory (or something similar) and then the GETSTART subdirectory within this.

Once you have entered the GETSTART subdirectory, you should have no trouble locating the text file BROCHURE.DOC. Double-click on its name and wait a few seconds for the file to load. Your GETSTART subdirectory may have slightly different files than our list in Figure 10. This doesn't matter—just find and select BROCHURE.DOC.

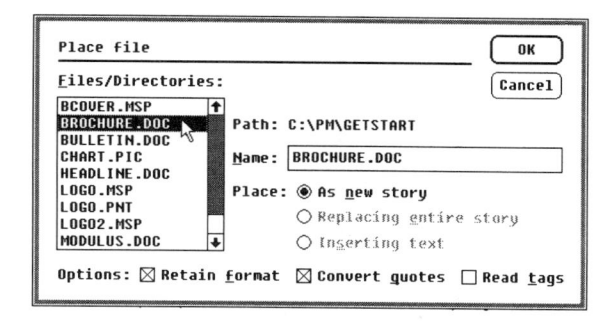

*Figure 10.* Double-click on the GETSTART subdirectory name from Figure 9, and double-click on BROCHURE.DOC from this figure.

*Module 2 Exercise - Loading Files*

Your mouse cursor will change shape after these first few seconds are up. It should be the same as shown in Figure 11—the manual flow mode. If it is not, go to the **Options** menu and choose the *Autoflow* command. To load this file onto the page, move the mouse cursor to the top left-hand corner of the page margins (Figure 11) and click the mouse once. The text will then flow onto the page (Figure 12).

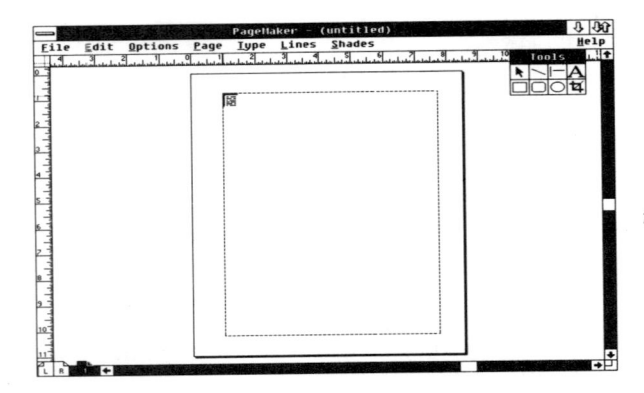

*Figure 11.* Note the shape of the mouse cursor denoting a file was successfully loaded. Position the mouse cursor from where you want the text to flow (normally the top of the page).

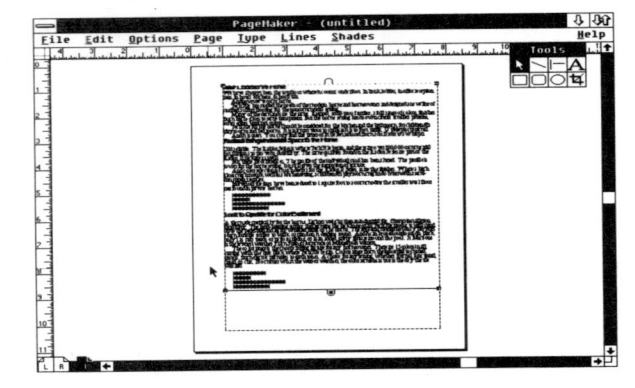

*Figure 12.* The text will flow across and down to fill the page.

5. Load in the graphic PHOTO.TIF from the GETSTART subdirectory and place it in the pasteboard area.

The *Place* command is again used to load in a file, no matter what format. This time, however, you will be immediately looking at the contents of the GETSTART subdirectory—as this is where we retrieved our last file.

72

*Module 2 Exercise - Loading Files*

Locate the file PHOTO.TIF, and double-click on the filename (Figure 13).

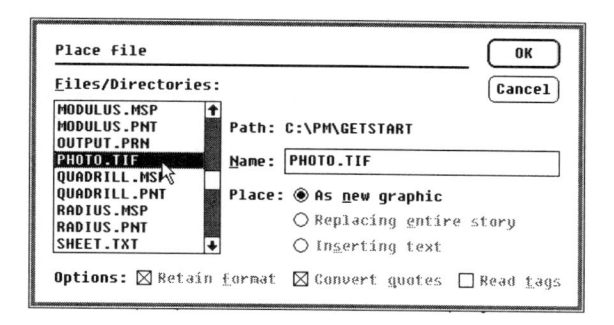

*Figure 13. Select the file PHOTO.TIF after selecting the Place command again. You will be taken to the same directory as you retrieved the last file from—in our case the GETSTART subdirectory.*

To place this file on the pasteboard area, move the mouse from the page and onto the area next to the page (see Figure 14). You can deposit the photo onto the pasteboard area using one of two techniques—either the one-click method (we used above for the text flow) or the box-draw method. To use the latter method, hold down the mouse button, move the mouse down and across to the right of the page, and release it when the box looks as big as you need (Figure 15).

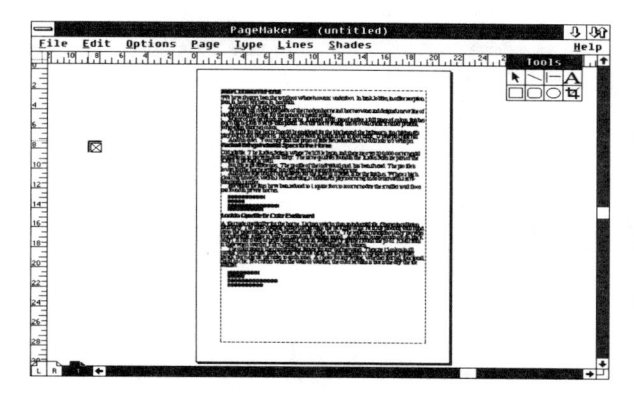

*Figure 14. Note again the different shape of the mouse cursor. Move it off into the pasteboard area, and either click the mouse button, or hold it down, drag the mouse down and across the screen, and release it. Either way the image file should appear on the screen.*

Module 2 Exercise - Loading Files

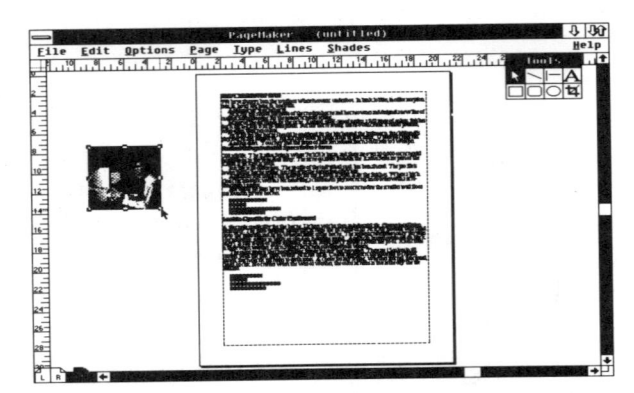

*Figure 15.* The photo on the page.

6. Change the page view to Actual size and scroll to the top right-hand corner of the page.

The page view is changed via the **Page** menu. Select the command *Actual size* from this menu (Figure 16).

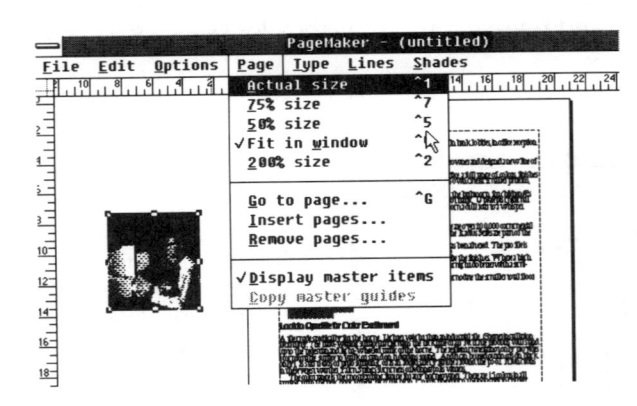

*Figure 16.* Changing to Actual size view can be done in a variety of ways, but this way is the most straightforward.

Initially, you will not be looking at the top right-hand corner of the page—in fact, it will more likely be the middle-left of the page. The scroll bars must be used to move the page around.

*Module 2 Exercise - Loading Files*

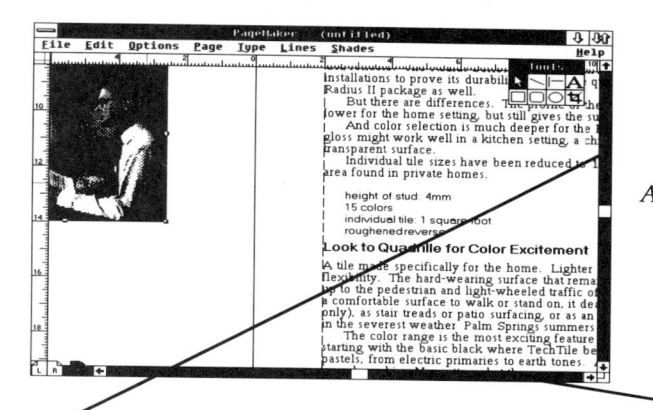

*Figure 17. Initially changing to Actual size will put you about half-way up the left-hand side of the page.*

The two areas on the scroll bar that move you to the top right are this area and this area. Two mouse clicks in each of these areas could be used to get you to the area we are after. You could, of course, use this arrow and this arrow, but that would be slower.

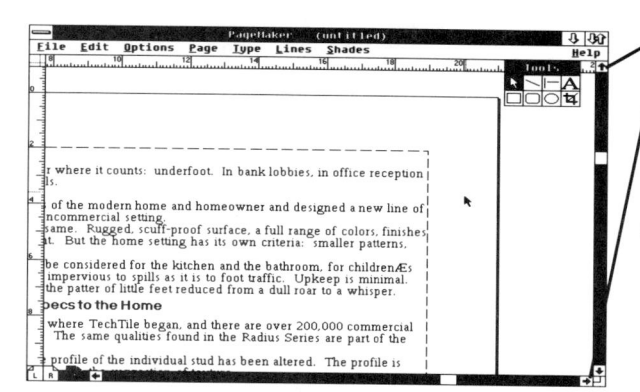

*Figure 18. We clicked twice in the areas indicated in Figure 17 to get this result —a look at the top right-hand corner of the page.*

After completing this exercise you should be familiar with the basic techniques involved in the use of PageMaker—how menus work, how dialog boxes work, how to load files, and how to move around the screen. This is a good start for moving to the next module.

# Module 3

# Manipulating PageMaker Text Blocks

# Manipulating PageMaker Text Blocks

As we have already seen, we can import text from other applications onto the PageMaker page. We need to have far more control over the text, however, than we did in the last module. We need to be able to manipulate a block of text in many different ways.

If you wish to follow along with us in this module, load any text onto the page. For example, select and load BROCHURE.DOC as outlined in the previous module. Use the load method discussed in Figures 25 and 26 of Module 2 to get your text onto the page similar to that shown in Figure 1.

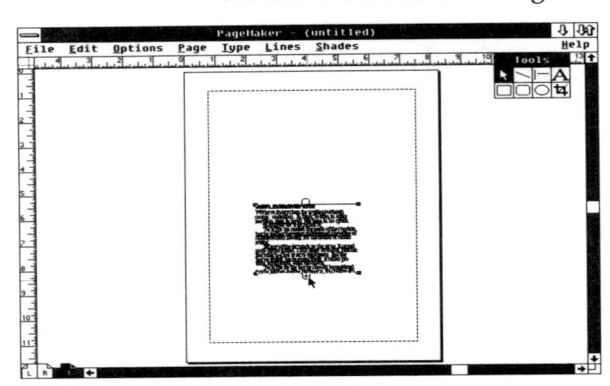

*Figure 1. Make sure that you have a block of text on your page similar to this if you wish to move through this module with us.*

Before we start this module, you must also make sure that you have the pointer (arrow) tool activated in the Toolbox. This will allow us to select and manipulate our text (Figure 1).

What we now have on the page in Figure 1 is referred to as a *text block*. We are not going to be looking at sentences, letters, and words in this module, but rather the manipulation of the whole block of text as one unit.

If it is not selected, click on the block of text, anywhere, just once. Once selected, you should see several things appear around the edge of this text block (Figure 2) including: a line above and below the text, a *"windowshade handle"* above and below the text, and a dot (or small square) in each corner of the text block. This indicates that the text block is selected. Each one of these selection indicators can be used in a different way to manipulate that text block.

*Module 3 - Manipulating PageMaker Text Blocks*

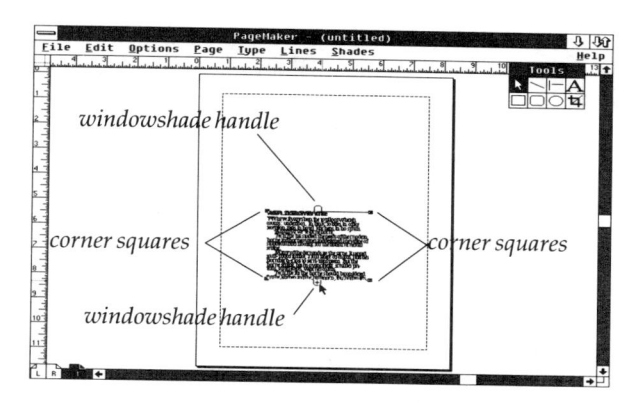

*Figure 2.* Note the features of the selected text. A line above and below, a windowshade handle above and below, and a dot or small square in every corner.

## Moving text

Any text block can be easily moved on the page without changing shape the block's shape in any way. There are two ways to do this. First, hold down the mouse button on the block of text, somewhere near the middle of the text. Hold the mouse button down and don't move the mouse for a few seconds. The arrow cursor changes to a four-arrow type, the handles and corner squares disappear and the text is bounded by dotted lines. Now move the mouse anywhere on the desk, with the mouse button still held down, and the text will move anywhere on the screen that you wish. This method is illustrated in Figure 3.

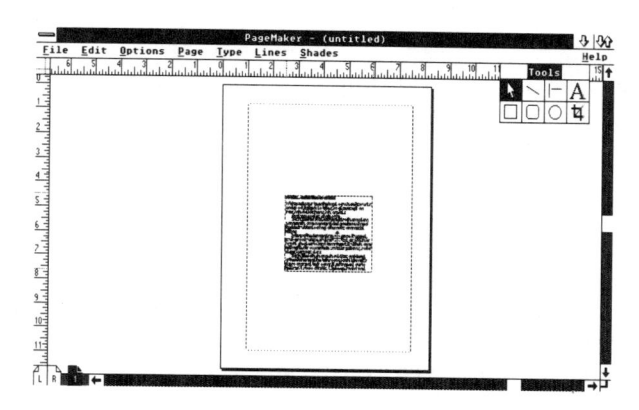

*Figure 3.* Here we have held down the mouse button on the text block, waited several seconds, and then moved the mouse. The entire text block moves with the mouse in the manner shown.

79

Alternatively, you can hold the mouse button down on the text and move the mouse immediately. What this will do is move the selected text block, but only in a boxed outline form. Once the mouse button is released, the text will reformat in its new position. This is illustrated in Figure 4.

Clicking anywhere outside the text block will *deselect* that block.

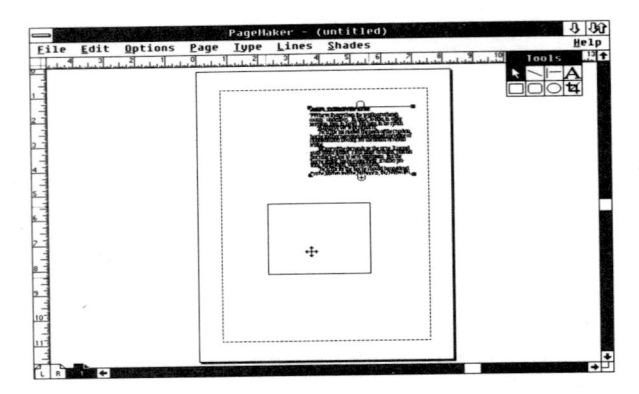

*Figure 4. Here we have held down the mouse button on the text block and moved the mouse immediately. Only a boxed outline of the text follows the mouse in this case—often a quicker, yet less exact way to move text.*

## Resizing text blocks

Text blocks can be resized as simply as they can be moved. Once again, there are several ways in which a text block can be resized. We will look at each one in turn.

People often think they must define their column width, number of columns, page breaks, and so on, from the word processor they used to create the text. However, all this kind of work is done from within PageMaker and can be altered at will, regardless of how the text was created in the word processor. The word processor is used basically as a text input medium—very little formatting work need be done at this early stage at all.

*Module 3 - Manipulating PageMaker Text Blocks*

## Resizing vertically

The method we are about to describe is used to resize a text block vertically—the width of the text block is not altered at all. Before we do this, however, let's get one thing straight—there is no way, using these methods, that you will lose any text. It may look as though text has disappeared, but rest assured, it will come back.

With reference to Figure 5, note the handles above and below the selected block of text. The top handle should be empty, while the bottom handle has a small plus sign in it. The plus sign indicates that this text block contains more text than is currently visible. If the sign was a hash symbol (#), this would indicate the end of a particular text block.

Let's now say that we want to lengthen this text block vertically. The way this is done is as follows. Hold the mouse button down on the bottom handle (with the plus sign). You must be fairly exact when doing this, and you must make sure that you do not simply click once—you must hold the mouse button down. Once you have done this, you can move the mouse up and down, keeping the button down, as much as you like. Wherever you release the mouse button is going to be the new length of the text block (see Figures 5 and 6). If you moved the mouse up, text will have disappeared from the page. However, if you moved the mouse button down, more text will have appeared on the page. (Unless, of course, the text file ran out of text; in which case the bottom handle would contain a hash symbol and no further text will appear.)

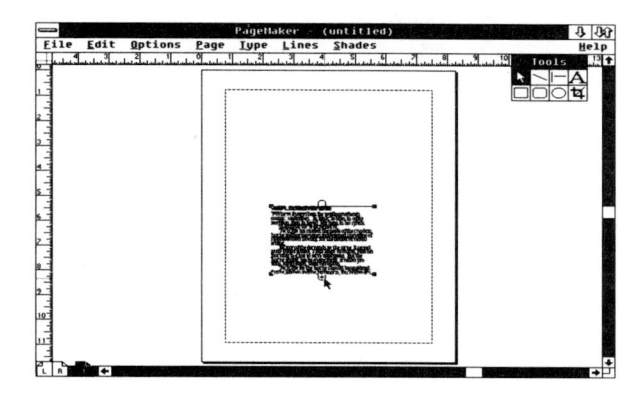

*Figure 5.* To resize the text block vertically, hold down the mouse button directly on top of the bottom handle (which contains a + symbol, indicating more text is contained in the text block than is visible).

*Module 3 - Manipulating PageMaker Text Blocks*

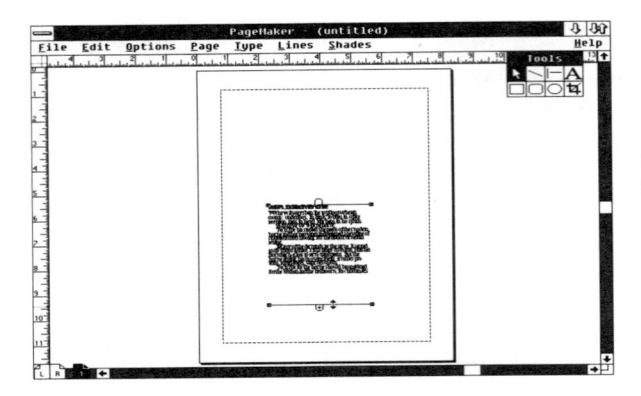

*Figure 6.* Hold the mouse button down on this symbol and move the mouse down or up. After releasing the mouse button, the text will reformat at its new size.

Alternatively, the text block could have been resized using the same method on the top handle. Holding the mouse button down on this handle will allow you to resize the text in the exact same way (Figure 7). However, if you shorten the text block from the top, the text will disappear from the bottom of the block. You cannot hide text from the top of a block using this method.

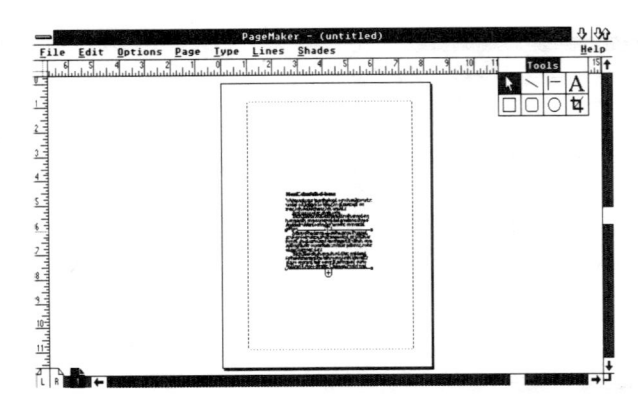

*Figure 7.* Text blocks can also be vertically resized by grabbing (holding down the mouse button on) the top handle and moving the mouse down.

Module 3 - Manipulating PageMaker Text Blocks

## Resizing horizontally

If you would like to horizontally increase or decrease the width of a text block, hold down the mouse button on any dot in any corner of the text block. You must be fairly exact when doing this, and you may miss the dot altogether at first. If you do, reselect the text block, and try again until you get it. You will know when you have selected it correctly when moving the mouse button causes the effect as shown in Figure 8 to appear.

This method of grabbing a corner dot with the mouse can, in effect, allow you to size text both horizontally and vertically.

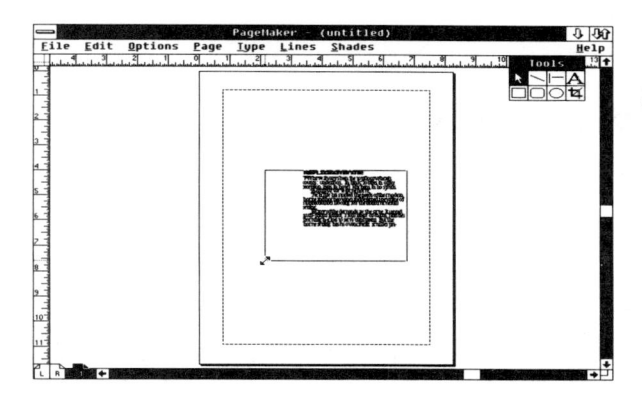

*Figure 8.* To resize text blocks horizontally, hold down the mouse button on any corner of a selected text block. In every corner of this block there should be a dot—this is what you should grab. As you move the mouse, a rectangle is created on screen indicating the new size of the text block. Text blocks can also be resized vertically in this fashion.

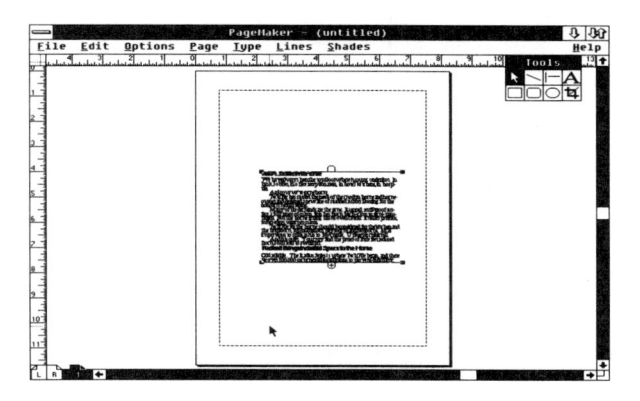

*Figure 9.* After we release the mouse button, the text block formats to the exact size of the rectangle of Figure 8.

83

Module 3 - Manipulating PageMaker Text Blocks

The Figure 8 box which appears on screen is letting you know the new dimensions of the text block as soon as you release the mouse button. You will find that the text block can be adjusted both horizontally and vertically at the same time, and the text will reflow immediately (Figure 9).

## Column guides

There are several guides that exist in PageMaker that can be used to exercise control over text blocks. Perhaps the first and most common type of guide that you will use is the column guide.

To adjust the number of columns on the page, select the *Column guides* command from the **Options** menu (Figure 10). You will be presented with the dialog box of Figure 11.

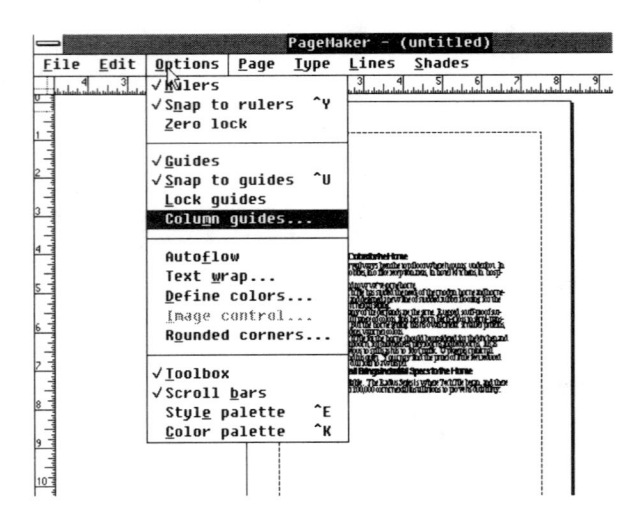

*Figure 10.* The Column guides command in the **Options** menu is used to select the number of columns for the page.

Within this dialog box, you first input the number of columns you want, and then the amount of space to be included between the columns. Upon clicking OK, you will notice some column guides have now been added to the page (Figure 12).

*Module 3 - Manipulating PageMaker Text Blocks*

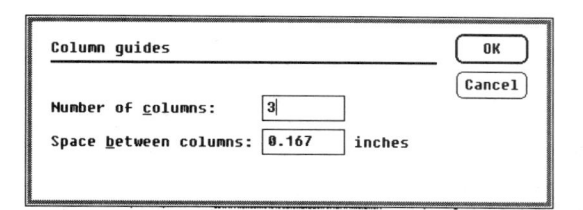

*Figure 11.* The Column guides command dialog box. Here we have defined three columns with 0.167 inches between each one.

Text will not immediately flow into these columns—it is up to us to flow the text into these columns. These column guides initially appear in the background. Text currently on the page stays at its previously defined width.

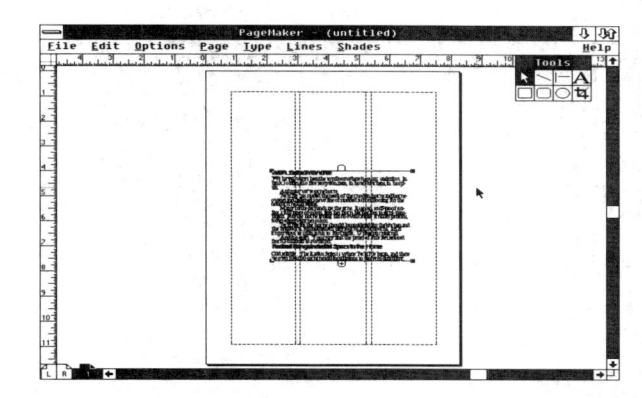

*Figure 12.* Although existing text on the page will not flow into the three columns automatically, the guides appear on the page, and any text now added to the page will flow into these new columns.

If you wish to continue following our operations, select your text as shown in Figure 12 and press the Delete (or Backspace) key. This text is then deleted. Choose BROCHURE.DOC again with the *Place* command, and flow it down column 1 of the page as shown in Figures 13 and 14.

Whenever a new text file is flowed, it will obey the bounds of a column guide. See Figures 13 and 14 which illustrate this point.

85

*Module 3 - Manipulating PageMaker Text Blocks*

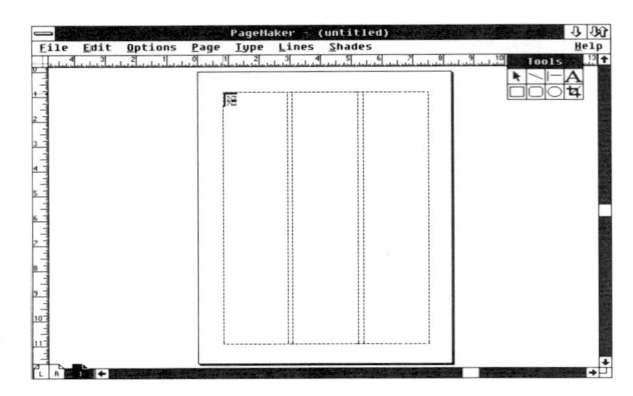

*Figure 13.* On a page defined with three columns, we are about to flow text down the page.

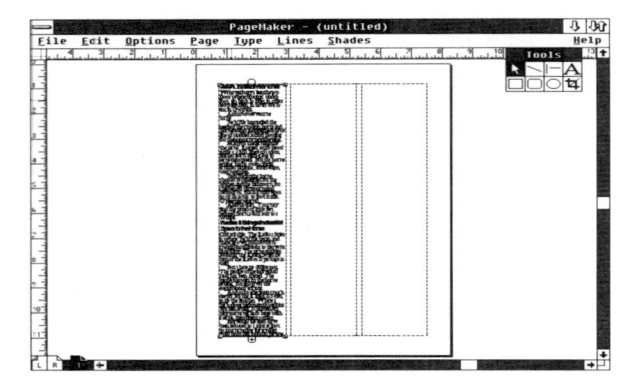

*Figure 14.* Note how the text flows down the first column rather than across the whole page, as it would if no columns were defined.

The *Column guides* dialog box only selects equal size columns. Irregular columns may be achieved by manually moving the column guides themselves. To do this, hold down the mouse button directly on a column guide, away from text if possible, and move the mouse button to the left or the right. You need to select the pointer tool and also wait a few seconds until the cursor changes to a horizontal double arrow. The column guide will move with the mouse. You cannot just pull one column guide. The set of column guides, as shown in Figure 15, moves together.

*Module 3 - Manipulating PageMaker Text Blocks*

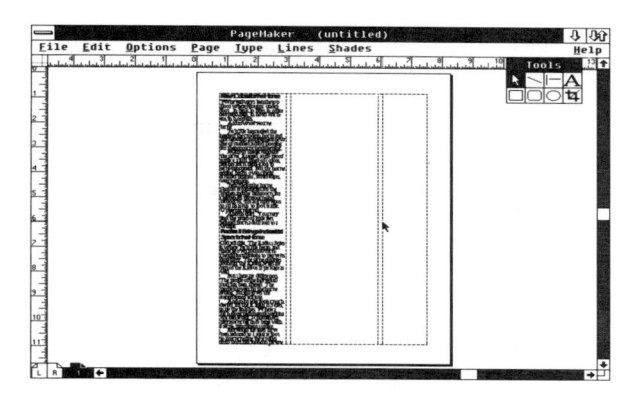

***Figure 15.*** *Irregular columns can be created by holding the mouse button down on a set of column guides and dragging it to the left or right.*
*Make sure the pointer tool is selected and that you wait for the double-headed horizontal arrows to appear.*

## Margin guides

We have already discussed margin guides, the guides we can see around the inside edges of the page, in Modules 1 and 2. These are defined when we start a particular publication however, they can be altered manually if we wish. To do this, hold down the mouse button on either the left or the right margin, and move the mouse to the left or the right. A dotted margin guide will follow the mouse, and where it is released will be the new text margin (Figure 16). Any text flowed onto this page will obey these margins.

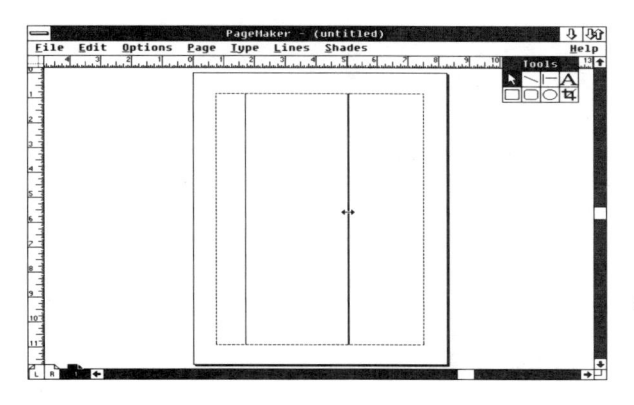

***Figure 16.*** *The left and/or right margin guides for the page can be altered from within a publication by holding down the mouse button on the left or right margin, and dragging them where necessary. To better illustrate this we have temporarily changed from three columns to one column through the Figure 11 dialog box.*

87

*Module 3 - Manipulating PageMaker Text Blocks*

All guides on the page, whether they be margin, column, or even ruler (which we look at in Module 5), are affected by several commands in the **Options** menu. Bear in mind, these guides never appear on the printed output. They are simply there to help control the layout of your document. The first command which modifies guides is the *Guides* command. This hides or shows all guides (Figures 17 and 18).

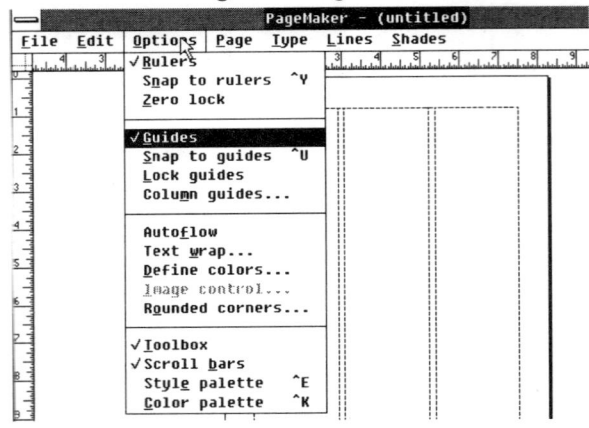

*Figure 17. Selecting the Guides command will alternately hide and show column guides on the screen. Note that with all such commands, a check to the left indicates that the command is on.*

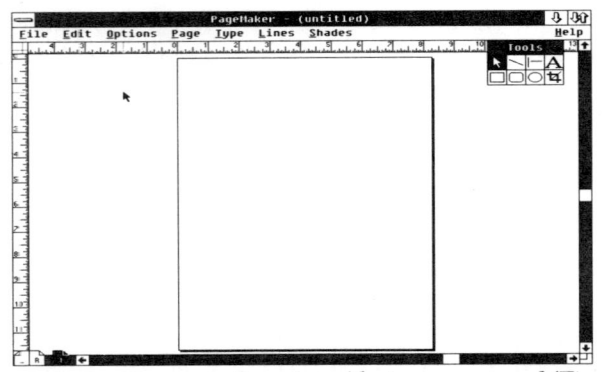

*Figure 18. Here the guides are hidden from the page—this gives a better indication of what the page is going to look like when printed.*

*Snap to guides* is a command (Figure 19) that toggles the ability for all text and graphics on the PageMaker page to "magnetically snap" to the various page guides whenever they are in close proximity. This feature is usually best left on, for it makes sure that all text and graphics blocks are flush with margins and each other. It is often turned off when working close to a guide that you do not want to to be flush with.

88

*Module 3 - Manipulating PageMaker Text Blocks*

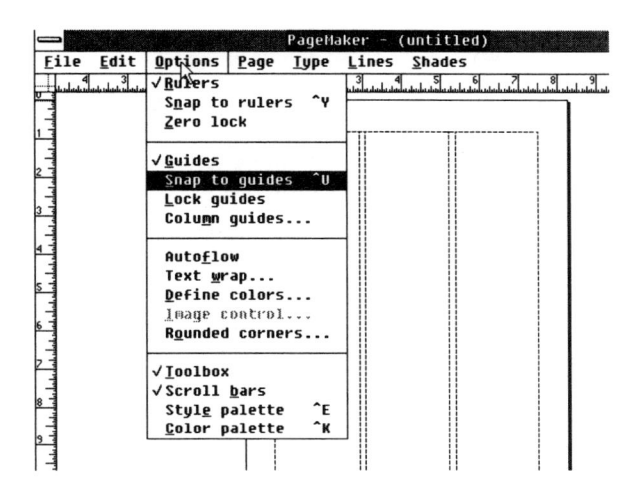

*Figure 19.* Selecting the Snap to guides command, which will be on by default, will allow text and graphics to snap flush to guides if they are close to those guides.

*Lock guides* is, as the name suggests, a lock for all guides on the page (Figure 20). With this command activated, no guides can be moved at all until this command is deselected. This makes sure you don't accidentally move painstakingly positioned guides on the page.

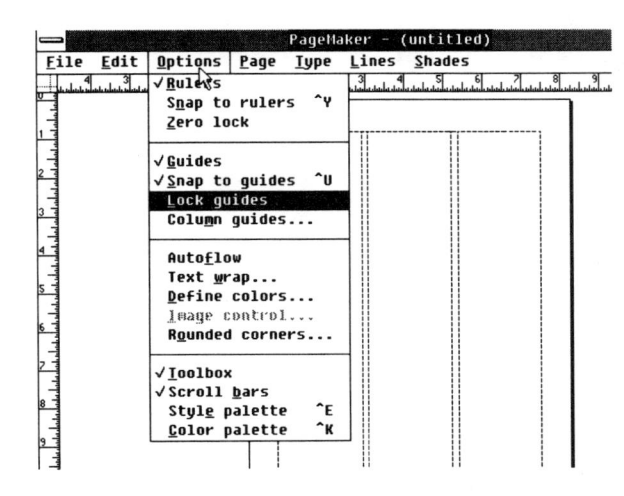

*Figure 20.* All guides can be locked into position using this command, to prevent accidental movement of precisely placed guides.

89

Module 3 - Manipulating PageMaker Text Blocks

## Warning about guides

All guides on the page can occupy a position above or below that of any textual or graphical objects on the page. What this means is: if you try to select text or graphics exactly where a guide is, the guide or the object may be selected first.

This can be controlled through the *Preferences* command in the **Edit** menu (Figure 21). The associated dialog box (Figure 22) provides you with a choice of setting the guides at the front or the back. Alternatively, even if the guides are set to the front, it is possible to choose the *Guides* command in the **Options** menu to temporarily hide the guides from the screen. The particular object can then be selected. Another way to select an object behind a guide is to hold down the Ctrl key while selecting.

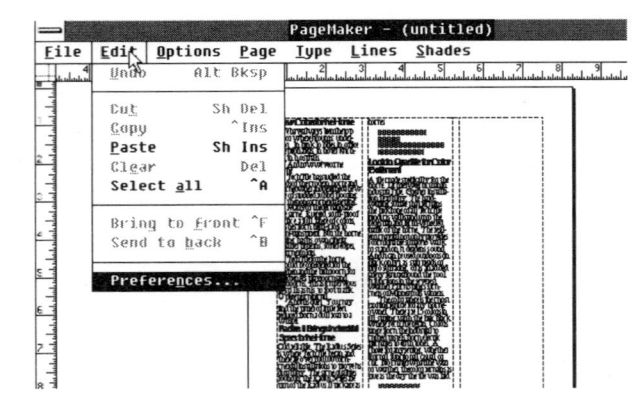

*Figure 21.* To control whether guides should be behind or in front of other objects on the screen, first choose the Preferences command from the **Edit** menu ...

*Figure 22.* ... then from the dialog box that appears, make your choice. We have chosen to have the guides appear at the front.

## Reflowing and following on text

By now, several questions about the movement of text may have entered your mind. How do we get to see all of a text file? How do we flow the same file down several columns? How do we continue a text file from one page to the next? We will look now at exactly how to do these things.

First, we will look at how to continue text from one text block to another. This will have to be done if you want to flow text down several columns on the same page, or even if you want to flow text from one page to another. As you might have guessed, there are again several ways to do this.

Figures 23 to 28 on the following pages show how to flow text manually into two columns across the page. If you wish to follow this approach, define three columns and select BROCHURE.DOC through the *Place* command in the **File** menu. After a few seconds your screen should look like Figure 23. Now flow the text down one column as shown in Figure 24. (Any text or graphics currently on the page can be erased by clicking on it to select it, and pressing the Delete or Backspace key.)

The first and easiest way to continue text from an existing block to a new one is as follows. Select the text block that contains the currently hidden text (such as column 1 of Figure 24). Click once on the bottom handle that contains a plus symbol (Figure 25). After doing this, you will have a new text paragraph mouse cursor, the same one that appears immediately upon loading a new file (Figure 26). You can now flow text anywhere or anyhow you like, with the knowledge that this new text block you are about to create follows on exactly where the text block you just selected leaves off.

Figures 27 and 28 show the results of flowing this text down the middle column.

Manual text flow by column requires that the *Autoflow* command in the **File** menu not have a check beside it. If you find that your text in Figures 23 to 28 flows automatically across multiple columns, then you are in *Autoflow* mode. Go to the **Options** menu and deselect this command. *Autoflow* is discussed later in this module.

*Module 3 - Manipulating PageMaker Text Blocks*

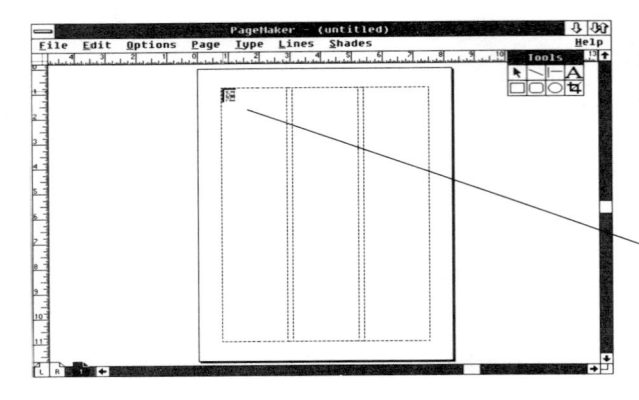

*Figure 23.* We want to flow text manually across two columns. The first step is to define three columns and load a text file. We have selected the BROCHURE.DOC file with the Place command and are ready to load text into the first column.
For manual mode to be in operation, your cursor needs to look the same as the one shown here.

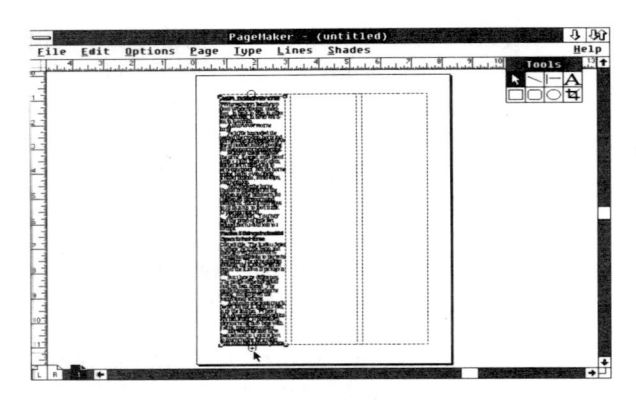

*Figure 24.* By placing the mouse cursor in the top left-hand corner of the first column and clicking the mouse button, the text has flowed down the first column, but stops there. With manual operation, it is up to us to grab the text from one column to continue its flow down the next column.

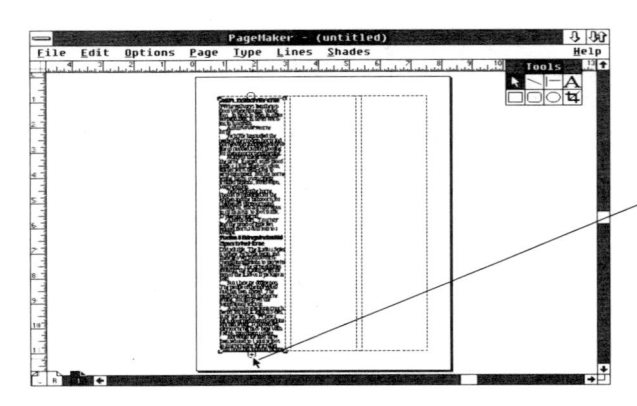

*Figure 25.* Move the mouse button directly over the bottom handle (the one that contains the + symbol) and click once.

*Module 3 - Manipulating PageMaker Text Blocks*

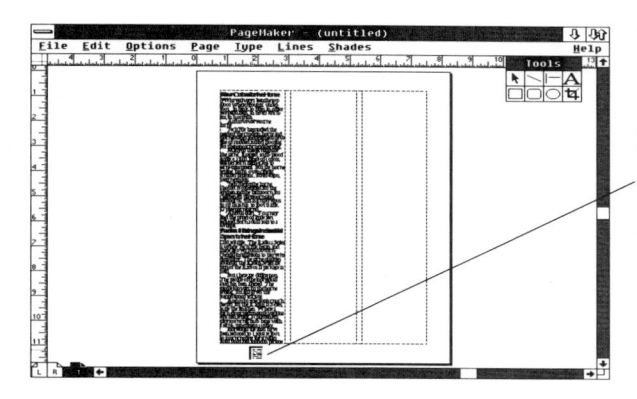

*Figure 26.* After clicking once, you will get this text symbol reappearing as the mouse pointer. If this does not appear, keep trying until it does. All it requires is a quick click.

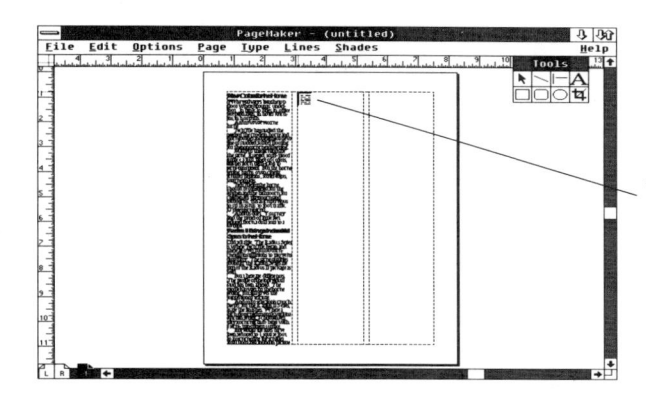

*Figure 27.* After getting the mouse cursor to this shape again, move it so that it appears at the top left-hand corner of the second column, and click the mouse button.

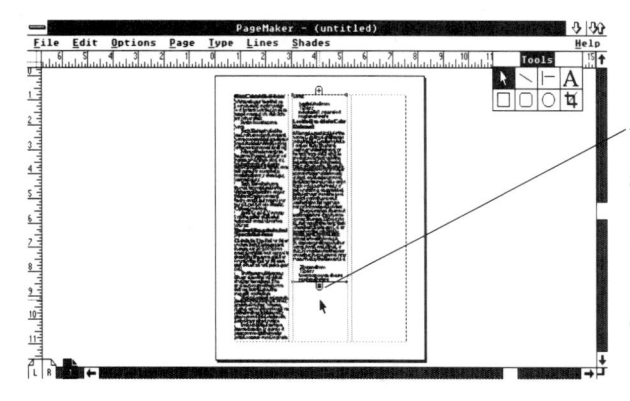

*Figure 28.* The text will flow down the second column. In our case the text in the file we are using ran out before it reached the end of the column. Apart from the fact that it does not fill the column, we are also aware of this because of the # symbol in the bottom handle of this second text block.

Module 3 - Manipulating PageMaker Text Blocks

If a text block contains the plus symbol in its bottom handle, this means that it can be clicked on again, and the rest of the following text can be flowed into a new text block. If you click on this handle by accident, and get the paragraph mouse cursor when you don't want it, simply reselect the selector tool, and it will disappear.

In our Figure 28, we know we have reached the end of the text file as the bottom handle of the second column contains a # symbol and not a + symbol.

## Automatic text flow

Text can be made to run across columns and pages automatically, without operator intervention. To do this, select the command *Autoflow* from the **Options** menu (Figure 29). When this command is selected, the mouse cursor will look like this 🔽 rather than like this 📄 (Figure 30). When you click the mouse to now flow the text, it will flow across columns and pages, fairly quickly, creating any pages it needs as it goes (Figure 31). This process, which can take a bit of time with large text files, can be stopped by clicking the mouse button.

In Figures 30 and 31, we have deleted any text on the page and are reflowing BROCHURE.DOC using the *Autoflow* command.

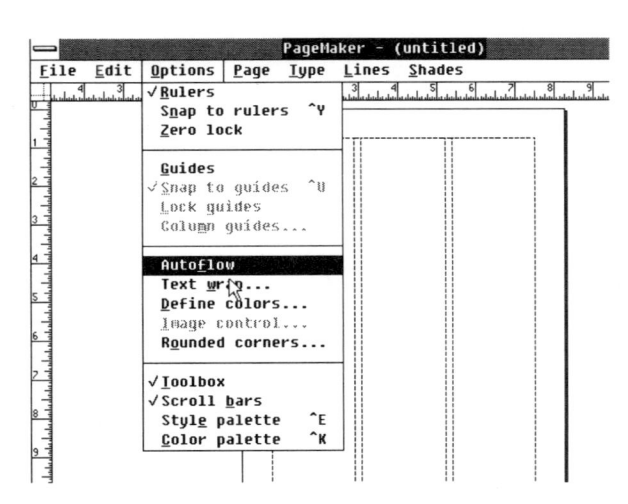

*Figure 29*. Selecting the Autoflow command in the **Options** menu, before text is flowed, allows text to run automatically across columns and pages.

94

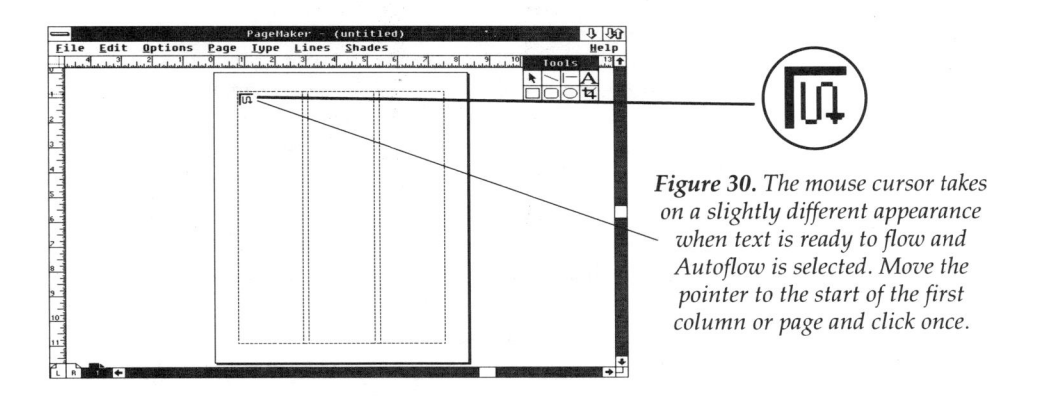

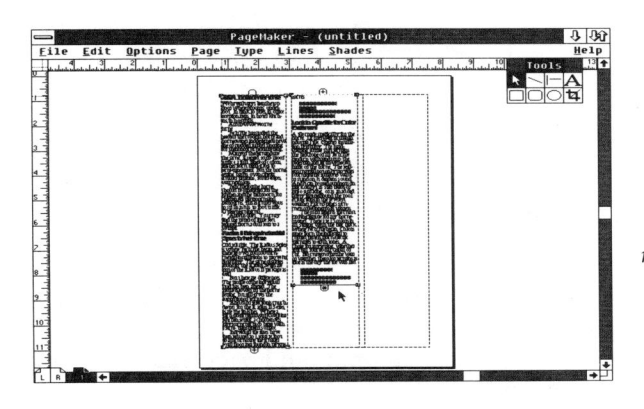

*Figure 30.* The mouse cursor takes on a slightly different appearance when text is ready to flow and Autoflow is selected. Move the pointer to the start of the first column or page and click once.

*Figure 31.* Text will flow across two columns without operator intervention at the end of every column. If this text file had been longer than one page in length, new pages would have been created automatically.

## Semi-automatic text flow

Semi-automatic text flow is just as it sounds—a midway point between manual and automatic text flow. In manual flow, you must click the loaded mouse cursor at the top of every column or page, go to the bottom of that column or page, click on the bottom windowshade handle to reload the cursor, go to the top of the next column or page, and repeat the steps. With automatic text flow you simply click the loaded mouse cursor on the first column or page and the rest is done automatically.

By holding down the Shift key as you are about to click the mouse cursor to flow the text for the first time (regardless of whether the *Autoflow* command has been selected), the mouse cursor will change appearance to look like this: (Figure 32). When it does, the text can be flowed down the first column or page and stop, yet the mouse cursor will be loaded automatically as the text finishes flowing down that column or page. You are then free to click at the top of the second column or page, without having to click on the bottom windowshade handle of the first column.

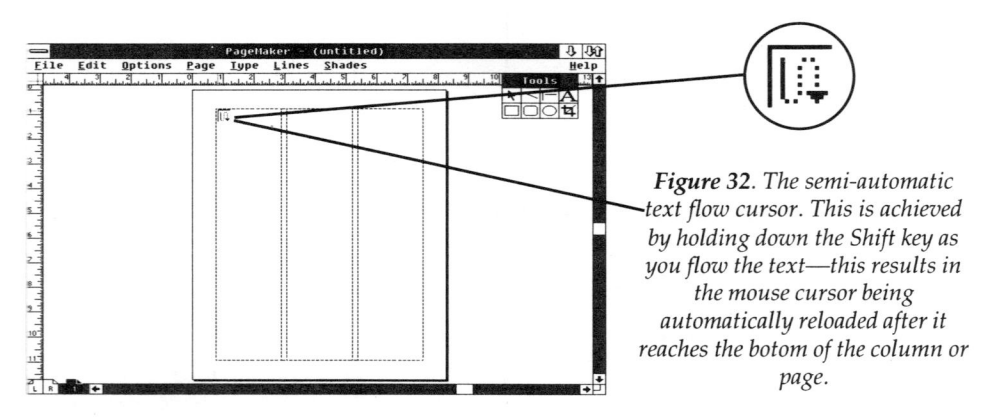

*Figure 32. The semi-automatic text flow cursor. This is achieved by holding down the Shift key as you flow the text—this results in the mouse cursor being automatically reloaded after it reaches the botom of the column or page.*

Semi-automatic text flow is perhaps best used when you want to flow text more quickly than you can manually, but not regularly across the full length of all columns and pages, as automatic text flow does by default.

# Temporarily changing text flow modes

### Automatic to semi-automatic

1. Select *Autoflow* on and click the mouse button after the text has started flowing.

2. Click on the + in the botom windowshade handle.

3. Hold down the Shift key, position the mouse cursor where text is to reflow and click on the mouse button.

The mouse icon changes to the semi-automatic icon and returns to automatic when the Shift key is released.

**Automatic to manual** follows similar steps except that the Ctrl key is used instead of the Shift key.

**Manual to semi-automatic**

1. Select manual text flow mode (*Autoflow* off in the **Options** menu).

2. Press the Shift key and click the mouse button.

The mouse icon changes to the semi-automatic icon and returns to manual when the Shift key is released.

**Manual to automatic** follows similar steps except that the Ctrl key replaces the Shift key. Text will flow to the end of file, or until you click the mouse button again.

## Resizing multiple text blocks

Anytime a text block is split up into several text blocks, any of the individual blocks can be resized and moved without ever losing any continuity of text between the blocks. When the first block in a series of blocks is resized, for example, all other blocks in that series will reformat to compensate for this resizing (see Figures 33 to 35).

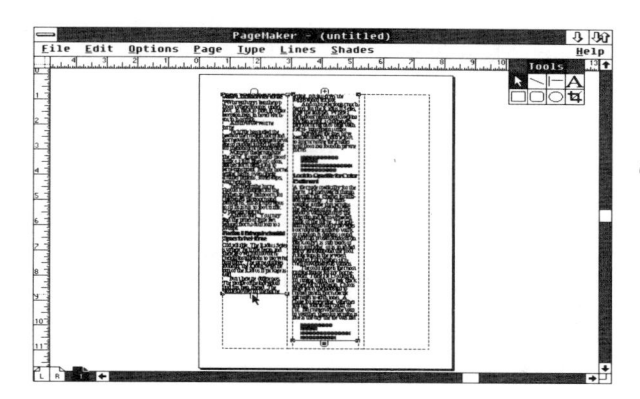

*Figure 33. Any text block in the sequence can be resized without drastic consequences or loss of text. Here we have resized the first column of the page in Figure 31. Note the second column has been changed automatically to compensate.*

## Module 3 - Manipulating PageMaker Text Blocks

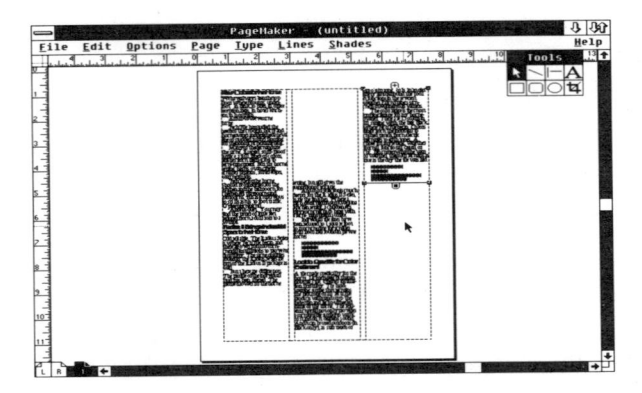

*Figure 34.* Here we have created a third column by reducing the middle column, clicking on the handle at the bottom, and clicking the mouse cursor at the top of the third column.

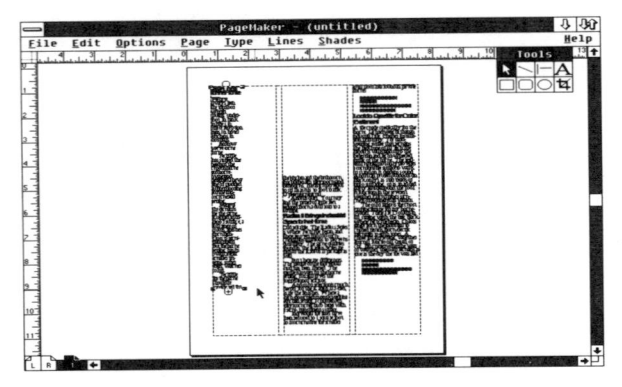

*Figure 35.* Here the first column has been narrowed, still without any loss in the flow or readability of the text.

## Removing text blocks

Text blocks can be selected with the pointer tool and then deleted using the *Cut* or *Clear* commands from the **Edit** menu. The Delete or Backspace keys also delete a text block once selected. When this happens, that text block is removed from the "chain." In other words, the text loses all continuity. Because of this, never use these commands to remove a text block if you want to keep text continuity.

The simple way to remove a text block is similar to the way we resized text blocks earlier. However, instead of resizing the text block a little, hold down the mouse button on the bottom middle handle, and pull the mouse cursor up to the start of the text block (Figures 36 to 39). The entire text block will disappear with only the two handles remaining, as shown in Figure 39.

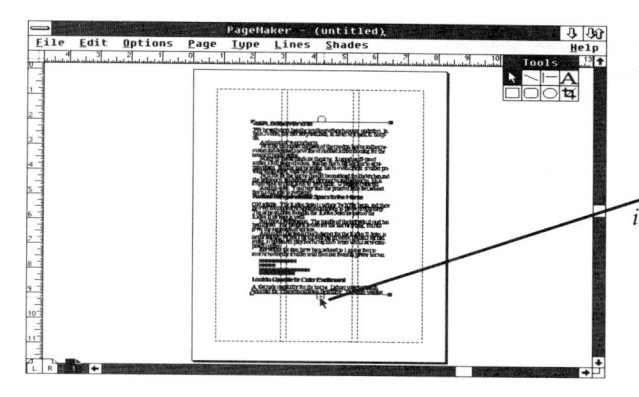

*Figure 36.* Let's say that we want to get rid of this text block. We initially act as though we are going to resize it.

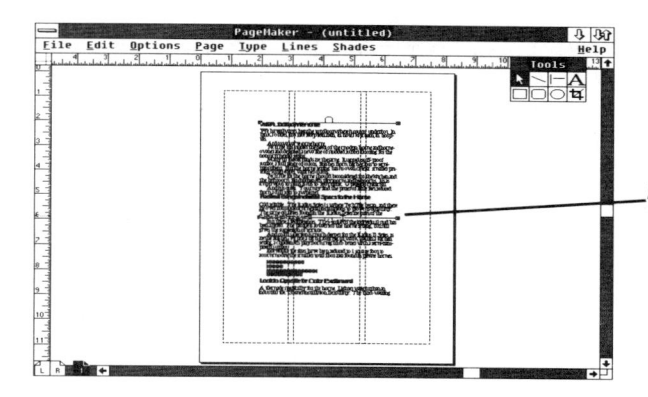

*Figure 37.* Hold down the mouse button on the bottom middle handle, and pull the mouse cursor up the page. However, instead of releasing the mouse button half-way up the column...

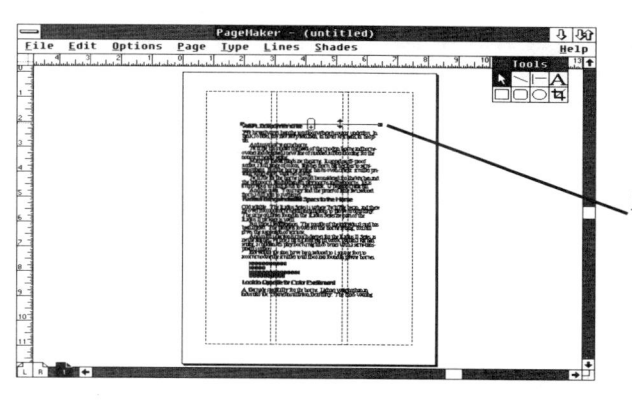

*Figure 38.* ...take it all the way to the top.

*Module 3 - Manipulating PageMaker Text Blocks*

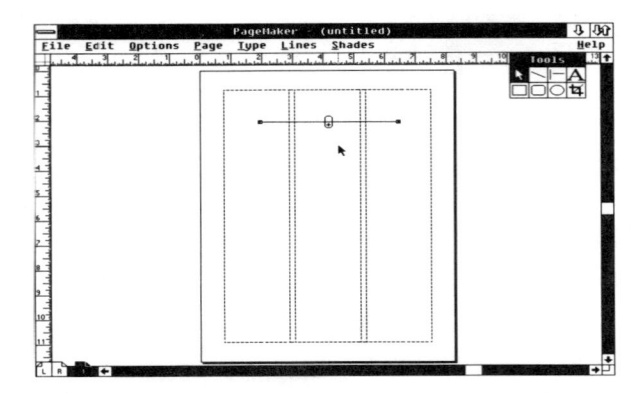

*Figure 39. After releasing the mouse button above the text block, the two handles will appear together on the page.*

When these two handles remain, there are two things you can do. First, if you click anywhere else on the page, they will disappear. Second, if you click on the bottom handle once, they will both still disappear, but you now have a loaded mouse cursor with which you can reflow the text elsewhere (Figure 40).

This method could have been used to remove the middle column of text in, say, Figure 35. Text continuity is not lost; all the text in the middle block that is removed using the above method, moves into the third column and, if necessary, onto another page.

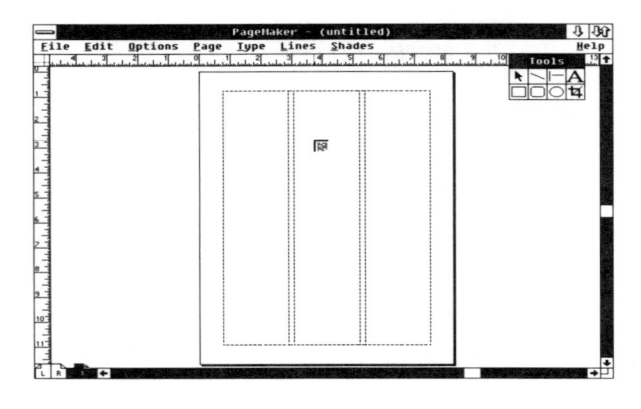

*Figure 40. If the mouse button is clicked on the bottom handle of the text block of Figure 39, the text can be completely reflowed. Text will never be lost, neither will continuity, if this method is used.*

## Module 3 Exercise

# Manipulating PageMaker Text Blocks

# Module 3 Exercise
# Manipulating PageMaker Text Blocks

In this exercise we will be flowing text into columns, and manipulating text files and blocks once we have loaded them in. We will be resizing the columns, horizontally and vertically, and reflowing the text.

This training material is structured so that people of all levels of expertise with PageMaker can use it to gain maximum benefit. In order to do this, we have structured this material so that the bare exercise is listed below this paragraph on just one page, with no hints. The following pages contain the steps needed to complete this exercise for those that need additional prompting. The **Manipulating PageMaker Text Blocks** module should be referenced if you need further help or explanations.

## Module 3 exercise steps

1. *Create a PageMaker document consisting of four A4 pages, 20 mm margins all around, and three columns on each of the four pages.*
2. *Load in the text file BROCHURE.DOC from the GETSTART subdirectory, and flow this file manually down the first column only of the first page.*
3. *Resize the text block in the first column so that it only flows halfway down that column.*
4. *Continue the text flow from halfway down the first column on the first page, to the top of the first column on the second page.*
5. *Move back to the first page and change the number of column guides to two. Resize the existing text block so that it fills the first column entirely. Continue the flow from the first column to the second.*

The steps to complete this exercise are located on the following pages.

Module 3 Exercise - Manipulating PageMaker Text Blocks

## The steps in detail

*1. Create a PageMaker document consisting of four A4 pages, 20 mm margins all around, and three columns on each of the four pages.*

The PageMaker publication itself is created by selecting the *New* command from the **File** menu (Figure 1).

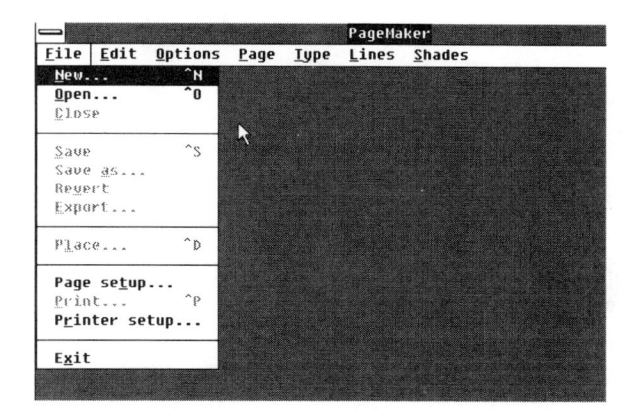

*Figure 1. The New command must be used to create a new PageMaker publication.*

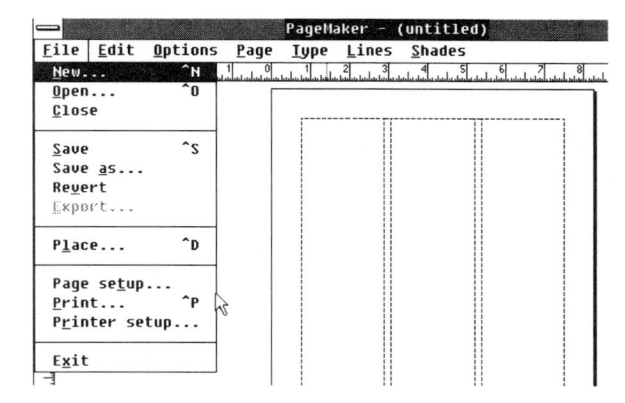

*Figure 2. If a publication is currently open, the New command must be used to open a new publication. This automatically closes the current document. In other words, only one PageMaker document can be open at a time.*

The A4 page size and the 20 mm margins are all set from the dialog box that appears upon selecting *New* (Figure 3). You should also set 4 for the number of pages within this dialog box.

103

*Module 3 Exercise - Manipulating PageMaker Text Blocks*

*Figure 3.* The New dialog box should be set up like this—an A4 page, four pages long, with 20 mm margins all around. If your dialog box says inches for margins, just put an m after each 20 to change to mm.

Once you have set up the box as per Figure 3, click on OK. The first page of the publication will then appear on screen.

To set the three column guides on the page you must use the *Column guides* command in the **Options** menu (Figure 4). From the dialog box that appears upon selecting this command (Figure 5), insert the number 3 for number of columns. The space between columns can be set at the figure indicated, 4.2 mm (or 0.167 inches if your measurements are in inches).

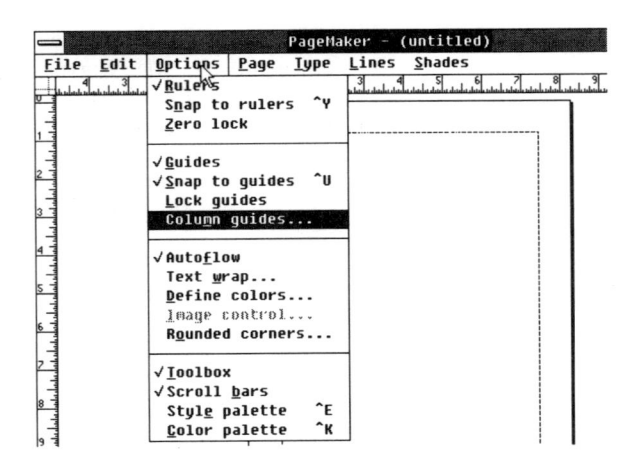

*Figure 4.* The Column guides command from the **Options** menu must be used to create column guides for the page.

*Module 3 Exercise - Manipulating PageMaker Text Blocks*

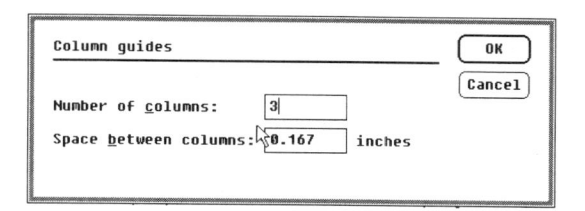

***Figure 5.*** *Insert a 3 for the number of columns for the page. The space between the columns, often called the "gutter," does not matter in this case.*

2. Load in the text file BROCHURE.DOC from the GETSTART subdirectory, and flow this file manually down the first column only of the first page.

To load in the file BROCHURE.DOC you must use the *Place* command from the **File** menu (Figure 6). If, after using this command, you are unsure as to how to locate the GETSTART subdirectory, review the steps in detail for step 4 of the Module 2 Exercise. Figures 7 and 8 briefly summarize the steps.

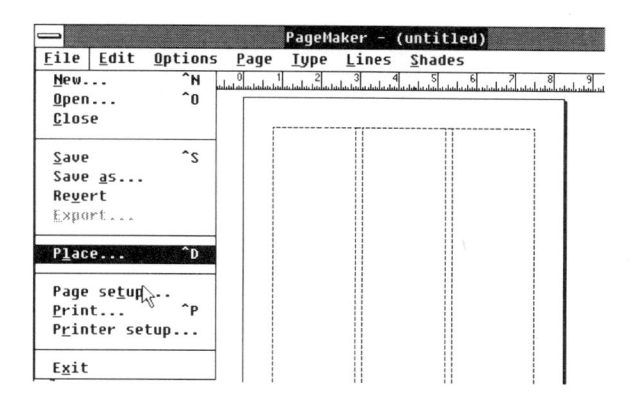

***Figure 6.*** *Choose the Place command to load in any files.*

105

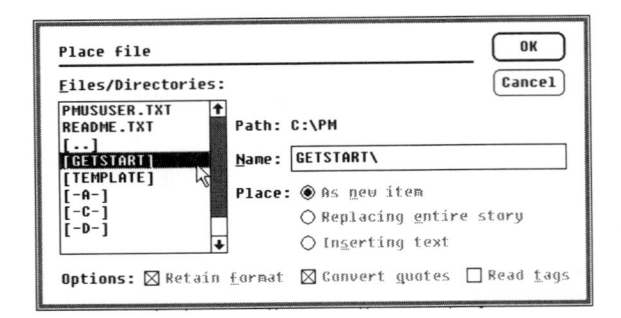

*Module 3 Exercise - Manipulating PageMaker Text Blocks*

*Figure 7.* This is the sight that will greet you after selecting Place. Double click on the GETSTART subdirectory to access the file.

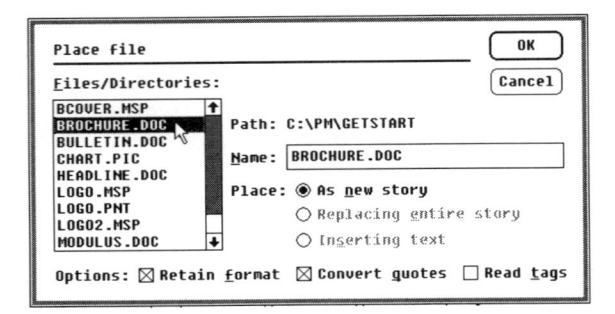

*Figure 8.* In this list of files, double-click on the filename BROCHURE.DOC

Before you flow the text down the first column, make sure that the *Autoflow* command has not been left on. Have a look at the **Options** menu, and if the command *Autoflow* has a check next to it, this means that it is on. Select the command and it will then turn off. If it does not have a check next to it (as in Figure 9), just exit the menu.

Once the text file is ready to load into memory, as in Figure 10, position the mouse cursor so that it appears in the very top left-hand corner of the first column of the page. From here, click the mouse button once. The text will flow down the first column and stop as shown in Figure 11.

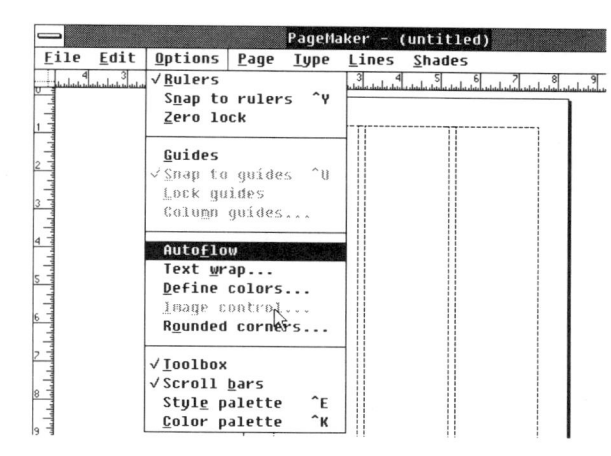

*Module 3 Exercise - Manipulating PageMaker Text Blocks*

*Figure 9.* Before you actually flow any text, make sure the Autoflow command in the **Options** menu has no check next to it. This will ensure that we are in manual mode and that the text only flows down one column at a time.

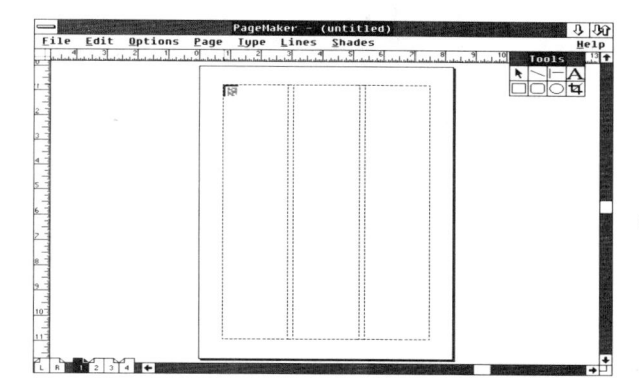

*Figure 10.* Position the mouse cursor at the very top left-hand corner of the first column and click the mouse button once.

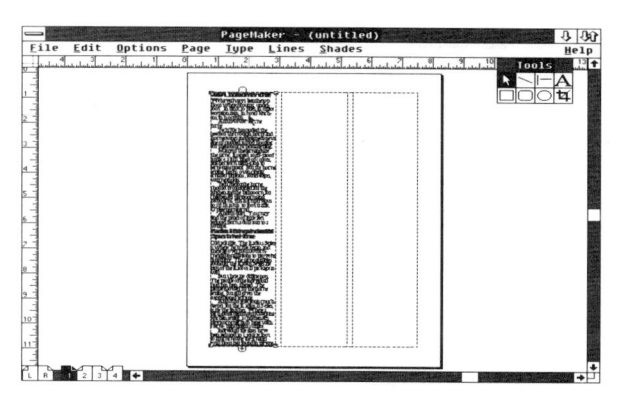

*Figure 11.* The text will flow down the first column and stop.

*Module 3 Exercise - Manipulating PageMaker Text Blocks*

3. *Resize the text block in the first column so that it only flows halfway down that column.*

Before you resize this first text block, make sure that the pointer tool has been selected. This is the tool in the top left-hand corner of the Toolbox.

Click once anywhere inside this text block to select it. Once selected, a handle will appear at the bottom of the text with a small + symbol in it. Move the mouse cursor over this handle and hold the mouse button down. (If all other handles of the text block suddenly disappear, it means that you were not quite on the bottom handle—reselect the text block and try again.) Once the mouse button is held down, move the mouse halfway up the column (Figure 12) and release the mouse button (Figure 13). The text will now reflow to stop exactly where you released the mouse.

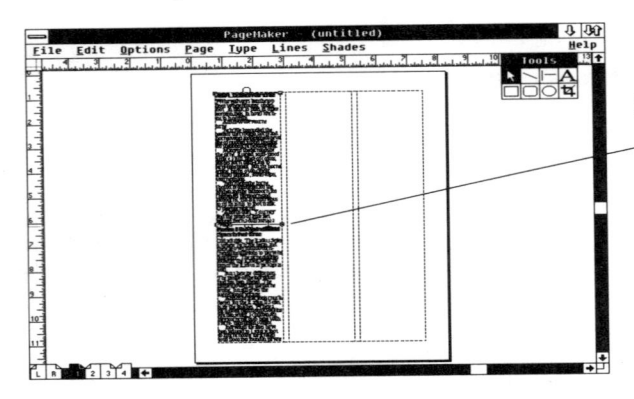

*Figure 12.* In this figure notice the position of the mouse cursor—which is actually now a two-sided arrow. We are in the process of resizing the column—achieved by holding the mouse button down on the bottom handle, and moving the mouse up the column.

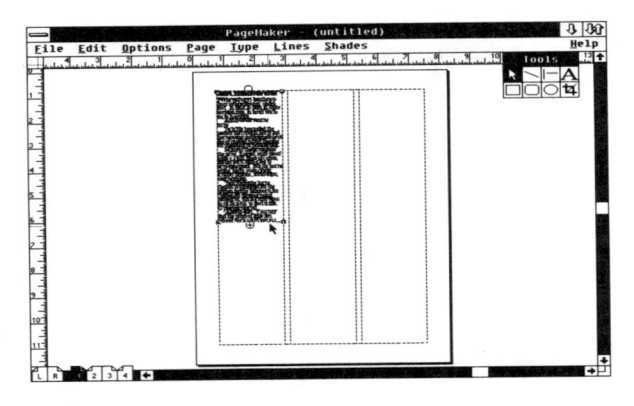

*Figure 13.* We release the mouse button when we think we have resized it far enough.

Module 3 Exercise - Manipulating PageMaker Text Blocks

4. *Continue the text flow from halfway down the first column on the first page, to the top of the first column on the second page.*

To continue text from one text block to another, regardless of where the second text block is going to flow, you must click once on the bottom handle of the existing text block (make sure this block is selected to make the handle visible). Once this is done, the mouse cursor will change appearance (Figure 14)—if it does not, try this again until it does.

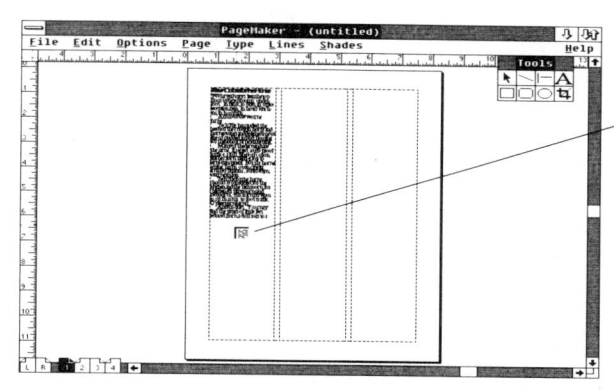

*Figure 14.* To continue text flowing somewhere else, locate the same handle that you held the mouse button down on to resize the column, but this time click on it once—so that the paragraph mouse cursor comes back.

After you have got the new mouse cursor, click on the Page 2 icon near the bottom left-hand corner of the page. You will move to page 2. Page 3 will also show on the screen (Figure 15), as we had Double-sided and Facing pages checked in our original dialog box of Figure 3.

Initially, page 2 will not have three columns. To give page 2 three columns, use the *Column guides* command from the **Options** menu, as we did for page 1 earlier.

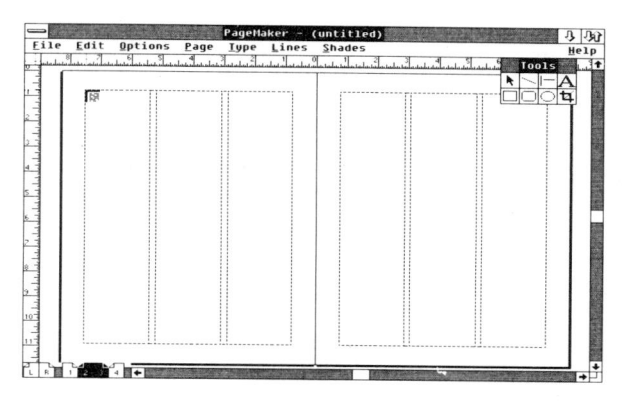

*Figure 15.* Click on the the number 2 page icon in the bottom left-hand corner of the screen. Because we are using the PageMaker Facing pages selection, we see page 3 as well.

## Module 3 Exercise - Manipulating PageMaker Text Blocks

Position the mouse cursor exactly as we did for page 1—at the top left-hand corner of the first column (Figure 15)—and click the mouse button once. Text will flow down the first column of the second page (Figure 16).

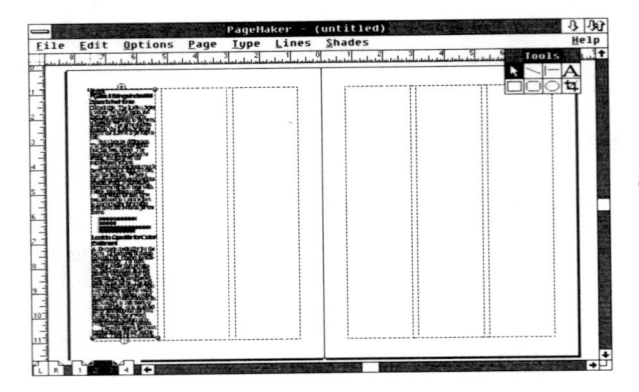

*Figure 16. As long as the mouse cursor was positioned correctly at the top of the left-hand column, and you clicked the mouse button once, text will flow down this column and stop.*

5. Move back to the first page and change the number of column guides to two. Resize the existing text block so that it fills the first column entirely. Continue the flow from the first column to the second.

Click on the page 1 icon to return back to page 1.

To change the number of column guides on this page, use the *Column guides* command in the **Options** menu. Change the 3 in this dialog box to a 2 (Figure 17).

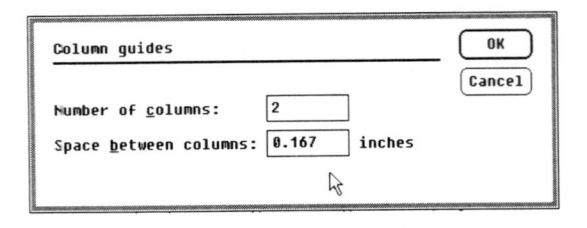

*Figure 17. After clicking on the 1 icon in the bottom left-hand corner to return to page 1, use the Column guides command from the **Options** menu to change the 3 columns to 2.*

*Module 3 Exercise - Manipulating PageMaker Text Blocks*

When you return back to the page, the text block will appear not to run into the newly-created columns (Figure 18). We must now resize the block so that it does. Because the text block begins in the correct place (the top left-hand corner of the first column) we only need to resize this text block using one of its handles—in this case, the bottom right-hand corner handle.

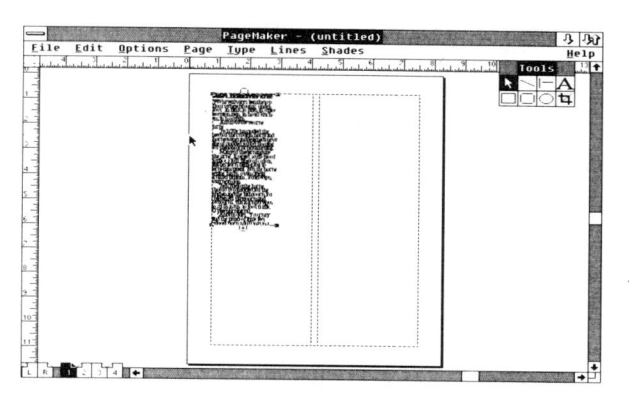

*Figure 18.* Because this text flowed when three column guides were on the page, it does not appear to fit the new two-column format. To resize it so that it does, you must first select the text block by clicking on it once. Now move to Figure 19.

Make sure the text block is selected, and locate the bottom right-hand handle (the small dot). Hold the mouse button down on this dot until the mouse cursor changes to a two-sided diagonal arrow, and move the mouse until the box that is created fills the entire column (Figure 19). Release the mouse button, and the text will reflow to fill the column (Figure 20).

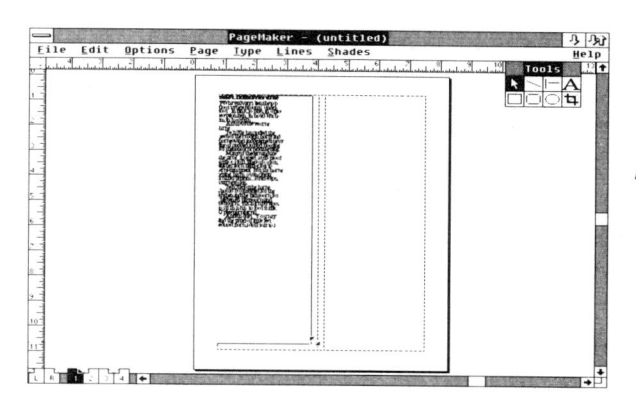

*Figure 19.* Hold the mouse button down exactly on the bottom right-hand corner of the text block, where a small handle will be. Drag the mouse diagonally down the page until the text block is resized exactly to fit the new column.

111

*Module 3 Exercise - Manipulating PageMaker Text Blocks*

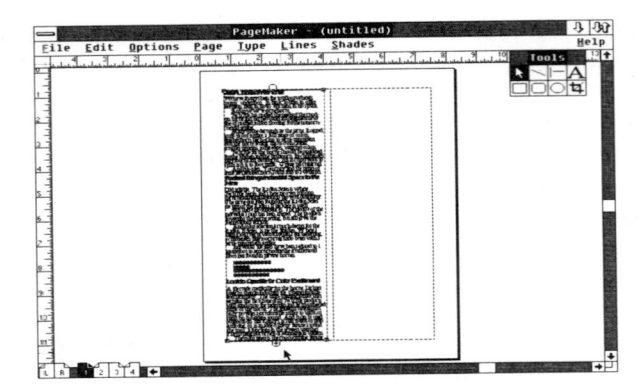

***Figure 20.*** *Upon releasing the mouse button, the text will reformat to fit the new column.*

To continue the flow from the first column to the second column, make sure that the first column has been selected. Now click once on the bottom handle of the first column where the plus sign is, so that the mouse cursor changes once again to the manual flow mode (Figure 21). Move the mouse cursor to the top left-hand corner of the second column and click the mouse button (Figure 22). The text will run out before the second column is filled (Figure 23).

In fact, depending on the style of the text as it comes into PageMaker, your text file may run out before even the first column is filled.

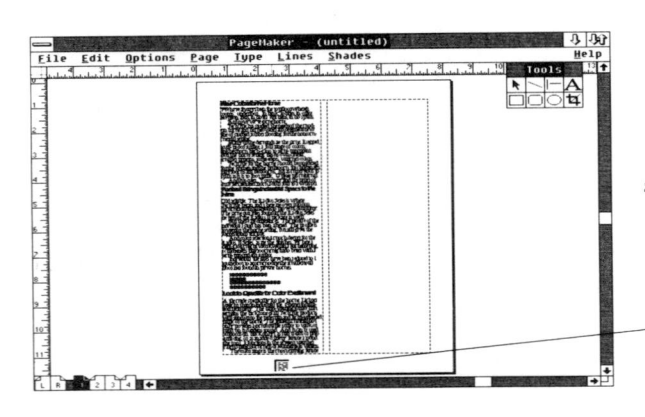

***Figure 21.*** *To continue the text flow from the first column to the second, click on the bottom handle of the first text block. (Note the position of the mouse cursor in Figure 20.) The mouse cursor will then change to the manual flow mode of this figure.*

112

*Module 3 Exercise - Manipulating PageMaker Text Blocks*

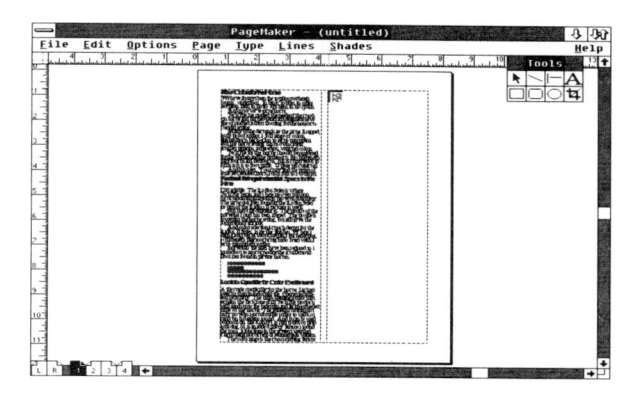

*Figure 22.* Position the mouse cursor in the top left-hand corner of the second column and click once.

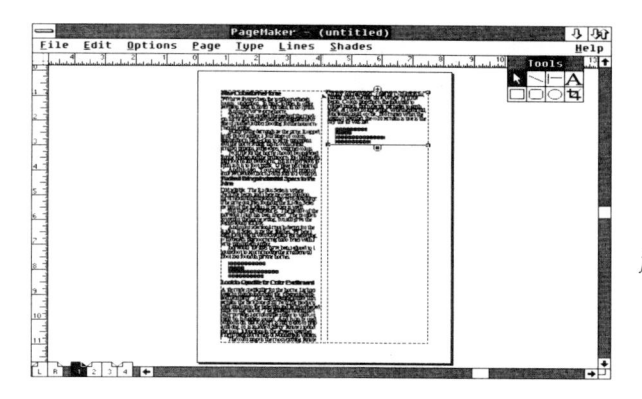

*Figure 23.* Text will then flow down the text column until the end. In this case the text file ends before the column does. Any text that we had flowed onto page 2 from step 4 has now moved back to page 1.

# Module 4

# PageMaker Text Editing

# PageMaker Text Editing

Any text file that is imported into PageMaker is not permanent —it can be deleted, edited, or added to, and also have its text attributes changed. Text can even be entered directly into PageMaker.

## Correcting errors

We will look first at how we can correct errors from any text on the PageMaker page or pasteboard area. This includes correcting simple errors, as well as deleting text and adding a few words or lines to text. If you wish to follow our examples in this module on your PageMaker program, load the file BROCHURE.DOC onto a three-column, A4 or letter page. Change to *Actual size* view and move to the top left-hand corner of the page (Figure 1). We will now make some corrections within this text.

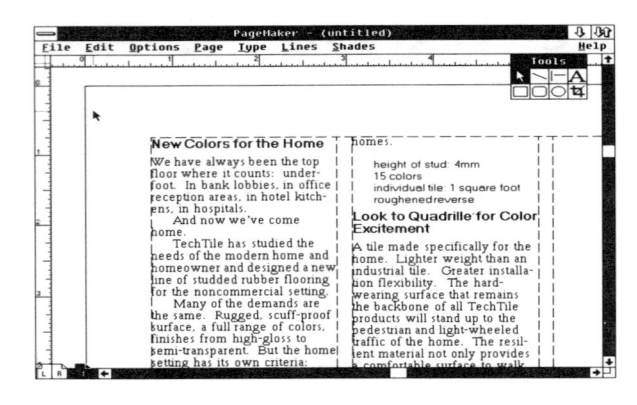

*Figure 1.* Load the file BROCHURE.DOC into three columns to follow this information section more clearly.

What we will be doing first is to correct a simple typing error— we want the first line of the story to read "New Color for the Home" rather than "New Colors for the Home."

To do this, we must first select the text tool from the Toolbox. This is the tool that looks like a letter A (Figure 2).

Upon selecting this tool, the mouse cursor will change appearance to look like the I-beam text cursor found in many word processors (Figure 2). Once this tool has been selected, we are free to start editing the text.

Module 4 - PageMaker Text Editing

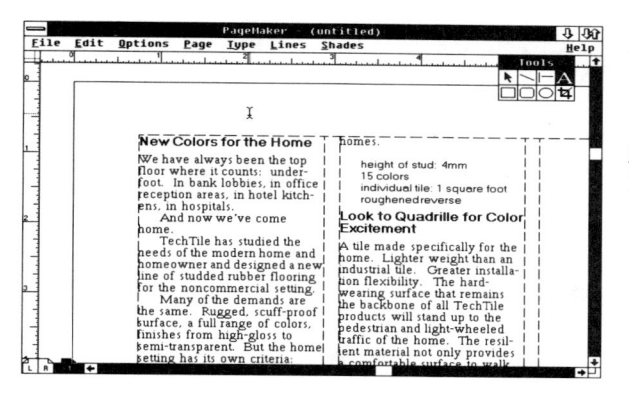

*Figure 2.* Select the A tool from the Toolbox to do any text editing. The cursor changes to the text editing I-beam.

If you have ever used any PC word processors, you will probably be fairly familiar with how editing works with PageMaker—in most cases it is similar to many of these other programs. For those unfamiliar with this approach, we will now go through the steps to edit text.

## Deleting letters

The first step is to insert the text cursor in the text. To do this, move the mouse cursor so that it is positioned just to the right of the letter s in the first line, "New Colors for the Home" (Figure 3). Now click the mouse button. A flashing cursor will appear just to the right of this s. Once this flashing cursor has been inserted in the text, the actual mouse is not used and it does not matter where the mouse cursor now lies. In fact, it is better to move it out of the way.

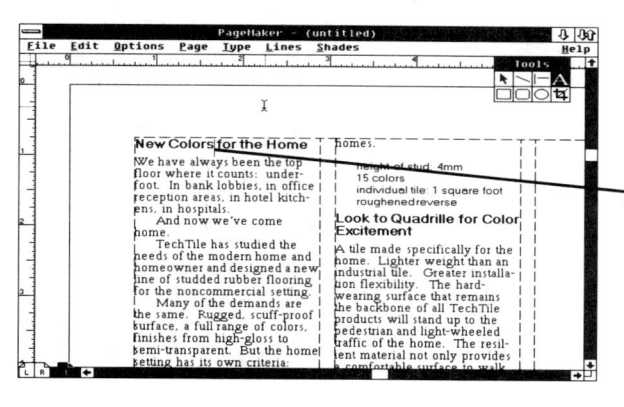

*Figure 3.* Move the mouse cursor to the right of the letter to delete, and click the mouse button once. A flashing text cursor will appear under the mouse cursor. Move the mouse cursor away.

117

*Module 4 - PageMaker Text Editing*

The keyboard now becomes the input tool, rather than the mouse. From here we can simply hit the Delete (or Backspace) key, and the letter to the left of the flashing cursor will disappear (Figure 4). Every time you hit the Delete key this will happen, so it can be used (though not efficiently) to delete words and even sentences. There are better ways to perform block deletions, as we will see below.

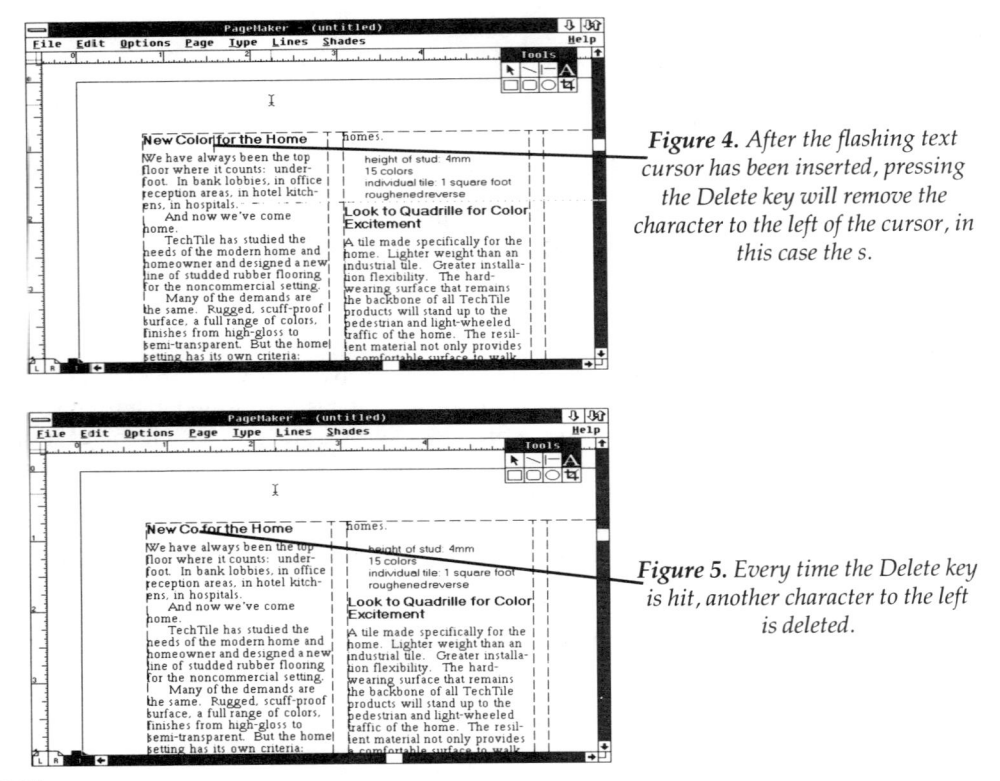

*Figure 4. After the flashing text cursor has been inserted, pressing the Delete key will remove the character to the left of the cursor, in this case the s.*

*Figure 5. Every time the Delete key is hit, another character to the left is deleted.*

## Adding text

Other keyboard keys can be used for inserting text once the text cursor is imbedded. Letters, words, sentences, and paragraphs can be added wherever the flashing text cursor appears in the text (Figure 6). New paragraphs are created by hitting the Return key.

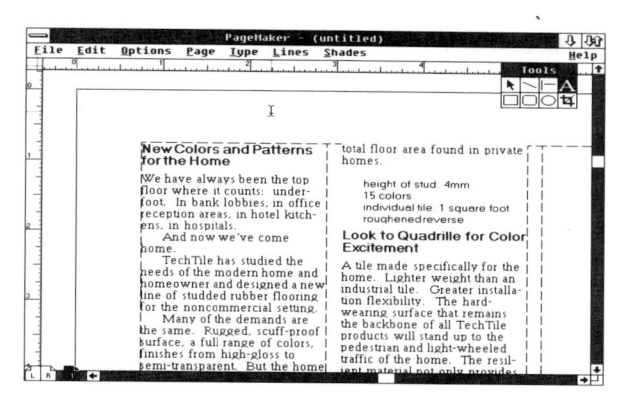

*Figure 6.* The keyboard can also be used to add letters to any imported text. Here we have added some text to the first headline paragraph.

## Moving the flashing cursor

The flashing text cursor obviously has to move around from time to time to allow you to correct errors all over the page. The text cursor can be moved in two ways. The first method involves the keyboard and is best used when the distance to move the flashing cursor is not far. The directional keys on the keypad are functional with PageMaker, so hitting the right direction key will move the flashing cursor one letter space to the right. The up direction key will move the mouse cursor one line up, the down key one line down, and so on (see Figures 7 and 8).

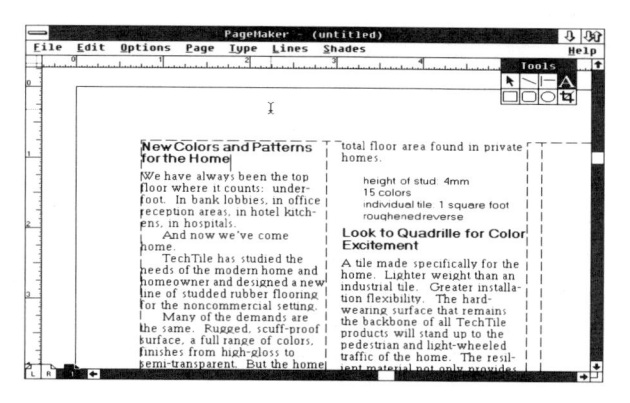

*Figure 7.* Note the position of the flashing text cursor now. We used the down arrow key on the keyboard to move the cursor down a line at a time.

*Module 4 - PageMaker Text Editing*

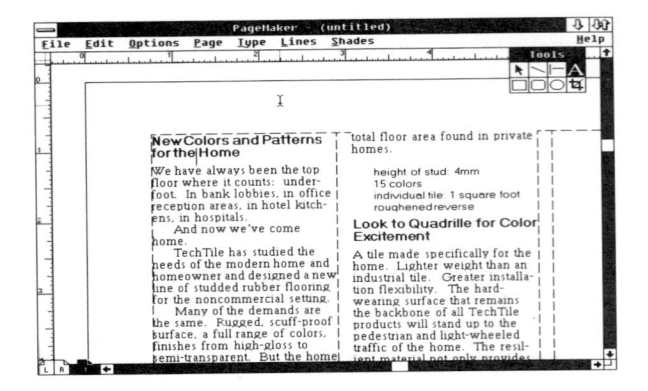

*Figure 8.* The text cursor has moved again, this time as a result of the left arrow key on the keyboard being tapped a couple of times.

The second method of cursor movement involves the mouse. This method is basically the same as how we inserted the text cursor in the text. Regardless of where the flashing text cursor appears in the text now, grab the mouse, and its cursor should reappear on the screen. Now move the mouse cursor to where you would like to reinsert the flashing cursor, and click the mouse button. The flashing cursor will move to this new position.

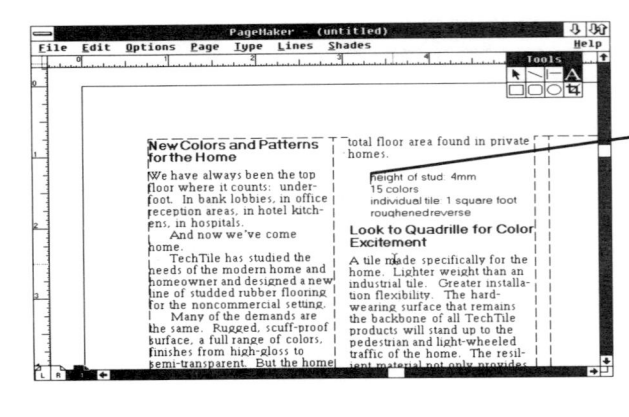

*Figure 9.* The mouse cursor can be found (it is hidden as text is added and deleted) by moving the mouse. It can be inserted anywhere else in the text in the same way it was inserted initially, as indicated in Figure 3.

## Deleting more than one character at a time

Obviously, using the Delete key to erase one character at a time is not a satisfactory way to delete any more than a couple of characters at once. There are other ways that words, paragraphs, and entire documents can be deleted and edited in one swift movement.

Before any more than one character can be acted on, it must be selected. There are several selection techniques you can use, depending on exactly how much text you would like to delete. The first technique we will look at must be used when you want to select an irregular amount of text—that is, an amount of text that is not exactly one word, one paragraph, or one file.

Move the mouse cursor to the start of the text you would like to select. Hold and keep holding the mouse button down as you do this. With the mouse button held down, move the mouse cursor to the end of the text you would like to select. As you move the mouse over the text, it will become highlighted in reverse video —indicating that this text is selected (see Figures 10 to 13).

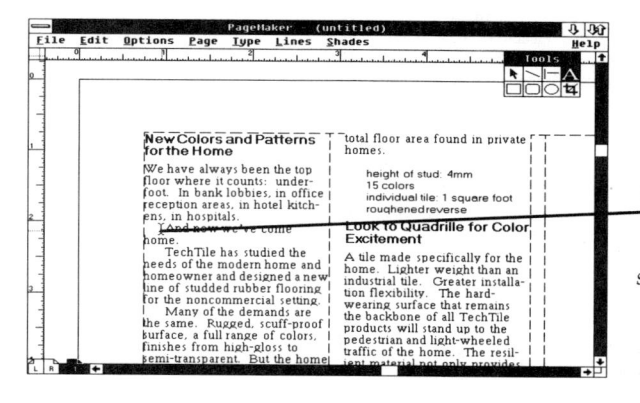

*Figure 10.* Here we are going to select the whole line that reads "And now we've come home." To do this, we move the mouse cursor so that it is positioned at the very start of the first word we want to select. Hold the mouse button down here.

121

*Module 4 - PageMaker Text Editing*

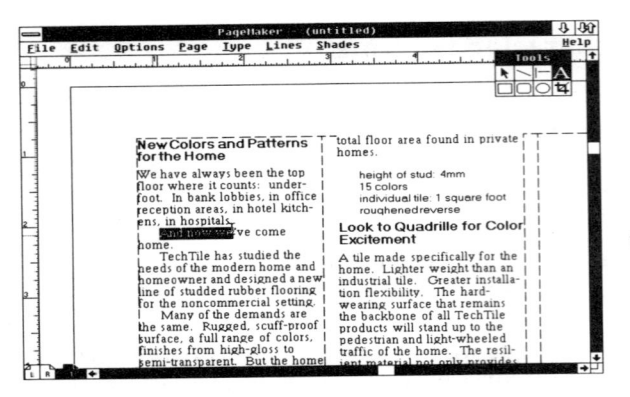

*Figure 11.* With the mouse button held down, move the mouse over the text. Everything the mouse passes is highlighted in reverse video. This indicates that the text is selected.

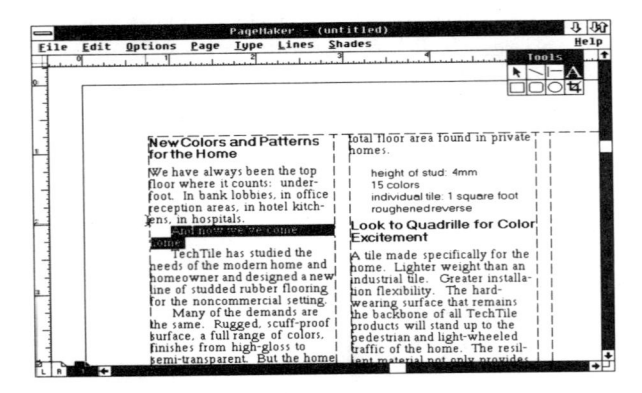

*Figure 12.* Release the mouse button when the desired text is selected.

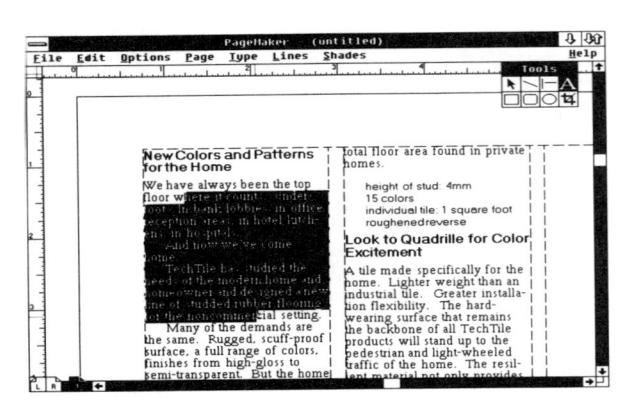

*Figure 13.* Any amount of text can be selected using the method shown in Figures 10 to 12, not just full words, paragraphs, or lines.

Module 4 - PageMaker Text Editing

There are several other methods which make it much quicker to select text. If, for example, you wanted to select one word, you may select that word by moving the mouse cursor anywhere over the word, and clicking twice. The entire word will become selected automatically (Figure 14).

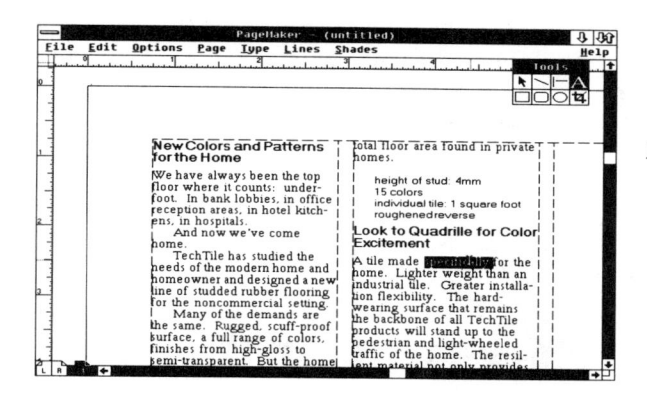

*Figure 14.* To select a single word, move the mouse cursor over the desired word and double-click the mouse. The entire word will be selected automatically.

An entire paragraph can be selected in a similar way. Move the mouse cursor over the paragraph you would like to select, and triple-click the mouse. The entire paragraph will become selected (Figure 15).

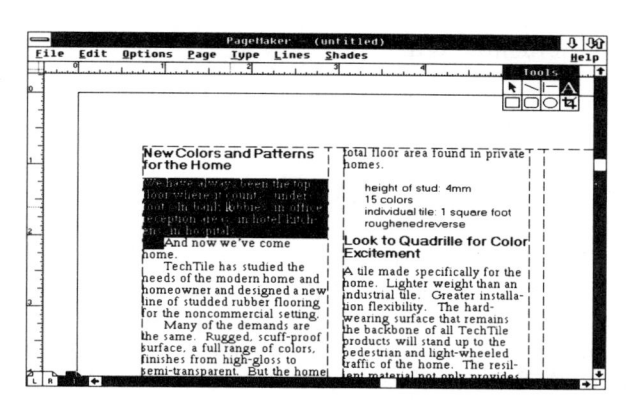

*Figure 15.* An entire paragraph can be selected in the same way as words—except a triple-click replaces the double-click.

123

*Module 4 - PageMaker Text Editing*

If you select any text with the double- or triple-click methods, you can still combine it with the original method of selection we talked about. After you double- or triple-click, keep the mouse button held down and run it over the text. Words or paragraphs will be selected as you go, depending on whether you double- or triple-clicked initially.

Any text selected in the above methods will be acted on as a group. If we decide to bold text for example (which we look at soon) all the selected text will become bolded. If we press the Delete key on the keyboard, all the selected text will be deleted.

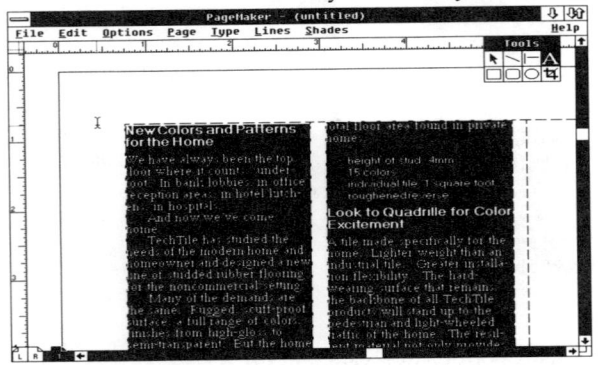

*Figure 16. An entire text file can be selected by inserting the text cursor anywhere in the text, and choosing the Select all command in the **Edit** menu. This selects an entire file—not just text on the screen, but even text that has not been seen yet.*

Another method for selecting irregular amounts of text is to insert the flashing text cursor at the start of the block, move to the end of the block, hold down the Shift key and insert the text cursor again. The entire block is selected. Finally, it is also possible to select the entire text file loaded or being loaded. Simply place the cursor anywhere in the text and choose the *Select all* command from the **Edit** menu (Figure 16).

Once selected, text can then be cut, copied, or pasted elsewhere. All these commands are in the **Edit** menu. The *Cut* command deletes text from the screen, *Copy* copies it, and *Paste* will reinsert at the text cursor the very last text block cut or copied.

The *Cut* and *Copy* commands store their text in a place called the *Clipboard*. The Clipboard only stores one block of text at a time. The last *Cut* or *Copy* command is the one that remains in the Clipboard and it is from here that the *Paste* command will take its text. If you wish to delete text without changing the contents of the Clipboard, then use the *Clear* command from the **Edit** menu.

## Changing text attributes

In this module we will be showing how to change text attributes using different commands within the **Type** menu. PageMaker 3 also offers a shortcut method for applying attributes to text using *style sheets*.

The basic theory discussed in this module, however, is important to understanding the concept behind style sheets, which are discussed in Module 11.

All text in PageMaker can have certain styles applied to it, regardless of whether or not a font and size was applied to the text at the word processor stage. To effect any changes to any text on the screen, the text must be selected using the techniques described above, and options from the **Type** menu applied to it.

Have a look now at the **Type** menu (Figure 17). We will look initially at the top six commands in this menu.

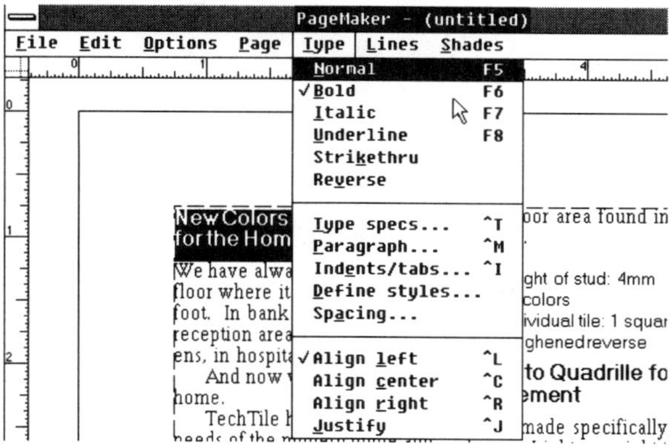

*Figure 17.* Several commands in the **Type** menu will change the selected text.

First, make sure that you have some text selected on the page, say the first paragraph, so you can see how the changes we are about to make alter the text.

Select any one of these first six commands from the **Type** menu. The selected text on the screen will instantly take on the attributes of the style that you choose. (If nothing does happen to the selected text, either you missed the command, or your printer does not support the type style you chose in the current type setting.)

*Module 4 - PageMaker Text Editing*

*Figure 18.* Here we choose the ***Type*** menu. A check appears next to the styles that the selected text already uses—here the selected text is already bold. We are now making the text italic as well.

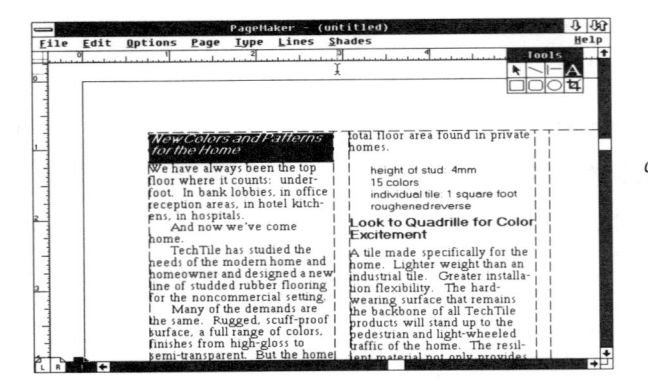

*Figure 19.* The text reflects the changes we made. Remember that if nothing happens, your printer may not support this type style.

*Figure 20.* Any number of type styles can be applied to selected text if your printer supports it. Here we have Bold, Italic, and Underline selected.

126

## Type specs command

More detailed changes can be made to text by using the *Type specs* command further down the **Type** menu (Figure 21). The type style change commands we have been looking at are generally used for simple shortcut commands.

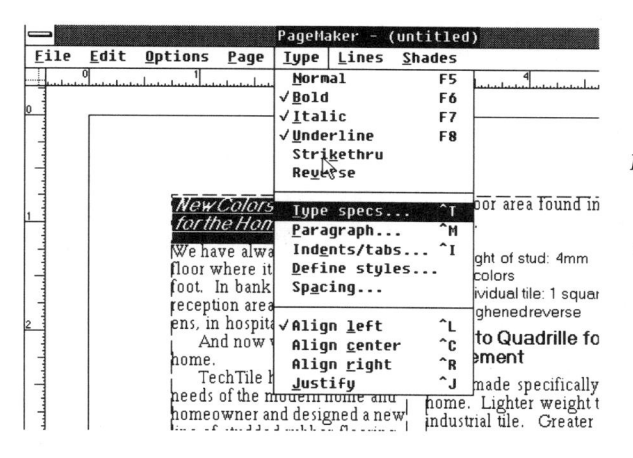

*Figure 21. Selecting the Type specs command will allow you to apply all the options found in the six commands above it plus more—all as a group.*

Within the dialog box that appears on choosing the *Type specs* command (Figure 22), there are several choices which must be made, some of them not so obvious.

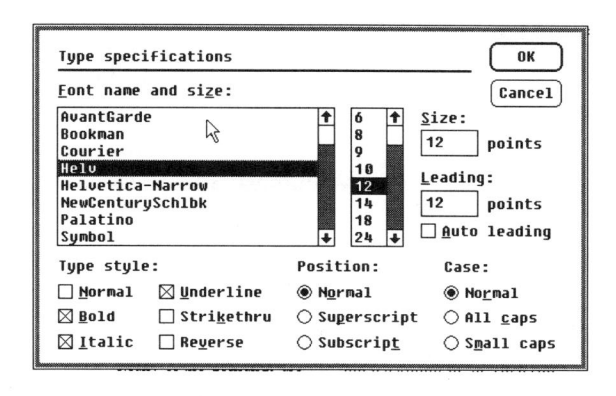

*Figure 22. This is the Type specs dialog box—reflecting all the current settings for the selected text.*

## Module 4 - PageMaker Text Editing

On the left side of the *Type specs* dialog box is a list of all the fonts available with your system. The font used by the currently selected text will be highlighted in reverse video (if there is a mixture of typefaces used by the selected text, no font will be highlighted within this dialog box). To change the font used, simply select the typeface you would like from the list.

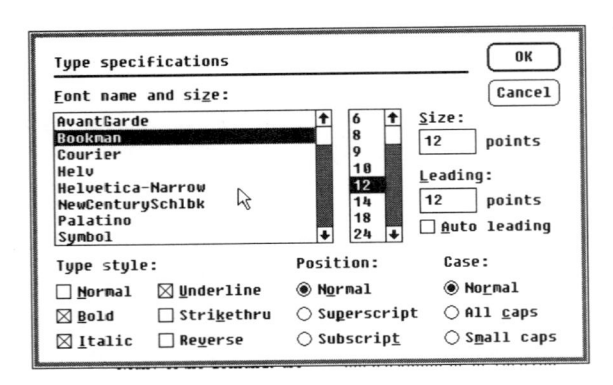

*Figure 23. Click the mouse button when the mouse cursor is over the typeface you would like to use. It then becomes highlighted.*

Beside the list of fonts are the size rectangles. The larger rectangle will list several point sizes that are available on your system, which you can click on to select. Alternatively, you can insert a custom size in the *Size* rectangle (if your printer supports this).

See Figure 24 for changes we have made to the size of the selected text. We have chosen 18 point.

128

*Module 4 - PageMaker Text Editing*

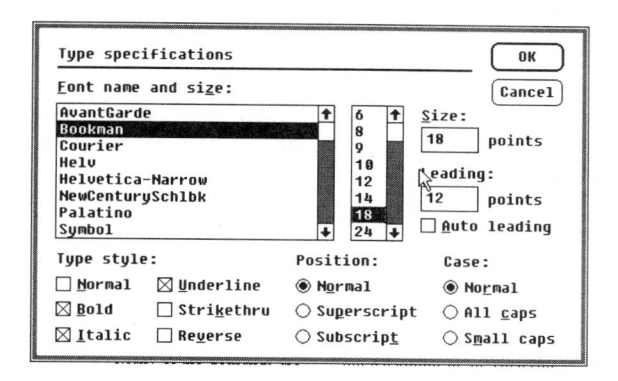

*Figure 24.* To change the size of the selected type, you can simply select a size from the list, or type in a size in the Size rectangle.

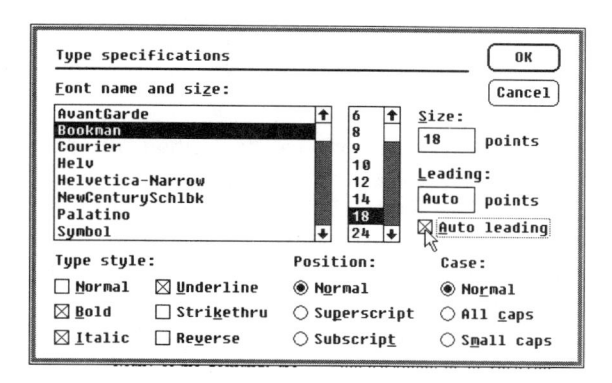

*Figure 25.* Leading can be altered by choosing Auto leading, or keying in a particular point size.

Underneath the Size rectangle is the *Leading* rectangle. You can insert a custom size for the leading in this rectangle (which is simply the line spacing), or leave it as *Auto* (it may already show Auto ).

If the word Auto is not in this rectangle, and you would like to use Auto leading, click on the *Auto leading* option below this rectangle (Figure 25).

129

## Module 4 - PageMaker Text Editing

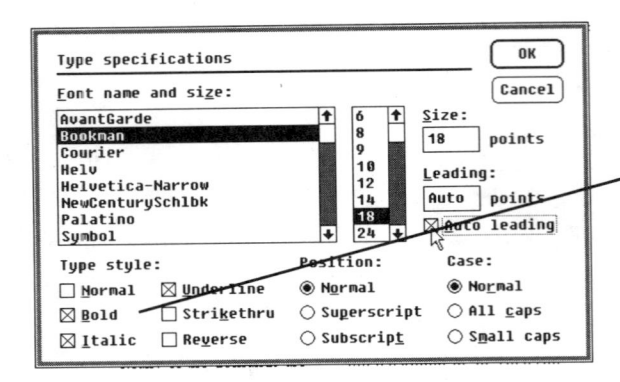

*Figure 26. The type style options at the bottom left are identical to the first six commands in the **Type** menu (Figure 21).*

To the bottom left of the dialog box are the *Type style* options (Figure 26). Type style is another method of altering the look of selected text. This will have the same effect as the first six commands in the **Type** menu. Any number of these type style changes can be selected together simply by clicking on the ones you want.

Alongside the Type style options are the *Position* options (Figure 27). Here you can select either *Normal, Superscript,* or *Subscript*—which is similar to keeping text *on* a baseline, slightly *above* the baseline, or slightly *below* the baseline, respectively. These types of commands are used when denoting footnotes and references, as well as in mathematical formulas.

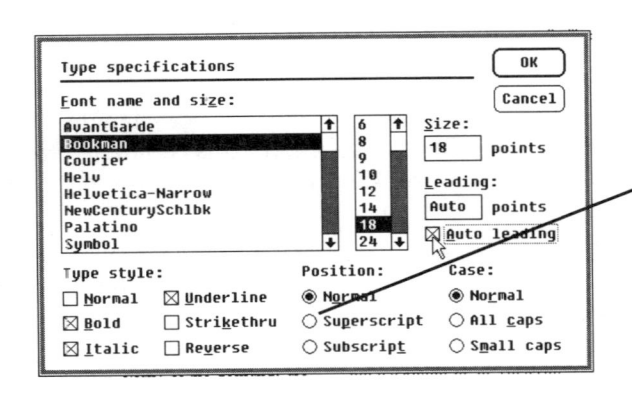

*Figure 27. The position of text, although generally set to normal, can be superscripted or subscripted for such things as footnotes, formulas, and so on.*

*Module 4 - PageMaker Text Editing*

Under the *Case* options (Figure 28), the *All caps* selection changes all letters to full-size capitals. The *Small caps* alternative changes lowercase letters to small capitals that are seventy percent the size of full-size capitals. The *Normal* selection reverts all text back to how it was originally placed or entered on the page.

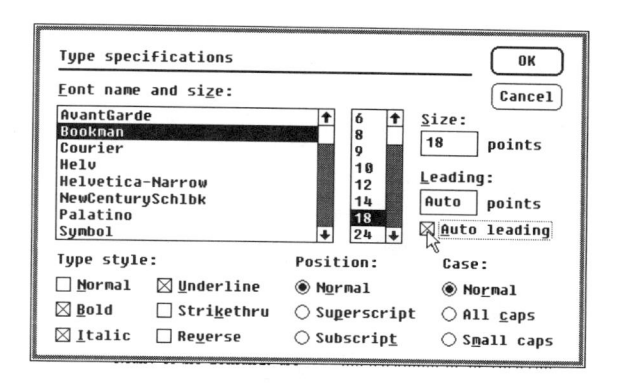

*Figure 28.* The Case of the text can be adjusted automatically—a quite handy feature for converting lowercase to uppercase, or vice versa.

After changing everything about the text you want to, either click the OK button, or hit Return on the keypad. All set changes will be applied to selected text. If no text was selected, and the pointer tool is active in the Toolbox, everything you set up will be the new default values for all text entered into this particular PageMaker publication via the keyboard.

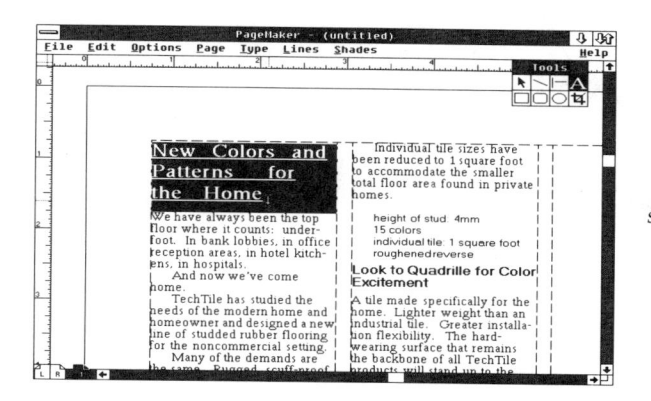

*Figure 29.* The result of all the settings we gave to this paragraph in Figures 23 to 28.

131

Module 4 - PageMaker Text Editing

**Some font, size and style examples:**

*Bookman 12 point italic*

**Times 14 point bold**

Avant-Garde 10 point normal

*Zapf Chancery 18 point italic*

# Helvetica 72 point
✺❀☐❄ ✦✤■✱✪❁▼▲

**New Century Schoolbook 36 point**

*Module 4 - PageMaker Text Editing*

## Paragraph command

All options in this command apply to entire paragraphs rather than just text. The entire paragraph does not have to be selected; all paragraphs partially selected, or the paragraph that contains the text cursor inserted in it, will be fully affected by this command.

Keep the first paragraph on the page highlighted and select the *Paragraph* command in the **Type** menu (Figure 30). You will be presented with the dialog box of Figure 31.

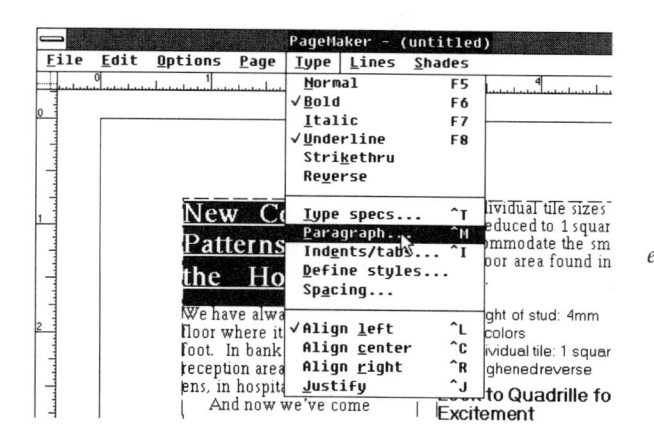

*Figure 30. The Paragraph command gives us access to a series of settings that apply to entire paragraphs rather than just selected text.*

*Figure 31. The dialog box that appears with the Paragraph command shows the current settings for the selected text (in our case the first paragraph). If several paragraphs are selected which use different settings, some boxes in this dialog box may be empty.*

133

*Module 4 - PageMaker Text Editing*

The first thing we can change about the selected paragraph is whether or not this paragraph should use the automatic PageMaker hyphenation. This is performed by checking the text against a supplementary dictionary, a built-in 110,000 word dictionary. If hyphenation is on, a cross will appear to the left of the word Auto on the *Hyphenation* line in Figure 31. To turn it off, click in the box to get rid of the hyphenation. Selecting the *Prompted* box will cause PageMaker, as it is hyphenating text, to prompt the user to hyphenate a word it feels needs hyphenating, but is unsure of how to hyphenate it.

The supplementary dictionary can accommodate up to 1,300 words. By editing the PMUSER.TXT (or PMUKUSER.TXT) document you can add, change, or delete words. The dictionary should be saved as a text-only document in the PM directory.

Below hyphenation in Figure 31 is the *Pair kerning* control. *Kerning* is the moving together of two very large letters that might otherwise appear too widely spaced. Generally, it is a good idea to leave kerning on (it is on if the check appears in the Auto above box next to Pair kerning). Being able to control the size above which text should be kerned allows you to kern perhaps only your headings, which may be 36 point, and not your subheadings, which may be 18 point or less.

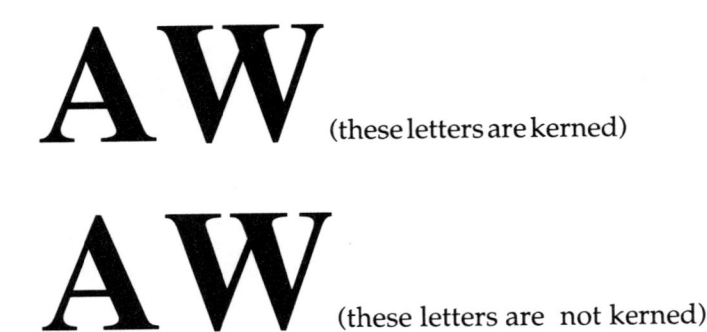

AW (these letters are kerned)

A W (these letters are not kerned)

134

*Module 4 - PageMaker Text Editing*

From the *Paragraph specifications* dialog box of Figure 31, you may also select which way your paragraph(s) should be aligned. Different effects are created by selecting either *Left* justified, *Right* justified, *Center*ed, or full justified. Click in the circle to the left of the *Alignment* selection (Figure 32) for the way you would like to align text. Some examples follow:

This paragraph is centered.

This paragraph is left justified.

This paragraph is right justified.

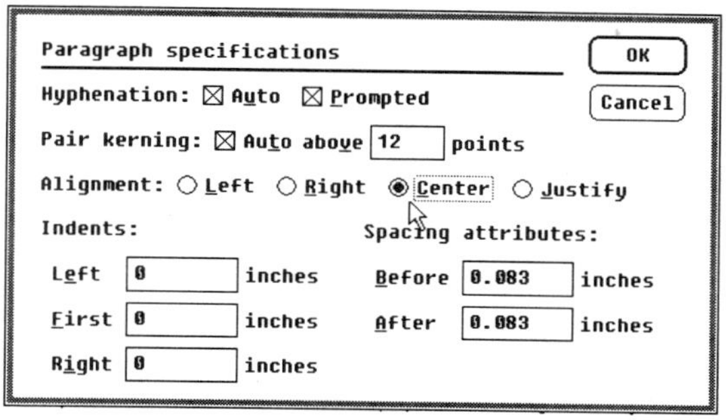

*Figure 32. If you want to change the alignment of the text, click the mouse button in the selected alignment circle on this line, either Left, Right, Center, or Justify. We have chosen Center.*

In the bottom left of the dialog box are the *Indents* selections. Each of the three indents, *Left, First,* and *Right,* affect the text in slightly different ways. The number in the rectangle next to the Left indent represents the distance that the entire paragraph will be indented from the left of the margin. It must be zero or a positive number. White space will run down the left of the paragraph for whatever measure is in this dialog box.

The First indent refers to how far the very first line in the paragraph is indented compared to the rest of the paragraph. A positive number here refers to a normal first line indent—a good way to denote the start of the paragraph. A negative number provides a *hanging indent,* where the first line is not indented, but all subsequent lines are.

## Module 4 - PageMaker Text Editing

The *Right* indent is the distance that the paragraph is indented from the right margin. This can only be set to zero or a positive number.

**Indenting and hyphenation examples**

This paragraph is indented 4 centimeters from the left and has the hyphenation turned off. Note the strange word spacing that may occur, as this paragraph is also fully justified.

This paragraph is indented 2 centimeters from the left and 2 from the right. It has the hyphenation turned on. The word spacing that occurs over a large block of text should look better than the paragraph above.

This paragraph has a hanging indent in which the second and subsequent lines are indented in from the first line. It also has a 2 centimeter indent from the right and a 2 centimeter indent from the left for the first line.

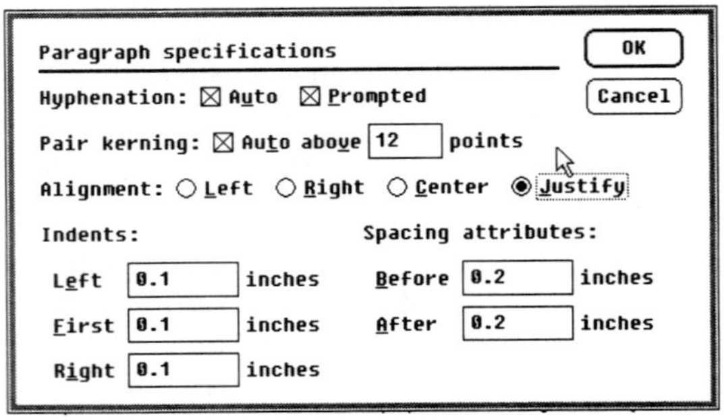

*Figure 33. Here we have justified the paragraph, set indents for the first line, to the left, to the right, and given space before and after the selected paragraph.*

*Module 4 - PageMaker Text Editing*

The *Spacing* selection, including *Before* and *After*, on the bottom-right of the *Paragraph* specifications dialog box, inserts white space above and below the selected paragraph. Body text, for example, may have some space before (or after) every paragraph to spread them out a little. Headings may have a quarter of an inch below them to break them from the rest of the text. Whatever the use, each figure above and below will be the amount of white space above and/or below paragraphs. In Figure 33, we have inserted 0.2 of an inch space above and below our paragraph. Figure 34 shows the results of the Figure 33 settings.

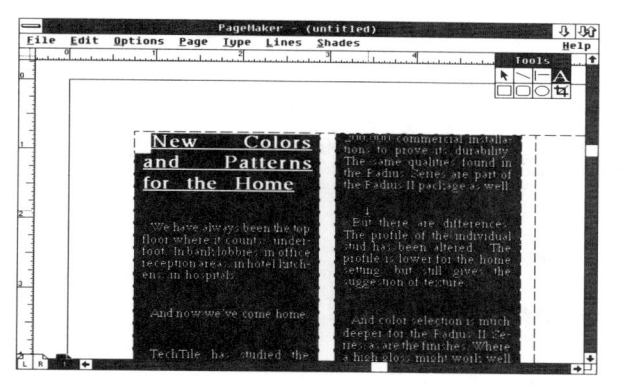

*Figure 34.* The results of our settings of Figure 33 applied to the entire text. The text is justified, indented from either side, and has 0.2 inch of space before and after each paragraph.

Shortcut paragraph alignment changes may be made using the four alignment commands at the bottom of the **Type** menu. These are used for quick alignment changes when it is not necessary to go to the full *Type specs* dialog box of Figures 22 to 28.

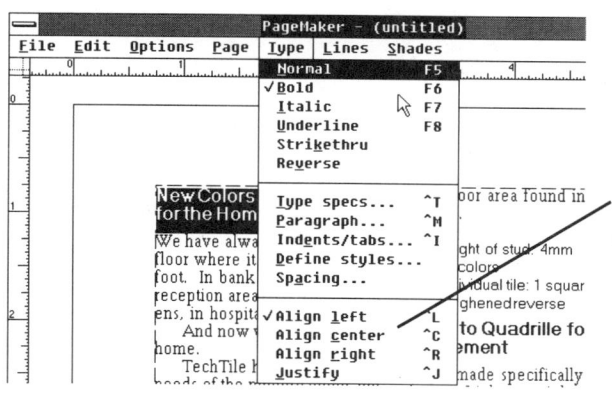

*Figure 35.* The various alignment commands can be used to quickly set the justification of selected text.

137

Module 4 - PageMaker Text Editing

## Indents/tabs command

As we discussed above, and as shown in Figure 33, it is possible to select Left, First, and Right indents of paragraphs using the *Paragraph* command in the **Type** menu. It is possible to do this as well, plus more, with the *Indents/tabs* command (Figure 36), also from the **Type** menu. The *Indents/tabs* dialog box, which results from selecting the command, is indicated in Figure 37.

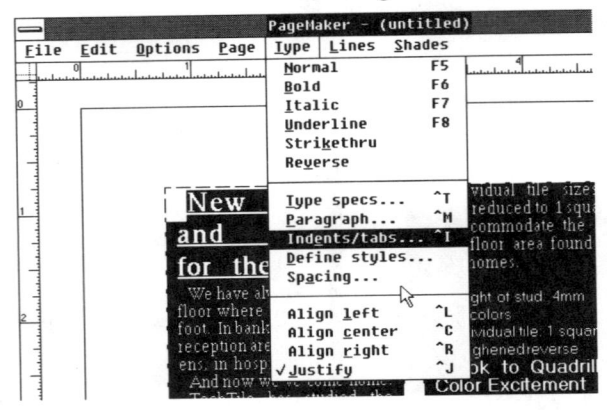

*Figure 36.* The Indents/tabs command from the **Type** menu can be used for setting tabs and indents. The latter capability is similar to that available with the Paragraph command.

Figure 37 shows the default PageMaker tab settings of one every one half of an inch. The vertical arrows represent left justified tabs. Right justified, centered, and decimal tabs are also possible, and are shown in Figure 38. In addition, this latter figure also shows left, right, and first indents.

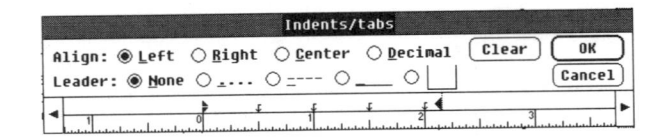

*Figure 37.* The Indents/tabs dialog box. Note the vertical tab arrows which are set by default to every one half of an inch.

*Module 4 - PageMaker Text Editing*

To change the default settings of Figure 37 requires the pointer tool in the Toolbox to be selected. Once the pointer is selected, it is simply a matter of going to the dialog box of Figure 37 and adjusting indents and tabs to your requirements. Wherever you then click on the page to type text, it will automatically assume the new default values. Text already on the page may have its indents and/or tabs changed by selecting it with the text tool, and then changing the settings in the *Indents/tabs* dialog box.

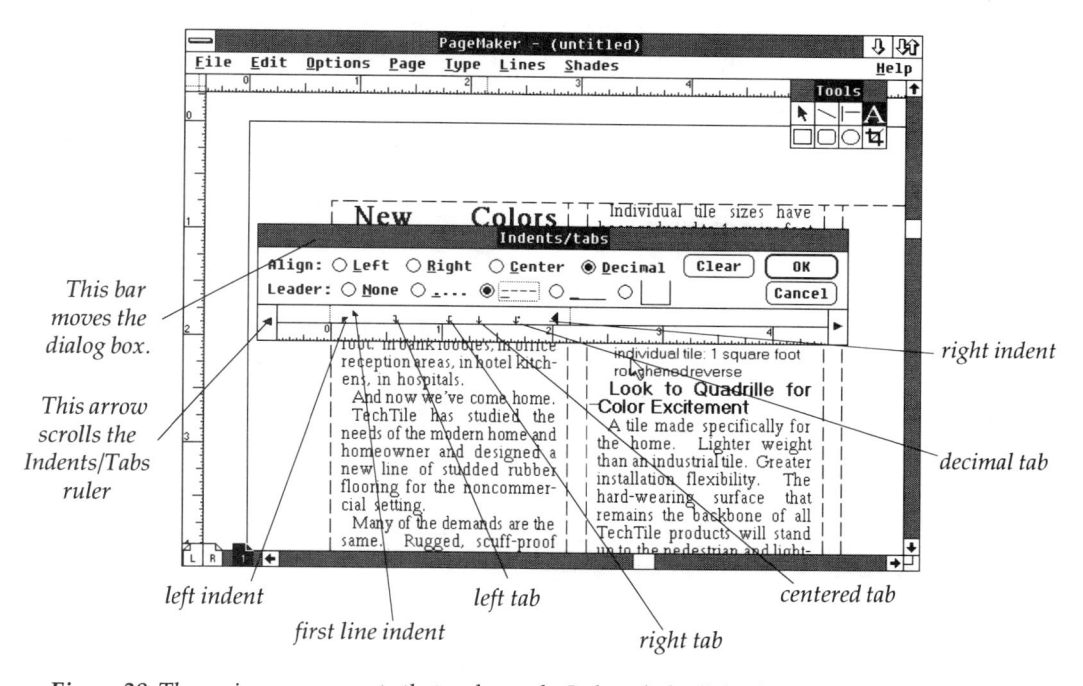

*Figure 38.* The various components that make up the Indents/tabs dialog box are indicated. One of the important points to note in this figure is the way we have aligned the zero point of the dialog box's ruler with the left-hand column guide for the left-most column. This makes it easier to set up indents and tabs for your column widths.

We will now provide some examples to illustrate the indents/tabs concept of PageMaker. Again, if you would like to follow along you may wish to reload BROCHURE.DOC into a single, three-column, A4 or Letter page. (It may be a little messy from some of our earlier experiments in this module.)

139

*Module 4 - PageMaker Text Editing*

In Figure 39, we have selected the first body text paragraph with the text tool, and then chosen the *Indents/tabs* command leading to the dialog box indicated in the figure. From this box we can see that there are no indents at all.

In Figure 40 we have set left, right, and first indents. If any tabs are set, they are deleted by simply grabbing them with the mouse and pulling them vertically downwards. Note the relationship between the *Indents/tabs* and *Paragraph* commands by comparing Figures 40 and 41. Figure 41 is the dialog box associated with the *Paragraph* command, while the first paragraph of Figure 40 is still selected. The values given for first, left, and right indents correspond with the settings shown in the *Indents/tabs* dialog box of Figure 40.

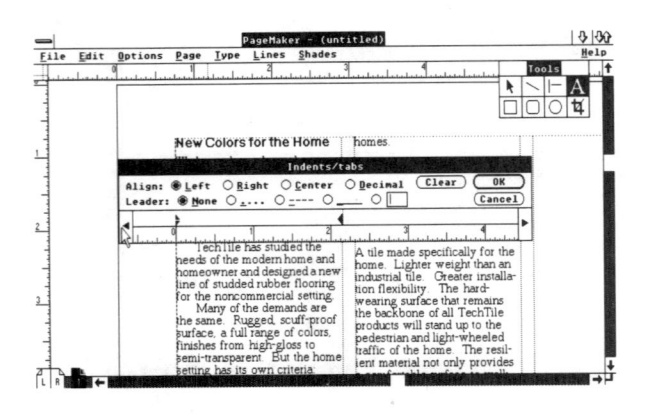

*Figure 39.* The initial paragraph we have selected has no indents set. Compare this to Figure 40 after we have made some adjustments.

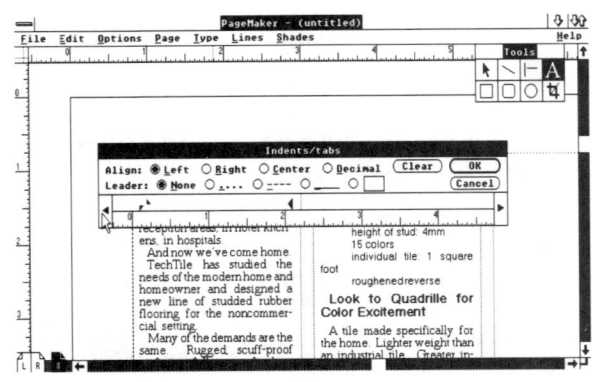

*Figure 40.* We have now set first, left, and right indents. Note that aligning the zero point of the ruler with the left margin allows us to pictorially view our settings and compare with the actual text.

140

*Module 4 - PageMaker Text Editing*

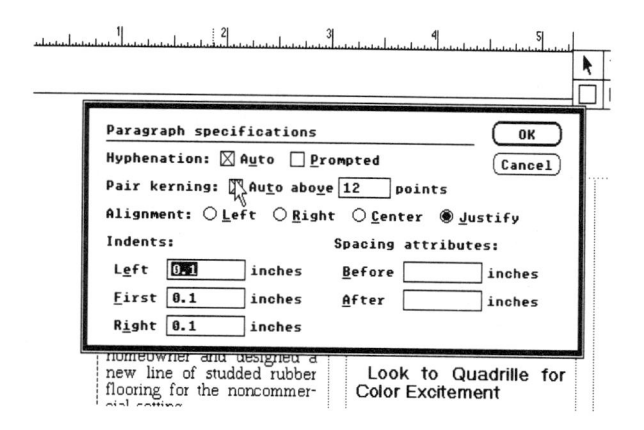

*Figure 41. Compare the settings of this Paragraph command dialog box with the same settings in the Indents/tabs dialog box of Figure 40. You'll see that the settings are identical, showing the relationship between the two commands.*

In our final two examples below, we have gone to the bottom of the third column to an empty area, clicked on the text tool, and then typed the numbers 1 to 5, with a tab after each one. The result, as shown in Figure 42, is simply tabs every one half of an inch, which is the default setting. We then selected this text and changed the tab settings. The new tab settings (now spaced every inch) and the result can be seen in Figure 43.

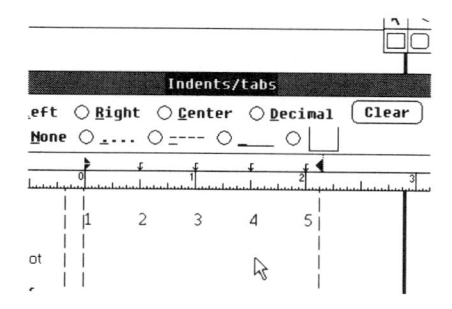

*Figure 42. By clicking on the text tool, and typing in the above numbers separated by tabs, we are using the default tab values of one every one half of an inch.*

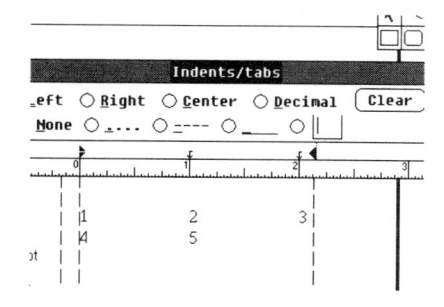

*Figure 43. Here we have selected the numbers keyed in in Figure 42 and have changed the tab settings to one every inch. This results in the changed settings as shown.*

141

Module 4 - PageMaker Text Editing

## Spacing

The *Spacing* command (Figure 44) works for an entire text file, not just selected text. This command is one that gives you a great deal of control over text spacing, but may not be required by all people. The default setting for text spacing is acceptable for the vast majority of uses. The *Spacing* attributes dialog box is shown in Figure 45.

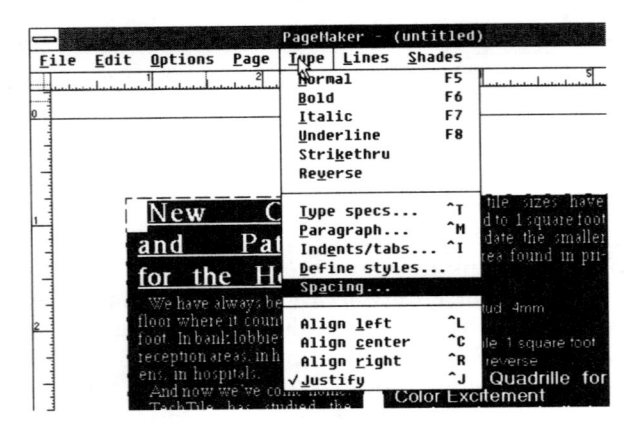

*Figure 44.* The Spacing command from the **Type** menu deals with very precise text spacing options.

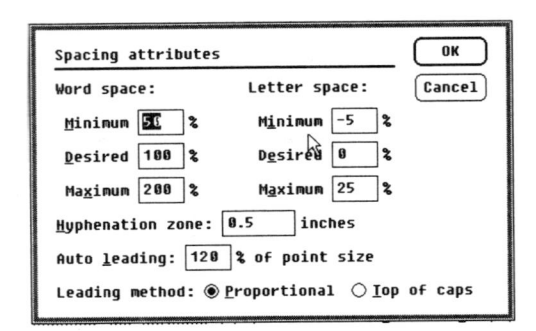

*Figure 45.* This is the Spacing attributes dialog box. Many people may prefer to leave this command alone, unless they have very precise requirements for text spacing.

(Do not confuse this *Spacing* command, which adjusts the amount of horizontal spacing between letters and words, with the Spacing selection in the *Paragraph* command of Figure 33. This latter selection, as we have discussed previously, simply adjusts the amount of vertical spacing before and after paragraphs.)

142

The dialog box of Figure 45 appears upon selecting the *Spacing* command. This dialog box is associated with adjusting the amount of spacing between words and letters. *Word Space*, the first selection, is used to set the space between words on the page. The designer of the font being used has set a value of 100% as the optimum space between words. The *Desired* space between words will be set by default at 100%. By decreasing this value, as well as the corresponding *Maximum* and *Minimum* values, the text will appear slightly tighter spaced. Increasing these values will cause the text to be more loosely spaced.

Word spacing works for both justified and unjustified text. The acceptable values that can be used here are:

- Minimum: 0 to 500%
- Desired: between minimum and maximum
- Maximum: 0 to 500%

*Letter space*, the next selection, is the figure that PageMaker is allowed to insert between letters in text when justifying. This selection does not apply to unjustified text. By having zero in all these three boxes, PageMaker will not insert extra spaces between letters at all. By putting a figure of 25 in *Maximum*, PageMaker is allowed to insert at maximum 25% of word space between letters if necessary. The *Minimum* and *Desired* figures can be negative.

The acceptable values that can be used for Letter space are:

- Minimum: -200 to 0%
- Desired: between minimum and maximum
- Maximum: 0 to 200%

See the examples on the next page of various word and letter spacing commands on text. These examples, showing the first body text paragraph of the BROCHURE.DOC file selected, illustrate that text spacing can be modified many ways, some of which are unacceptable, and some of which are useful for various applications. The look of the text, in many instances, is up to the individual.

Remember that *Spacing* selections apply to the whole text file not just the selected text.

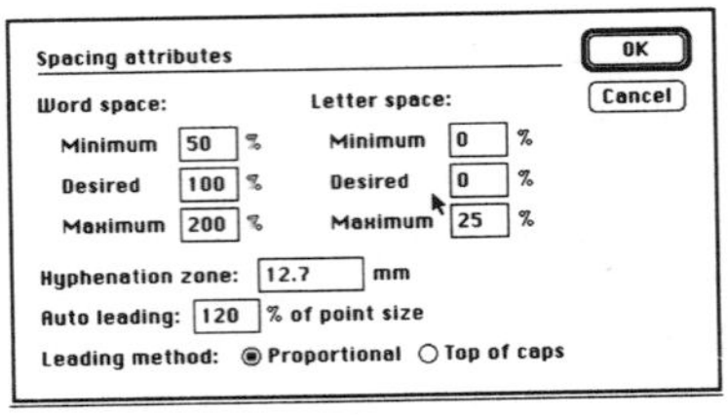

## Module 4 - PageMaker Text Editing

*Figure 46.* The paragraph on the right shows the results of the PageMaker default settings on the left.

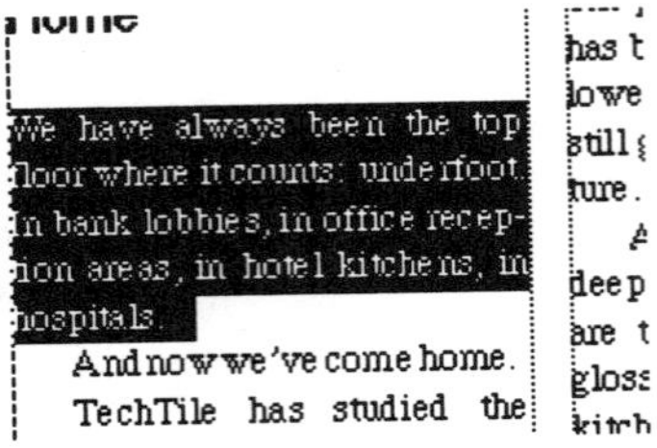

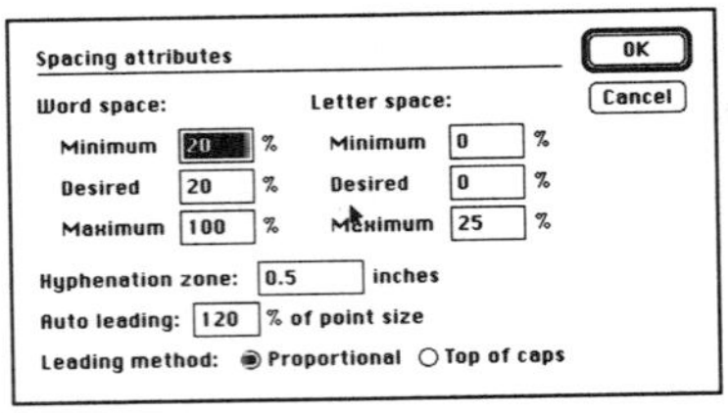

*Figure 47.* We have tightened up on the word spacing settings on the left to give the results on the right.

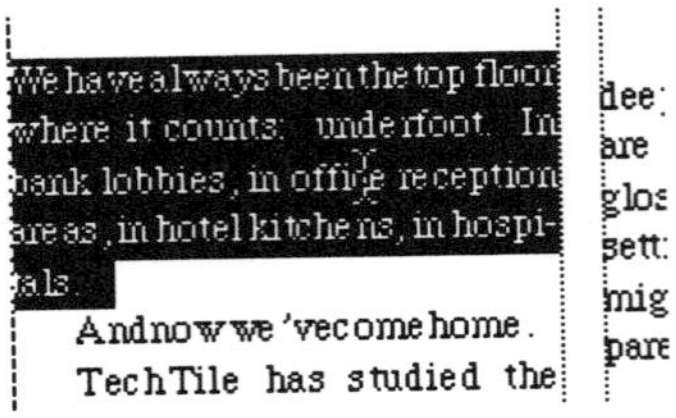

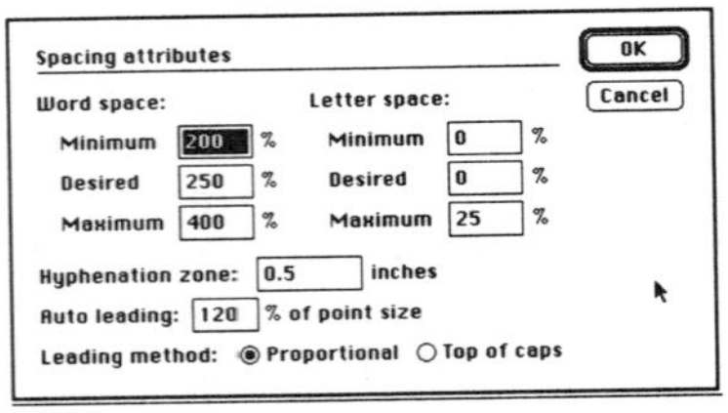

*Figure 48.* We have now loosened the word spacing to produce the results on the right.

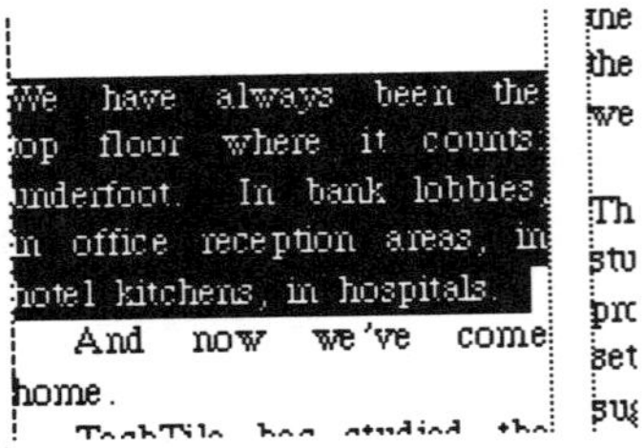

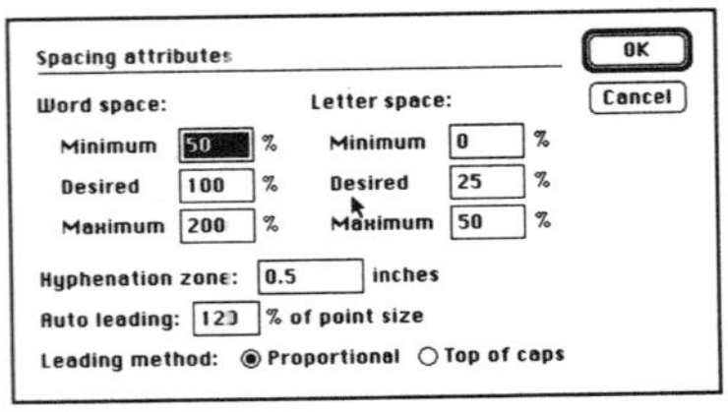

*Figure 49.* We have now adjusted the letter spacing by allowing more space between letters. The result is on the right. Compare to Figure 46 which uses the same word spacing.

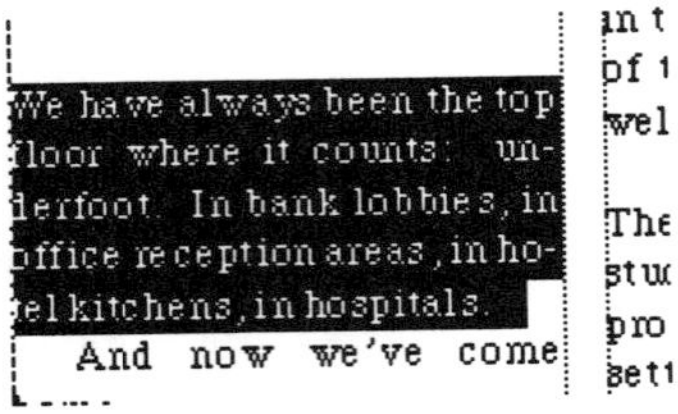

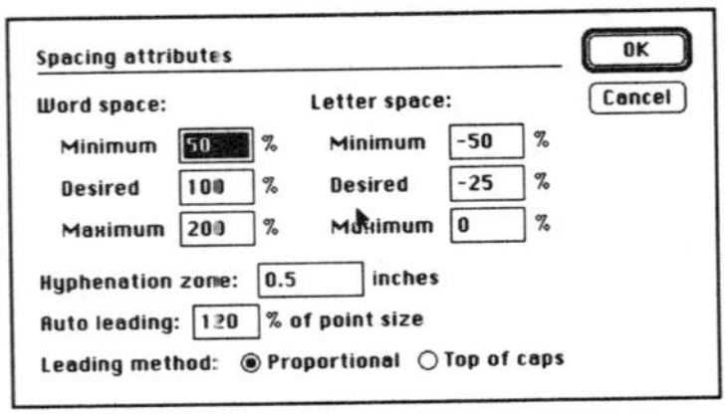

*Figure 50.* Letter spacing has now been tightened to provide the results as shown.

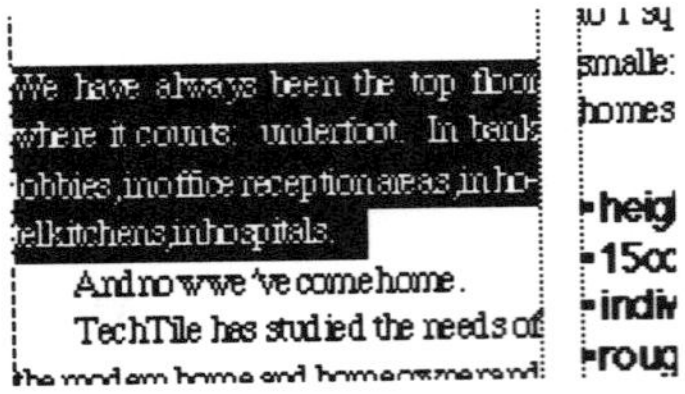

144

The final parts of the *Spacing* command dialog box concern hyphenation and leading.

The *Hyphenation zone* (again refer back to Figure 45) is the area at the end of a line that a word must start to be hyphenated. This selection is only applicable for unjustified text. The larger this hyphenation zone is, the more likely hyphenation is to occur. If you want less hyphenation to occur than is occurring presently, make the hyphenation zone smaller.

The value set for Auto leading in Figure 45 is the amount PageMaker uses by default (120%) when Auto leading is selected for text through the *Type specs* command. The figure is taken as a proportion of the text size, so to achieve leading at around ten percent of the text size, insert 110 in this rectangle.

A *Leading method* must be selected—either *Proportional* or *Top of caps*. Both use different parameters to judge the leading distance. Proportional is based on the largest character in the line—a line of 10 point text that contains a 14 point character will be leaded based on the 14 point character. It is the preferred method of use.

The Top of caps method is included for compatibility with earlier PageMaker versions and should not be used for new work.

## Define styles command

This command is described in Module 11—PageMaker Style Sheets.

Module 4 - PageMaker Text Editing

# Creating new text files

Rather then creating your files wholly and solely from a word processor and then loading them into PageMaker, files of considerable length can be created totally from within PageMaker itself. PageMaker, of course, does not contain the many features found in dedicated word processors, nor is it as fast, but it is quite capable of inputting relatively large files. All the captions in this book were input directly into PageMaker rather than created in a word processor with the rest of the text.

To create your own PageMaker files is extremely simple. Select the text tool from the Toolbox, click on the page where you would like to add some text, and start typing. A flashing text cursor will appear where the cursor was clicked. After typing, text will then appear on the page in its own text block (see Figures 51 to 53). You may wish to start a new publication for this step.

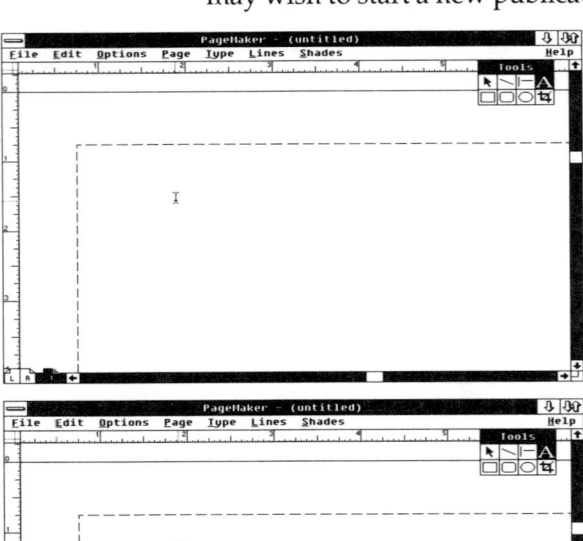

*Figure 51.* We are about to add text to an empty page using the PageMaker text tool, which we have just displayed.

*Figure 52.* Move to the area on the page you would like to start typing, and click the mouse button once. A flashing text cursor will appear, in this case at the left margin.

*Module 4 - PageMaker Text Editing*

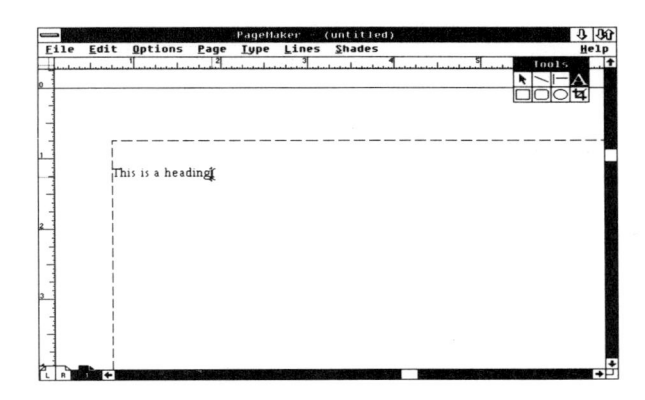

*Figure 53.* After the flashing text cursor has been inserted, you are free to add text as you see fit.

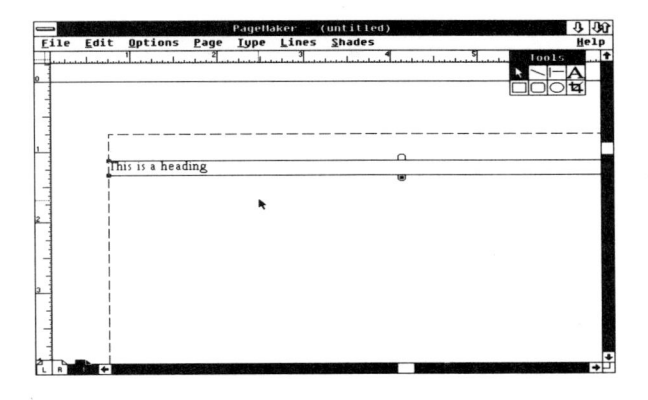

*Figure 54.* This new text file we have created occupies its own text block, as every new text file does (note the change of tool in the Toolbox).

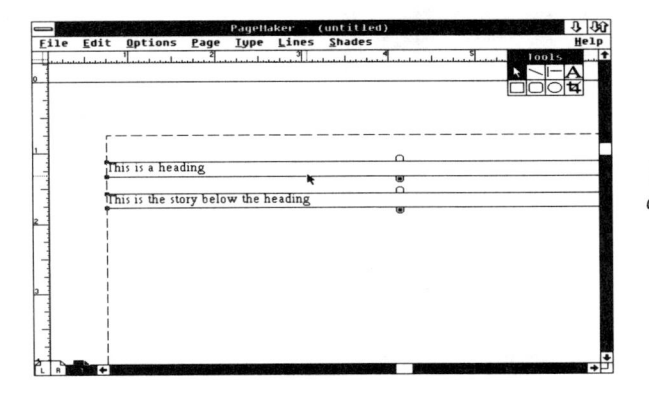

*Figure 55.* Every time the mouse cursor is clicked in a new position and text is entered, a new text block is created.

147

## Module 4 - PageMaker Text Editing

Another method of defining a text block for keying in your own text is the *drag-place* method. With this approach, you select the text tool and draw an imaginary box on the screen starting from the spot where the text is to commence. While you are dragging the mouse down the page, the outline of the box will appear on screen (Figure 56). You make the box width equal to the width that you would like the text block to be. Once you release the mouse, the box outline disappears and the text cursor is automatically positioned at the top-left corner of the required text block. Any text now typed in will keep to the bounds of the imaginary box (see Figure 57).

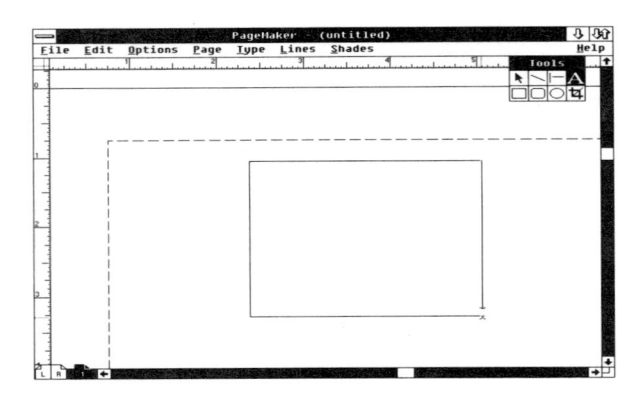

*Figure 56.* This imaginary box drawn with the mouse while the text cursor is active, is defining the bounds of a new text block. Text keyed into this block is shown in Figure 57.

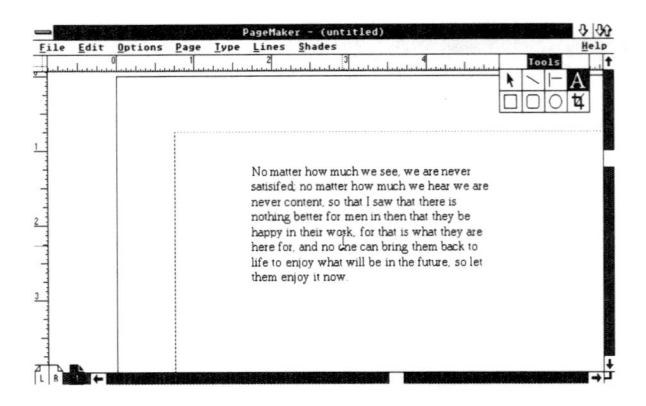

*Figure 57.* This text has been keyed into the text block drawn in Figure 56. With this approach the width of the block is more important than its length. The width constrains the width of the text. The length doesn't affect the amount of text you can type or paste in.

*Module 4 - PageMaker Text Editing*

If you attempt to add text in an area that looks blank, but is in fact part of another text block, PageMaker will think that you are trying to edit that text block, and the flashing cursor will not appear where you want it to—it will appear imbedded in the text of that text block. You will only be editing an existing text block rather than creating your own (Figures 58 and 59).

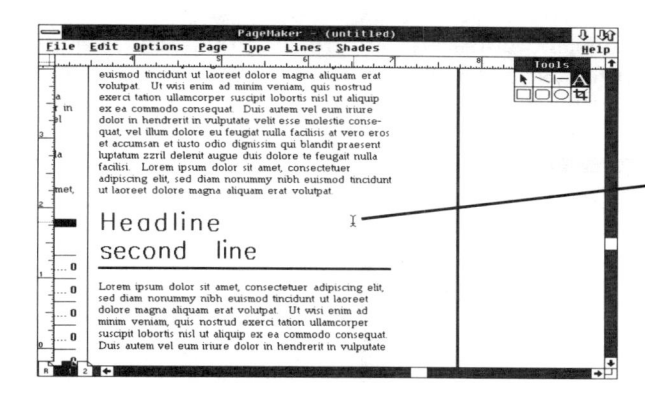

***Figure 58.** If we tried to create some text directly under the text cursor where it is situated in this figure, it could not be done...*

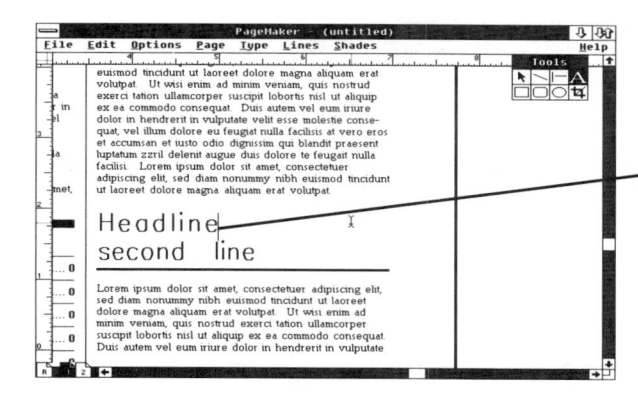

***Figure 59**... because the text cursor was clicked inside an existing text block, and PageMaker assumes you want to edit the text in this block.*

*Module 4 - PageMaker Text Editing*

Even if there are no other text blocks on the page, the flashing cursor may not always appear where you clicked the mouse cursor. Where it does end up depends on how the defaults for text are set. (Defaults are looked at in another module.) For example, if you tried to click the mouse cursor in the center of an empty page, and the default text setting is left justified, the flashing cursor will appear to the left side of the page. If you want the text centered, type it in, select it, and center it. Alternatively, go to the **Type** menu, and choose *Align center*.

For these reasons it is often easier to move off to the side of the page to create smaller text files. Quite often such things as headings, captions, footnotes, etc., are created in this way. After they have been formatted off the side of the page, move them into position on the page. Figures 60 to 63 illustrate this approach.

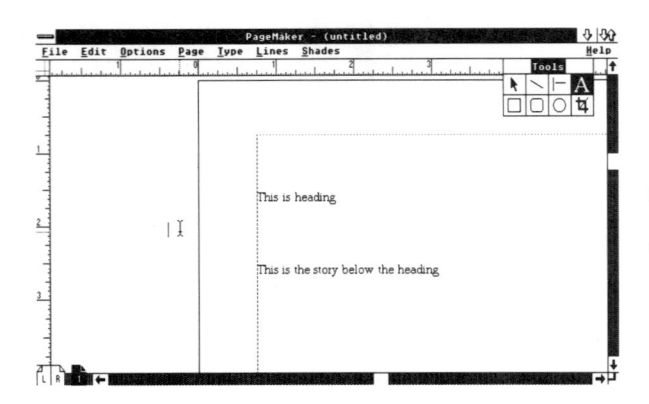

*Figure 60.* It is often easier to create small text blocks, for such things as headings or captions, off the actual page in the pasteboard area and move them onto the page later.

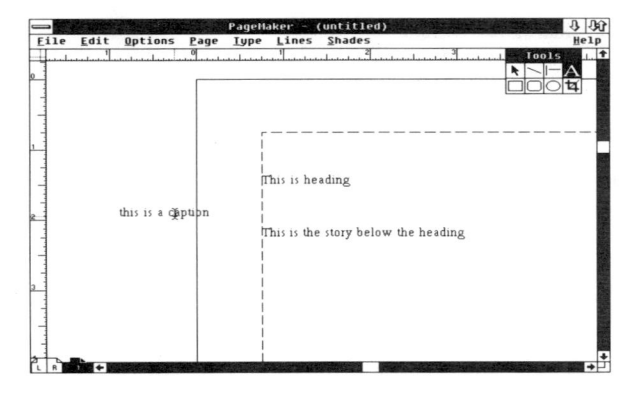

*Figure 61.* This text we have added on the side of the page will now also occupy its own little text block...

150

*Module 4 - PageMaker Text Editing*

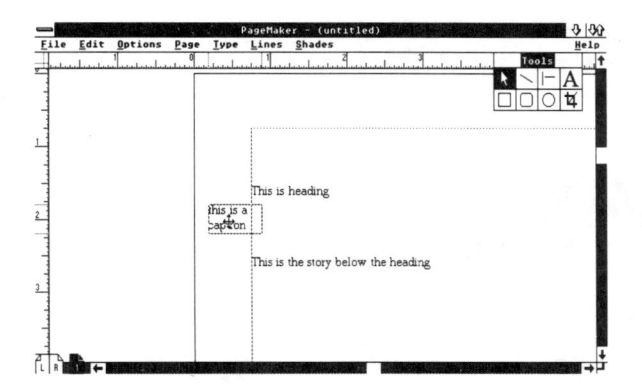

*Figure 62*... *which can now be moved onto the page from the pasteboard area using the pointer tool...*

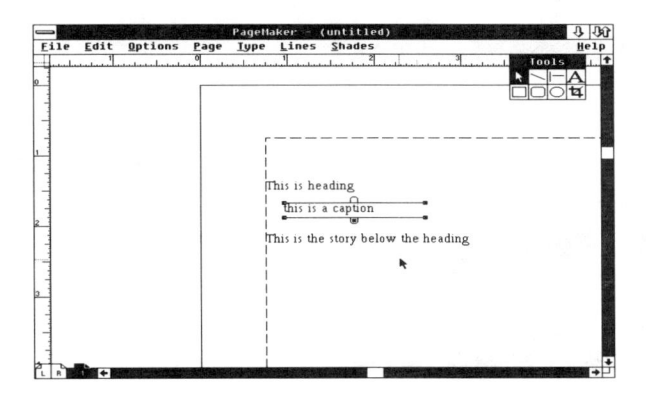

*Figure 63*... *as we have done here.*

## Exporting Text

Text from within PageMaker, whether it was imported or created within PageMaker, can be exported in word processor format for use in a word processor or other such application.

The first step is to select the text you would like to export to a file. If you wish to export a whole file, choose *Select All* from the **Edit** menu before you choose *Export*—otherwise, simply select the text you would like to export (perhaps just a few words or paragraphs as shown in Figure 64).

After performing either of these steps, choose the *Export* command from the **File** menu (Figure 65). The Figure 66 dialog box will appear.

151

*Module 4 - PageMaker Text Editing*

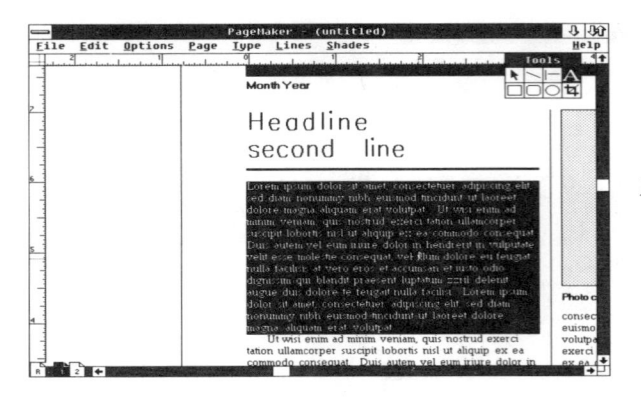

*Figure 64.* Here we have selected a single paragraph to export to a word processor file.

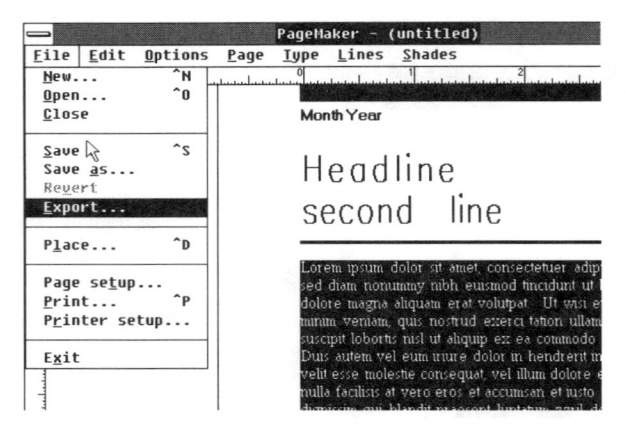

*Figure 65.* After selecting the text to export (in Figure 64), choose the Export command from the **File** menu.

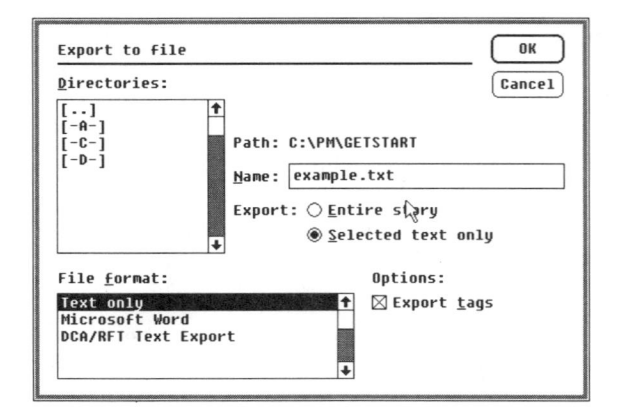

*Figure 66.* The Export command dialog box.

152

Insert the name of the word processor file you wish to create in the rectangle provided, as well as the format underneath this rectangle. The format you choose will depend on exactly what word processor you have or what you want to use the WP file for. We have chosen Example.txt in Microsoft Word 3.0 format (Figure 66).

Module 4 Exercise

# PageMaker Text Editing

# Module 4 Exercise
# PageMaker Text Editing

In this exercise we will be editing text—moving through correcting simple errors, selecting text, and applying simple style and formatting information.

This training material is structured so that people of all levels of expertise with PageMaker can use it to gain maximum benefit. In order to do this, we have structured this material so that the bare exercise is listed below this paragraph on just one page, with no hints. The following pages contain the steps needed to complete this exercise for those that need additional prompting. The **PageMaker Text Editing** module should be referenced if you need further help or explanations.

## Module 4 exercise steps

1. *Open up the publication PRODSPEC.PT3 from the GETSTART subdirectory.*

2. *The heading for this publication reads "TechTile Industrial Product Specifications." The company has decided to reword it to "TechTile Commercial Product Information." The words Industrial and Specifications must be deleted one at a time, and replaced by Commercial and Information, respectively.*

3. *To distinguish between the two different series of tiles, the company has decided to bold the information on the Radius Series, and italicize the information on the Quadrille Series.*

4. *All specifications must be centered rather than left justified. The major heading for the document must be centered and use the font Palatino. Change its size to 18 point.*

5. *Change the leading for the series of paragraphs which form the specifications of the Radius Series to 12 points. This will help the two columns align.*

6. *The first paragraph in the Radius Series and Quadrille Series information must have a first line indent of 0.2 of an inch.*

The details for completing these steps are found on the following pages.

*Module 4 Exercise - PageMaker Text Editing*

## The Steps in Detail.

*1. Open up the publication PRODSPEC.PT3 from the GETSTART subdirectory.*

Opening up an existing publication is a little different from starting a new one yourself. The command used to open a publication is the *Open* command from the **File** menu.

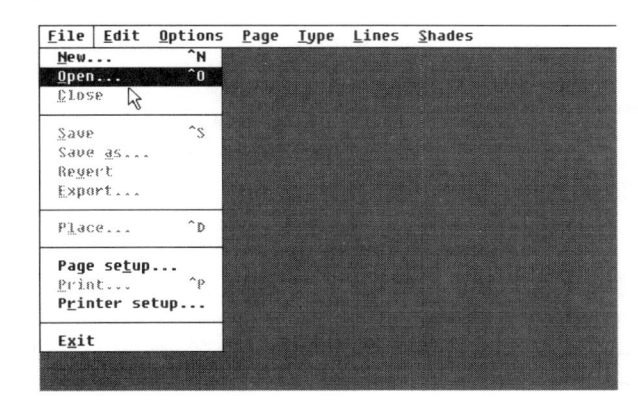

*Figure 1. The Open command must be used to access an existing publication.*

After choosing this command you are presented with a dialog box similar to when we choose the *Place* command. However, this time only saved publications are there for you to choose, whereas before we were searching for files. Locate the GETSTART subdirectory (Figure 2), which will be listed in this dialog box, and double-click on it. Within that subdirectory is the PRODSPEC.PT3 publication (Figure 3). Double-click on its name. This publication is, in effect, actually a PageMaker *template*—a special type of publication. For this exercise this doesn't matter. Templates are described in Module 9.

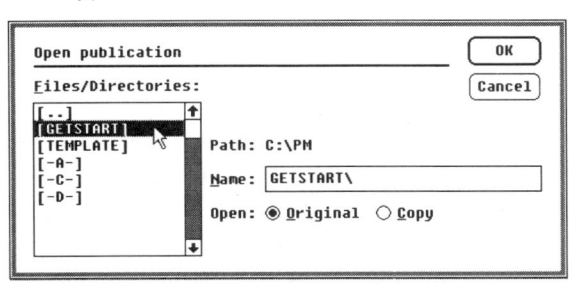

*Figure 2. Once again, this publication is located in the GETSTART subdirectory.*

157

*Module 4 Exercise - PageMaker Text Editing*

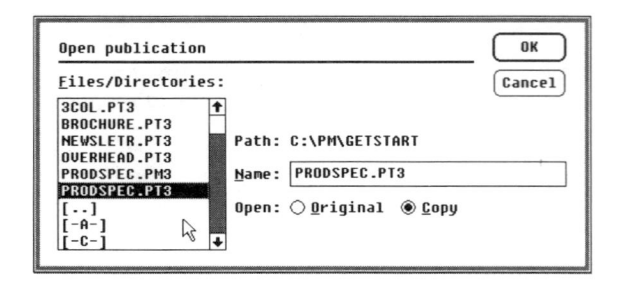

*Figure 3.* Locate the publication entitled PRODSPEC.PT3, and double-click on it.

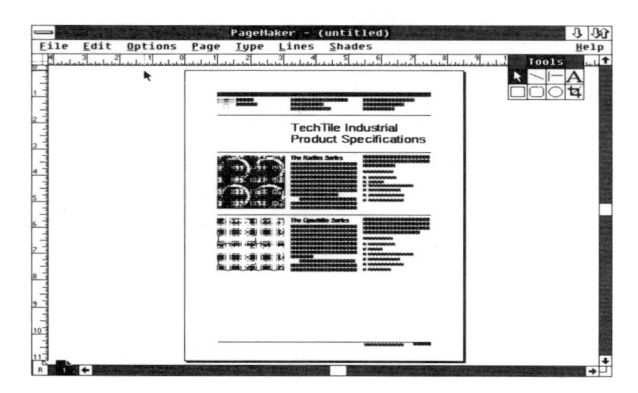

*Figure 4.* PRODSPEC.PT3 will look like this when set to Fit in window view.

2. The heading for this publication reads "TechTile Industrial Product Specifications." The company has decided to reword it to "TechTile Commercial Product Information." The words Industrial and Specifications must be deleted one at a time and replaced by Commercial and Information, respectively.

There are several ways that we can delete and replace these two words. First, however, change to *Actual size* view and use the scroll bars to move the page so that you can actually read this heading (Figures 5 and 6).

*Module 4 Exercise - PageMaker Text Editing*

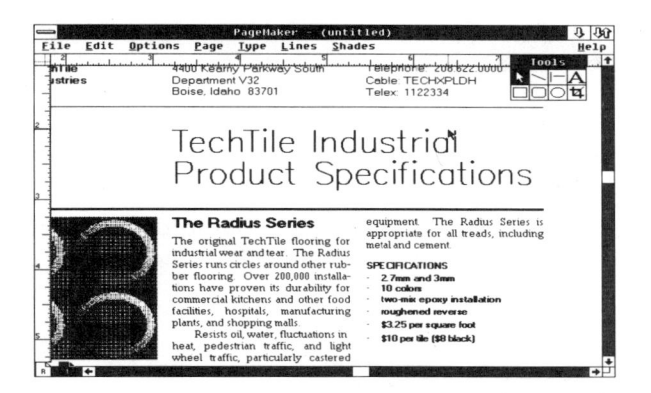

*Figure 5.* Change to Actual size view so that the text can be read.

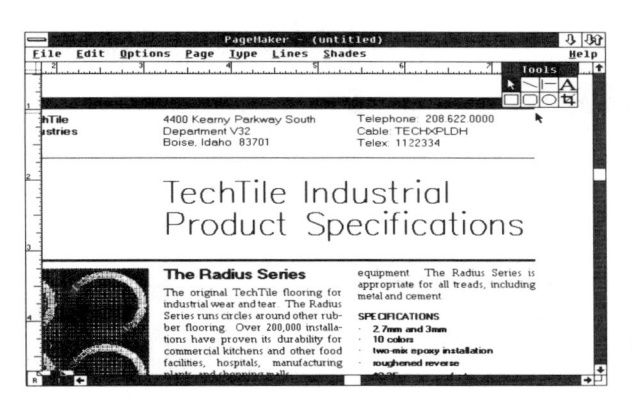

*Figure 6.* The scroll bars may have to be used to move the page around so that you can read the heading.

Make sure the text cursor is selected before you start (see the Toolbox in Figure 7). When it is, move the mouse cursor over the first word we are going to replace—Industrial. Now double-click the mouse and the word will become selected (Figure 7). If it does not, wait a second and double-click the mouse again, until it is highlighted in reverse video.

If, by mistake, you selected the whole paragraph (by triple-clicking the mouse), click outside the paragraph to deselect it, and double-click on Industrial again.

*Module 4 Exercise - PageMaker Text Editing*

Once Industrial is highlighted, you can type in the replacement word—Commercial. There is no need to delete the existing word first—just type the new one in. As soon as you touch the first key on the keyboard, the highlighted word disappears—to be replaced by the new characters you are typing (Figure 8). This applies whenever a selection of text is highlighted within PageMaker. Any text keyed in simply replaces the highlighted text.

The method described above is now used to replace the word Specifications in the heading. The steps are highlighted in Figures 10 to 12.

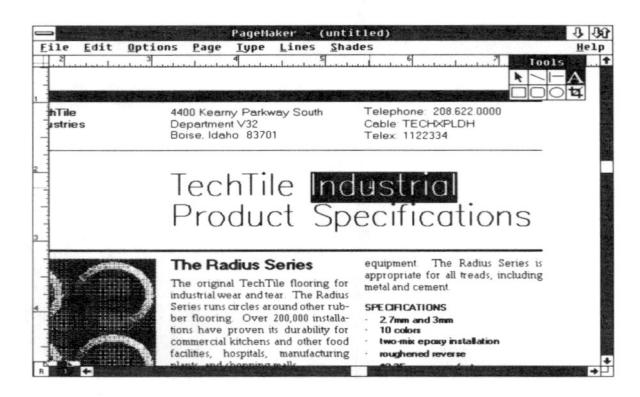

*Figure 7.* Making sure that the text cursor is selected (note the **A** tool selected in the Toolbox), move the mouse cursor over the word Industrial, and click the mouse twice quickly. The word will become selected.

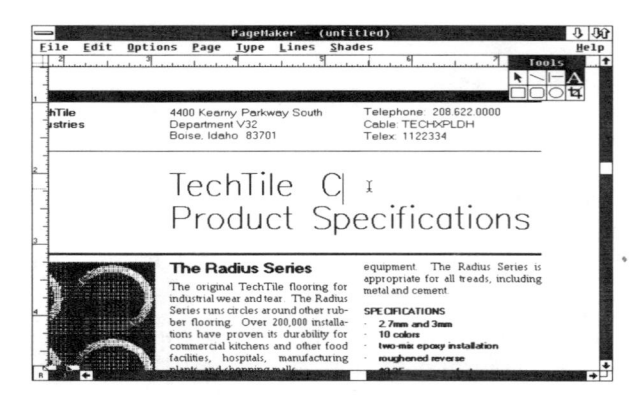

*Figure 8.* As soon as you start typing the new word in, the old word disappears. Continue typing until the new word or words have been entered.

160

*Module 4 Exercise - PageMaker Text Editing*

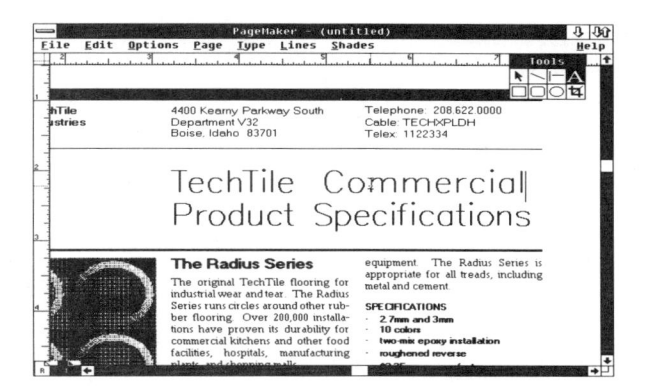

*Figure 9.* The completed word.

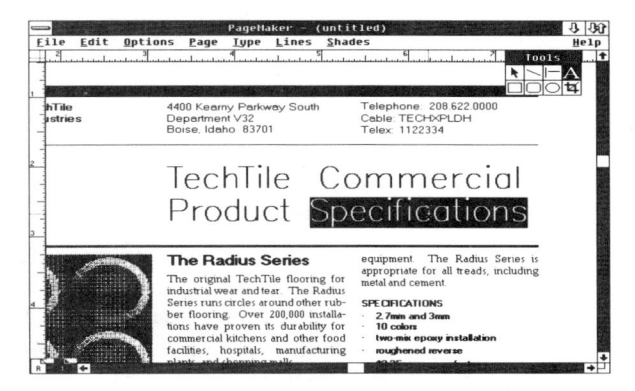

*Figure 10.* The same steps can be followed to replace the word Specifications. Double-click on this word, and type in the new word straight away.

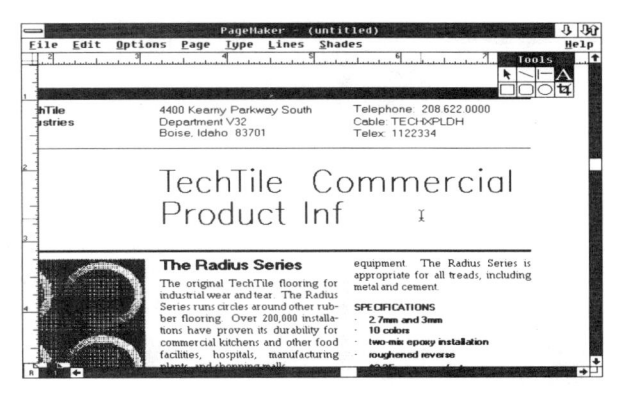

*Figure 11.* In the process of typing in the new word...

161

*Module 4 Exercise - PageMaker Text Editing*

*Figure 12.* ... and completion. The heading has been reworded with a minimum of fuss.

3. To distinguish between the two different series of tiles, the company has decided to bold the information on the Radius Series, and italicize the information on the Quadrille Series.

Move the screen around so that you can see fully the first block of text we are going to edit (the two paragraphs in the middle column under the subheading "The Radius Series"). Once again, there are several ways that we can select this text, as this is what we must do before we can bold it.

The most straightforward way to select the text is as follows. Making sure the text cursor is still selected, move the mouse cursor to the start of the text you would like to select (Figure 13). Hold the mouse button down here and keep it down. Now run the mouse cursor over the text, releasing the mouse button only when it appears to the right of the very last letter you would like to select. The entire two paragraphs will be highlighted (Figures 14 and 15).

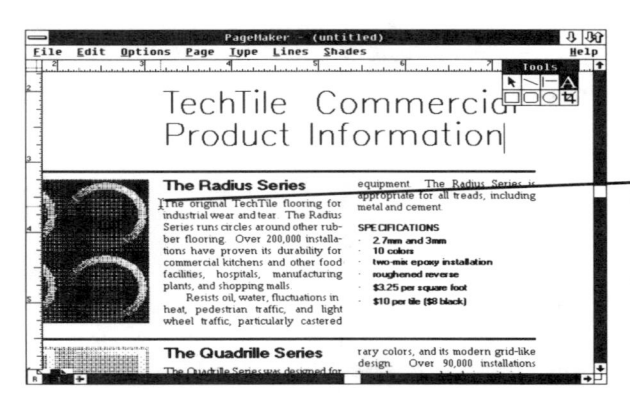

*Figure 13.* We are now going to select the two paragraphs below the heading "The Radius Series." To do this, we move the mouse cursor to the very start of the text we want to select, hold the mouse button down, and move to Figure 14.

162

Module 4 Exercise - PageMaker Text Editing

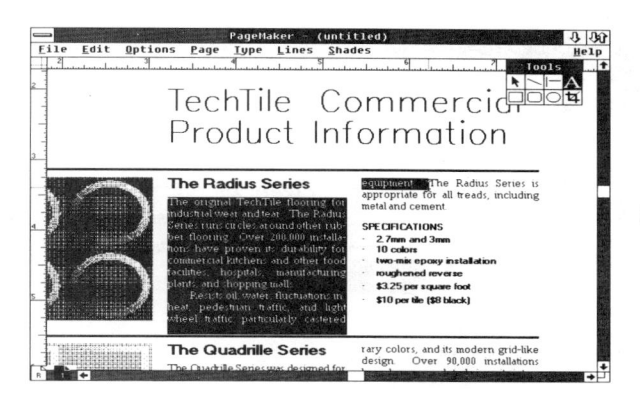

*Figure 14.* Run the mouse cursor over the text, keeping the mouse button held down, and all text will become highlighted as you go.

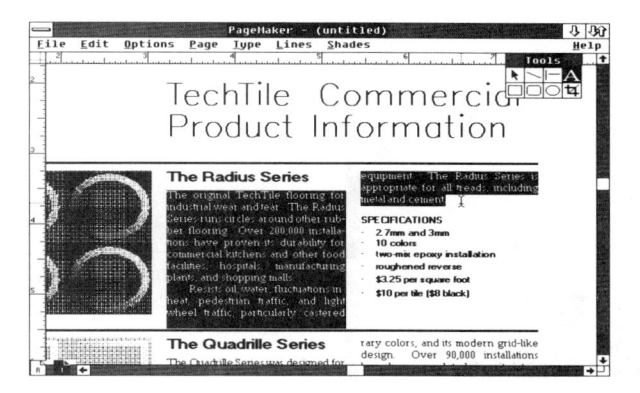

*Figure 15.* Release the mouse button when the mouse cursor is to the right of the very last letter you want to select. All letters in between the start and end points will be selected.

If your hand slipped off the mouse, or for any other reason you were unsuccessful, click once at the beginning and try again.

Two other methods could have been used to select the text. You could have clicked once to insert the text cursor at the start of the text to select, held down the Shift key, and clicked at the end of the text block. You could also have triple-clicked on the first paragraph, held the mouse button down on the third click, and moved the mouse anywhere into the second paragraph. If you are unsure of either of these methods, stick to the first method described.

Once the text is selected, select the style *Bold* from the **Type** menu (Figure 16).

163

Module 4 Exercise - PageMaker Text Editing

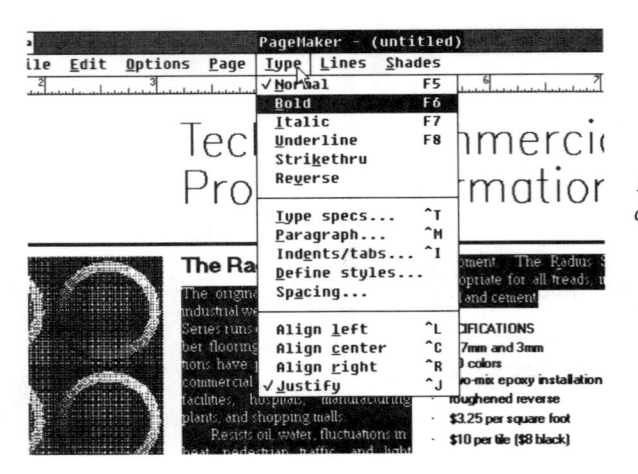

*Figure 16.* After selecting the text, choose the Bold style from the **Type** menu.

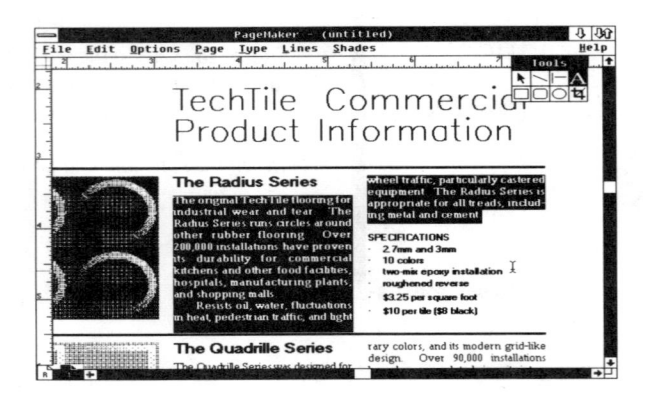

*Figure 17.* The entire two paragraphs that were selected now change to bold on the screen.

The two paragraphs have now changed to bold style (Figure 17).

After having successfully completed this, move down the page a little to view the next two paragraphs (underneath the heading "The Quadrille Series"), and select those as well, using the methods described earlier in this step. This time however, select the style *Italic* from the **Type** menu. See Figures 18 to 20 for the steps involved.

*Module 4 Exercise - PageMaker Text Editing*

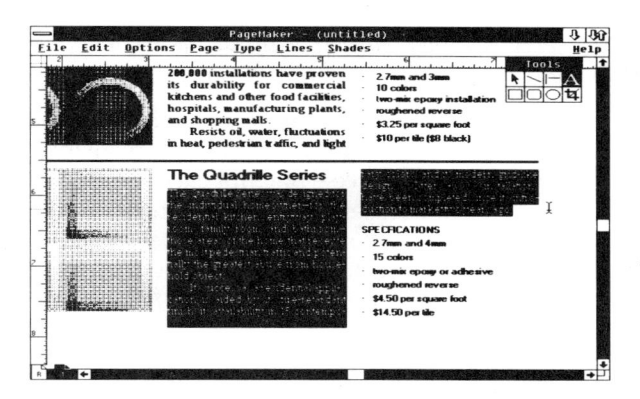

*Figure 18.* Use the right-hand scroll bar to move yourself down the page enough to select the next two paragraphs, under the heading "The Quadrille Series." Use the same method as described earlier to select the text.

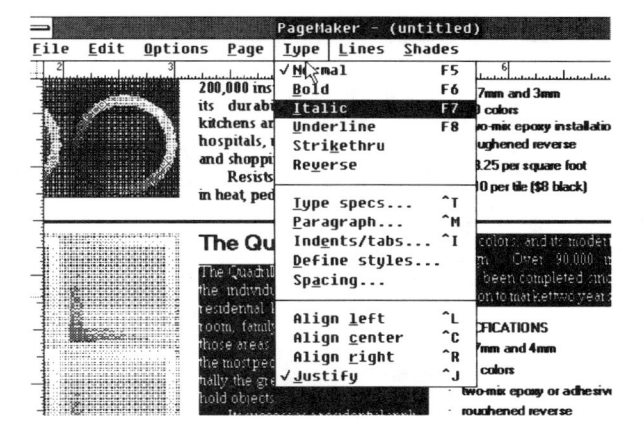

*Figure 19.* After selecting the text, use the Italic command from the *Type* menu.

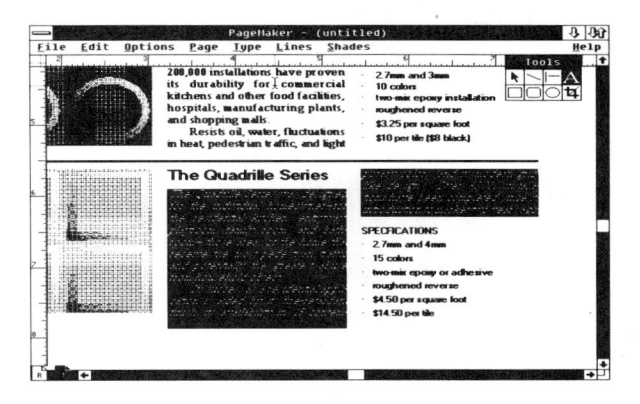

*Figure 20.* The italicized text.

165

Module 4 Exercise - PageMaker Text Editing

4. All specifications must be centered rather than left justified. The major heading for the document must be centered and use the font Palatino. Change its size to 18 point.

The specifications are the small paragraphs that appear after the information on the tiles. Move the page around so that the specifications are visible, and select them all. (This will have to be done twice—once for each series of tiles—only one block can be done at a time). After selecting the specifications (Figure 21 shows the Radius Series specifications), select the *Align center* command from the **Type** menu (Figure 22). All selected paragraphs will be instantly centered.

Repeat this step yourself for the Quadrille Series specifications.

*Figure 21.* Our next task is to alter the justification of the specifications. Locate the first group of specifications next to the Radius Series, and select them all.

*Figure 22.* Use the Align center command from the **Type** menu to center the selected text.

166

*Module 4 Exercise - PageMaker Text Editing*

Now for the final part of this step. Move the page so that you can read the major heading that, from Step 2, reads "TechTile Commercial Product Information," and select it (Figure 23). To change the size and font of the text, choose the *Type specs* command from the **Type** menu (Figure 24).

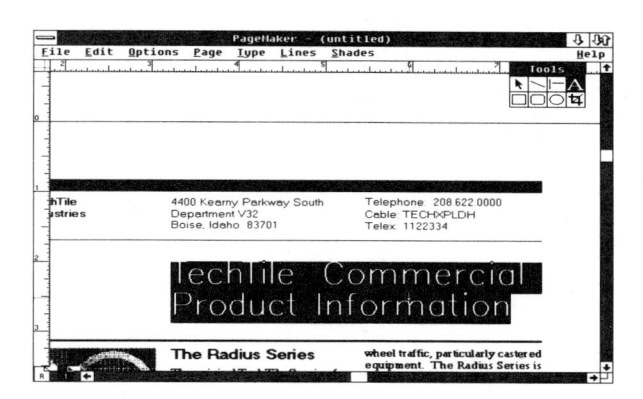

*Figure 23. Use the scroll bars once again to move the page up a little to read the heading. Select the heading as shown.*

*Figure 24. After selecting the heading, select the Type specs command from the **Type** menu.*

*Module 4 Exercise - PageMaker Text Editing*

Within the dialog box that occurs when choosing the *Type specs* command (Figure 25), select the Palatino font from the list of type faces to the left of this dialog box (Figure 26).

If your printer does not support Palatino, then choose Times (or a similar font).

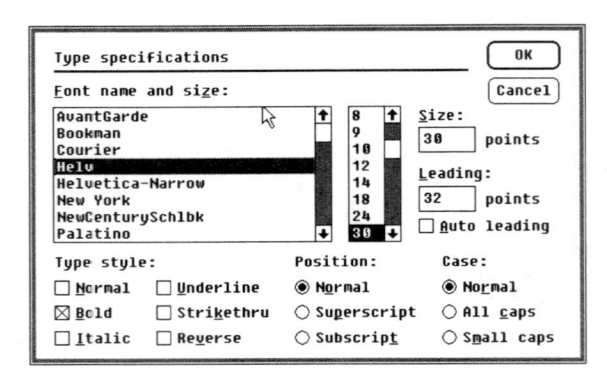

*Figure 25. The Type specs dialog box will initially return the current type face, size, etc., of the selected text.*

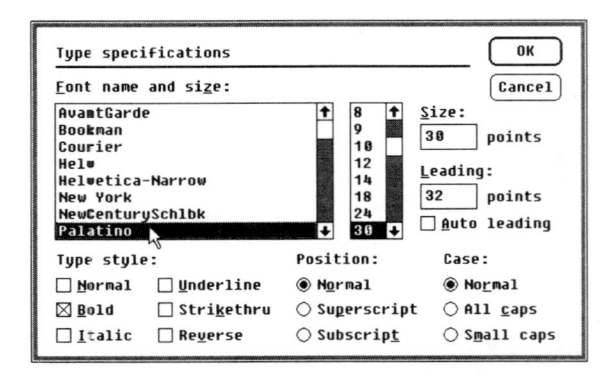

*Figure 26. To change the font being used, select a new typeface from the list that appears. Choose Times or a similar font if your system does not contain the font Palatino.*

168

*Module 4 Exercise - PageMaker Text Editing*

To change the size of the text, simply type in the new size of 18 point (Figure 27) in the Size box. Figure 28 shows the results of Figures 26 and 27. If your system does not support 18 point, then choose the next highest figure.

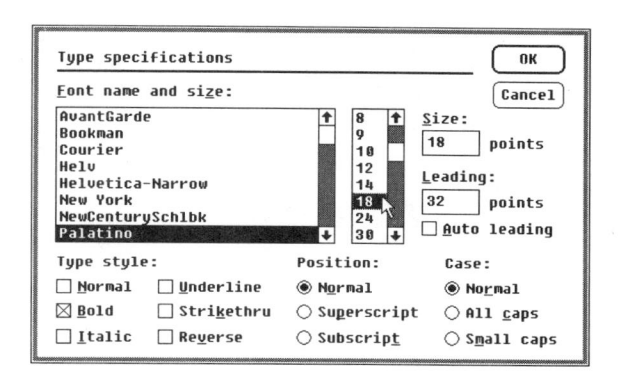

*Figure 27. The new size for the text, 18 point, has been keyed into the Size box.*

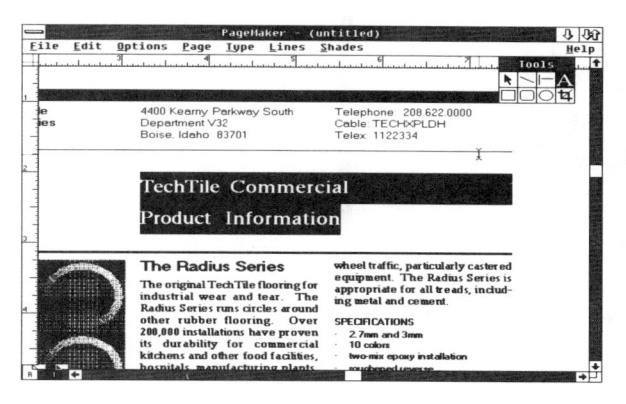

*Figure 28. Here we see the result of the heading after the Type specs command has been adjusted in Figures 26 and 27. We next must center this heading.*

To center the heading, make sure it is still selected, and choose the *Align Center* command in the **Type** menu (Figure 29). The result is shown in Figure 30.

169

*Module 4 Exercise - PageMaker Text Editing*

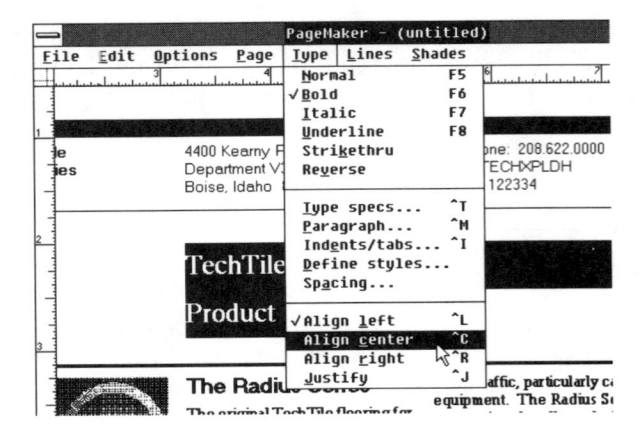

*Figure 29.* Centering the heading is achieved via the Align Center command in the **Type** menu.

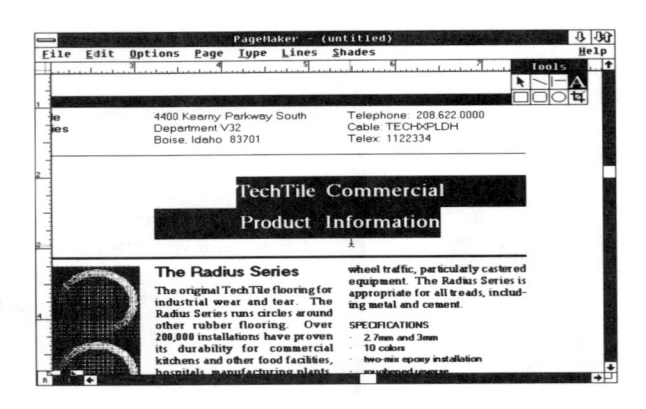

*Figure 30.* The result.

5. Change the leading for the series of paragraphs which form the specifications of the Radius Series to 12 points. This will help the two columns align.

After scrolling to a position to see these specifications, select the entire specifications block using the text tool (Figure 31). We must then use the *Type specs* command (Figure 32).

170

*Module 4 Exercise - PageMaker Text Editing*

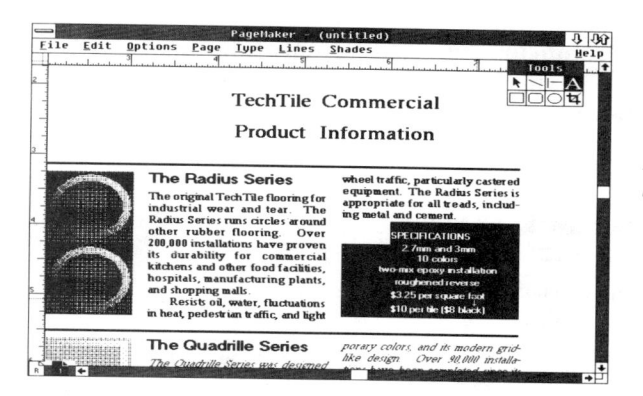

*Figure 31.* Select the specifications block for the Radius Series in order to change its interline spacing (leading).

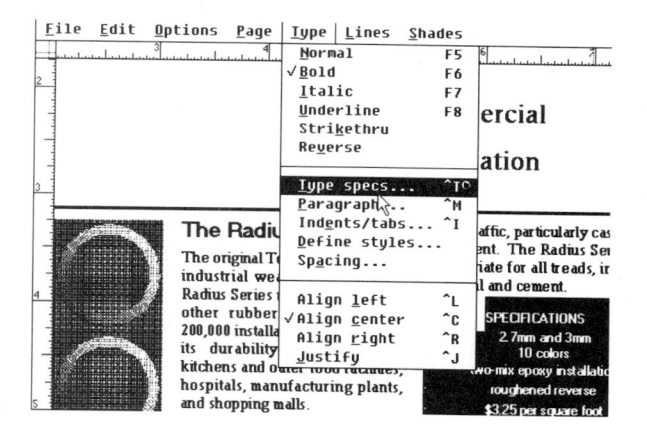

*Figure 32.* To change the leading of selected text we must use the Type Specs command from the **Type** menu.

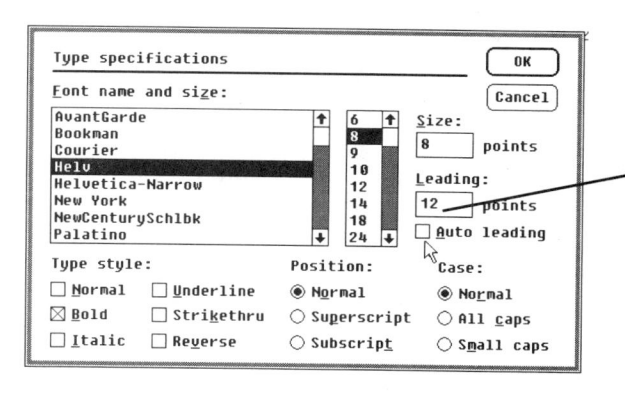

*Figure 33.* In the Type specs dialog box, change the leading figure to 12 by keying in the number 12 at the Leading box.

171

*Module 4 Exercise - PageMaker Text Editing*

Within this *Type specs* command, select the current leading figure and change it to 12 points (Figure 33). The space between the lines will change to reflect this new figure after selecting OK (Figure 34).

*Figure 34.* The change of leading in the specifications closely aligns the two columns.

6. *The first paragraph in the Radius Series and Quadrille Series information must have a first line indent of 0.2 of an inch.*

First, you must locate and select the paragraph mentioned (Figure 35). After doing this, you must select the *Paragraph* command from the **Type** menu (Figure 36).

*Figure 35.* Select the first paragraph in the Radius Series as such.

Module 4 Exercise - PageMaker Text Editing

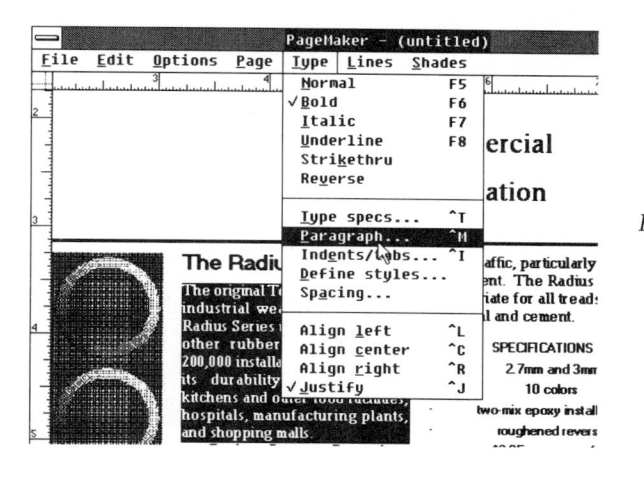

*Figure 36.* Now select the Paragraph command in the **Type** menu in order to change the indents of the paragraph.

Within this command you must alter the number for First (which at the moment should read 0) under the Indents boxes. Change this figure to 0.2 (if units are in inches)—see Figure 37. If in another unit, insert 0.2i. The first paragraph of the Radius Series now reflects the 0.2 inch first line indent (see Figure 38).

Repeat these steps for yourself after selecting the first paragraph of the Quadrille Series.

*Figure 37.* Change the First rectangle to contain the figure 0.2 (inches). This will cause the first line of the selected paragraph to be indented this distance.

173

*Module 4 Exercise - PageMaker Text Editing*

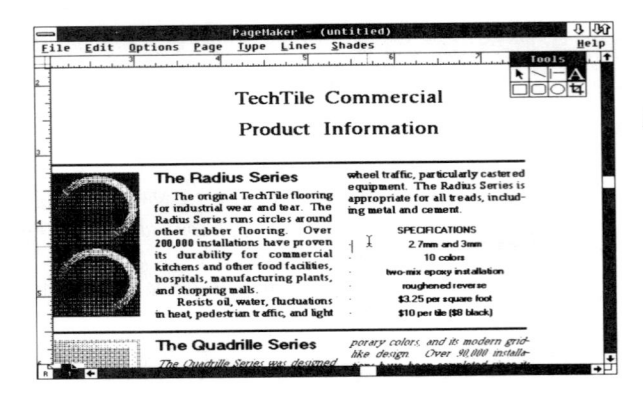

*Figure 38.* The paragraph that was selected now reflects the first line indent we set. Repeat the last few steps yourself (Figures 35 to 37) after selecting the first paragraph of the Quadrille Series.

# Module 5

# PageMaker Internal Graphics

# PageMaker Internal Graphics

Most of the time, third-party packages will be used to create the complex and professional quality graphics that can be used within PageMaker. There are packages available for the PC that make graphics a reality for all types of users—a reality that most of the time cannot be achieved via PageMaker alone.

This is not to say that PageMaker can't create a large array of graphics internally—because it can. When it comes to preparing simple graphics, such as borders, underlines, boxes, circles, simple graphs, and charts, you may not need to look any further than PageMaker itself.

Figure 1 is an example of how graphics can be created within PageMaker in very little time.

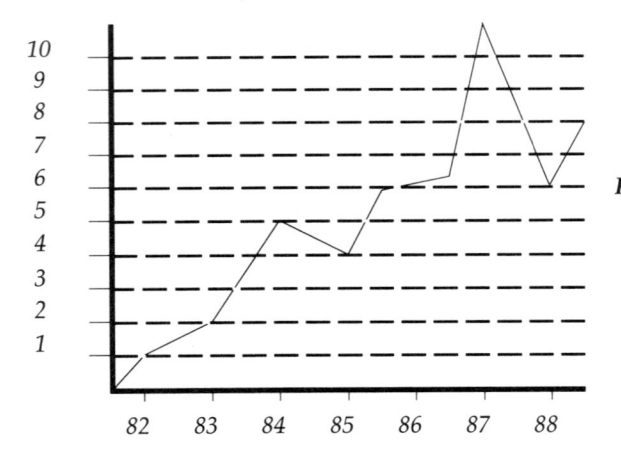

*Figure 1. A simple graph created using the PageMaker graphic tools.*

All of the PageMaker graphics tools are found in the Toolbox (Figure 2). They include two straight-line drawing tools, two rectangular drawing tools, and the oval drawing tool. The way these tools are used is quite simple.

*Module 5 - PageMaker Internal Graphics*

Simply select the tool you would like to use from the Toolbox. Let's say we select the square-corner drawing tool first (Figure 3). The mouse cursor changes its appearance to a crosshair.

*Figure 2. The Graphic Tools.*
The diagonal- and perpendicular-line drawing tools
The square-corner drawing tool
The oval drawing tool
The rounded-corner drawing tool.

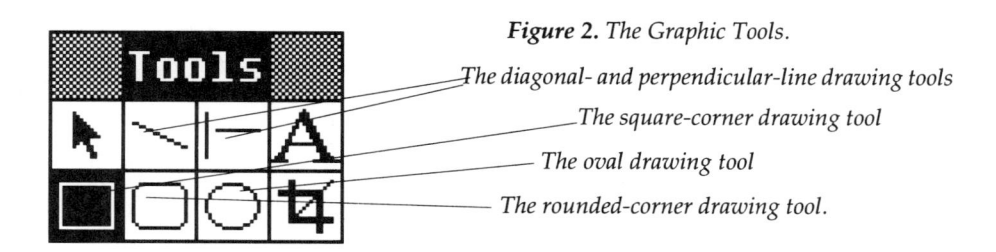

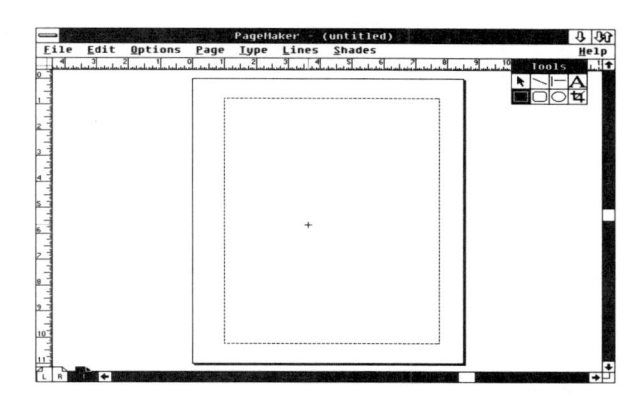

*Figure 3.* When any graphic tool is selected, the mouse cursor changes to a crosshair.

Hold down the mouse cursor where you would like to start drawing the graphic. Dragging the mouse in any direction will cause a box to appear, which will become permanent when the mouse button is released (Figures 4 and 5). All other graphics can be created in exactly this same manner—by selecting it in the Toolbox, and dragging the mouse along the page. Experiment with all the graphic drawing tools to see the results you get, as we have done in Figure 6.

177

*Module 5 - PageMaker Internal Graphics*

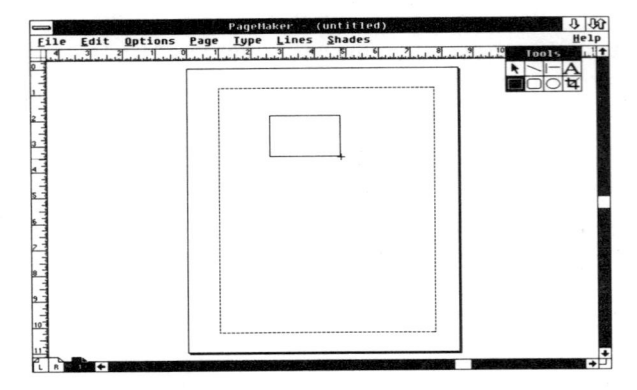

***Figure 4.*** *To create a graphic once you have selected a tool (in this case the square-corner drawing tool), hold the mouse button down and drag the mouse across the page. In our case, a rectangle is created.*

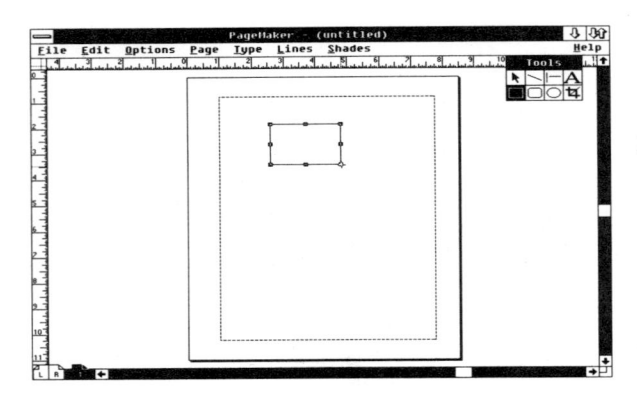

***Figure 5.*** *Release the mouse button when the graphic is the correct size. It will then become selected. Note the small square dots (called handles) around the edge of the graphic.*

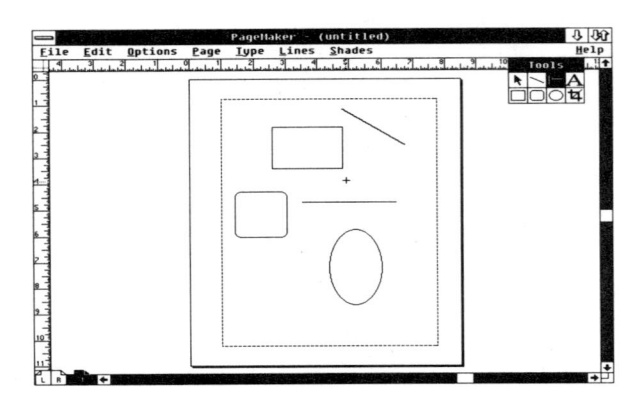

***Figure 6.*** *Here is an example of a graphic from each of the graphic drawing tools.*

## Altering graphics

Whenever you draw a graphic, you will notice that the graphic is selected (Figure 5)—that is to say, it has several small square dots, or handles, around its edge. However, whenever you create another graphic, this new object becomes selected and the previously selected graphic is deselected.

To manipulate a graphic on the page, it must first be selected. This is done by activating the pointer tool in the Toolbox and clicking with the arrow on the border of the graphic. Once selected, a graphic will display the handles around its border (Figure 7). Alternate graphics can be selected simply by clicking anywhere on their border.

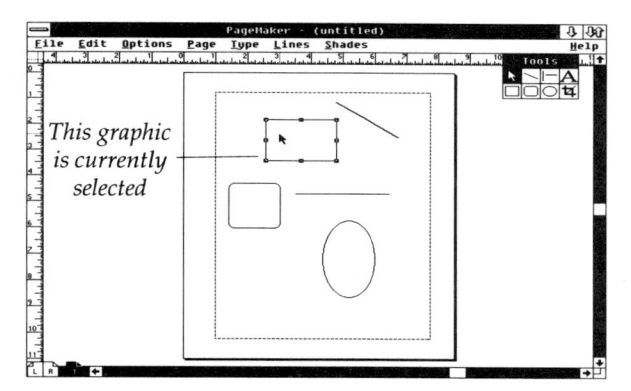

*This graphic is currently selected*

*Figure 7.* To select a graphic, you must first make sure the pointer tool is currently active (note the Toolbox), and click on the border of the graphic you would like to select.

## Changing borders and fills

After selecting a graphic, there are several things that can be done with it. First, we will look at how we can change both the border and/or the *fill* for that graphic. If you have created a graphic using either of the line drawing tools, you will only be able to adjust the line thickness, because a line has no fill at all.

Make sure a rectangular graphic is selected on screen, similar to Figure 8, and study the commands in the **Lines** and **Shades** menus. Most of the choices in these menus are self-explanatory—line thickness and patterns can be set by selecting the one that appeals to you, as can the shade and pattern to fill a selected graphic. Figures 8 to 14 illustrate some examples.

*Module 5 - PageMaker Internal Graphics*

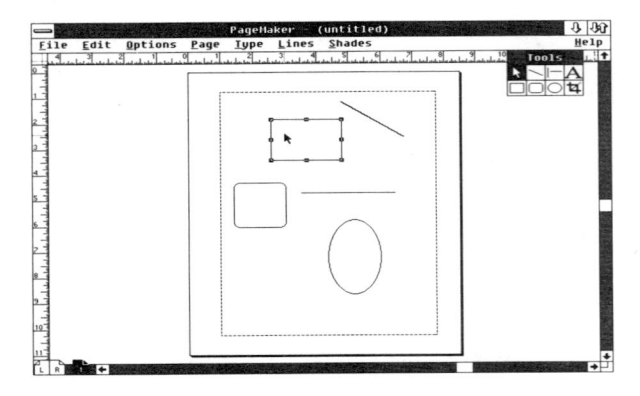

*Figure 8.* The process of changing the appearance of a graphic begins by selecting the graphic you would like to change.

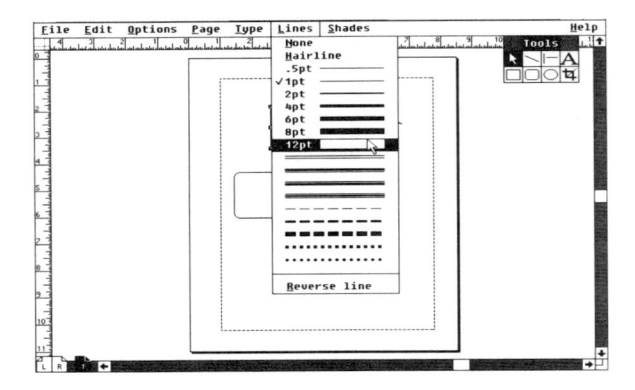

*Figure 9.* After selecting the graphic, move to the **Lines** menu and select the desired line thickness.

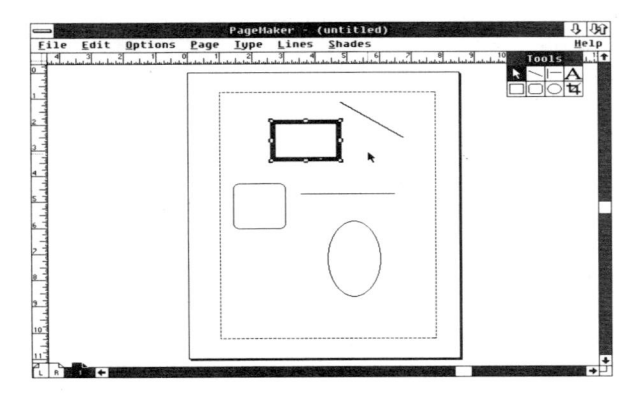

*Figure 10.* The graphic will reflect on screen the new line thickness. A small change may sometimes not look like a change due to the resolution of the screen.

*Module 5 - PageMaker Internal Graphics*

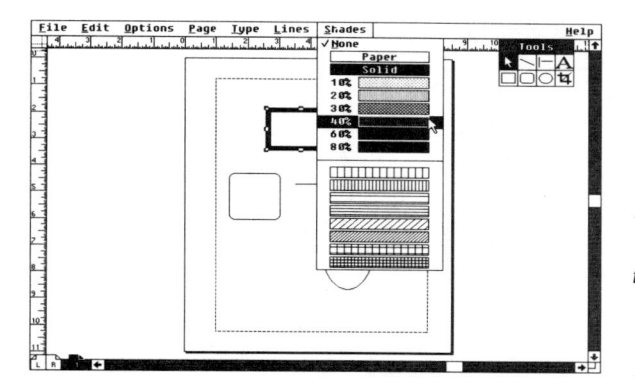

*Figure 11.* The same idea works when changing the fill pattern of a graphic. Make sure it is selected, then move to the **Shades** menu and select a shade or pattern.

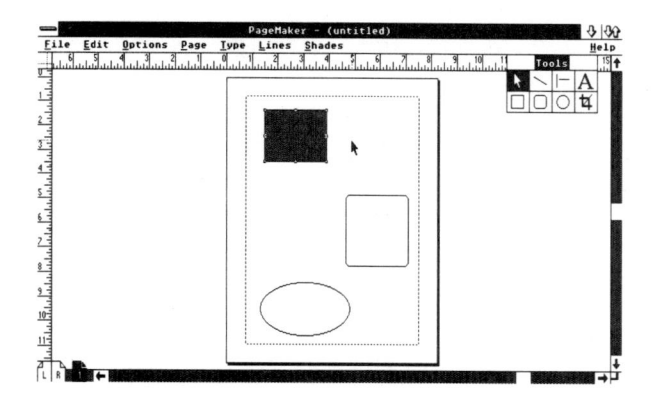

*Figure 12.* The selected graphic will reflect the new pattern or shade on screen.

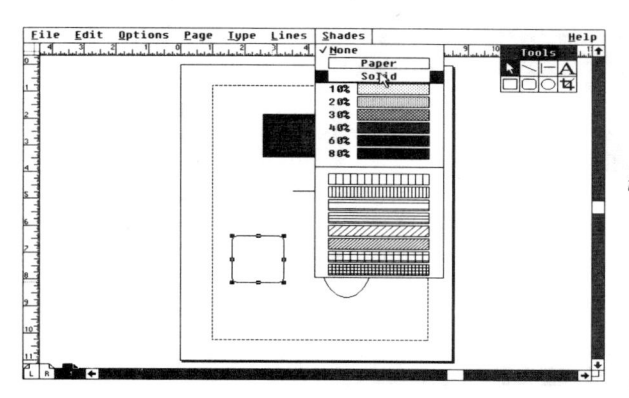

*Figure 13.* Here we have selected the rectangle near the bottom of the screen, and are in the process of choosing the Solid option, which will be black.

*Module 5 - PageMaker Internal Graphics*

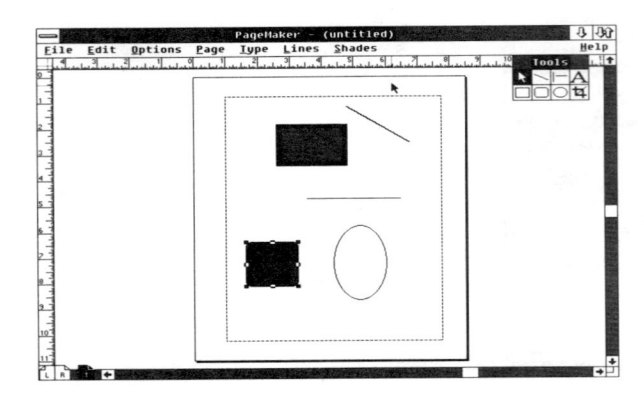

*Figure 14.* The color black is shown on screen filling the selected rectangle.

# Moving

Any graphic can be moved in exactly the same way as a text block. Hold down the mouse button on the border of the graphic if it is hollow, or anywhere in the graphic if it has a fill pattern, and move the mouse. The graphic will be dragged along with the mouse and will stay where the mouse button is released.

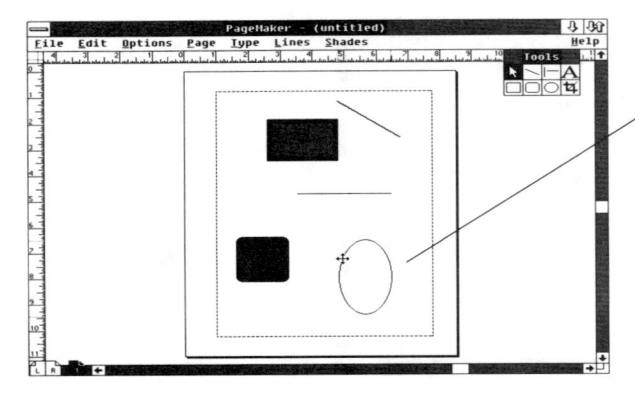

*Figure 15.* The ellipse has been selected and is in the process of being moved. Note the shape of the mouse cursor. Wherever the mouse cursor is released will be the new position for the graphic.

*182*

Module 5 - PageMaker Internal Graphics

## Resizing

Any graphic can be resized in any direction much the same way as a text block can. Only in the case of a graphic, there are more dots around the edge, giving more flexibility in resizing. To resize, first select the graphic using the pointer tool, hold down the mouse button on any handle around the edge of the graphic, and drag it in any direction you like. Release the mouse button when the graphic has been sized correctly.

You will notice, as you experiment with the resizing of graphics, that the handle you grab will determine in which direction the graphic can be resized, horizontally, vertically, or diagonally. See Figures 16 to 18 that illustrate this point.

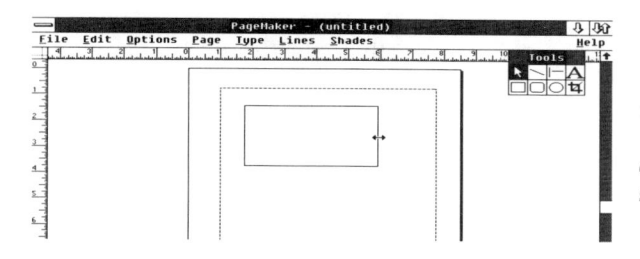

*Figure 16.* Holding the mouse button down on a side handle means that the graphic can only be resized in that direction (in this case the width of the graphic can be shortened or lengthened, depending on the movement of the mouse).

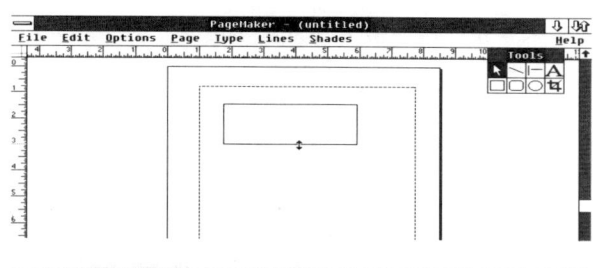

*Figure 17.* Here we have selected the bottom handle—allowing us to size the graphic vertically.

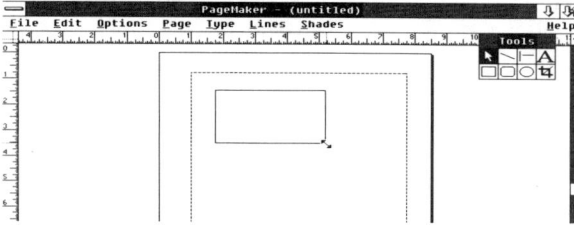

*Figure 18.* We have now selected a corner handle to size the rectangle diagonally.

183

## Editing

Any selected graphic can be deleted, copied, cleared, or pasted to and from the PageMaker screen, similar to text, by using the editing commands in the **Edit** menu. *Cut* will remove the selected graphic from the screen, and keep it in a temporary memory (called the *Clipboard*). The graphic is not yet lost, although it is not visible. *Copy* will put a copy of the selected graphic into the Clipboard and not remove it from the screen.

*Paste* will transfer the graphic from the Clipboard back to the middle of the screen. Once the graphic is in the Clipboard, it can be pasted any number of times back onto the page. This can have several advantages, one of which is in duplicating a selected graphic any number of times. A graphic can be cleared from the screen, without being transferred to the Clipboard, by selecting the *Clear* command from the **Edit** menu. The Backspace and Delete keys operate identically to the *Clear* command.

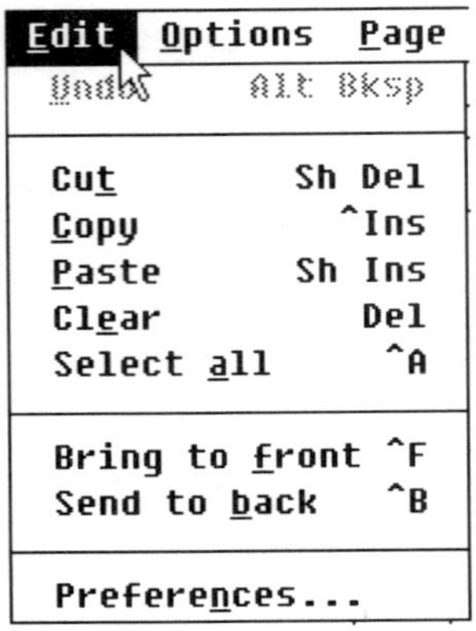

*Figure 19.* Cut removes a selected graphic from the screen and puts it into memory (the Clipboard). Copy copies the selected graphic from screen to the Clipboard (the screen graphic is not altered in any way). Paste transfers whatever is in the Clipboard back to the middle of the screen. And the Clear command removes a graphic from screen and does not put it into the Clipboard.

Be aware when using the Clipboard, that it will only hold one graphic at a time. Every time you cut or copy something to this temporary memory, the previous element in that memory is removed for good.

Figures 20 to 22 provide examples of using the *Copy* command with graphics.

*Module 5 - PageMaker Internal Graphics*

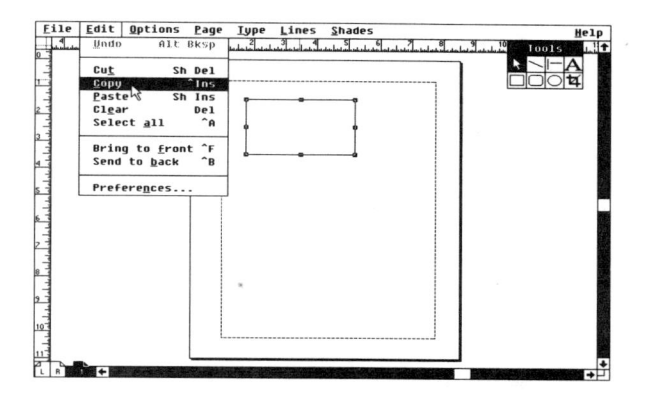

***Figure 20.*** *The graphic on this page has been selected. Let's assume that we now select the Copy command. The graphic is then copied to the Clipboard.*

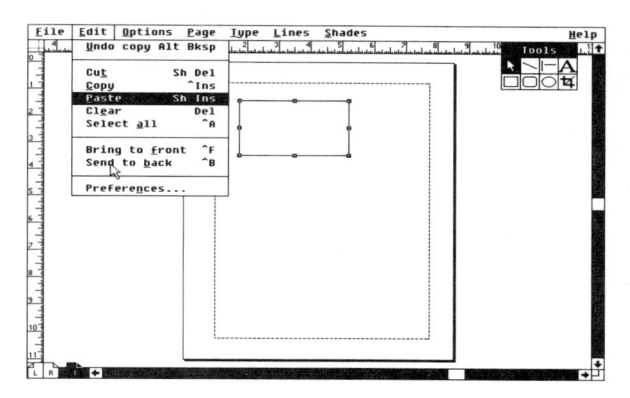

***Figure 21.*** *Immediately after choosing Copy we can choose the Paste command (it does not have to be immediately after, but before something else is cut or copied, or the computer is turned off).*

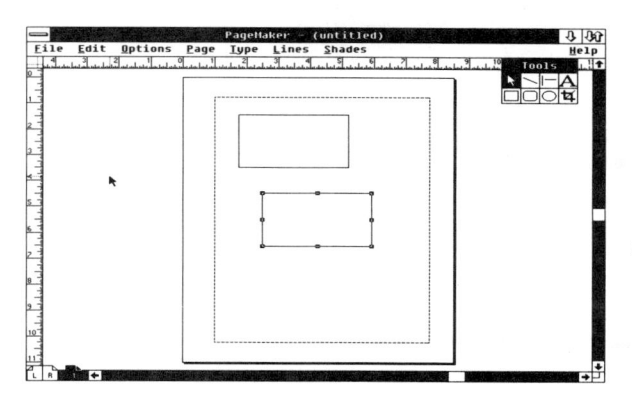

***Figure 22.*** *After choosing Paste, whatever was in the Clipboard is pasted back to the middle of the screen. This process can be repeated to obtain multiple copies of any graphic.*

Module 5 - PageMaker Internal Graphics

## Changing the printing order of graphics

It's very easy to create graphics that either overlap each other, or overlap text on the page. Using two other commands in the **Edit** menu, *Send to back* and *Bring to front*, the order of the graphics overlap can be changed. Study Figures 23 to 28 to see examples of this technique.

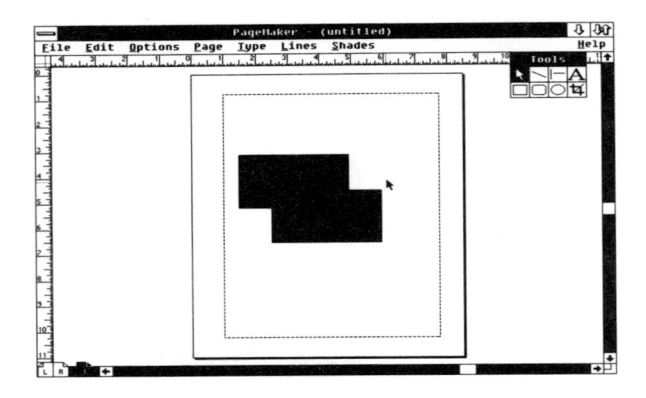

*Figure 23.* Here we have two graphics that overlap each other. Let's say we now want to change the order of the overlap so that the black graphic is on top.

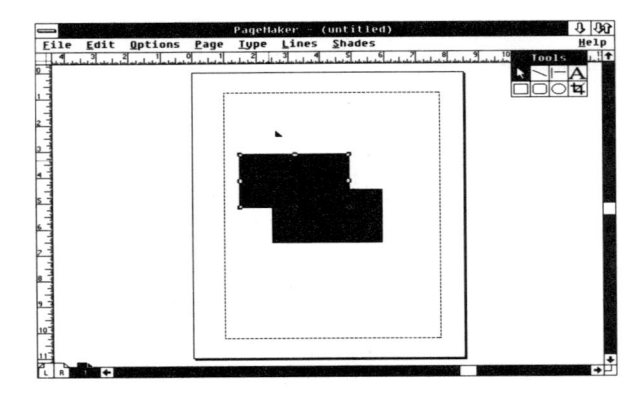

*Figure 24.* We could actually select either graphic here, but we will start with the black graphic on the bottom (note the white handles).

186

*Module 5 - PageMaker Internal Graphics*

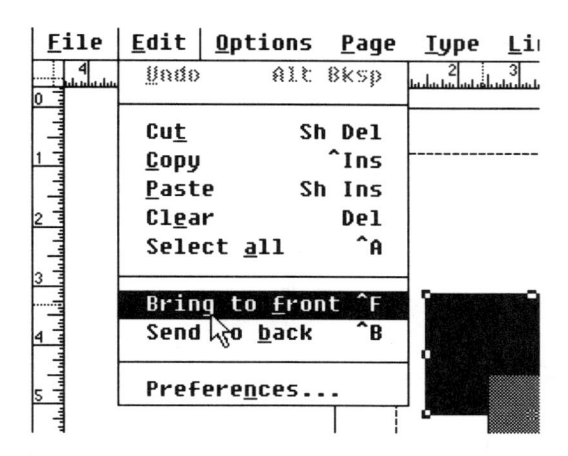

*Figure 25. We select the command Bring to front from the **Edit** menu (because the graphic we have selected is on the bottom).*

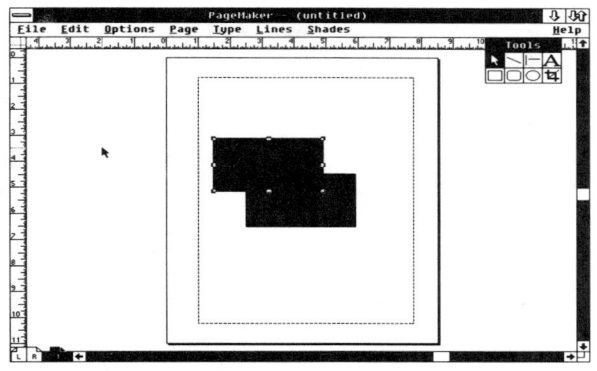

*Figure 26. The change can be seen immediately—the black graphic is now on the top.*

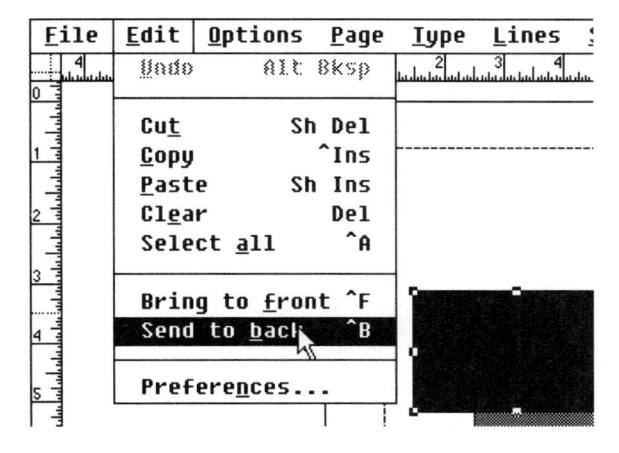

*Figure 27. If we now wanted to send the black graphic to the back again, we would need to select the Send to back command (because the black graphic is still the selected object).*

Module 5 - PageMaker Internal Graphics

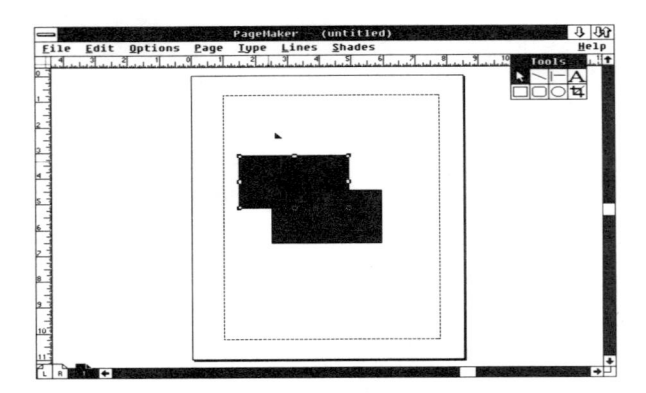

*Figure 28. After selecting the command in Figure 27, the shaded graphic now sits on top again.*

## Transparent and solid graphics

Graphics can be filled with transparent and solid selections from the **Shades** menu (Figure 13), as well as a range of shaded options. It is important when using the *None* and *Paper* selections to understand the difference between *None*, which is hollow, and *Paper*, which is usually white. Both look white on the screen.

Note the two overlapping diagrams in Figure 29. In both cases the white rectangle is on the top. In the example towards the top of the page, the rectangle has a fill selected from the **Shades** menu as *None*, while in the bottom example, the white rectangle has a fill selection of *Paper*.

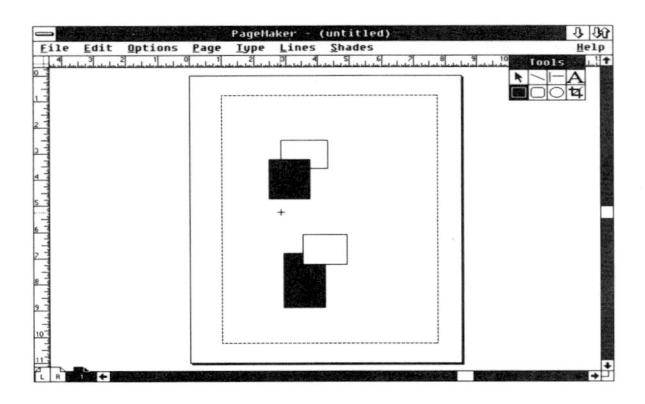

*Figure 29. The white rectangle at the top of the page has a fill selection of None. It is hollow and the black rectangle underneath can be seen completely. The bottom rectangle has a fill selection of Paper (which is usually white), and therefore covers the black rectangle underneath it.*

## Rounded-corner drawing tool

It is possible to draw both squares and rectangles with rounded corners. This is done by selecting the rounded-corner drawing tool from the Toolbox (see Figure 2).

This tool is used in exactly the same manner as the square-corner tool. One additional thing to remember is the *Rounded corners* command available in the **Options** menu. This command offers a choice of radii for the rounded corners of the rectangle or square. Figure 30 shows an example of the rounded-corner tool, and Figure 31 illustrates the dialog box activated with the *Rounded corners* command.

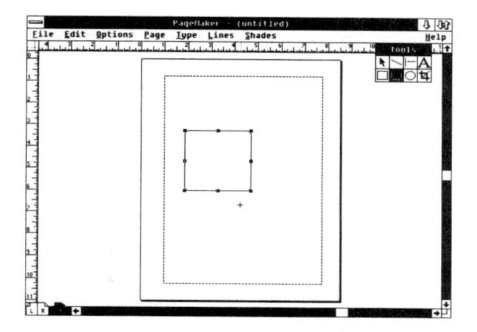

*Figure 30. This rectangle was drawn using the rounded-corner drawing tool. The actual radius of the corners can be set using the dialog box of Figure 31. This radius was set close to 90 degrees.*

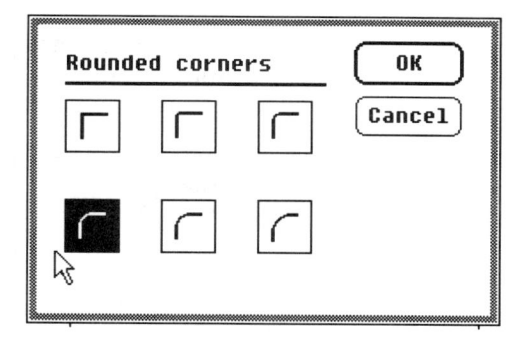

*Figure 31. This is the Rounded corners dialog box associated with the Rounded corners command from the **Options** menu. You simply choose the radius that suits you.*

## Line drawing tools

The diagonal- and perpendicular-line drawing tools are indicated in the Toolbox diagram of Figure 2. The perpendicular tool draws lines at 45-degree increments, while the diagonal tool allows straight lines at any angle. The diagonal tool acts like the perpendicular tool when the Shift key is held down.

The thickness of the lines can be set using the **Lines** menu (see Figure 9). Some examples are shown in Figure 32.

*Module 5 - PageMaker Internal Graphics*

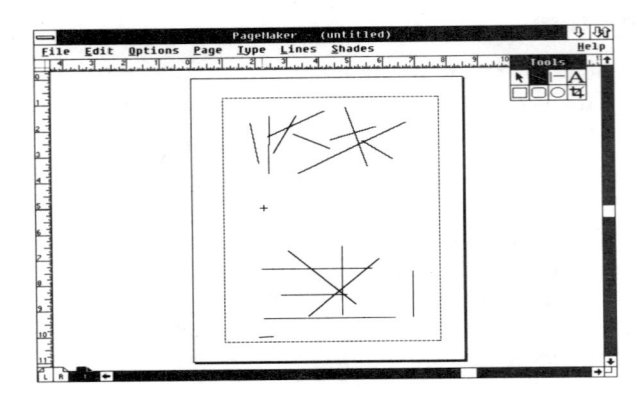

**Figure 32.** *Examples of the two different line drawing tools are shown.*

# Rulers

One element of PageMaker that makes the creation and manipulation of graphics a lot easier is the PageMaker rulers. They are activated by the *Rulers* command in the **Options** menu (Figure 33).

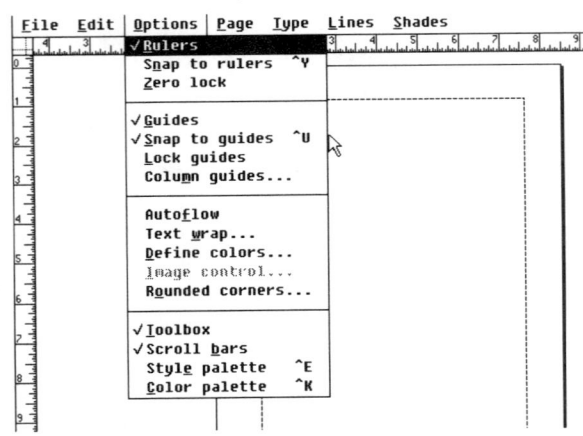

**Figure 33.** *Selecting the Rulers command from the **Options** menu will cause rulers to appear down the left and across the top of the page.*

As you select this command, you will notice a ruler appear down the left and across the top of the page (Figure 34). These rulers will use units that are controlled by the *Preferences* command in the **Edit** menu. The rulers will always reformat to give accurate measurements on the screen, irrespective of the current PageMaker view. The increments in these rulers change depending on the current page view.

*Module 5 - PageMaker Internal Graphics*

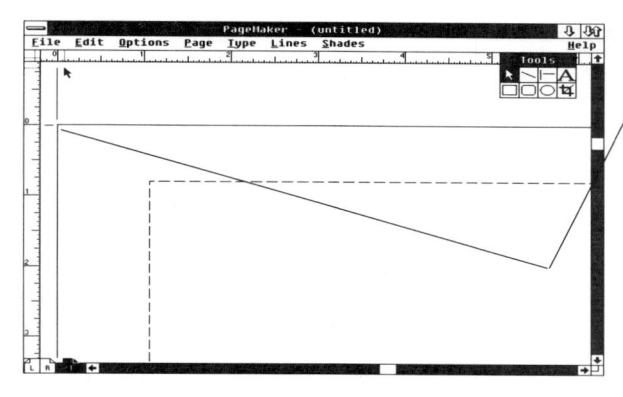

*Figure 34.* Note that the zero point of the ruler, both vertically and horizontally, is aligned with the top left-hand corner of the page. If the increments on your ruler look a little different from this figure, you may have other units set up in the Preferences command in the **Edit** menu. We currently have inches selected.

We can also change exactly where the zero points of both the horizontal and vertical rulers start. By default, the zero point of both these rulers starts at the top-left corner of the actual page. Move to *Actual size* view through the **Page** menu and look at the top-left corner of the page to check this (Figure 34).

To change the zero point of the ruler, move the mouse button to the top-left corner where the two rulers intersect (see Figure 35), and hold the mouse button down. Keep this button held down, and slowly move the mouse cursor back onto the page. A crosshair will follow the mouse cursor back down the page (Figure 35). Wherever the mouse button is released is the new zero point of the ruler, both horizontally and vertically. The rulers will reformat to show this as the mouse button is released (Figure 36).

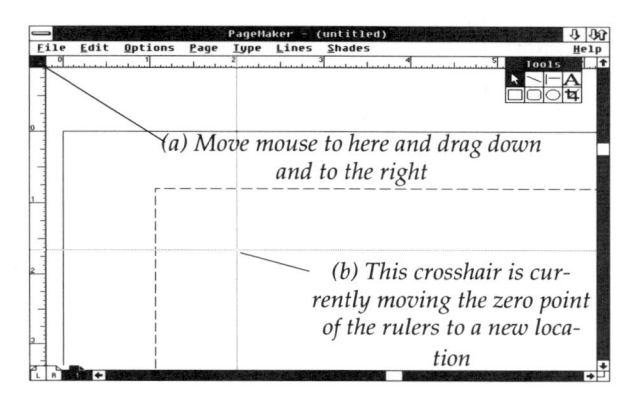

*Figure 35.* To change the ruler's zero point, hold the mouse button down in the intersecting square of both rulers and pull the mouse back out onto the page. A crosshair indicating the new zero point of the rulers replaces the mouse cursor. Release the mouse button when the crosshair is positioned correctly.

*191*

*Module 5 - PageMaker Internal Graphics*

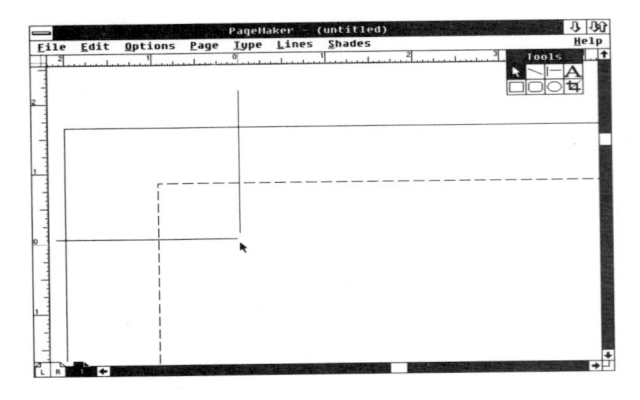

*Figure 36.* Note the new position of the ruler zero points after Figure 35.

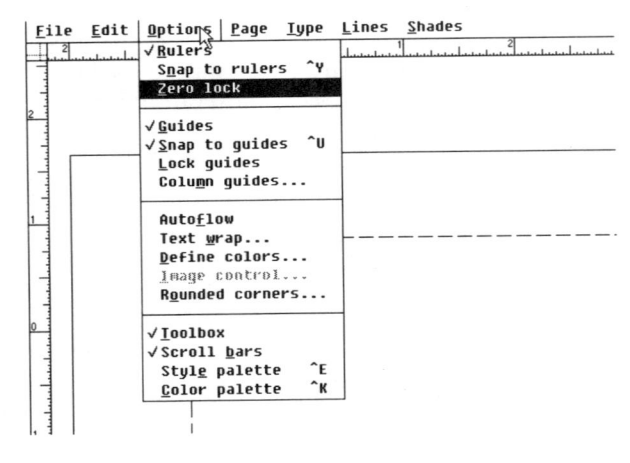

*Figure 37.* The zero point of the rulers can be locked into position by selecting the Zero lock command from the **Options** menu.

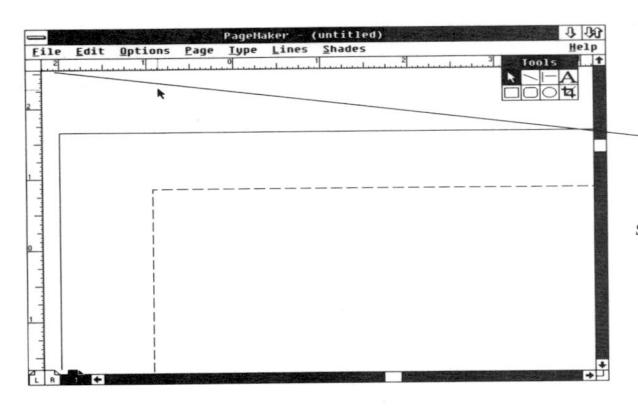

*Figure 38.* After selecting the command in Figure 37, the intersection of the two rulers now shows a blank square (compare this with Figure 36).

Additional features are available with the rulers. Ruler guides can be "pulled" from the rulers, horizontally and vertically, allowing a form of grid to be set up—a grid that graphics can snap to, and hence precisely align themselves very easily.

To use these ruler guides, hold the mouse button down in either ruler, and pull the mouse cursor back down onto the page. As long as the mouse cursor is released on the page, rather than the pasteboard area that surrounds it, a dotted line parallel to the ruler from where this guide originated will be visible on the page (Figure 39).

Multiple guides can be pulled from either ruler (Figures 40 to 42), and it is quite easy to set up a grid with these guides. All guides can be precisely positioned by aligning them with the measurements of the other ruler. More exact alignment is possible at larger page views. Any ruler guide can be moved around on the screen by holding the mouse button down on it and dragging it to a new position (Figure 41). If you want to get rid of one or more ruler guides, simply pull them right off the page (Figure 42) and they will disappear.

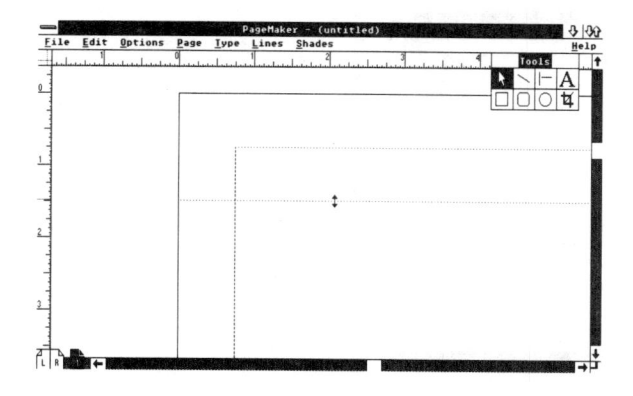

*Figure 39.* Ruler guides can be pulled from the rulers onto the page by holding the mouse button down in a ruler and dragging it down onto the page.

*Module 5 - PageMaker Internal Graphics*

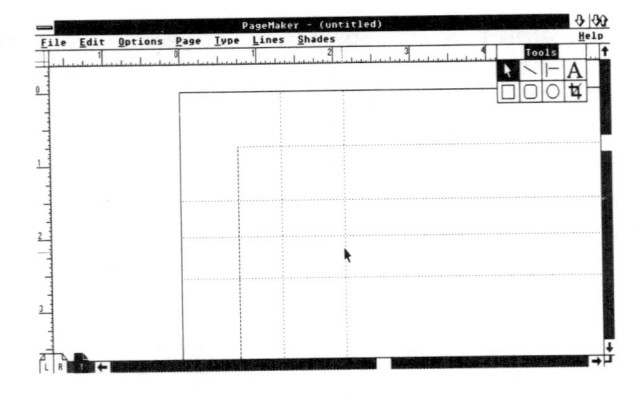

***Figure 40.*** *Here we have built up quite a few guides from both the vertical and horizontal rulers, creating a grid.*

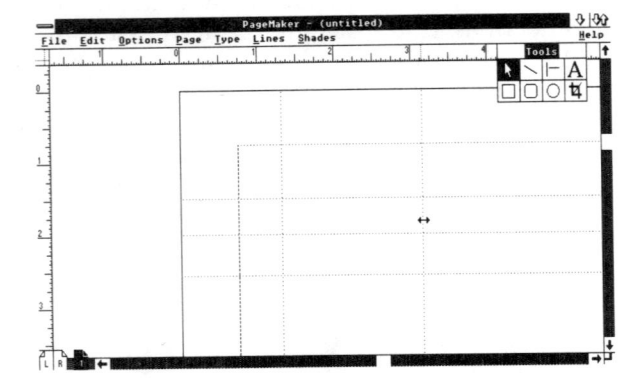

***Figure 41.*** *Any guide can be repositioned by holding the mouse button down on it and moving it to a new position.*

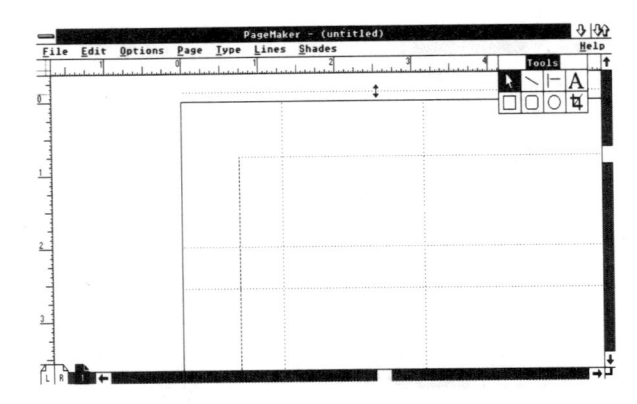

***Figure 42.*** *To remove a ruler guide from the page, simply move it so that it is no longer on the page. It will not remain on the pasteboard area when the mouse is released.*

194

*Module 5 - PageMaker Internal Graphics*

## Multiple selections

So far, we have talked about selecting only one graphic at a time. It is possible, however, to select multiple graphics in a number of different ways. The easiest way to select all graphics on a page is to choose the *Select all* command in the **Edit** menu (Figures 43 and 44). Any operation, whether it be editing, line, or fill changes, will then apply to all selected graphics.

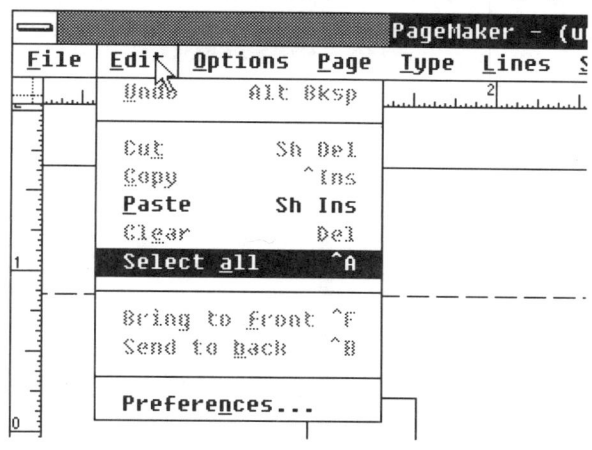

*Figure 43. The Select all command can be used to select all the graphics on a page, but remember that this command will also select any text blocks that may be on the screen.*

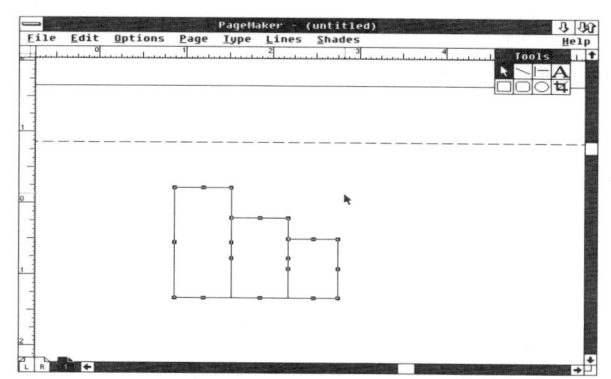

*Figure 44. Here are all the graphics selected from Figure 43 using the Select all command. These graphics can now be deleted, moved, copied, have their line or fill attributes changed, all as a group.*

Generally, as you select a graphic, the one currently selected becomes deselected. However, if you hold down the Shift key on the keyboard as you select other graphics, all graphics will remain selected. Once again, any future operations will then apply to all selected graphics.

195

Another way to select a group of graphics is to draw an imaginary box around them. Pretend that you are drawing a box around a group of graphics, but make sure that the pointer tool is currently active. A dotted box will be drawn as the mouse button is held down (Figure 45), and once released, any graphics that are entirely enclosed by this imaginary box will be selected.

If you ever have trouble selecting a graphic because it is behind a guide (ruler, margin, or column) or a block of text, try holding down the Ctrl key as you attempt to select the graphic. This will often allow hidden or hard to get at graphics to be selected.

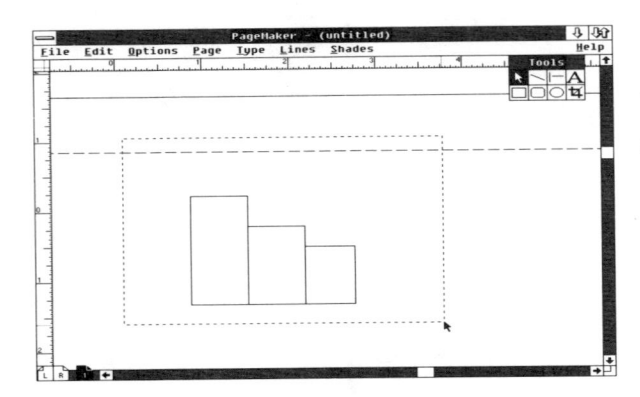

*Figure 45. Drawing an imaginary box around a set of graphics will also select multiple graphics. Make sure the pointer tool is selected, and draw a border around the graphics you would like to select. Upon releasing the mouse, all the graphics within the border will be selected.*

## Setting the graphic default

Every graphic you create initially has a line thickness setting and a shade setting. It would be a nuisance to have to change every graphic you create to use the line thickness you want, rather than the one that is set.

Setting the default lines and shades value for graphics is achieved by selecting the pointer tool from the Toolbox, making sure that no graphic is currently selected, and choosing the required values from the **Lines** and **Shades** menus. Although you will see no immediate change on screen, every graphic that is created from now on will use the **Lines** and **Shades** values you have just set by default.

## Maintaining aspect ratio

When you create a rectangle, an ellipse, or a line, you will find it extremely difficult to create a square, a circle, or in some cases a straight line. Combine the use of the mouse with the *aspect ratio* of the screen and this is almost impossible. PageMaker, however, allows you to use a technique that automatically maintains the correct aspect ratio.

When you create a graphic, or even if you are resizing a graphic, hold down the Shift key as you do so. The graphic will snap to its correct shape (square or circle) immediately. Make sure that you release the mouse button before you release the Shift key, otherwise the aspect ratio may be lost.

Using all these features of PageMaker together means that fairly complex graphics are quite easy to achieve. No freehand drawing is possible, so any freehand drawings must be created in other packages. Try not to get too involved, however, in very complex graphical creations in PageMaker, as many graphics, although quite possible to create in PageMaker, may be created much more easily, and perhaps a little better, in third-party packages.

Bar charts are a good example. Although possible in PageMaker, a number of graphing programs produce such charts automatically by simply entering the actual data.

## Wraparounds

All internally-created PageMaker graphics can be set up as regular or irregular wraparounds. The method by which this is done is identical to the method for imported graphics, and is explained in detail in modules 6 and 7 (regular wraparounds in module 6, and irregular wraparounds in module 7). All facets of wraparounds described in these modules can be applied to internally-created graphics.

## Module 5 Exercise

# PageMaker Internal Graphics

# Module 5 Exercise
# PageMaker Internal Graphics

In this exercise we will be creating simple graphics from within PageMaker.

This training material is structured so that people of all levels of expertise with PageMaker can use it to gain maximum benefit. In order to do this, we have structured this material so that the bare exercise is listed below this paragraph on just one page, with no hints. The following pages contain the steps needed to complete this exercise for those that need additional prompting. The **PageMaker Internal Graphics** module should be referenced if you need further help or explanations.

## Module 5 exercise steps

1. *Create a new, one-page publication using an A4 page, and 20 mm margins.*
2. *Assign three columns to the first page.*
3. *Load in the text file BROCHURE.DOC using the Autoflow method.*
4. *Insert a border of 2 points thickness around the outside of the page, with a spacing of 5 mm, (0.2 inches) horizontally and vertically, between the margins and the border.*
5. *Insert intercolumn rules of 2 points thickness.*
6. *Change the first paragraph (heading) to 18 points bold Palatino or Times.*
7. *Create a box behind the heading using a 2 point outline and a 10% shade background.*
8. *Draw a box in the bottom right-hand corner of the third column, 5 cm (2 inches) high, with a 2 point thickness border.*
9. *Load in the graphic PHOTO.TIF from the GETSTART subdirectory (within the PageMaker directory), and place it initially into the Pasteboard area to the right of the page. Proportionally reduce its size to fit into the box of step 8, and then move it into this box.*
10. *Select the box and the photo from steps 8 and 9, delete from page 1, and place them into the top left-hand corner of page 2.*

The steps to completing this exercise are on the following pages.

Module 5 Exercise - PageMaker Internal Graphics

# The Steps in detail.

*1. Create a new, one-page publication using an A4 page, and 20 mm margins.*

The new publication is created using the *New* command (Figure 1). Set up the associated dialog box as shown in Figure 2.

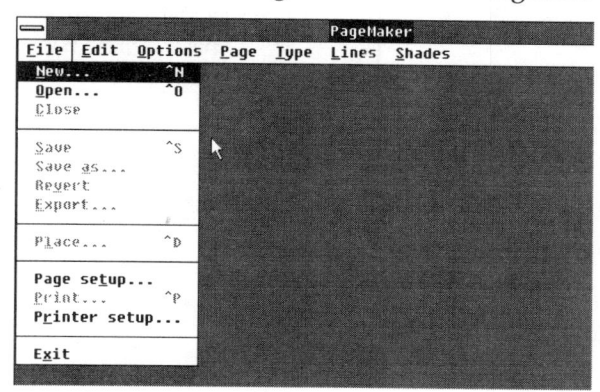

*Figure 1. Use the New command to start a new PageMaker document.*

*Figure 2. Set the page size to A4 in the New dialog box, one page long and 20 mm margins all around. If you wish to work in inches, use 0.75 inch margins.*

*2. Assign three columns to the first page.*

The page is assigned columns using the *Column guides* command from the **Options** menu (Figure 3). Insert 3 in the *Column guides* command dialog box (Figure 4).

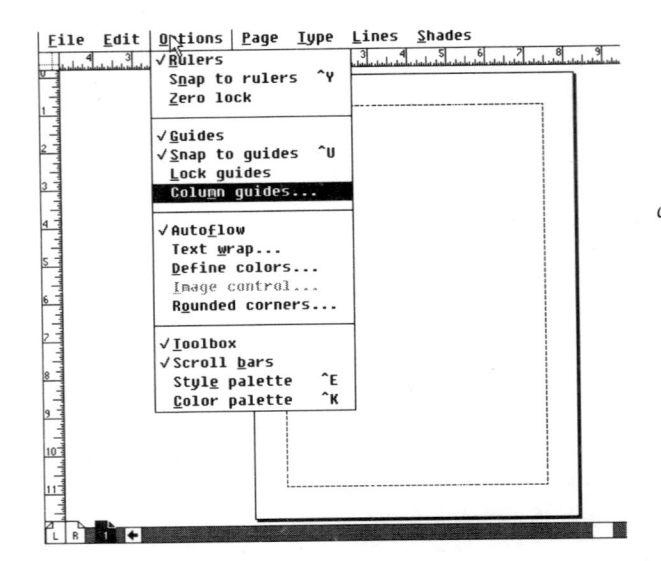

## Module 5 Exercise - PageMaker Internal Graphics

*Figure 3.* The Column guides command from the **Options** menu allows you to set columns on the page.

*Figure 4.* Set 3 columns for the page from the Column guides dialog box.

3. *Load in the text file BROCHURE.DOC using the Autoflow method.*

Use the *Place* command to load in the BROCHURE.DOC file from the GETSTART subdirectory. Locate this subdirectory, and the BROCHURE.DOC file within it, and double-click in it (Figures 5 to 7).

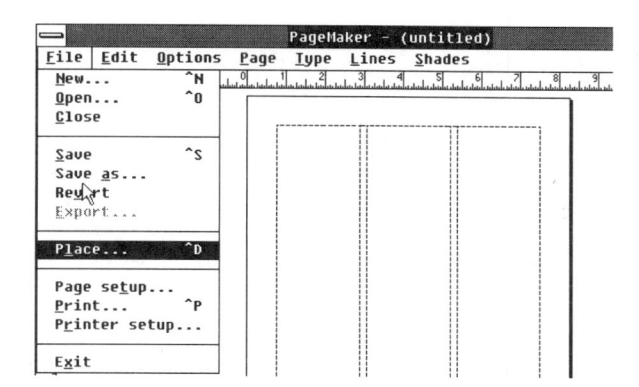

## Module 5 Exercise - PageMaker Internal Graphics

*Figure 5.* The Place command is used to insert text into PageMaker.

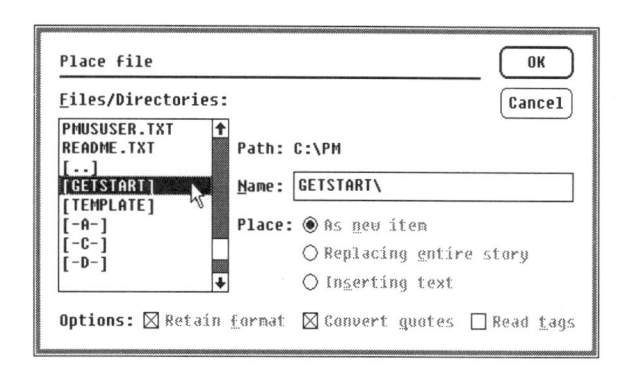

*Figure 6.* BROCHURE.DOC is located in the GETSTART subdirectory within the PageMaker directory

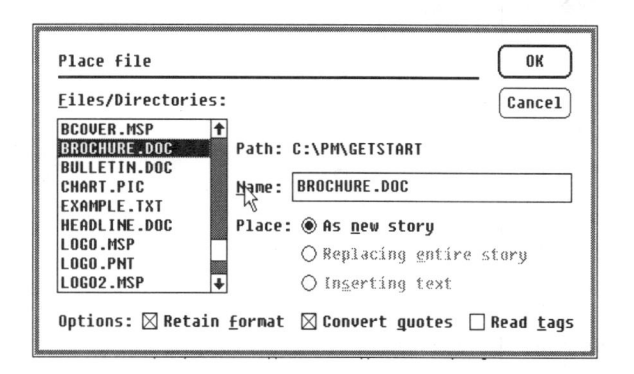

*Figure 7.* Double-click on the file BROCHURE.DOC

203

Module 5 Exercise - PageMaker Internal Graphics

To use the *Autoflow* method to flow the text, make sure this option is selected within the **Options** menu (Figure 8). It is selected when a check appears next to the command. If it has a check, leave it, and if it doesn't, select it. The mouse cursor will then appear as shown in Figure 9.

Position this mouse cursor at the top of the first column (Figure 9) and click once. After a few seconds text will have flowed into two columns (Figure 10) on the page. Depending upon the style selected (if any), your text may flow further than this. If it does, adjust it to look similar to Figure 10 by deleting the third column, and reducing the size of the text block in column two.

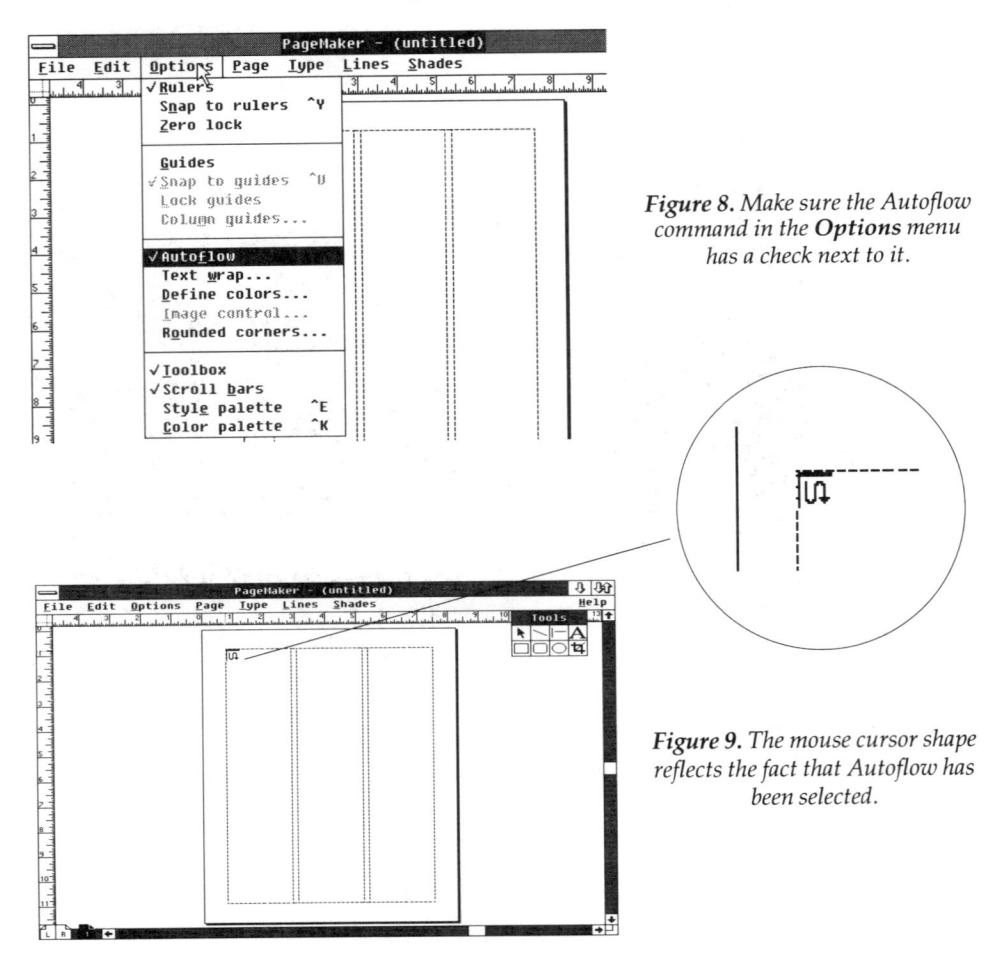

*Figure 8. Make sure the Autoflow command in the **Options** menu has a check next to it.*

*Figure 9. The mouse cursor shape reflects the fact that Autoflow has been selected.*

204

*Module 5 Exercise - PageMaker Internal Graphics*

4. *Insert a border of 2 points thickness around the outside of the page, with a spacing of 5 mm (0.2 inches), horizontally and vertically, between the margins and the border.*

A border around a page is best created using either the square-corner or rounded-corner drawing tool. Select either of these two tools from the Toolbox. We have chosen the square-corner tool in Figure 10.

Position the mouse cursor (which will now look like a crosshair) just above the top left-hand margin (Figure 10). Hold down the mouse cursor and move it to below the bottom right-hand margin. Release the mouse button (Figure 11).

In this example we have aligned the border by eye, approximately 5 mm outside of all margins. To be more exact, you could display the rulers and adjust the settings more precisely.

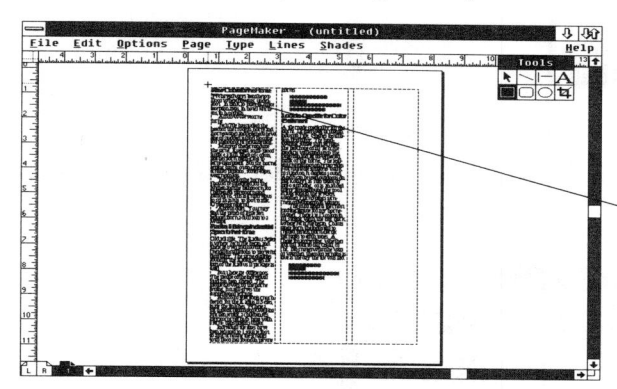

*Figure 10. Select the square-corner drawing tool from the Toolbox and move the mouse cursor just above and to the left of the first column.*

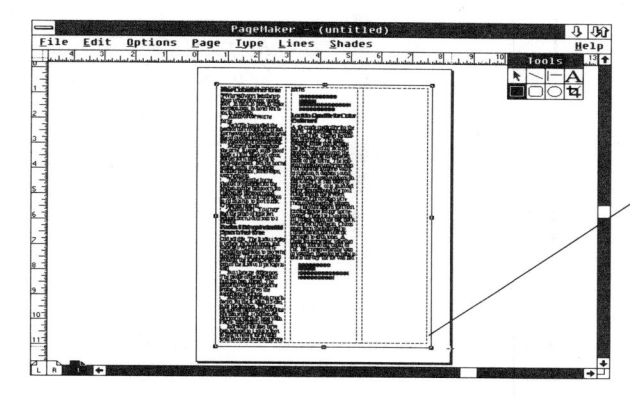

*Figure 11. Hold down the mouse button and drag the mouse to the bottom of the right-hand column.*

Module 5 Exercise - PageMaker Internal Graphics

What the rectangle looks like now depends on how the default was set. However, there are two commands that should be chosen to ensure that the graphic is correctly set. The first command is to make sure that the graphic has no fill whatsoever (Figure 12).

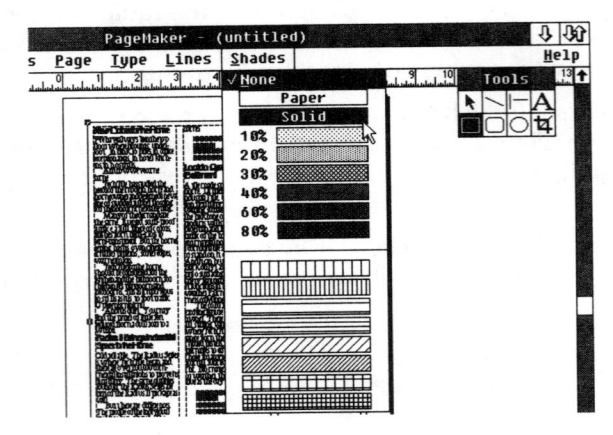

*Figure 12.* To make sure the setting for the shading is correct, use the **Shades** menu to set the fill to None.

The second command makes sure that the border of the graphic is set at 2 points thickness (Figure 13).

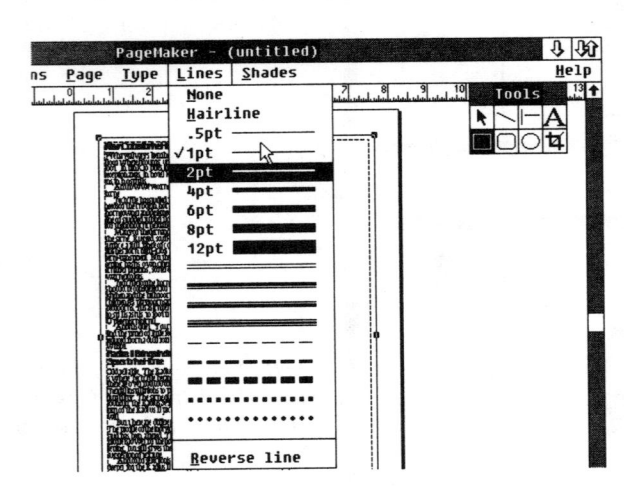

*Figure 13.* Use the **Lines** menu to set the thickness of the outline to 2 points.

After using these two commands the border of the page will be set correctly.

206

*Module 5 Exercise - PageMaker Internal Graphics*

5. *Insert intercolumn rules of 2 points thickness.*

Intercolumn rules are inserted using the perpendicular-line drawing tool. Select this tool now from the Toolbox (Figure 14).

Before we create the intercolumn guides, try this helper. Turn the *Snap to guides* command from the **Options** menu off. It is off when there is no check alongside it. This ensures that the line drawn does not snap to either side of the column guide, but is drawn down the middle. Move the mouse cursor to the top, between the first set of column guides (Figure 14). Hold the mouse button down, drag the mouse to the bottom of this column, and release the button (Figure 15). Repeat this operation for the second set of column guides.

Set the line thickness for this rule to 2 points, as shown in Figure 16. Make sure the border is selected to do this.

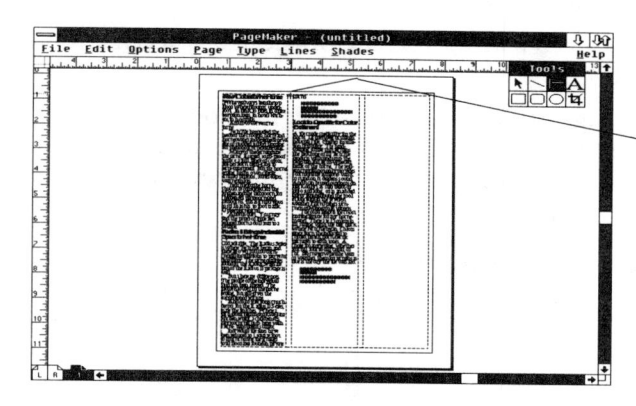

*Figure 14.* To create intercolumn rules, select the perpendicular-line drawing tool, and move it to the middle and top of the first set of column guides.

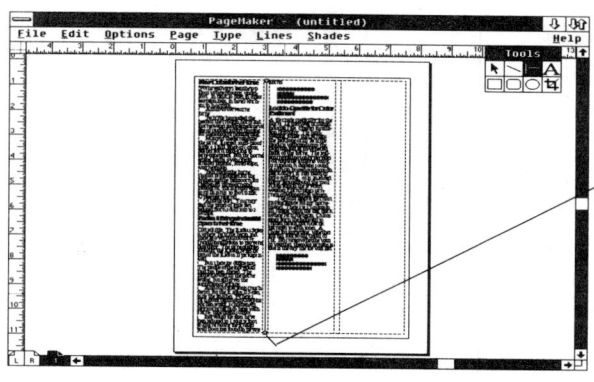

*Figure 15.* Hold down the mouse button and drag it down to the bottom of the column. Repeat this for the second set of column guides.

## Module 5 Exercise - PageMaker Internal Graphics

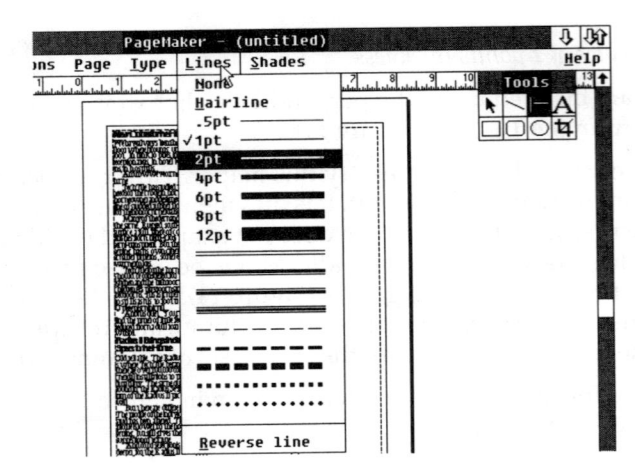

*Figure 16.* Set the line thickness for the intercolumn rules to 2 points.

6. *Change the first paragraph (heading) to 18 points bold Palatino or Times*

This step has to be achieved with the text cursor selected. Select this tool from the Toolbox (Figure 17).

To select the first paragraph, use the triple-click method. Move the mouse cursor anywhere over the first paragraph and click the mouse button three times in succession. The paragraph will be highlighted in reverse video (Figure 17).

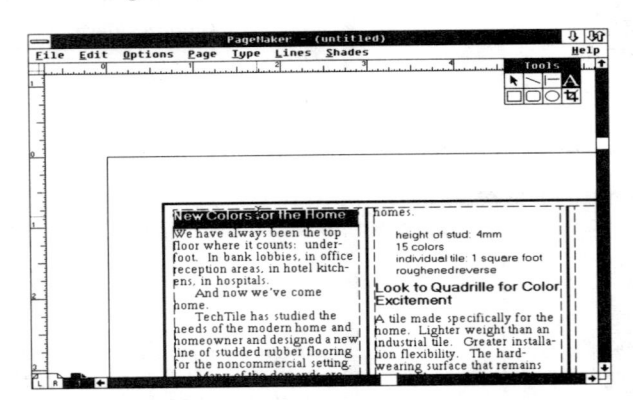

*Figure 17.* Select the heading to change its specifications.

Select the *Type specs* command from the **Type** menu to set the specifications for this paragraph (Figure 18). Set up the dialog box that appears upon selecting this command, as shown in Figure 19. The new heading is shown in Figure 20.

*Module 5 Exercise - PageMaker Internal Graphics*

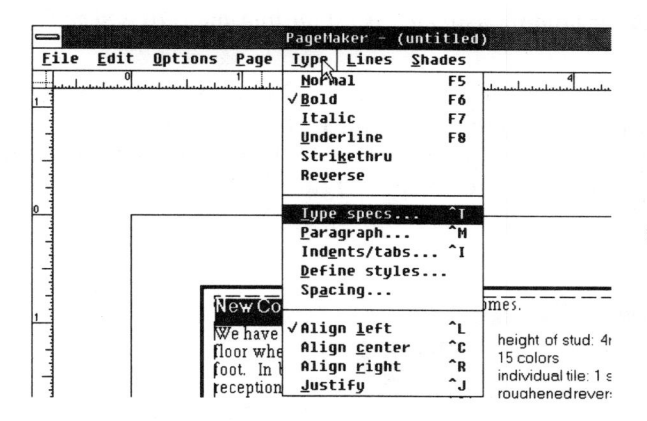

*Figure 18.* The Type specs command can change the specs for the text.

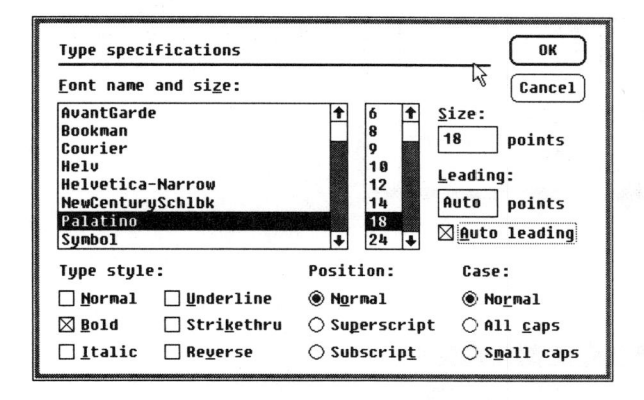

*Figure 19.* Set up the Type specs dialog box as illustrated to 18 point Palatino and bold. Choose Times if your system does not include Palatino.

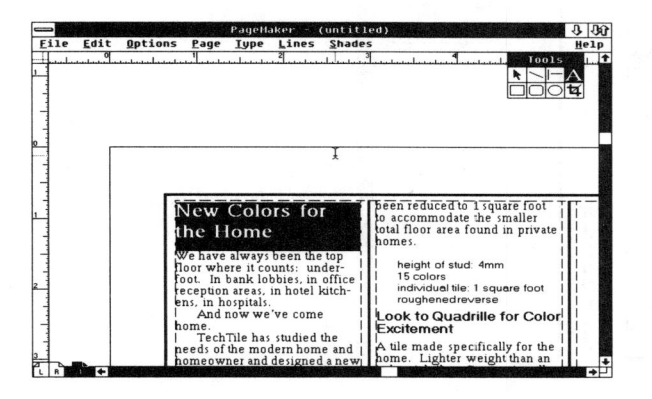

*Figure 20.* The new heading resulting from the settings of Figure 19.

209

## Module 5 Exercise - PageMaker Internal Graphics

7. *Create a box behind the heading using a 2 point outline and a 10% shade background.*

Select the square-corner drawing tool from the Toolbox, and draw a rectangle to completely cover the first paragraph as shown in Figure 21. Use the **Lines** menu to set the outline at 2 points (Figure 22) and the **Shades** menu to set the background for this graphic to 10% (Figure 23).

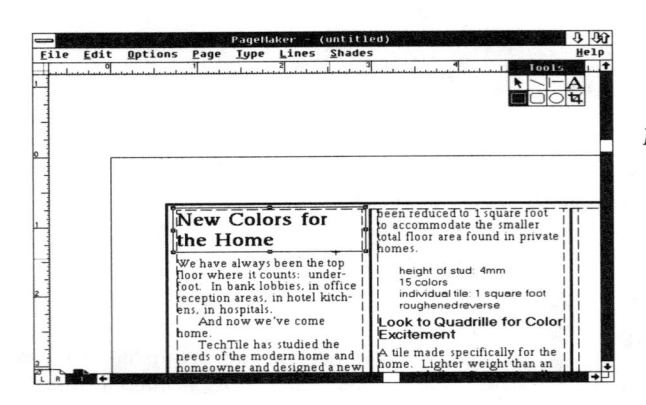

*Figure 21. Select the square-corner drawing tool, hold the mouse button down, above and to the left of the heading, and drag it to the bottom-right of the heading.*

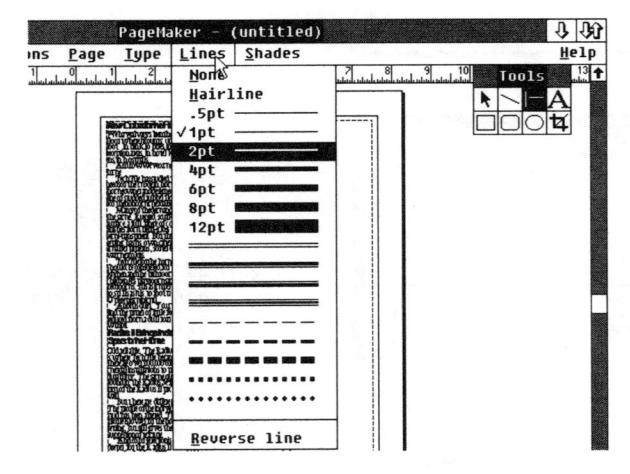

*Figure 22. Set the thickness of the box outline to 2 points.*

210

*Module 5 Exercise - PageMaker Internal Graphics*

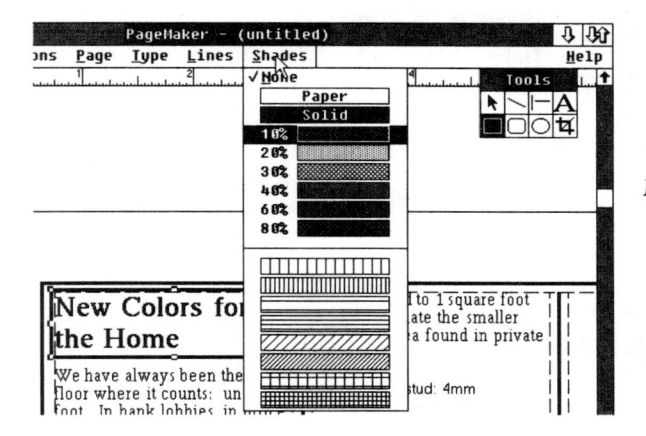

*Figure 23. Also make sure that the shade for the rectangle is set to 10%.*

At this stage the rectangle will be sitting on top of the text with the text unreadable (Figure 24). Make sure the rectangle is selected, and choose the *Send to back* command from the **Edit** menu (Figure 25). The text will immediately appear over the graphic (Figure 26).

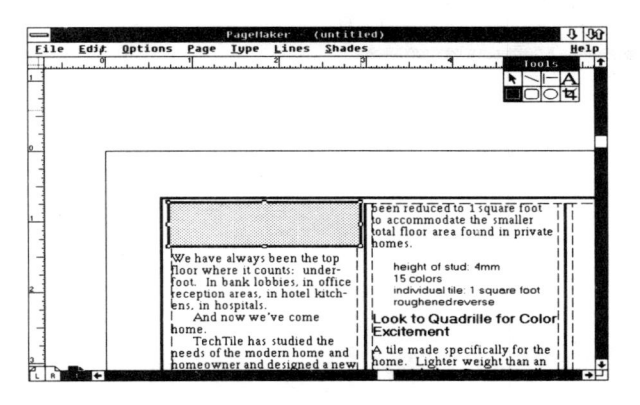

*Figure 24. Don't panic if your heading disappears. Choose the Send to back command from the **Edit** menu as shown in Figure 25.*

211

*Module 5 Exercise - PageMaker Internal Graphics*

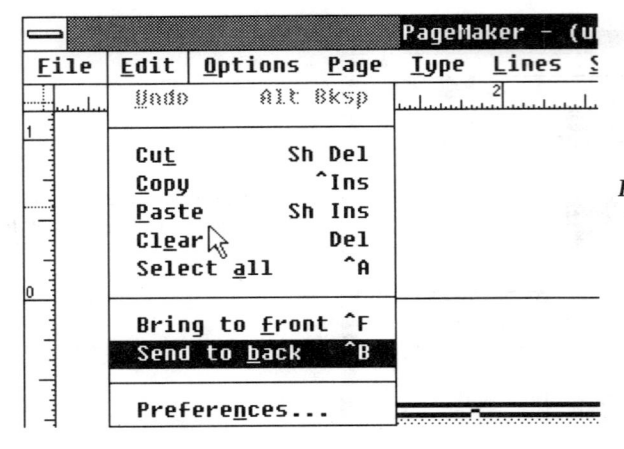

*Figure 25.* Make sure the rectangle is selected, and choose this command from the **Edit** menu.

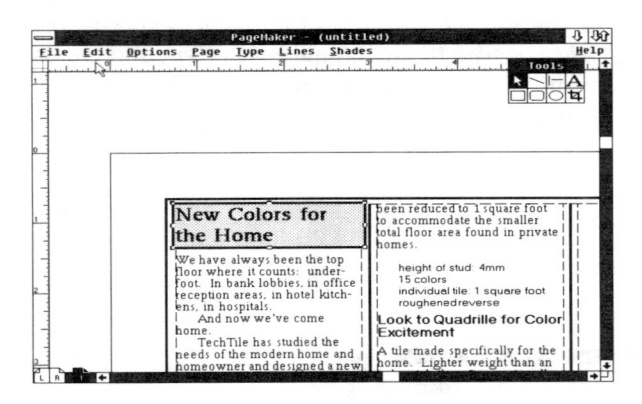

*Figure 26.* The heading reappears as the rectangle has now been sent behind the text.

## Module 5 Exercise - PageMaker Internal Graphics

*8. Draw a box in the bottom right-hand corner of the third column, 5 cm (2 inches) tall, with a 2 point thickness border.*

To ensure that we get the vertical dimension of 5 cm correctly placed, we have chosen to first show rulers through the *Rulers* command in the **Options** menu. We have then gone to *Actual size* view from the **Page** menu and set up two ruler guides in the bottom right-hand corner, as shown in Figure 27. A horizontal guide is set at the bottom margin of 27.7 cm. Another guide is set at 22.7 cm for our 5 cm box height. If you are using inches, set up ruler guides in a similar fashion to Figure 27, but 2 inches apart.

By using the square-corner drawing tool, we now draw the box as shown in Figure 28. The **Lines** menu was then used to adjust the border thickness to 2 points.

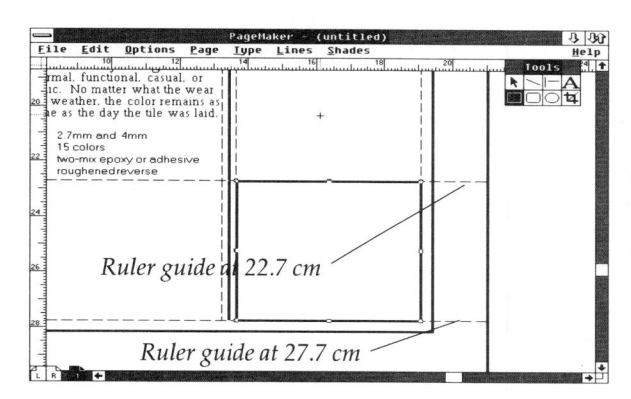

*Figure 27. We are now positioned in Actual size view at the bottom right-hand corner of the page. Two ruler guides are set up at 27.7 and 22.7 cm to help draw the 5 cm tall box at the bottom of this last column.*

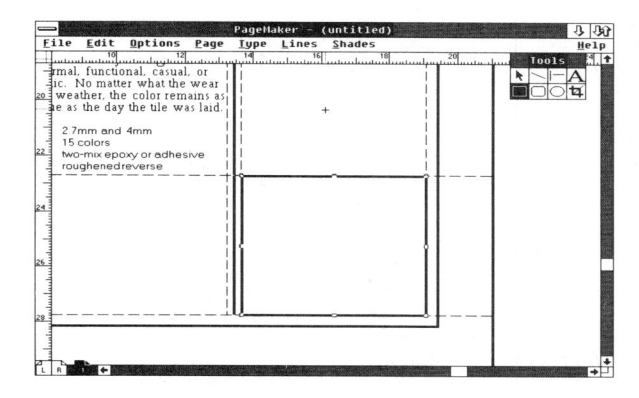

*Figure 28. The box has now been drawn using the ruler and column guide as alignment tools. If the Snap to guides command was on, the box outlines would have automatically snapped to the correct positions. The border was also set to 2 points thickness using the **Lines** menu.*

213

*Module 5 Exercise - PageMaker Internal Graphics*

9. *Load in the graphic PHOTO.TIF from the GETSTART subdirectory (within the PageMaker directory), and place it initially into the Pasteboard area to the right of the page. Proportionally reduce its size to fit into the box of step 8, and then move it into this box.*

In Figure 29 we have now changed back to *Fit in window* view through the **Page** menu. The PHOTO.TIF picture is selected through the *Place* command in the GETSTART subdirectory, and the cursor is positioned as shown in Figure 29. At this point all you need to do is click the mouse to get the result shown in Figure 30.

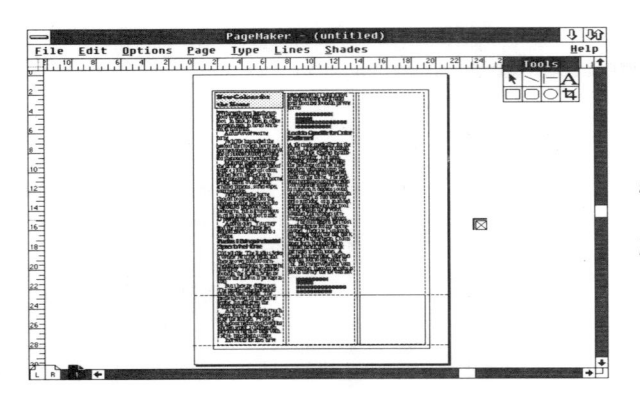

*Figure 29. This is Fit in window view. PHOTO.TIF has been selected from the GETSTART subdirectory using the Place command, and the mouse cursor is positioned to now load the picture onto the Pasteboard.*

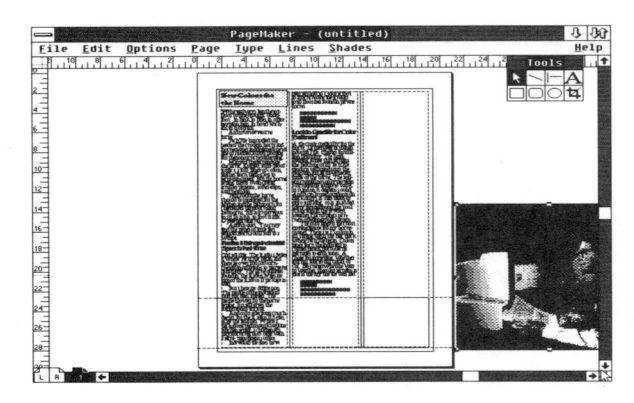

*Figure 30. The mouse has been clicked and the picture is loaded onto the Pasteboard area.*

Module 5 Exercise - PageMaker Internal Graphics

The picture now needs to be proportionately reduced to fit into the box. This is achieved by selecting the picture, holding down the Shift key, grabbing the bottom-right handle with the mouse button down, and diagonally dragging upwards and to the left. The result of this operation is indicated in Figure 31. You may need to move your page to the left to get to the bottom right-hand corner of the picture.

Now place the mouse in the middle of the picture, hold down the button, and move it into the box, as shown in Figure 32. With this figure we are back to *Actual size* view for a better look.

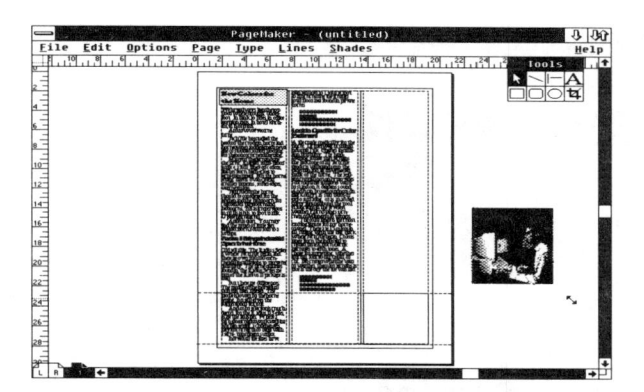

*Figure 31. The picture is being proportionately reduced to fit into the box.*

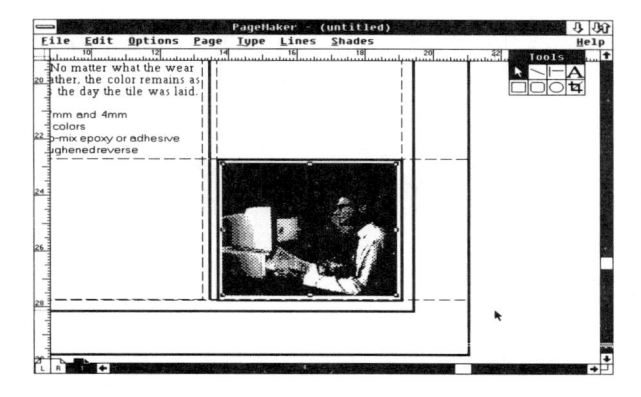

*Figure 32. Actual size view of the picture now placed inside the box.*

## Module 5 Exercise - PageMaker Internal Graphics

10. *Select the box and the photo from steps 8 and 9, delete from page 1, and place them into the top left-hand corner of page 2.*

To achieve this last operation, we need to go through the following steps:

- Insert a new page, as our publication is only one page long.
- Select and cut the picture and the box from page 1.
- Move to the new page 2.
- Paste the picture into page 2. It will initially be pasted into the center of the page.
- Move the picture to the top of the first column.

Figures 33 to 38 show the steps that are required.

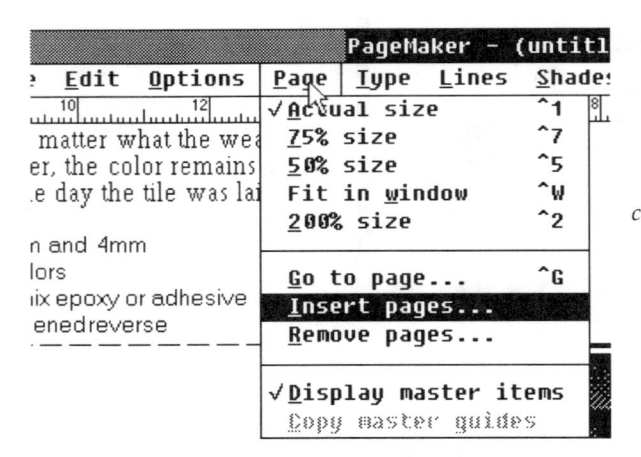

*Figure 33. The Insert pages command is selected from the* **Page** *menu.*

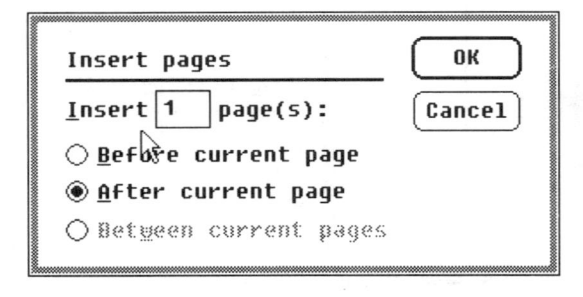

*Figure 34. The Insert pages dialog box is then filled out as shown.*

216

*Module 5 Exercise - PageMaker Internal Graphics*

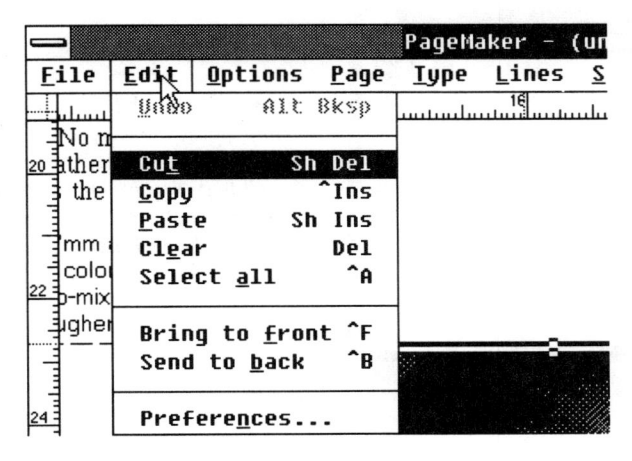

*Figure 35.* The picture and box were both selected, and the Cut command chosen from the **Edit** menu. The simplest way to select both items together is to hold down the Shift key to select the second item. If you have trouble selecting the box because it is aligned with ruler and margin guides, hold down the Ctrl key as you select.

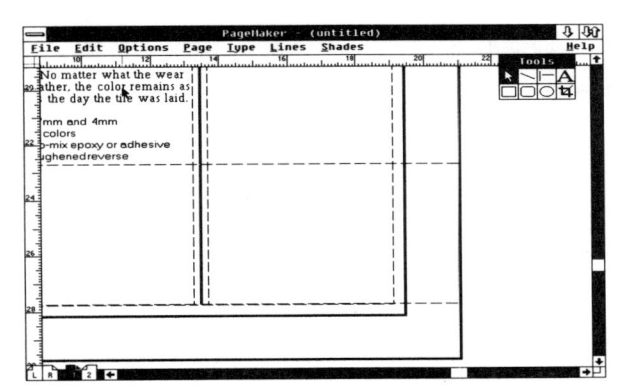

*Figure 36.* After the operation of Figure 35, the picture and the box are both deleted from page 1.

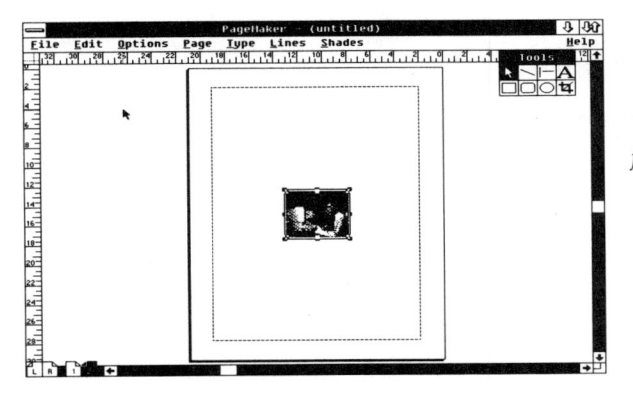

*Figure 37.* We have moved to page 2 and chosen the Paste command from the **Edit** menu, with the result that the picture and box are pasted into the middle of the page. This is the way PageMaker always pastes graphic objects stored in the Clipboard.

217

*Module 5 Exercise - PageMaker Internal Graphics*

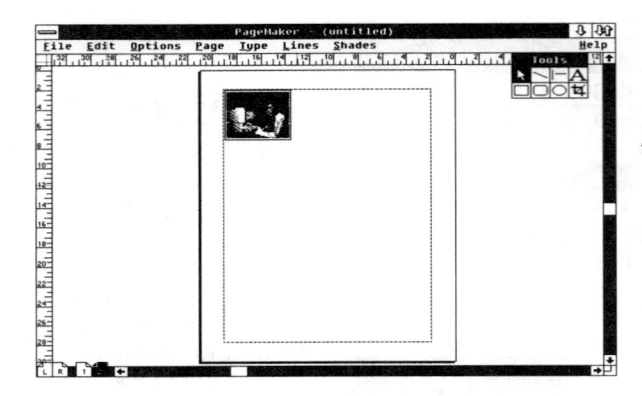

***Figure 38.*** *To finish this final step, we simply grab the picture with the mouse, hold the button down, and move it to its required position in the top left-hand corner. The mouse is then released.*

# Module 6

# Introduction to Imported Graphics

# Introduction to Imported Graphics

A large variety of graphics programs can be used in conjunction with PageMaker to create very professional presentations with your PC. In this module we will look at the types of graphics we can import, how we import them, how we size them, crop them, move them, and generally alter them. In a later module we will look at more complex things that can be done with imported graphics—irregular wraparounds and shading, basically.

There are four different types of graphics that can be imported into PageMaker. The type of graphic that you import depends generally on the type of graphics package that creates it.

*Paint-type* or *bit-map* graphics are the pictures that come from files created by paint-type packages. These graphics are formed as a collection of *pixels*—where pixels are the physical units on your screen that can be individually turned on or off. Programs that produce these types of files include Windows Paint, PC Paintbrush, and Publisher's Paintbrush.

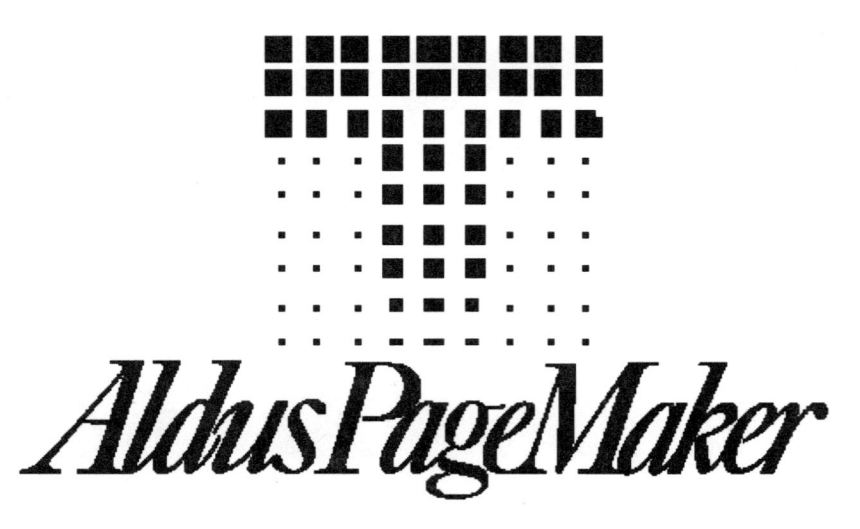

*Figure 1.* These graphics can be imported from programs such as Windows Paint.

*Module 6 - Introduction to Imported Graphics*

*Draw-type* or *object-oriented* graphics are based on a sequence of drawing commands that describe the graphic. Programs that produce these type of graphics include Windows Draw, In-a-vision, AutoCAD, and .PIC files from Lotus 1-2-3. These graphics are *output device resolution dependent*—meaning that the print resolution depends on the output device. These are generally much higher quality pictures than can be achieved with Paint-type programs.

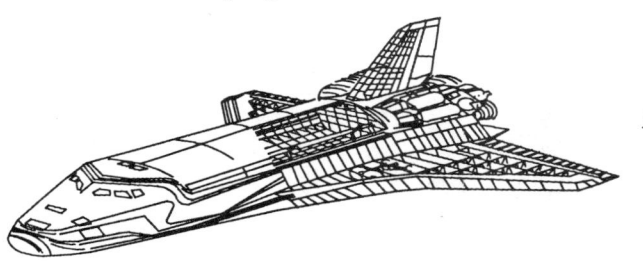

**Figure 2.** *AutoCAD line-art.*

*Encapsulated PostScript* (EPS) graphics are quite possibly the highest quality graphics of the lot—produced at the moment by graphics programs such as Headline, Arts & Letters, and Snap-Shot. These types of graphics use PostScript code to create the pictures—so that unless a screen image is created when the actual graphic is created, only a box will appear on screen. Most packages do, however, create a screen image to match the PostScript code. These graphics are limited in resolution only by the output device.

**Figure 3.** *Both text and graphics can be manipulated and created in EPS-format graphics. This image has been imported from Corel Headline.*

*Module 6 - Introduction to Imported Graphics*

*Scanned images* are usually those in the TIFF format—although they can be imported in other formats. These images usually print at a maximum resolution of 300 dpi, and are normally created by the specialist scanning programs that come with the many scanners available today.

*Figure 4. A scanned image.*

# Importing graphics

Before you can import any graphics into PageMaker, you must make sure that the graphics are in the correct format for importation. Using a program like Corel Headline does not automatically mean that the graphic will slip directly into PageMaker. By default, the image will be saved in the Headline format—not the EPS-format required. Most other programs also have a choice of which format to save the graphic under.

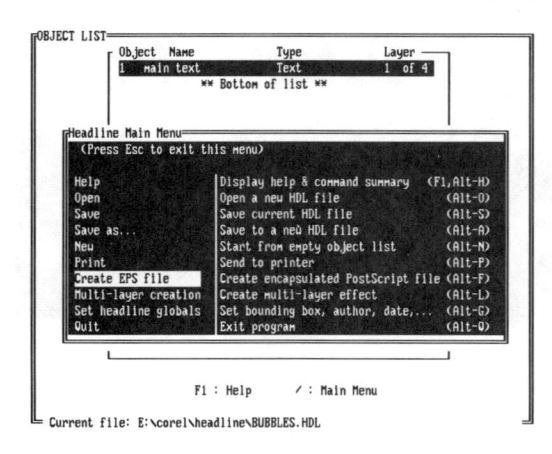

*Figure 5. Many programs (Corel Headline in this case) require that a special type of file be created before they can be imported into programs like PageMaker. In this figure, we are about to create an EPS (Encapsulated PostScript) file—a format compatible with PageMaker.*

*Module 6 - Introduction to Imported Graphics*

All graphics are imported into PageMaker the exact same way as are text files—via the *Place* command in the **File** menu. Once imported, however, the mouse cursor takes on a different appearance—depending on the type of graphic that is imported. Figures 7 to 10 indicate the different mouse appearances depending upon the type of graphic being imported.

*Figure 6.* The Place command is used to import all files into Page-Maker—both text and all varieties of graphics.

*Figure 7.* An imported Paint-type graphic will cause the mouse cursor to take on this appearance.

*Figure 8.* A draw-type or object-oriented graphic causes this cursor...

*Figure 9.* ...an EPS-format file this cursor...

*Figure 10.* ...and a TIFF scanned image this cursor.

223

*Module 6 - Introduction to Imported Graphics*

Once the mouse cursor has changed its appearance to indicate a graphics file has been loaded into memory, as shown in Figure 11, there are two ways to place it—as there are with text. The first way, preferable for text files but definitely not for graphics files, is simply to click the mouse button where you want the graphic to load. The graphic will certainly load, but could be very large, and quite probably nowhere near the size that you wanted it to be. Extra time must then be spent to resize the picture.

In Figures 11 and 12, we are loading in the TILES.PNT graphic from the GETSTART subdirectory using the above method. Figures 13 and 14 use a different method, described on the following page.

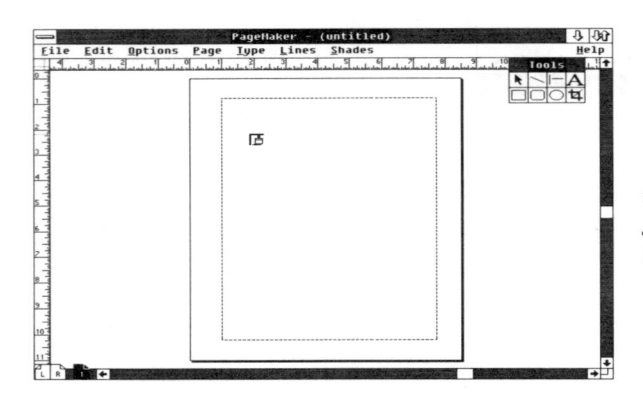

*Figure 11.* The easier, but not necessarily the better, way to load a graphic from this point is simply to position the mouse cursor and click the button.

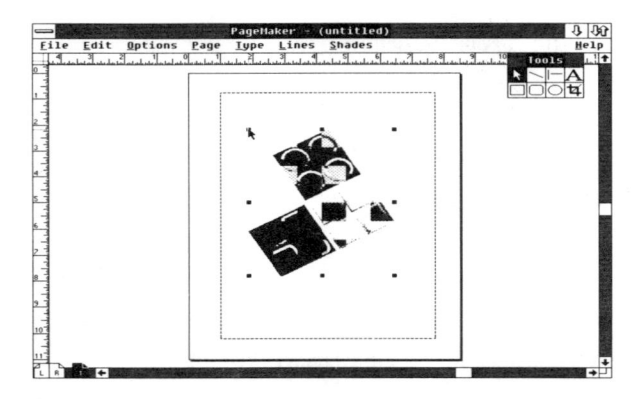

*Figure 12.* We were lucky here in that the graphic appeared at this size. Often the graphic appears much larger than this, causing extra work to resize it.

*Module 6 - Introduction to Imported Graphics*

A better way to load a graphic file onto the page is to pretend that you are working with the square-corner drawing tool, even though the mouse cursor is loaded with one of the graphic options shown in Figures 7 to 10. Draw a box exactly the same size as you would like the picture. Depress the mouse button and drag the mouse down and across the screen (Figure 13)—release it only when the box is big enough. A temporary box will appear as the mouse button is held down. When the mouse button is released, the graphic will appear in that box (Figure 14).

With this approach, the graphic may not initially be in the correct proportion. See the Proportional resizing section later in this module to return it to the correct aspect ratio.

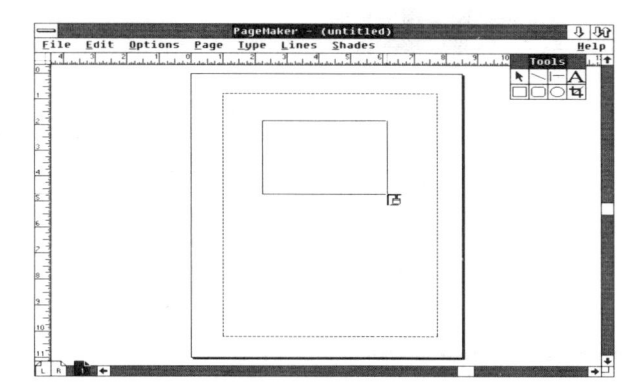

*Figure 13. A better way to load the graphic is to draw an imaginary box the size you would like to see the graphic. This is done by holding down the mouse button and drawing a box.*

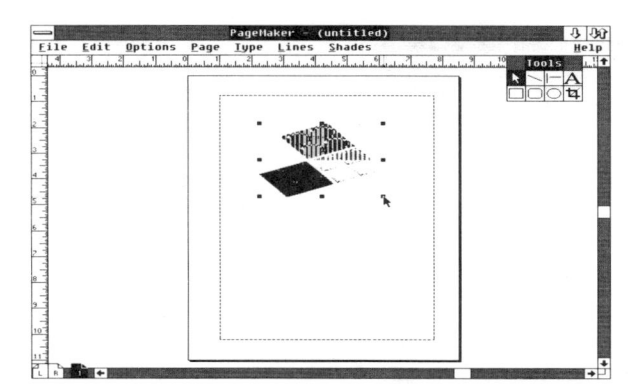

*Figure 14. Once the mouse button has been released, the graphic is loaded at exactly the same size as the box.*

Module 6 - Introduction to Imported Graphics

## Moving graphics

Once the graphic is placed on the screen, chances are it may have to be moved from one area of the screen to another. To do this, you must hold the mouse button down inside the graphic, and move the mouse to the new position. If you moved the mouse immediately after holding it down, only a box representing the graphic outline will be moved with the mouse (Figure 15). However, if you keep the mouse still for a few seconds before moving it, the entire picture will move with the mouse (Figure 16).

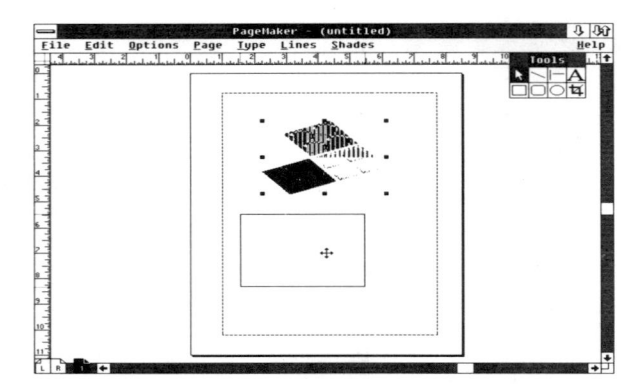

*Figure 15.* Here we held the mouse button down on the graphic and moved the mouse immediately. Hence only the outline of the graphic has been moved. The graphic will take up its new position as the mouse button is released.

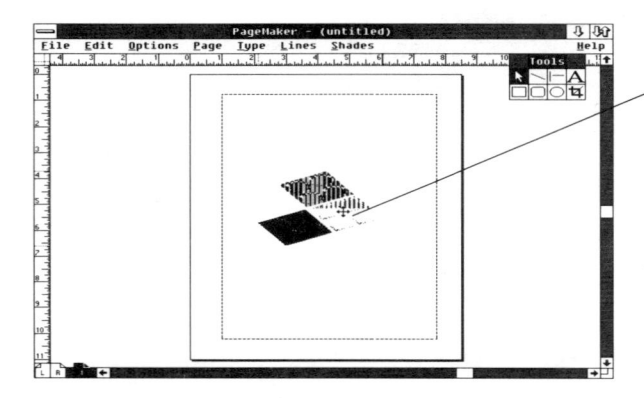

*Figure 16.* We are in the process here of moving this graphic across the screen. Locate the mouse cursor and note its shape (a four-headed arrow). This move was achieved by holding the mouse button on the graphic, keeping it still for a few seconds, and moving the mouse.

*Module 6 - Introduction to Imported Graphics*

## Simple wraparounds

Before we discuss resizing and cropping the imported images, we will look at the options for setting the *wraparound* for this image—or simply controlling how the text flows around the picture. This is achieved via the *Text wrap* command in the **Options** menu (Figure 17). This command works in exactly the same way for graphics created within PageMaker.

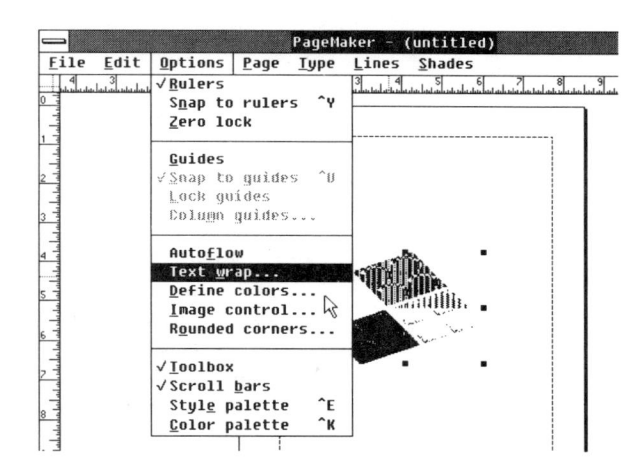

*Figure 17. Simple text wraparound control is achieved via the Text wrap command. Choosing this command causes the dialog box of Figure 18 to appear.*

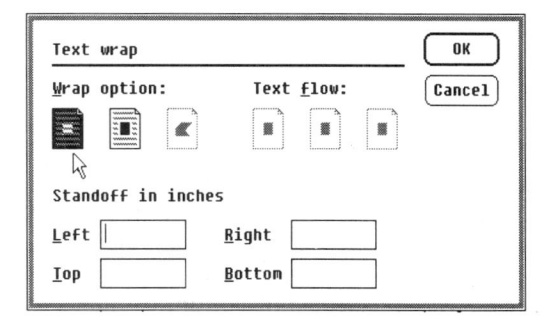

*Figure 18. The Text wrap dialog box.*

The commands in this dialog box are very visual and straightforward. You make decisions as to how the text will flow around this graphic, and how far the text must stay away from the graphic.

227

*Module 6 - Introduction to Imported Graphics*

Your first decision determines the *Wrap option*, and you have three choices. Within this dialog box, you may only choose between the first two. The choice is simple—do you want the text to flow around the graphic or not? If the answer is no, then select the first box (Figure 19). When this is done, all commands under *Text flow* in this dialog box become unusable and you have finshed with this command. However, if your answer is yes, select the second box (Figures 20 and 21). The third box is explained in a later module.

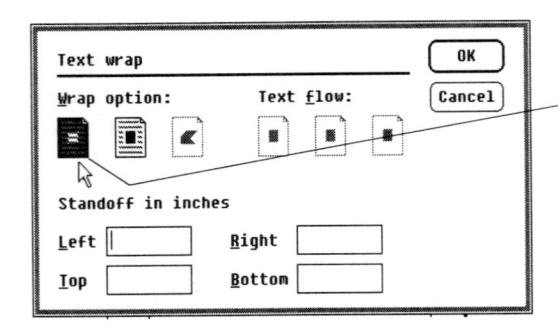

*Figure 19. If this box is selected under Wrap option, no other choices are made available. In essence, you have asked the text to ignore this graphic on the screen— to just run right over it.*

When the second box is selected, you must make a choice as to the *Text flow* (i.e., the three page icons to the right of the dialog box). Under this heading there are three options also, which are all very straightforward. The first choice causes text to stop flowing when it reaches a graphic, and not continue unless manually restarted. The second choice causes the text to completely jump the graphic—i.e., stop when it reaches the graphic, yet continue underneath (Figure 20). The third box will cause the text to flow as best it can around the graphic—not irregularly, but straight up and down the outsides of the graphic (Figure 21).

*Module 6 - Introduction to Imported Graphics*

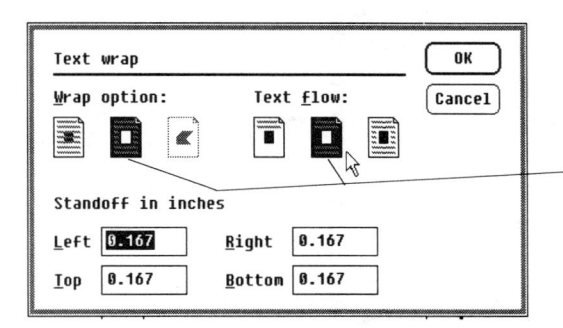

*Figure 20.* When the middle boxes from both the Wrap option and Text flow have been selected, text will jump over a graphic—not down its sides, but completely jump the graphic. Alternatively, selecting the first box for Text flow in this instance would cause the text to stop whenever it came to a graphic.

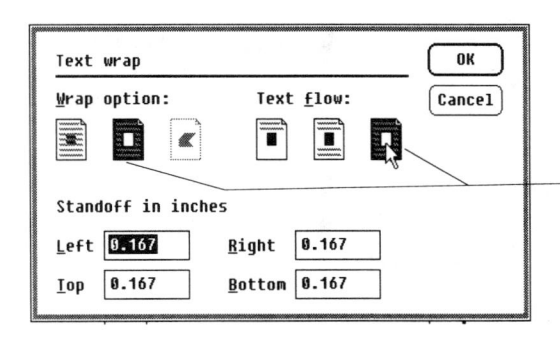

*Figure 21.* This combination of selections causes text to run regularly around the graphic—down the sides, and as close as it can, given the standoff values inserted below these boxes.

If you chose the middle Wrap option (Figures 20 and 21), you must also define a *standoff* for this graphic. This is the area around the graphic that the text cannot flow into—in effect, a margin for the graphic. Insert your own figures here or keep the default values.

If you selected this command without a graphic being selected, then everything you set up in that command will become the default. If, however, a graphic was selected, the settings will only apply to that particular graphic.

*Module 6 - Introduction to Imported Graphics*

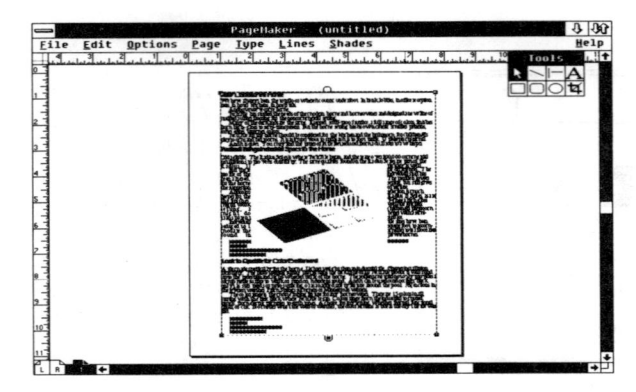

*Figure 22. Here we see the practical result of a graphical wraparound. The graphic here was set up as in the dialog box of Figure 21.*

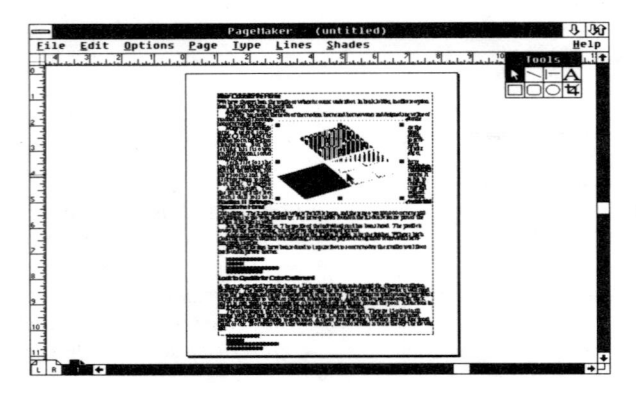

*Figure 23. Once the wraparound has been set up, the graphic can still be moved around and the text will reflow around it.*

# Graphic resizing

Any imported graphics are resized in exactly the same way as are graphics created in PageMaker. Each graphic contains six handles around its edge which are used to resize the graphic in the direction of the handle. However, you must be careful when resizing.

Depending on the Wrap option you set for this graphic in the *Text wrap* command, you may have two sets of handles around the graphic. The inner handles are the normal graphic selection handles, with the outer handles being associated with the middle Text wrap option of Figures 20 and 21. These outer handles,

*Module 6 - Introduction to Imported Graphics*

connected by a dotted line, are indicating the Wrap option selected, as well as the standoff. In the next module we will be looking at the use of these handles, so make sure that you select the inner ones (these will quite likely be a little harder to see). If you would like to get rid of the outer handles altogether, move to the *Text wrap* command, and click on the first Wrap option as per Figure 19. The outside handles for that graphic will then disappear.

Figures 24 to 26 give examples of graphic resizing.

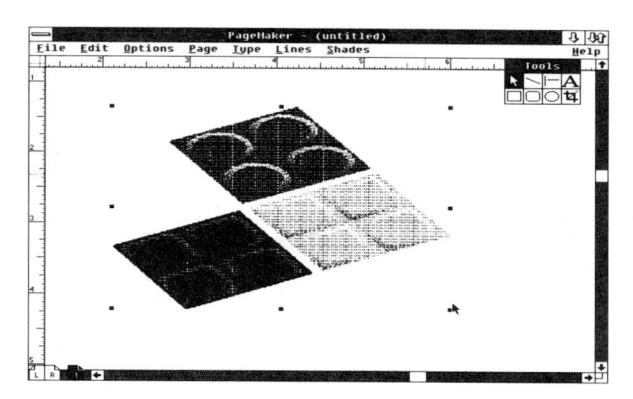

*Figure 24. Resizing the graphic is achieved using the handles that appear around the selected graphic. The pointer tool must also be selected.*

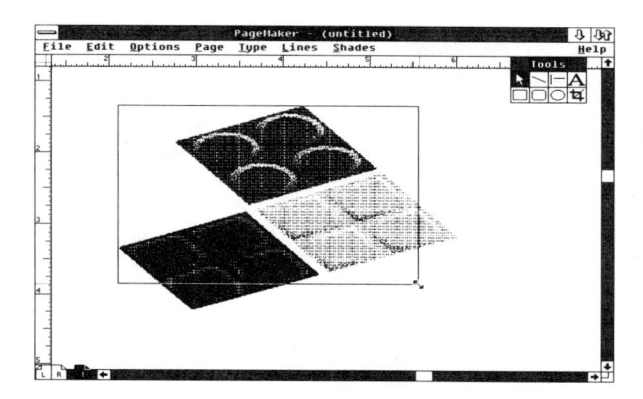

*Figure 25. Hold the mouse button down on any handle until the mouse cursor changes to a two-sided arrow. Whatever direction the arrows are pointing in are the directions that the graphic can be resized. Here we are resizing it diagonally.*

231

Module 6 - Introduction to Imported Graphics

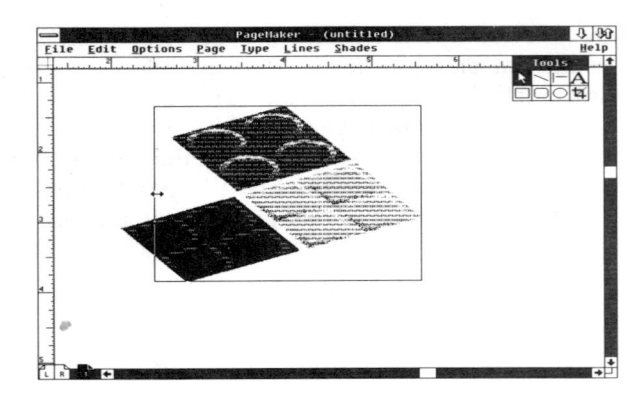

*Figure 26.* Holding the mouse button down on a side arrow allows us to resize the graphic horizontally.

## Proportional resizing

If the Shift key is held down as the graphic is resized it will snap to its correct aspect ratio. Make sure you let go of the mouse button before the Shift key. If you hold down the Ctrl key as well as the Shift key, the graphic will be resized according to your printer's resolution, so that it will look better when printed. You will notice the graphic snapping to certain size increments as the Ctrl key is held down.

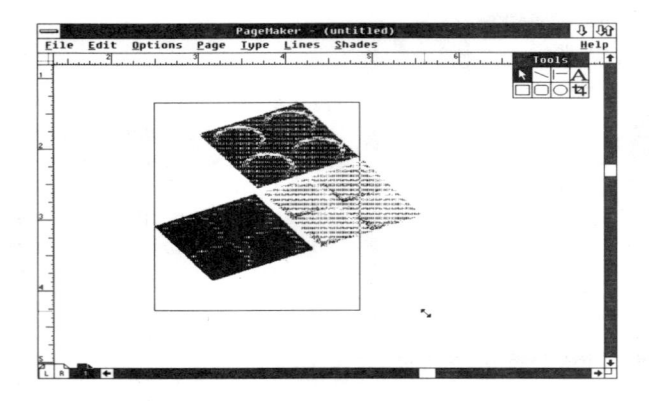

*Figure 27.* Hold down the Shift key, and the Ctrl key if necessary, to proportionally resize a graphic. It will snap to its correct aspect ratio and size (according to your printer's resolution).

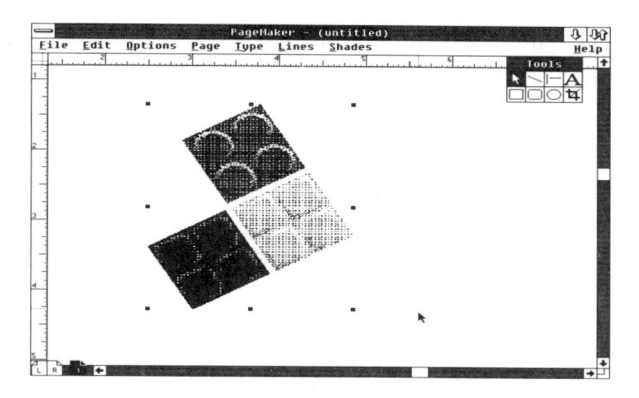

*Figure 28. Release the mouse button first, and the graphic will snap to the correct size.*

## Graphics cropping

Graphics are *cropped* (you may find it easier to think of it as chopped) in almost exactly the same way as they are resized, except that a different tool is used. The cropping tool is located in the bottom right-hand corner of the Toolbox (Figure 29).

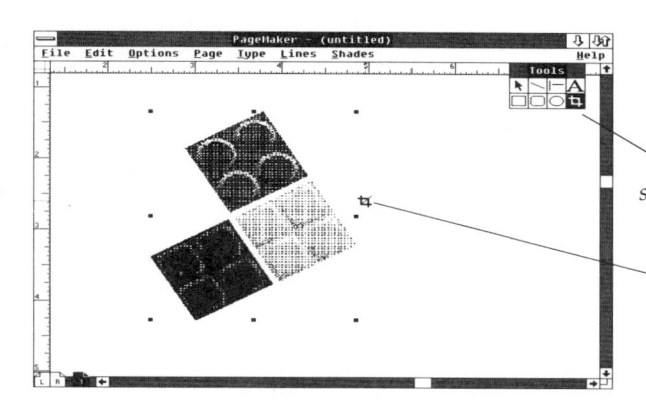

*Figure 29. The cropping tool is selected from the bottom right hand corner of the Toolbox.*

The cursor changes to that of the cropping tool.

Once this tool is selected, locate the graphic you would like to crop. Don't worry, the removal of parts of graphics is never permanent using this method—any hidden part of the graphic can be recovered at any later stage. Click once on the graphic to be cropped (using the cropping tool instead of the pointer tool) to make sure it is selected. Now decide from which side you would like to start cropping.

## Module 6 - Introduction to Imported Graphics

Locate one handle on the side of the graphic, position the cropping tool over it with the handle showing through, and hold the mouse button down. Keep the mouse still for a few seconds until the cursor turns into a two-headed arrow, and then move the cursor towards the center of the graphic. This is much the same as how we resized the graphic—yet you will note that there is a dramatic difference as the mouse is moved. Depending on which handle of the graphic you selected, different parts of the graphic will disappear.

We have selected the right-hand side, middle handle in Figure 30, and are in the process of cropping towards the center of the graphic. Figure 31 shows the result of cropping from both the top and the right.

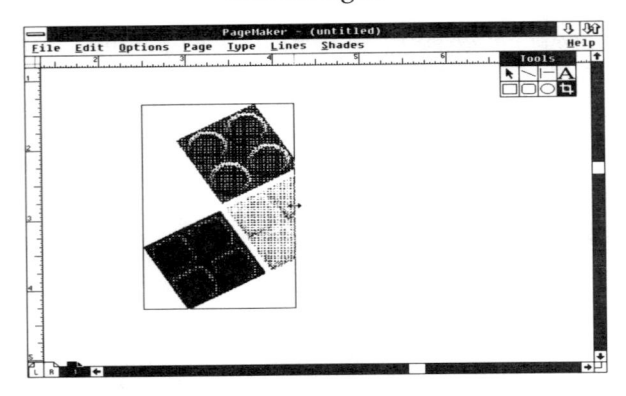

*Figure 30. Proceed as though you are going to resize the graphic, yet use the cropping tool. The difference will soon become apparent.*

To reverse the crop at a later stage, reselect the cropping tool, and select the cropped side's handle, and move the mouse away from the graphic.

Once a graphic has been cropped, another technique can be used to alter what has been cropped. This is particularly effective if the graphic has been cropped considerably. Position the cropping tool in the center of a cropped graphic, hold down the mouse button, and move it around. The cursor changes to a hand (Figure 32). Rather than the entire graphic being moved, the image itself is moved, as if behind a window—we are merely altering which part of the graphic is showing and which is hiding.

Any cropped graphic can still be moved, resized, and have the text wrap altered.

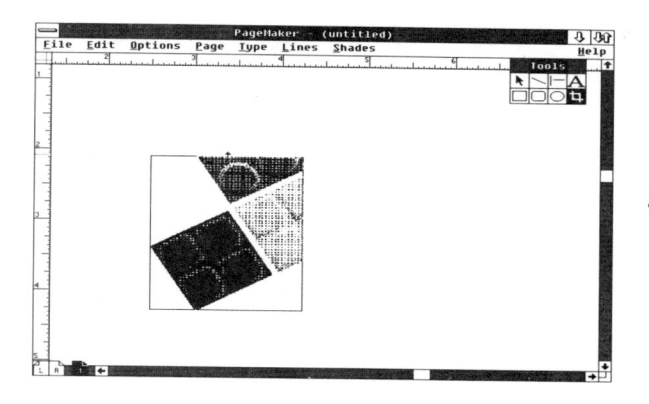

*Figure 31.* We have cropped this graphic from both the top and the right-hand side.

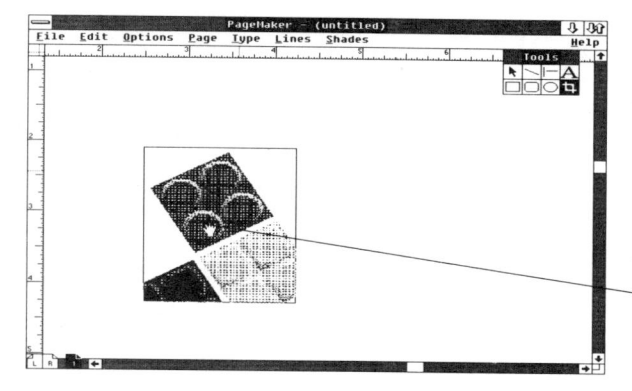

*Figure 32.* We can move the cropped graphic around as if behind a window by holding down the cropping tool positioned in the middle of a cropped graphic, and moving the mouse around.

Note the cursor changes to a hand.

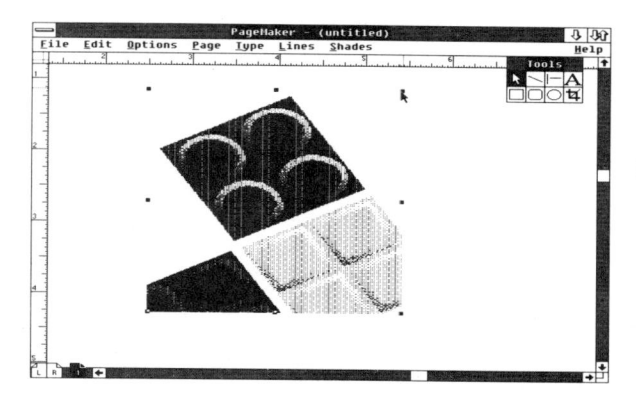

*Figure 33.* After a graphic has been cropped, it can still be resized, moved, and have wraparounds applied to it.

Module 6 Exercise

# Introduction to Imported Graphics

# Module 6 Exercise
# Introduction to Imported Graphics

In this exercise we are going to import a photograph, then manipulate it by resizing, moving, and cropping it. We will also load some text to automatically wrap around the graphic.

This training material is structured so that people of all levels of expertise with PageMaker can use it to gain maximum benefit. In order to do this, we have structured this material so that the bare exercise is listed below this paragraph on just one page, with no hints. The following pages contain the steps needed to complete this exercise for those that need additional prompting. The **PageMaker Introduction to Imported Graphics** module should be referenced if you need further help or explanations.

## Module 6 exercise steps

1. Load the picture PHOTO.TIF onto an A4 or Letter page (your choice).
2. Resize this picture so that it measures 4 inches by 4 inches exactly.
3. Resize the picture proportionally so that it is 4 inches high.
4. Crop the picture so that only the computer screen and the man's head are visible.
5. Load the text file BROCHURE.DOC onto two columns on the opening page.
6. Move the photo into the middle of the screen.
7. Make BROCHURE.DOC wrap around all sides of the photo.
8. Make space for a border around the photo, and then create a border.

The steps for completing this exercise are on the following pages.

*Module 6 Exercise - Introduction to Imported Graphics*

## The steps in detail.

*1. Load the picture PHOTO.TIF onto an A4 or Letter page (your choice).*

The file PHOTO.TIF is located in the GETSTART subdirectory in the PageMaker directory. Locate and load this picture through the *Place* command in the **File** menu. Load this file onto the page by either clicking the mouse button once, or holding the mouse button down and drawing an imaginary square.

See Figures 1, 2, and 3 to perform these steps.

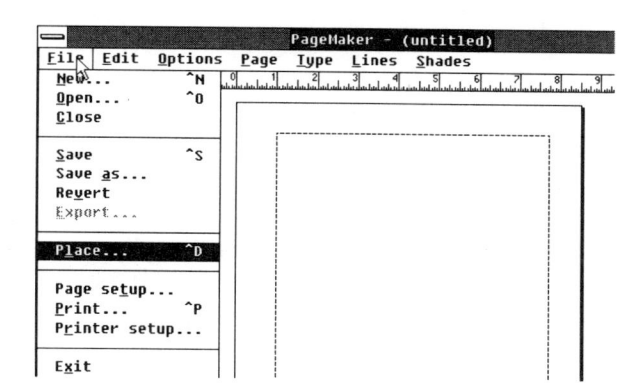

*Figure 1.* Select the Place command from the **File** menu to load the file PHOTO.TIF.

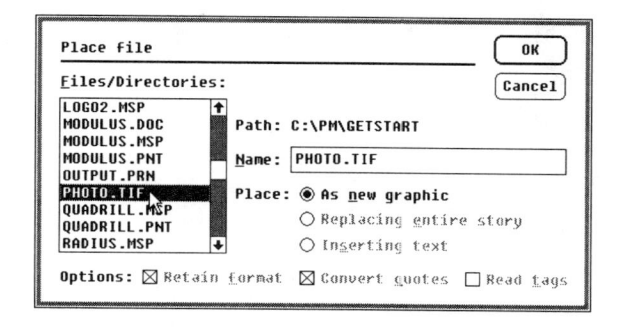

*Figure 2.* Select the file PHOTO.TIF from the GETSTART subdirectory.

239

*Module 6 Exercise - Introduction to Imported Graphics*

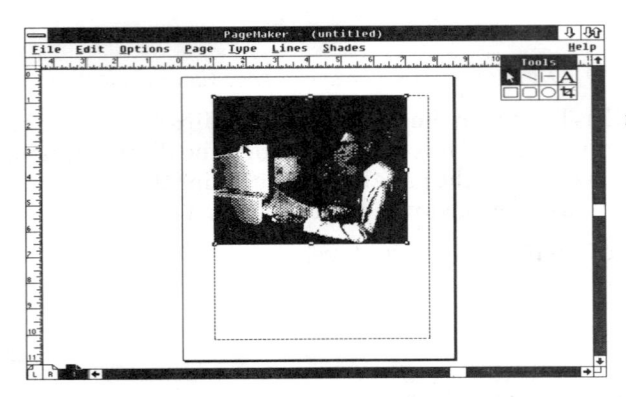

*Figure 3.* The file PHOTO.TIF is now loaded on the page—the actual size that it appears on the page depends on the method you used to load it.
In this case we just clicked the mouse button in the top-left corner of the margins to let it flow to its actual size.

2. Resize this picture so that it measures 4 inches by 4 inches exactly.

To make sure the photo is the correct size, you should first invoke the PageMaker rulers. Using these rulers and the accompanying guides, create a grid on the page of 4 by 4 inches. Figures 4 to 6 provide explanations.

Now grab the bottom right-hand handle, and resize the image (Figure 7) so that the bottom right-hand corner snaps to the bottom right-hand corner of the grid (Figure 8). The picture is now exactly 4 inches by 4 inches.

Note ruler
zero point at margins

*Figure 4.* In order to create the grid to contain the file we must first perform a few steps—use the Rulers command from the **Options** menu to display the rulers (the Preferences command in the **Edit** menu can be used to ensure inches are used in the ruler), and move the zero point of the ruler to the top left margin of the page.
The zero point of the ruler is moved by holding down the mouse button in the area where the two rulers intersect, and dragging the mouse to the spot on the screen where the new zero point will be.
We have also moved to 75% view to see the graphic better.

*Module 6 Exercise - Introduction to Imported Graphics*

*Figure 5.* After the zero point of the ruler is in the correct spot, we must now pull a ruler guide from both the vertical and horizontal rulers to align with the 4 inch mark in both rulers. Hold the mouse button down in a ruler to first obtain a guide. Here we have just pulled a ruler guide from the vertical ruler to align with the 4 inch horizontal ruler mark.

*Figure 6.* Here we have added a horizontal ruler guide, also at the 4 inch mark. (Make sure your zero point in the ruler is at the same place as ours).

*Figure 7.* We can now resize the picture (make it smaller) to fit it into the 4-inch square grid. We have moved down the page slightly to see the bottom of the picture (while still seeing the grid), and began resizing by holding the mouse button down on the bottom right-hand handle and moving this corner up to the intersection of the two 4-inch ruler guides.

241

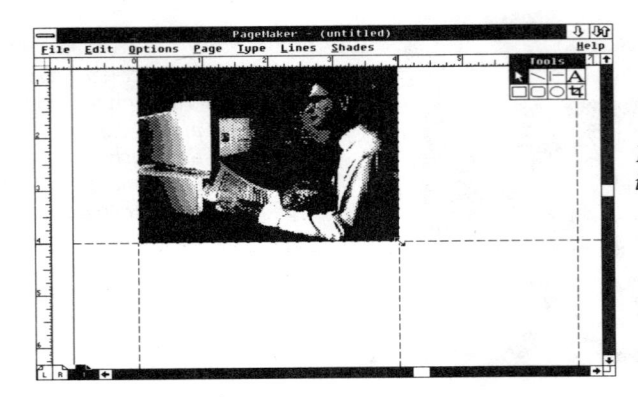

*Module 6 Exercise - Introduction to Imported Graphics*

**Figure 8.** *We have now reached the intersection of the two ruler guides. The picture has now been resized exactly to the 4-inch-square grid.*

3. Resize the picture proportionally so that it is 4 inches high.

Although we have resized the picture so that it is exactly 4 inches by 4 inches, it is not necessarily in its correct proportion. To make sure that it is, we must resize the picture with the Shift key held down. Once the picture is in the grid, hold the mouse button on the bottom right-hand corner of the picture as though you were about to resize it. Now, with the mouse button held down, hold down the Shift key.

The picture moves to its true proportion as shown in Figure 9.

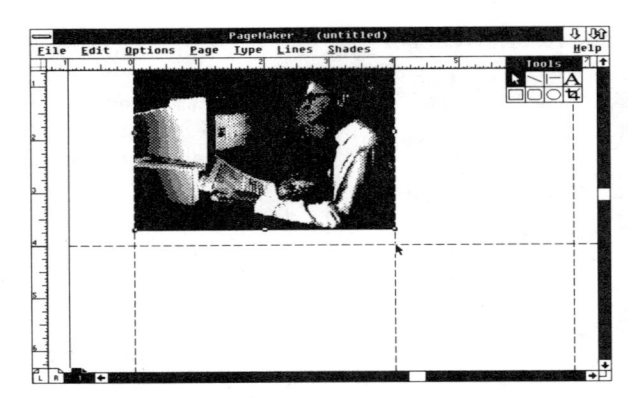

**Figure 9.** *The true proportion of the picture at 4 inches width. Note how the height is now less than 4 inches. Although similar to what it was before, this is the result of holding down the mouse button on the bottom right-hand corner handle of Figure 8, and holding down the Shift key. The mouse was not moved at all, and was released before the Shift key was.*

*Module 6 Exercise - Introduction to Imported Graphics*

To now make the image proportionally 4 inches high, we need to hold down the Shift key and grab the bottom-right handle of the picture again, and move it down until it snaps to the horizontal 4-inch ruler guide as shown in Figure 10. This will ensure that the picture is exactly 4 inches high, and as long as you release the mouse button before you release the Shift key, the picture will be proportionally accurate.

Note that with Figure 10, for the picture to be in proportion at 4 inches high, it is a little wider than 4 inches.

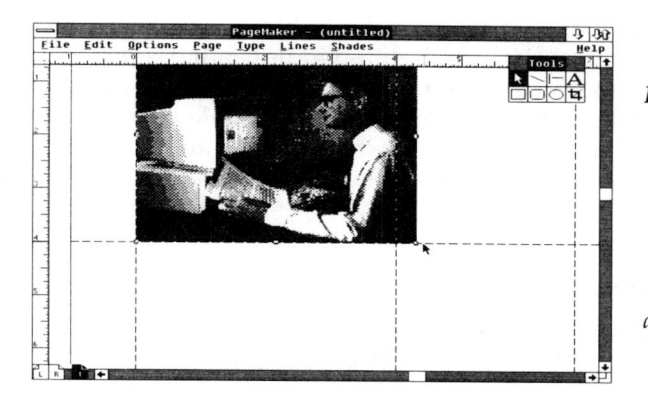

*Figure 10. In this figure, as before, we have held down the mouse button and Shift key to keep the proportions correct. This time, however, we had to make the picture a little wider (by moving the mouse down and to the right) until the bottom of the picture aligned with the 4-inch, horizontal ruler guide.*

243

## Module 6 Exercise - Introduction to Imported Graphics

4. *Crop the picture so that only the computer screen and the man's head are visible.*

Before we can crop the picture we must select the cropping tool from the Toolbox. This is the tool to the bottom-right of the Toolbox (Figure 11).

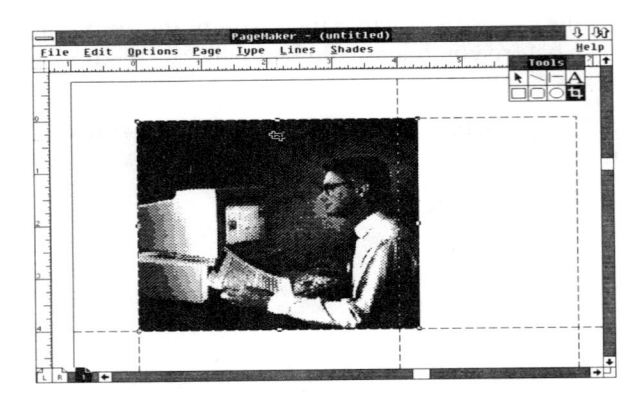

***Figure 11.*** *Select the cropping tool from the bottom right-hand corner of the Toolbox.*

Select the picture simply by clicking on it once with the cropping tool. From here, act as if you are going to resize the picture—hold down the cropping tool so that the middle of this tool is over the top-middle handle (Figure 12). From here, you may have to wait a second or two before you can do anything as PageMaker readies itself for the crop. After the double-arrowed, vertical mouse cursor appears (Figure 12), keep the mouse button held down and move towards the center of the picture. The picture will not resize but will be cropped.

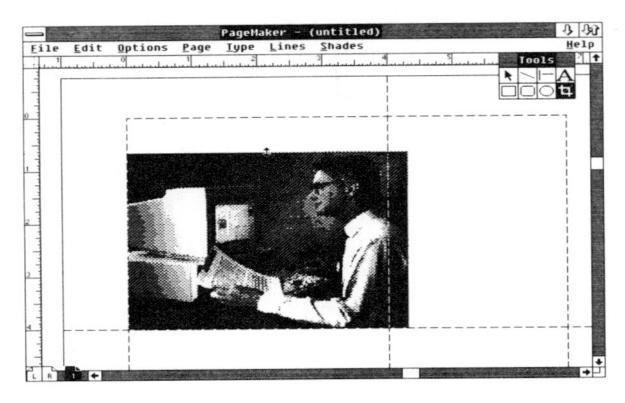

***Figure 12.*** *Hold down the cropping tool over the top-middle handle of the selected picture (click on it with this tool to select it), and proceed as though you were resizing the picture. As you can see, the picture is actually cropped.*

*Module 6 Exercise - Introduction to Imported Graphics*

After cropping from one side, you then move to the other handles and cut additional sides off of the picture. Continue cropping the picture from all four sides until only the man's head and computer screen are visible (Figure 13).

*Figure 13. Here is a close up of the cropped photo. We have cropped the picture from all sides—leaving only the man's head and computer screen visible.*

5. *Load the text file BROCHURE.DOC onto two columns on the opening page.*

The first step is to make sure that you have two columns on the page. This is achieved using the *Column guides* command from the **Options** menu. Select the command, and from the resulting dialog box, choose 2 columns. Change to *Fit in window* view as shown in Figure 14.

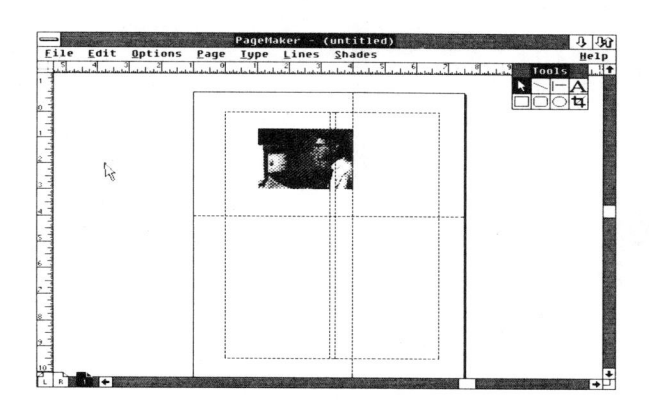

*Figure 14. Move back to Fit in window view to load the text file, and also add two columns to the page via the Column guides command in the **Options** menu.*

Use the *Place* command from the **File** menu to look into the GETSTART subdirectory and find the BROCHURE.DOC file (Figure 15). Select this file and flow it into the two columns on the page (Figure 16). Depending on the selected style, this text may only flow down one column.

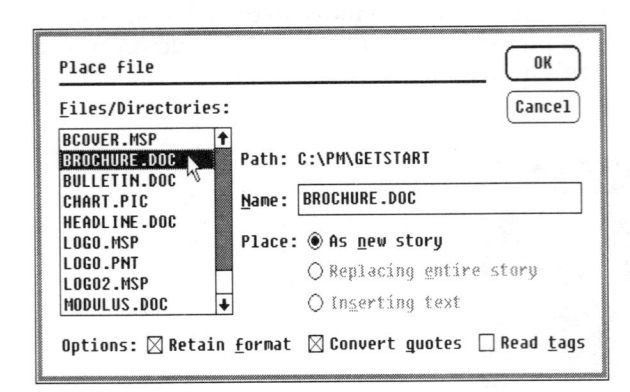

*Module 6 Exercise - Introduction to Imported Graphics*

*Figure 15. We are loading the file BROCHURE.DOC from the GETSTART subdirectory.*

How the text reacts when it comes to the picture will depend on the setting for the picture wraparound. So far it doesn't really matter. In our case, in Figure 16, the text has run through the graphic.

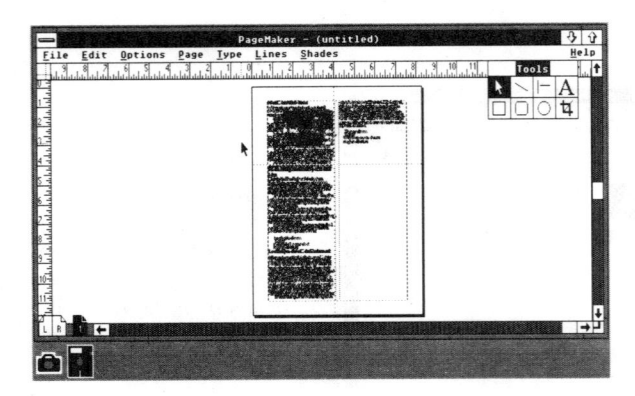

*Figure 16. In our case, after loading the file, the text has run all over the graphic. Whether or not yours does this does not really matter at this stage—although it does mean that the Ctrl key may have to be held down on the keyboard in order to select the graphic for step 6.*

6. *Move the photo into the middle of the screen.*

Select the picture with the pointer tool and move it into the middle of the screen (Figure 17). The text may have to reflow around the picture. If the text flows over the picture, as it has in our example, you may have to hold down the Ctrl key as you attempt to select the graphic.

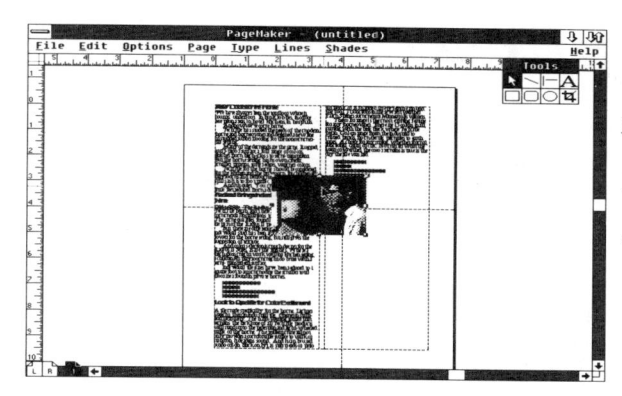

Module 6 Exercise - Introduction to Imported Graphics

*Figure 17.* Here we have moved the photo down to the middle of the page—remember, if the text covers the photo, you will have to hold down the Ctrl key as you select the photo.

7. Make BROCHURE.DOC run around all sides of the photo.

To do this, we must first make sure that the picture remains selected (if it is not, simply click on it). Now, move to the *Text wrap* command in the **Options** menu (Figure 18).

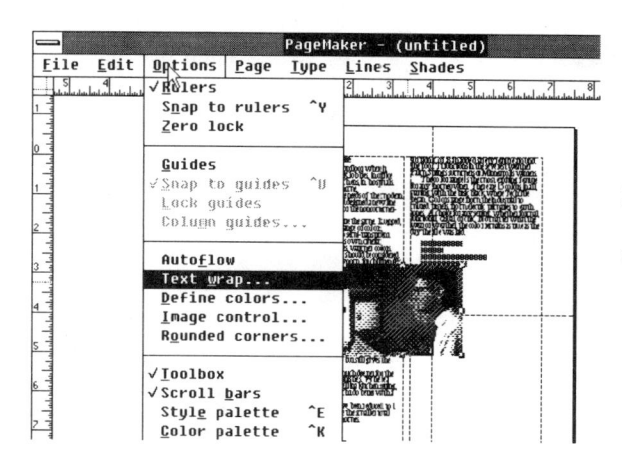

*Figure 18.* Making sure the photo is still selected, choose the Text wrap command from the **Options** menu.

Within the dialog box that appears (Figure 19), set the wraparound so that the text will flow around all sides of the picture regularly. See the settings of Figure 19 if you are unsure of how this is done.

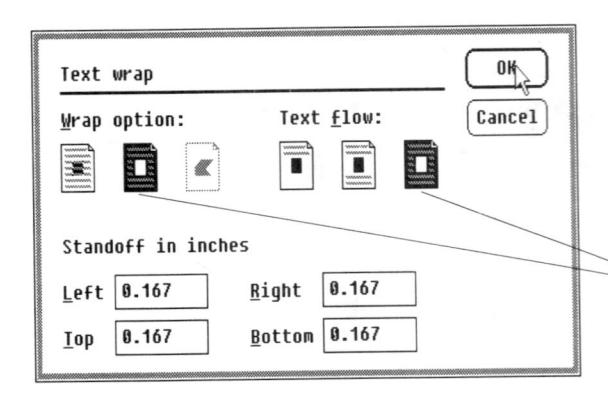

## Module 6 Exercise - Introduction to Imported Graphics

*Figure 19. Within this dialog box, make sure these options are selected. The left option ensures that the text flows around the graphic, and the option to the right determines how the text flows around the graphic.*

After setting up the dialog box as in figure 19, your page should look something like Figure 20.

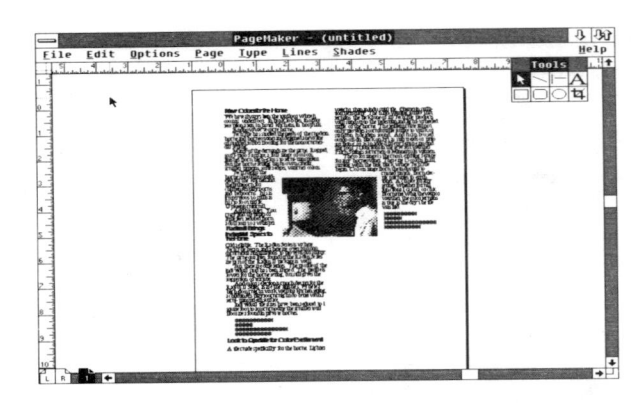

*Figure 20. Here we can see that the text has indeed wrapped around the graphic.*

8. *Make space for a border around the photo and then create a border.*

To make space for a border around the picture, we must once again move to the *Text wrap* command in the **Options** menu (keep the picture selected). It may be that the space for the border has already been created, but we will look at how to alter the space around the picture. Figure 21 shows the *Text wrap* dialog box again.

Notice the space above, below, and around the picture in Figure 20. This will be the forced white area around the graphic. Increase this slightly to provide a larger area around the picture for our border. Change the settings for *Standoff in inches* from the Figure 19 dialog box to those shown in Figure 21.

*Module 6 Exercise - Introduction to Imported Graphics*

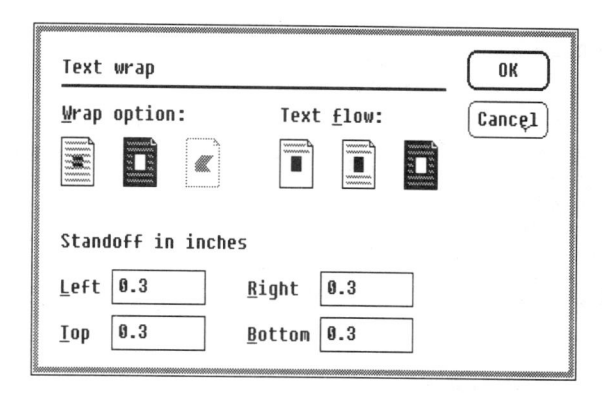

*Figure 21.* Note the figures at the bottom of this dialog box that determine how close the text can flow to all sides of the graphic. We have increased these figures slightly from Figure 19 to push the text further away from the photo. Figure 22 shows the result.

Once you OK these changes, you will be returned back to the page. Move to *Actual size* view so that you can see the picture and the text (Figure 22). You will now see an increased amount of white space around the picture.

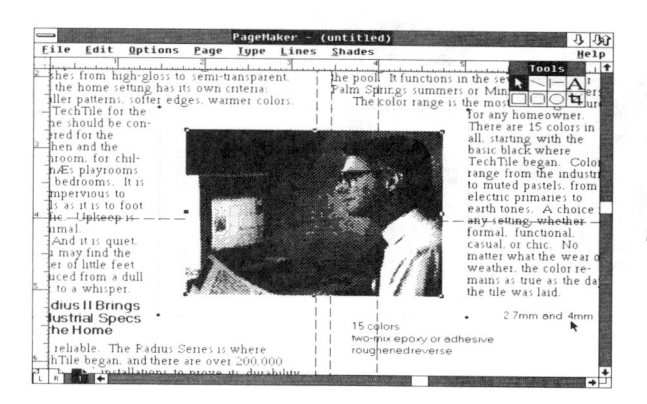

*Figure 22.* The result—quite a distinct white space between the photo and the text—equivalent to the numbers we inserted in Figure 21.

Now, grab the rectangle drawing tool from the toolbox and draw a rectangle around the picture (Figure 23). If the rectangle has a shade or a color, it will overlay the picture. If it does, and you cannot see the picture, choose the *Send to back* command from the **Edit** menu. You may, after choosing this command, like to apply a shade, color, and/or line thickness to the outline. The result is shown in Figure 24.

249

*Module 6 Exercise - Introduction to Imported Graphics*

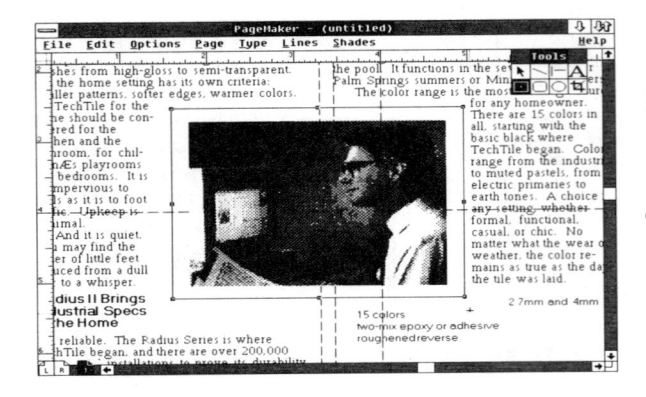

***Figure 23.*** *Select one of the graphics tools from the Toolbox (in this case the rectangle) and draw a box around the photo. If the box you create sits on top of the graphic and you cannot see it, immediately choose the Send to back command from the* **Edit** *menu.*

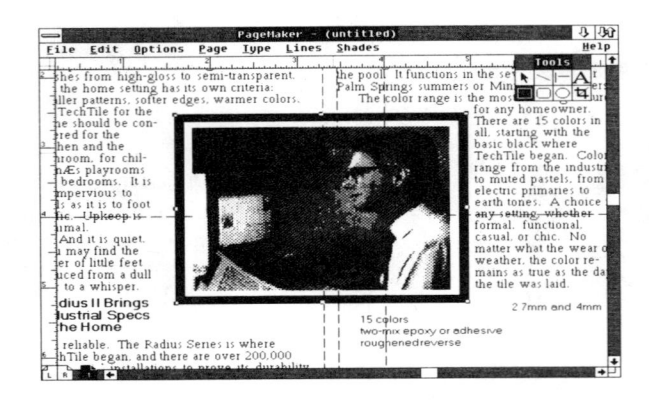

***Figure 24.*** *We increased the thickness of the line using the* **Lines** *menu and gave the box a background shade using the* **Shades** *menu (and sent it to the back) to make it look a little different.*

250

# Module 7

# PageMaker Advanced Picture Formatting

# PageMaker Advanced Picture Formatting

## Introduction

We described in the last module how we can import pictures, and also how we can resize and move these pictures in various ways. In this module we are looking at more complex wraparounds, and also how we can alter the composition of the picture itself.

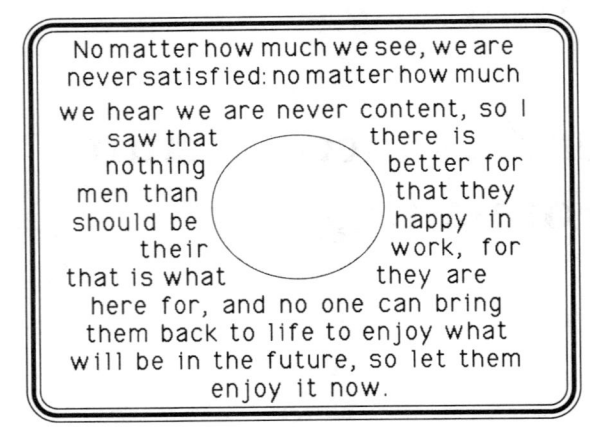

*Figure 1. An example of an irregular wraparound achieved using PageMaker 3's advanced techniques.*

## Irregular wraparounds

In module 6, we looked at creating simple wraparounds with graphics using the *Text wrap* command in the **Options** menu. Depending on your choice here, text can be made to skip over a graphic, stop at a graphic, run through a graphic, or wrap regularly around the border of the graphic. We will now learn how to make text wrap *irregularly* around the edge of the graphic.

For this example, load the text file BROCHURE.DOC into a three-column page, and load the picture file TILES.PNT somewhere on top of this text. Make the graphic initially about 4 inches (10 cm) square (see Figure 2 for details).

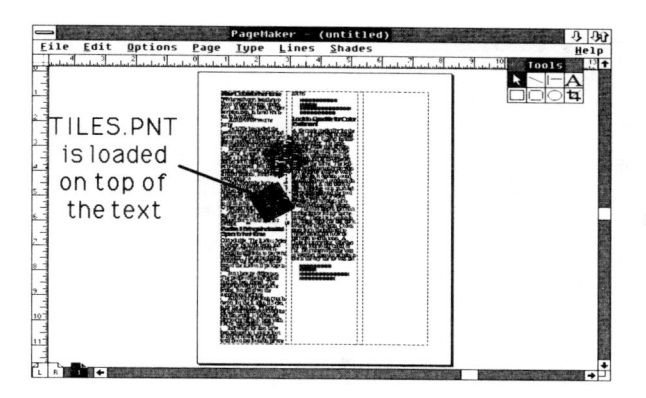

*Figure 2. The file BROCHURE.DOC may not fill three columns, but should read something like this. Depending upon your Text wrap option, your text may run through the TILES.PNT graphic as ours does, or it may wrap around it.*

Every picture, when selected (click on it), will have two sets of handles around it. The inside handles are the ones used to resize the picture. We have already looked at the use of these handles in previous modules. The outside handles, connected by dotted lines, are used to create a wraparound for the graphic. Each outside handle is called a *vertex* by PageMaker. Before these handles can be used, however, the *Text wrap* command must be set up in a similar fashion to Figure 3.

Depending upon what you may have been doing, your *Text wrap* option could be the same, or different to this figure. In any case, set it up as in Figure 3.

Now size the graphic so that it fits across two columns as shown in the *Actual size* view of Figure 4.

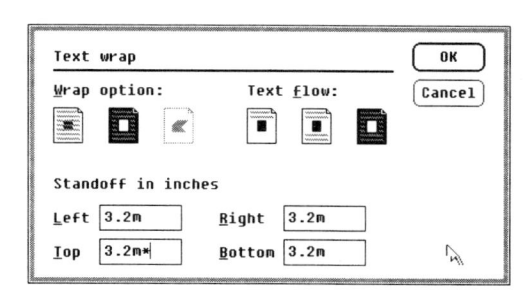

*Figure 3. To make sure that the text wraps correctly around the image loaded in, alter the Text wrap command so that it reads the same as shown here. Your image should be selected before moving to this command.*

*Note that even though the preference is set for inches, we have inserted 3.2 millimeters by putting an m after the numbers. Choose 0.125 if you wish to stay in inches.*

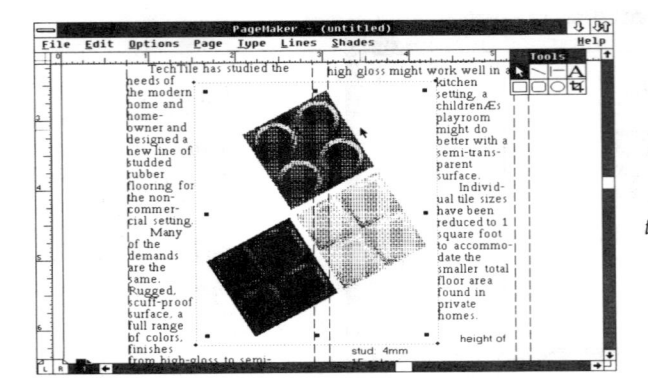

*Module 7 - PageMaker Advanced Picture Formatting*

**Figure 4.** *Size the graphic so that it fits nicely across two columns. Text will flow down both sides of the graphic as long as you followed the instructions in Figure 3.*

Initially, the outside set of handles around a selected graphic consists of dots or vertexes in every corner. You can hold the mouse button down on any of these corners, as if you were going to resize the graphic, and change the shape of the wraparound. Move the top right-hand dot a little to the right (Figure 5) and watch how, after a few seconds, the text will change its flow to compensate for this movement (Figures 6 and 7). Any of the four corner dots can be moved in this way, and the text will change its flow each time.

The text flow can be altered so that it bears no relevance to the graphic originally within it.

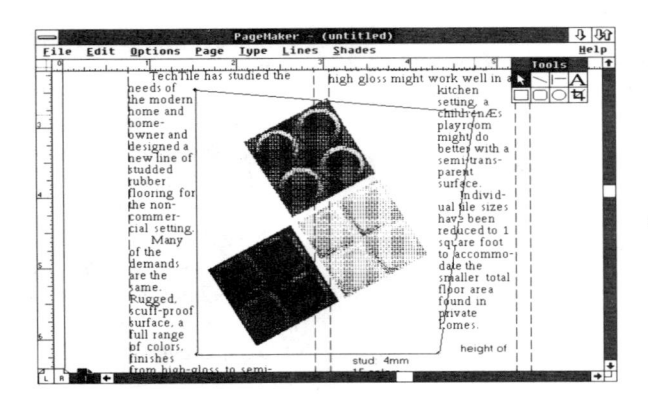

**Figure 5.** *Here we are in the process of altering the position of the right-hand, outside text flow margin of the graphic. See the next figure to see the result of this movement.*

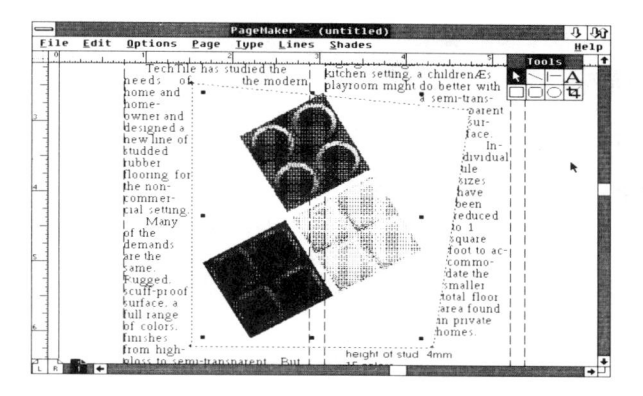

*Module 7 - PageMaker Advanced Picture Formatting*

*Figure 6.* After moving one of the outside dots slightly, the text reformats to compensate for this movement.

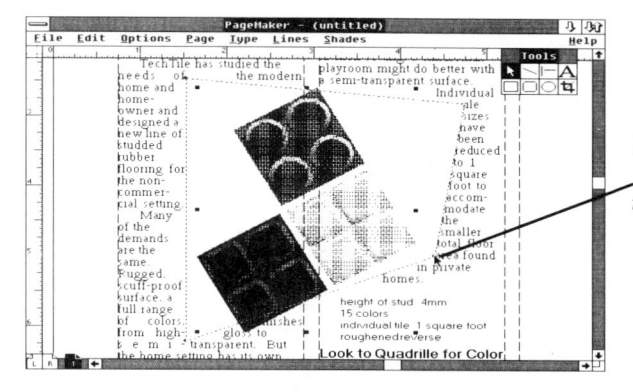

*Figure 7.* Here we have also moved the bottom right-hand corner dot up almost a centimeter. Notice how much text has reformatted to compensate for this.

Moving the four dots in this way will alter the way the text flows, but will hardly create an irregular wraparound. We need to have more than four dots or vertexes to achieve a correct irregular wraparound. We can actually create more to suit our purpose.

Move the mouse cursor to a point on the dotted outline where another vertex would come in handy. Think of it as moving to a point where a bend in the outline would be necessary. Click once, and a new vertex will be created (Figure 8). After clicking once, hold the mouse button down on this vertex and move it around. You will notice that there is now a new bend in the outline of the graphic (Figure 10).

255

*Module 7 - PageMaker Advanced Picture Formatting*

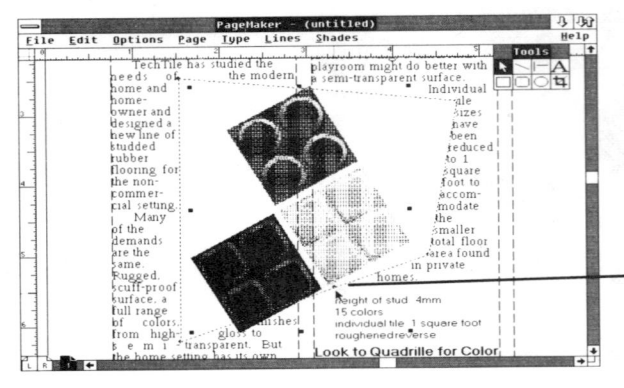

*Figure 8.* *We have decided that the dotted outline, in order to best hug the graphic, needs a bend exactly where the mouse is. All we do is click on that spot, and a new vertex, with all the properties of the corner vertexes, appears.*

This vertex can be moved in any direction, including along the line itself. As many vertyexes as are needed can be created to make an irregular wraparound. Simply click on the dotted outline of the graphic wherever you need to bend the line.

Figures 10 to 12 show additional manipulations to make the text run exactly as we would like. With this irregular wraparound created, the graphic can still be resized and moved, using the inside handles, without losing the actual shape of the wraparound (Figure 13).

Every time a vertex is moved or created, the text reflows to compensate. If this is slowing you down, hold down the space bar as you move or create vertices. The text will only reformat when the space bar is released. You can move several vertices before the space bar is released.

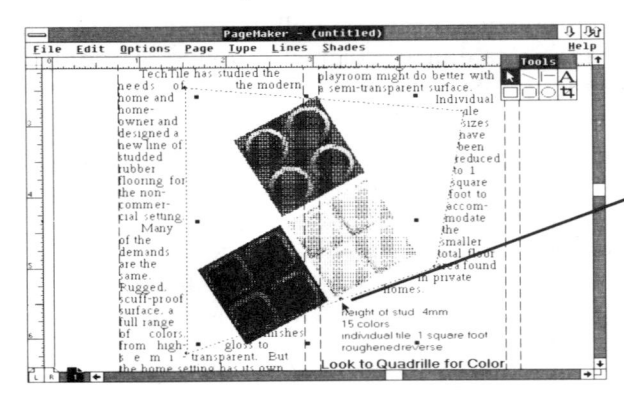

*Figure 9.* *This little dot (vertex) can now be used as another corner.*

256

*Module 7 - PageMaker Advanced Picture Formatting*

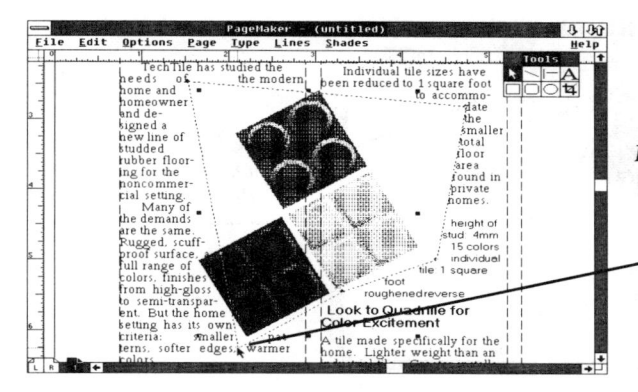

*Figure 10.* We can also move down the left-hand corner vertex thanks to that new vertex we created in Figure 8.

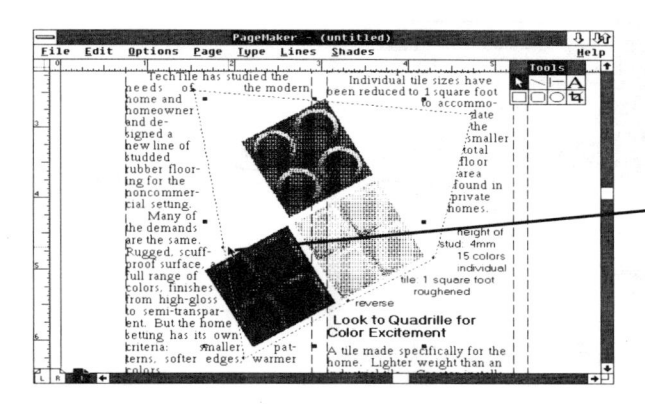

*Figure 11.* We have created another vertex, simply by clicking on the dotted line where we felt it necessary.

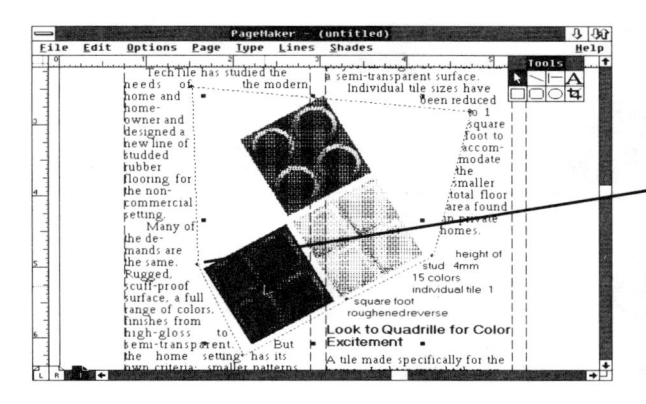

*Figure 12.* The vertex created in Figure 11 is moved to the left a little.

*Module 7 - PageMaker Advanced Picture Formatting*

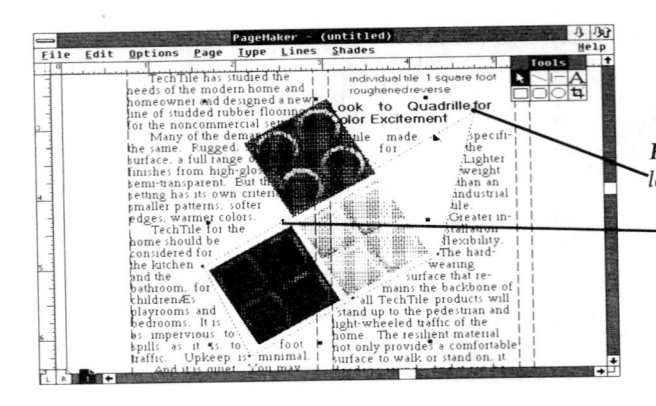

*Figure 13.* Here we moved the top left hand handle all the way across to the right, and also created a vertex here.

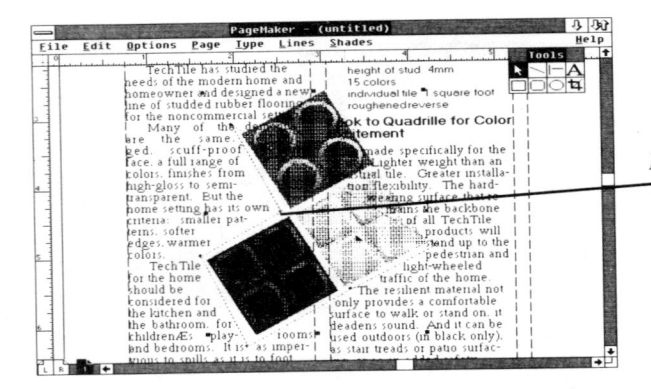

*Figure 14.* This vertex once again is used as a corner.

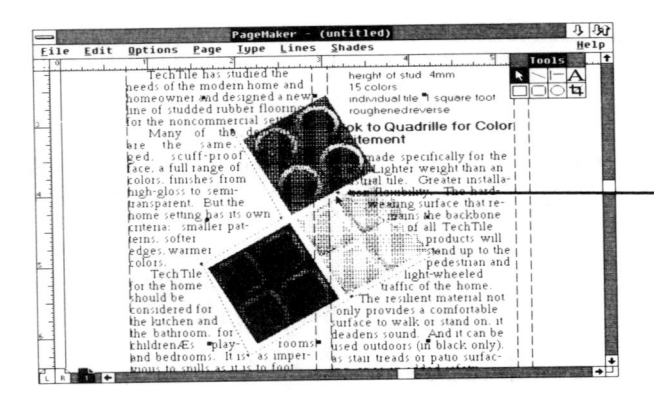

*Figure 15.* Another vertex is created here—the picture is beginning to take shape.

Module 7 - PageMaker Advanced Picture Formatting

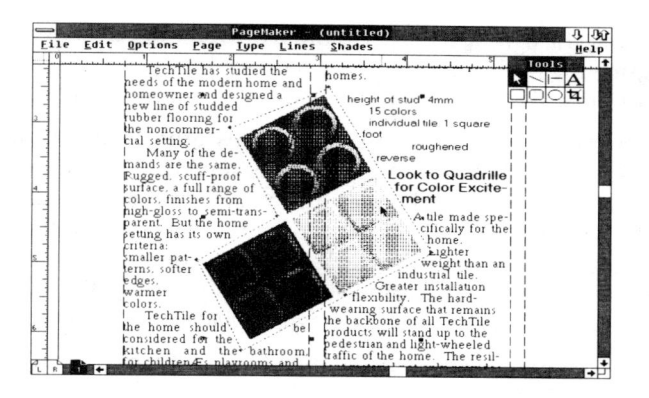

*Figure 16.* The final result—text has run irregularly around the graphic.

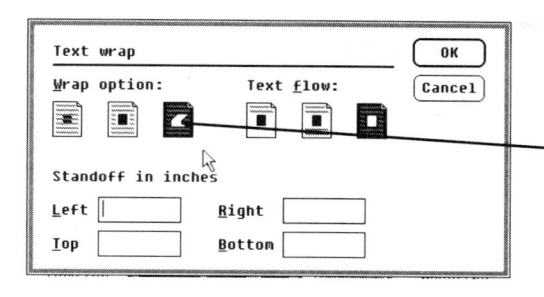

*Figure 17.* Once the text wraparound has been manually altered, the dialog box for the Text wrap command from the **Options** menu will reflect that change. This option will then be automatically selected.

## Altering the appearance of graphics

Several controls exist to alter the appearance of certain imported graphics, such as scanned images or paint-type graphics created in any of the packages compatible with PageMaker. Graphics imported in EPS-format, draw-type package images, or internally created graphics cannot be altered in this way.

The controls for altering these graphics are contained within the *Image control* command in the **Options** menu. Before this command can be activated, a graphic must be on the screen and be selected.

Several attributes of an imported graphic can be altered. These include the lightness, contrast, gray levels, and screen pattern of the graphic.

259

*Module 7 - PageMaker Advanced Picture Formatting*

Adjusting the *lightness* of a graphic will affect the entire image. Blacks, for example, can be lightened until they appear a light shade of gray; light images darkened to appear totally black.

Adjusting the *contrast* of an image involves lightening dark areas and darkening light areas. A high-contrast picture would be one where there are very dark areas and very light areas—without much in between. A low-contrast picture is one where there is little difference between the dark areas and the light areas of a picture—for instance, a photo that is taken in poor light. Contrast can be increased or decreased using the *Image control* command.

In this example we have loaded the LOGO.MSP graphic (on the top), and the PHOTO.TIF file from the GETSTART subdirectory. These are shown in Figure 18.

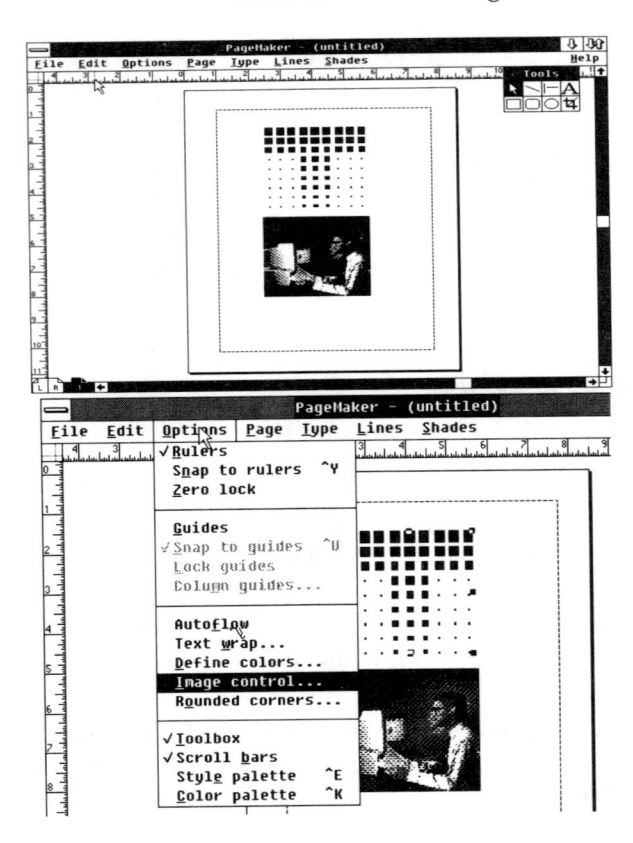

*Figure 18.* Here we are going to alter two different types of imported graphics—a black and white image on top, with a sixteen levels of gray image below it.

*Figure 19.* Select the image you would like to alter, and choose the Image control command from the **Options** menu. We have selected the black and white image on top to look at first.

260

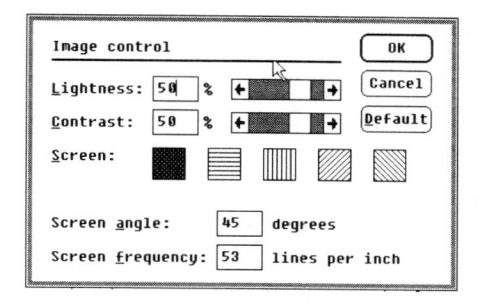

Module 7 - PageMaker Advanced Picture Formatting

*Figure 20.* The image control dialog box. Normally the lightness is set at 0%. Here we have altered it to 50% to get the result in Figure 21. (A slightly lighter box).

The *Image control* dialog box appears identically for all images on the PC—regardless of the number of gray scales contained in the image.

The first thing we will look at in this dialog box are the two scroll bars at the top—one representing lightness, the other contrast. Each of these bars can be moved either to the left or the right to increase or decrease brightness and/or contrast.

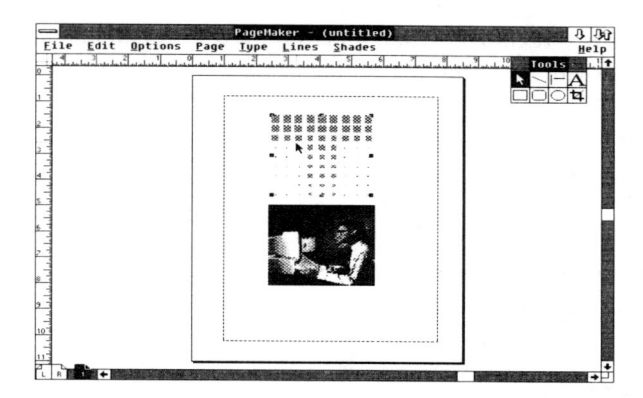

*Figure 21.* By changing the lightness to 50%, the top graphic appears and prints as a shade less than black.

The lightness initially is initially set at 0%. This can be altered from -100% to 100%—where -100% is a totally black image, and 100% is a totally white image.

Contrast initially is set at 50%, where 0% is a one-color image, 100% is a black and white image (no shades of gray), and -100% is a reversed black and white image (no shades of gray, but a negative of 100%).

*Module 7 - PageMaker Advanced Picture Formatting*

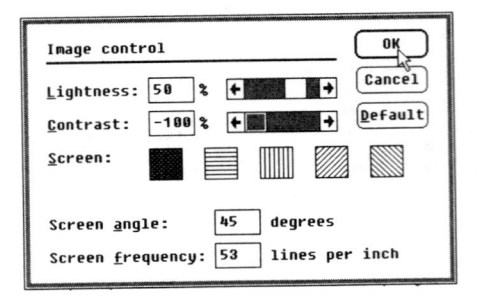

*Figure 22. We can turn the black and white image into a reverse image by turning contrast to -100%. With lightness at 50% and contrast at -100%, the result can be seen in Figure 23.*

Below these lightness and contrast commands are the several preset screening choices that can be applied to the selected graphic. Selecting any one of these five boxes will result in a slightly different pattern to be interlaced with the image.

The vertical lines, for example, add several straight up and down lines throughout the image. Examples of the effects that can be created by using these screen selections can be seen in Figure 30.

Underneath the preset screening selections are tools that allow you to create your own custom screen for the selected image. Using the two rectangles that appear here, a screen of lines at any angle and of any frequency per inch (from 10 to 300) can be added to enhance the picture. This feature will involve a little experimentation to get the correct look for the picture.

Figures 23 to 30 provide further examples of these operations.

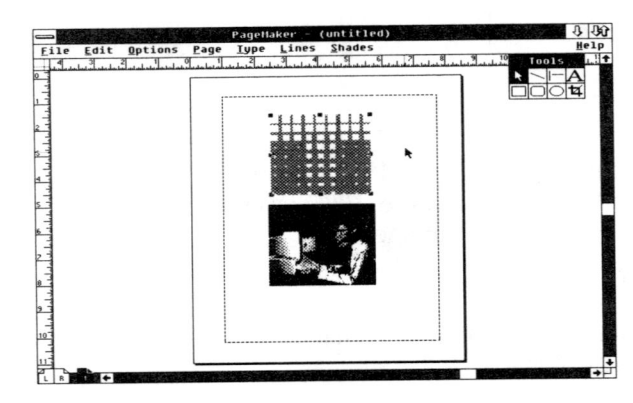

*Figure 23. The results of Figure 22. The figure is reversed.*

262

*Module 7 - PageMaker Advanced Picture Formatting*

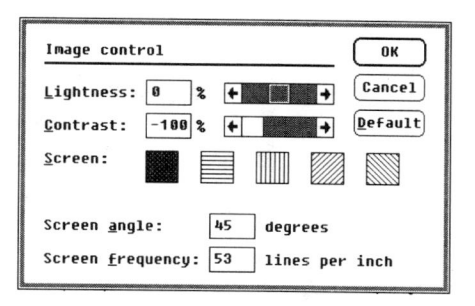

*Figure 24.* We are now adjusting the lightness of Figure 23 back to zero to give the result of Figure 25.

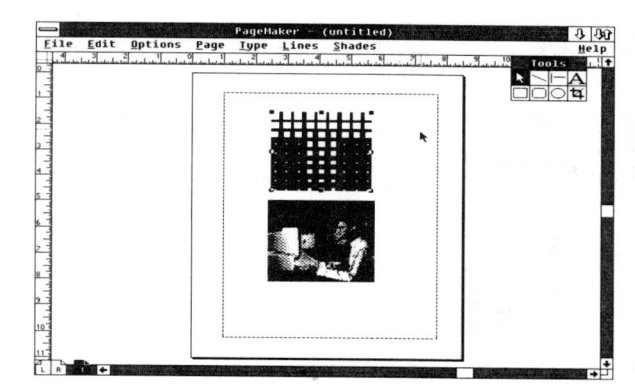

*Figure 25.* Here the blacks appear as black, rather than a shade less than black.

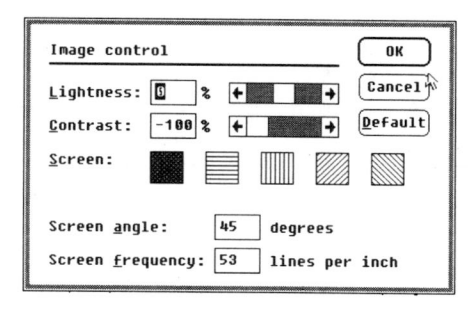

*Figure 26.* We have now selected the photo and changed its contrast from 50% to -100%. See Figure 27.

263

*Module 7 - PageMaker Advanced Picture Formatting*

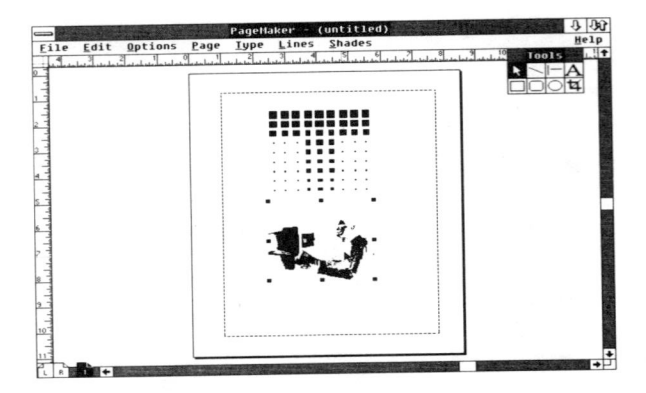

*Figure 27.* The photo is now reversed black and white.

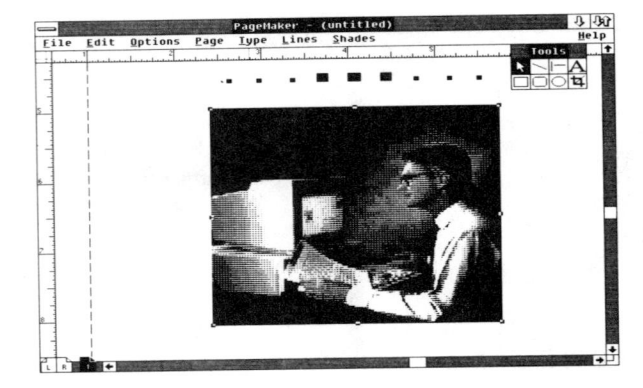

*Figure 28.* Back to 0% lightness and 50% contrast.

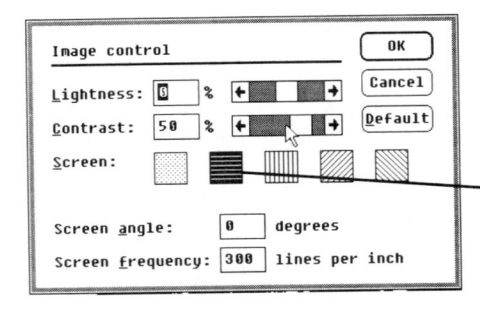

*Figure 29.* Random screening of the photo can be achieved by clicking the mouse in the different boxes.

*Module 7 - PageMaker Advanced Picture Formatting*

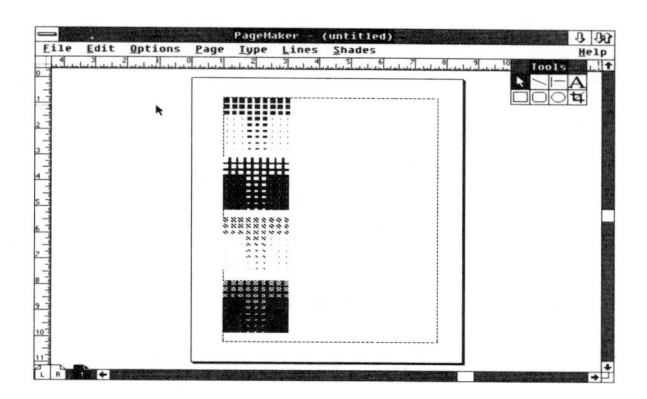

***Figure 30.*** *Some examples of what can be done to the average black and white graphic.*

265

# Module 7 Exercise

# PageMaker
# Advanced Picture Formatting

# Module 7 Exercise - PageMaker Advanced Picture Formatting

In this exercise we are importing different types of pictures into PageMaker and looking at the sort of advanced options that are available to alter the look and properties of these pictures. We will also be working with irregular wraparounds of graphics.

This training material is structured so that people of all levels of expertise with PageMaker can use it to gain maximum benefit. In order to do this, we have structured this material so that the bare exercise is listed below this paragraph on just one page, with no hints. The following pages contain the steps needed to complete this exercise for those that need additional prompting. The **PageMaker Advanced Picture Formatting** module should be referenced if you need further help or explanations.

## Module 7 exercise steps

1. In this exercise we are going to load three files from the GETSTART subdirectory—PHOTO.TIF, TILES.PNT, and BROCHURE.DOC. Load these files now so that BROCHURE.DOC is in two columns on the page, and the two graphics are positioned on the page, each about 3.5 inches square. Text must also wrap regularly around these graphics. If you are unsure about what we mean here, look at Figure 1 on the next page.

2. Select the file PHOTO.TIF, and change it from a sixteen shades of gray photo to a black and white image. Also reverse the image—turn white black and black white.

3. For the second graphics file, TILES.PNT, create a wraparound with this image that will cause the text to wrap irregularly around the image—to hug the image. (See Figure 2 on the next page if you are unsure about what we mean here.)

The steps for completing this exercise are on the following pages.

*Module 7 Exercise - PageMaker Advanced Picture Formatting*

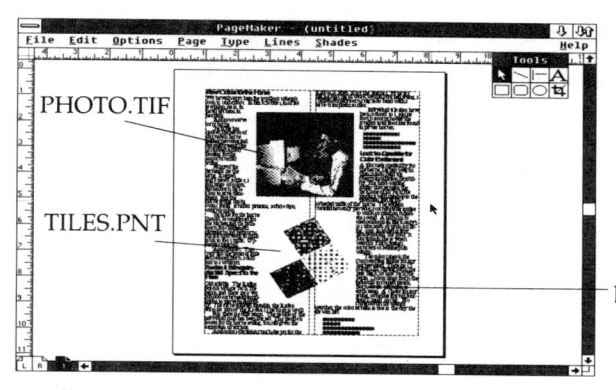

*Figure 1.* This is the result we want after step 1.

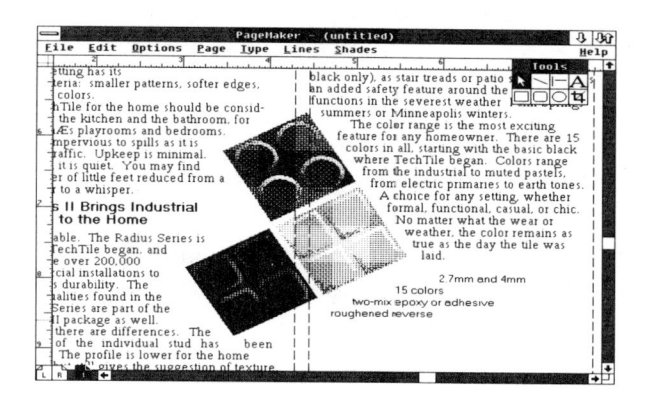

*Figure 2.* This is the result we want after step 3.

# The Steps in detail.

1. *In this exercise we are going to load three files from the GETSTART subdirectory—PHOTO.TIF, TILES.PNT, and BROCHURE.DOC. Load these files now so that BROCHURE.DOC is in two columns on the page, and the two graphics are positioned on the page, each about 3.5 inches square. Text must also wrap regularly around these graphics. If you are unsure about what we mean here, look at Figure 1 above.*

Module 7 Exercise - PageMaker Advanced Picture Formatting

To achieve the page shown in figure 1, follow these steps:

Select *New* to create the publication, and choose an A4 or Letter size page.

Use the *Column guides* command in the **Options** menu to create two columns (Figure 3).

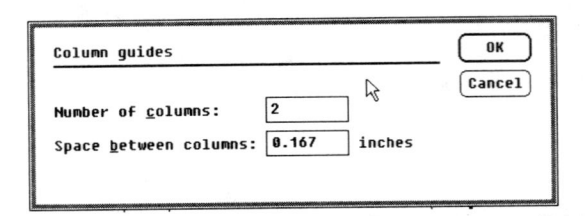

*Figure 3. In the Column guides dialog box, insert the 2 for the number of columns.*

Load the file BROCHURE.DOC from the GETSTART subdirectory into these two columns (Figures 4 and 5).

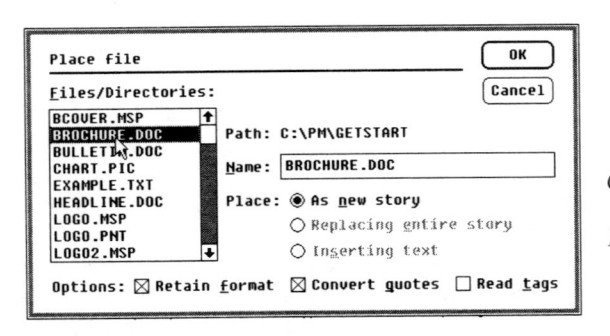

*Figure 4. Load the file BROCHURE.DOC from the GETSTART subdirectory. This is the dialog box obtained from the Place command in the **File** menu.*

270

*Module 7 Exercise - PageMaker Advanced Picture Formatting*

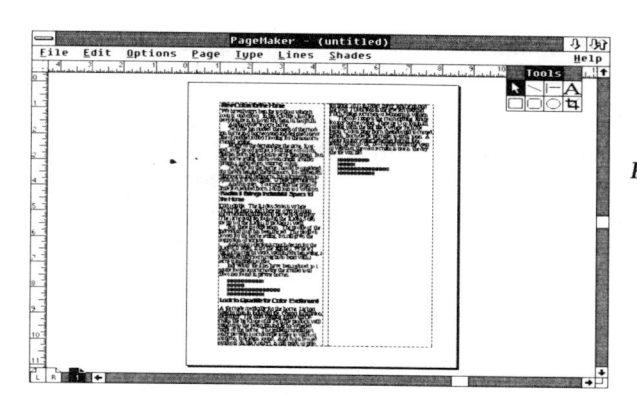

*Figure 5.* The BROCHURE.DOC file must be loaded into two columns on an A4 or Letter size page.

Before loading any pictures, move to the *Text wrap* command in the **Options** menu and set up the dialog box for a regular wrap as illustrated in Figure 6. Make sure the pointer tool is selected, and make sure also that no text block is selected—as the *Text wrap* command will only apply to that text block.

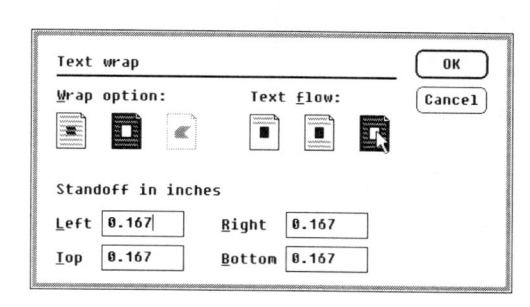

*Figure 6.* It is a good idea to set the Text wrap dialog box up as such, before actually loading any pictures. This ensures that all pictures, when loaded, automatically take on this setting.

Load both PHOTO.TIF and TILES.PNT onto the page using the *Place* command from the **File** menu. Position them approximately as shown in Figure 1. Resize these pictures, if necessary, so that they are approximately the size of those in this figure.

If the text did not wrap around the pictures as in Figure 1, the step you took in Figure 6 failed. Simply select each picture, choose the *Text wrap* command, and set up the dialog box as in Figure 6 for each picture.

*Module 7 Exercise - PageMaker Advanced Picture Formatting*

2. Select the file PHOTO.TIF, and change it from a sixteen shades of gray photo to a black and white image. Also reverse the image—turn white black and black white.

Select the file PHOTO.TIF on the page by clicking on it, and choose the *Image control* command from the **Options** menu (Figure 8). If this command cannot be chosen, make sure that the correct graphic is selected on the page. The Image control dialog box of Figure 9 then appears. Also change to *Actual size* view as shown in Figure 7.

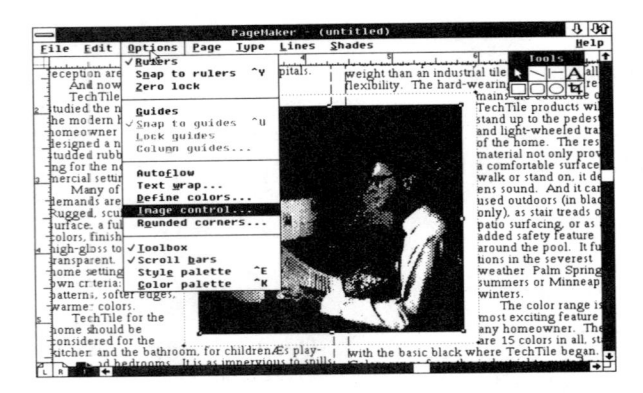

***Figure 7.*** *Select the file PHOTO.TIF. Also make sure that you are in Actual size view, or something similar, so that you can see the changes we make to this picture.*

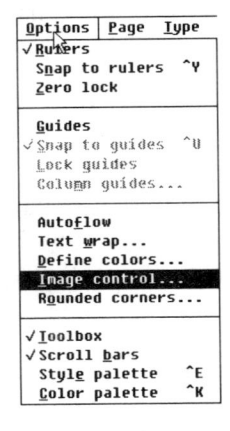

***Figure 8.*** *After selecting the file, choose the Image control command from the **Options** menu.*

272

*Module 7 Exercise - PageMaker Advanced Picture Formatting*

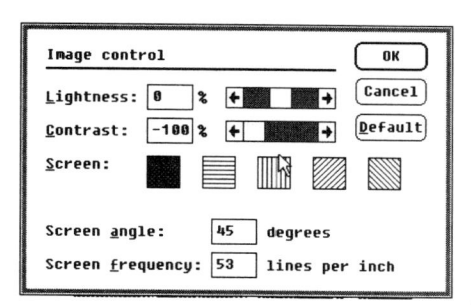

*Figure 9.* The Image control dialog box.

From within the *Image control* dialog box (Figure 9), we can change the lightness and contrast of the selected image quite easily by moving the scroll bars either to the left or to the right. However, in this exercise we are asked only to do two things—change the image to a black and white, and reverse the image.

This can actually be done in one step on the PC. Using the Figure 9 dialog box, simply alter the contrast scroll bar to read -100%. The 100% contrast is to turn it black and white (as opposed to shades of gray), and the - sign is to reverse the image.

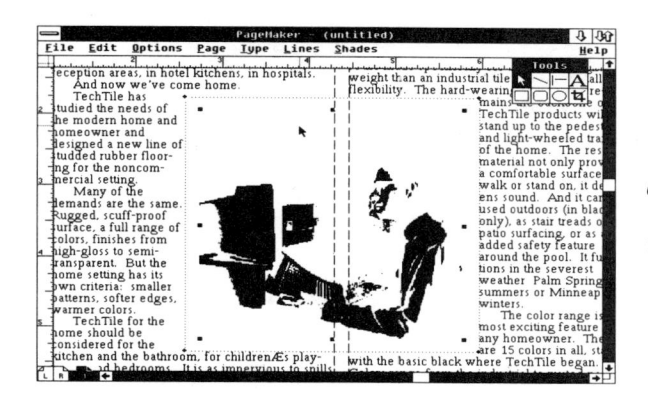

*Figure 10.* Simply change the reading for contrast to -100% by either inserting this number in the contrast reading dialog box, or by moving the white box in the scroll bar all the way to the left.

273

## Module 7 Exercise - PageMaker Advanced Picture Formatting

3. For the second graphics file, TILES.PNT, create a wraparound with this image that will cause the text to wrap irregularly around the image—to hug the image. (See Figure 2 if you are unsure about what we mean here).

Stay in *Actual size* view and move down the page to view the graphic TILES.PNT. Also, select the image so that you can see the handles around the image (Figure 11). There should be two sets of handles around the image.

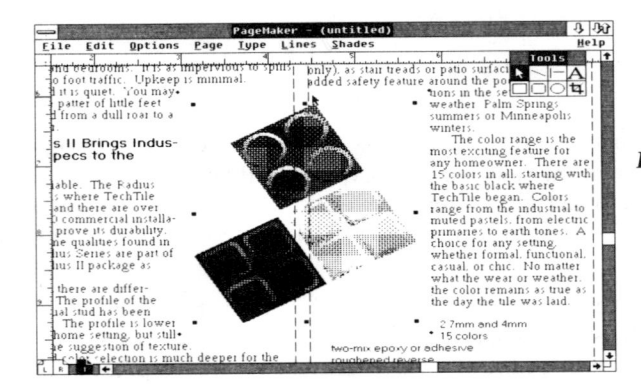

*Figure 11.* TILES. PNT at Actual size view. Note the two sets of handles showing.

The outside diamond handles that are joined by the dotted lines are called *vertexes*. These control the irregular wraparound. We will use these to create our wraparound.

Every time you click the mouse button on the dotted line a new vertex is created. Several of these vertexes will have to be created at strategic points on the dotted line in order to create the wraparound. See Figures 12 to 14 as starting points for turning Figure 11 into Figure 2.

274

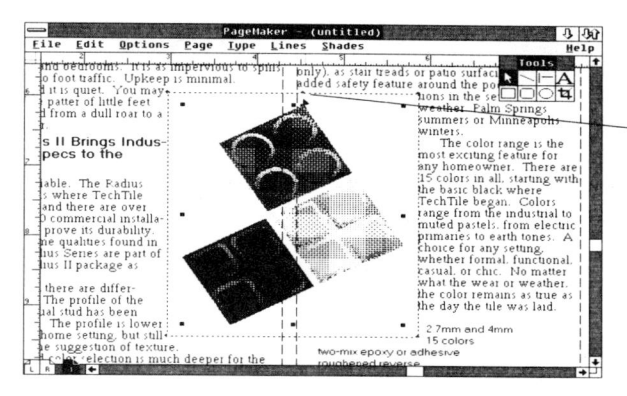

*Module 7 Exercise - PageMaker Advanced Picture Formatting*

***Figure 12.*** *To add a corner or vertex to the dotted line, we simply click on it. In this figure we have added another corner (it looks at the moment like another handle on the dotted line) in the middle of the top horizontal line.*

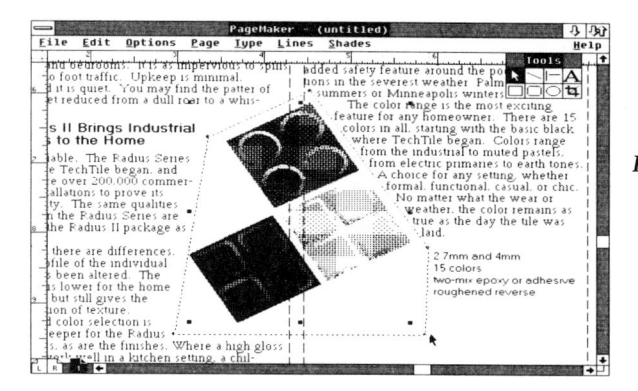

***Figure 13.*** *Here we have moved the handle from the top-right corner down a little.*

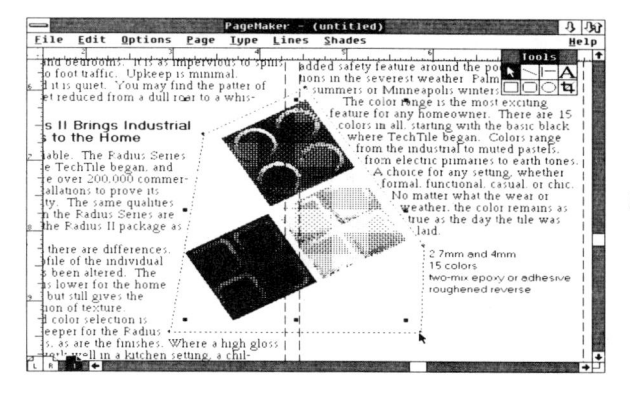

***Figure 14.*** *We are about to move another handle. Continue moving handles and creating vertexes until you get the result shown in Figure 2.*

275

Module 8

# PageMaker Master Pages

# PageMaker Master Pages

## Theory

*Master Pages* are used when text, graphics, page numbers, headers, footers, and whatever must be repeated on many pages throughout the document. They save having to repaste or recreate the same item on multiple pages.

## Master page icons

Along the bottom left-hand corner of the screen are the page number icons. We have looked at these icons before as we changed, created, and deleted pages. However, there are two extra icons that read L and R. These icons stand for the left and right master pages. There will only be one R icon if your document is not set up as a Double-sided publication in the *Page setup* command from the **File** menu. As you click on either of these icons, you will be presented with either one or two blank pages; for two pages to show, you need the Facing pages option selected from the *Page setup* command. These pages are the master pages, and on the screen they look like any other page (Figure 1).

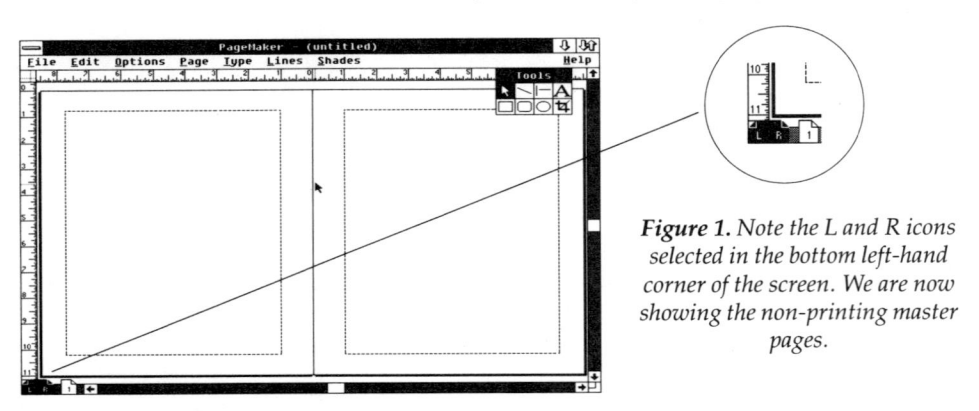

*Figure 1.* Note the L and R icons selected in the bottom left-hand corner of the screen. We are now showing the non-printing master pages.

When presented with the master pages, remember three things. These master pages are exactly like any others in the way graphics, text, and columns, etc., are applied to them. Anything you place on these pages, however, will repeat on all pages throughout the publication. These pages do not print. To print the contents of a master page, you first display them on a standard page and print from there.

## Document changes and guides

These master pages are much like any others—they can have columns applied, have ruler guides inserted, and have their margins altered, either as individual left or right pages, or together. If we apply three columns to the right master page, all right-hand pages in the publication, existing or not, will use these three columns. The same applies to the left-hand page. Consequently, if every page in your 100-page book needs three columns, you only need define these columns on the master pages. You can change these column guides individually on each page after the master pages have been set. This flexibility allows you to change any specific page to look a little different from the others.

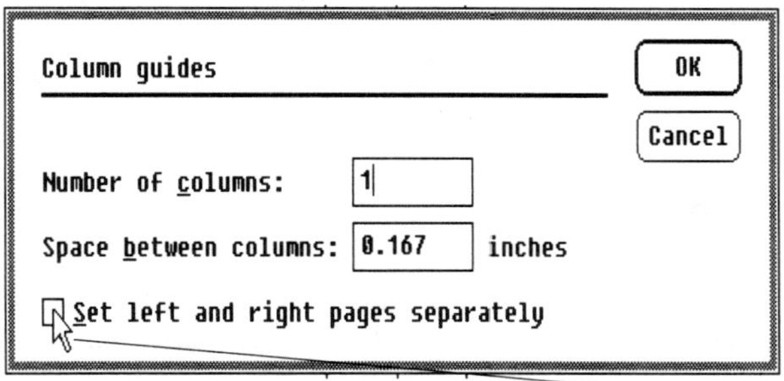

*Figure 2.* Here we are defining the number of column guides for both left and right master pages. This dialog box allows both left and right to be defined in one operation.

If we click the bottom left-hand square, we get the slightly different dialog box of Figure 3.

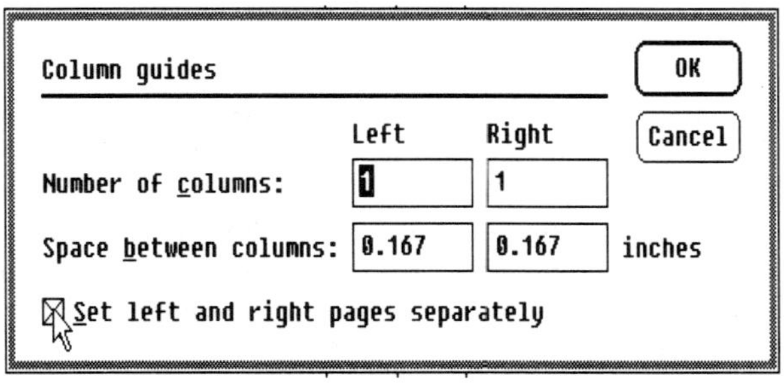

*Figure 3.* In this instance, it is now possible to set different columns for left and right pages.

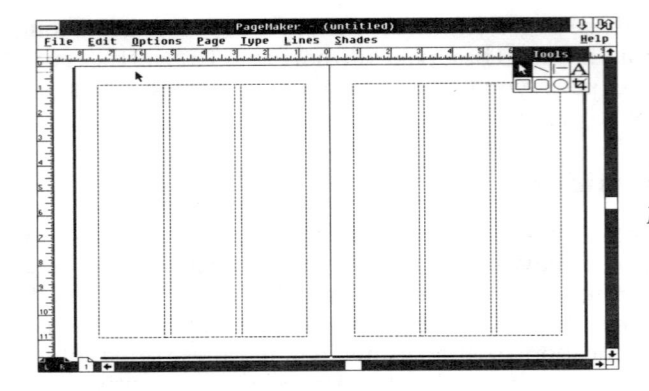

*Figure 4.* These column guides are a result of inserting a 3 for the Number of columns in the Figure 2 dialog box.

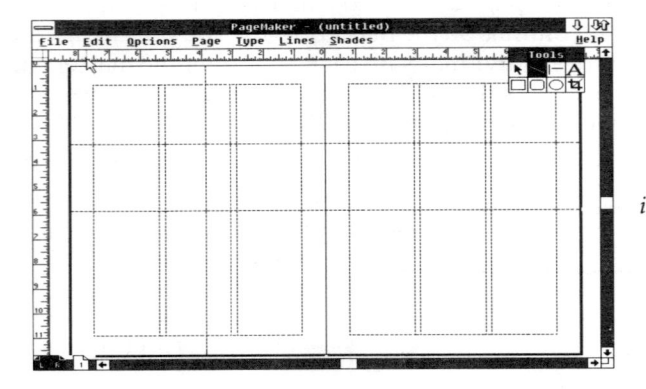

*Figure 5.* One vertical and two horizontal ruler guides have been included on the master pages. These will , like the column guides, appear now on each page.

Any non-printing margin guides and/or ruler guides added to these pages will also be seen on all corresponding pages in the publication (Figure 5).

## Text and graphics additions

As you might have guessed, any text or graphics that are placed on the master pages (which is done in exactly the same way they are placed on any page in the document) will repeat on every page. In this way a company logo, motto, and/or address and phone number, can be placed on one or both of the master pages. These will then repeat exactly as they appear on the master pages on every page in the document. Borders for pages can also use master pages effectively.

*Module 8 - PageMaker Master Pages*

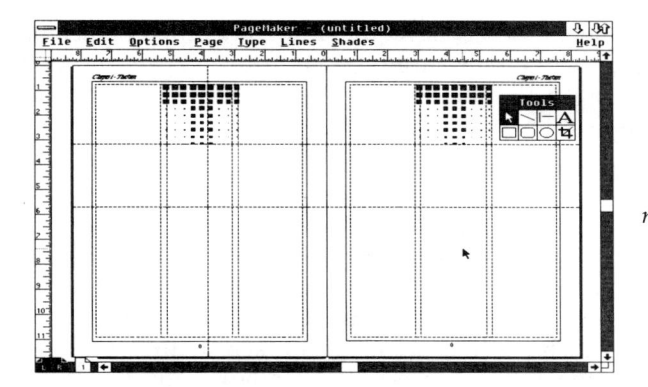

*Figure 6.* We have just placed the graphic LOGO.PNT onto both master pages and sized it as shown.

## Headers, footers, and page numbers

*Headers* and *footers* are the repeating bits of information that appear at the top and bottom of every page in a book or magazine. These often include such items as the book name, chapter name, chapter number, date, and/or page number. To define these items for a document, simply create them on the master pages.

In Figure 7, we are positioned in *Actual size* view at the top-left corner of the left master page. A heading that we would like repeated on each page has been keyed in.

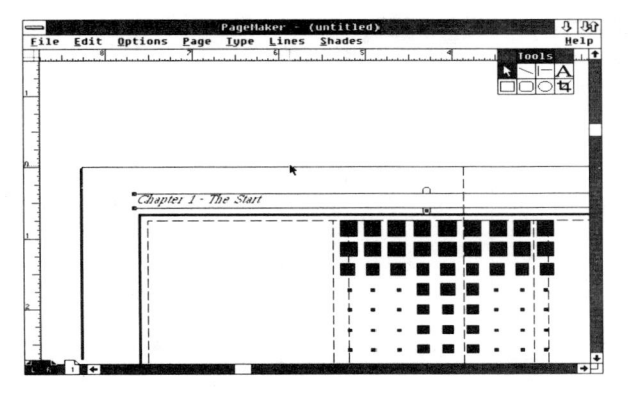

*Figure 7.* A header, "Chapter 1— The Start" has been keyed in and placed just above the border on the top left-hand corner of the left master page.

We have also keyed in the same header on the top right-hand corner of the right master page.

*Module 8 - PageMaker Master Pages*

Page numbers, however, require a slightly different technique. This is because they need to be updated on every page throughout the publication. Putting a number on the master page will result in that same number being literally translated on every page.

To achieve an automatically updated page number, instead of typing the actual number, hold down the Ctrl and Shift keys, and type a 3 (you must first select the text (A) tool from the Toolbox, and place it on the page where you want the page number to appear). On the master page, this will appear as the numeral zero (Figure 8), but will appear as the correct number on all other pages (Figure 11). The correct number is taken as the number that appears on that page's icon box. To alter the number that this uses, select the *Page setup* command in the **File** menu, and see the instructions given in Figure 10.

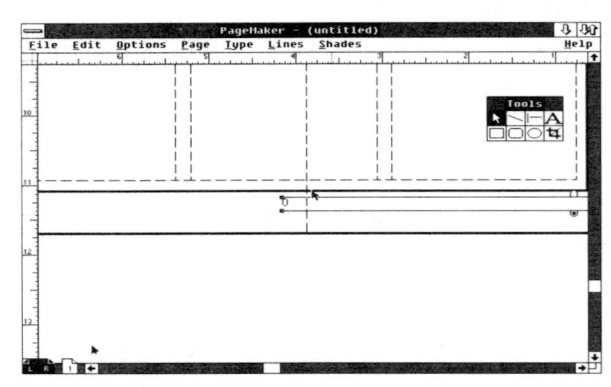

*Figure 8.* An automatic page number has been added to the bottom of a master page. It always shows as the symbol zero on the master page. This is achieved by inserting the mouse cursor and pressing Ctrl-Shift-3, when in text mode.

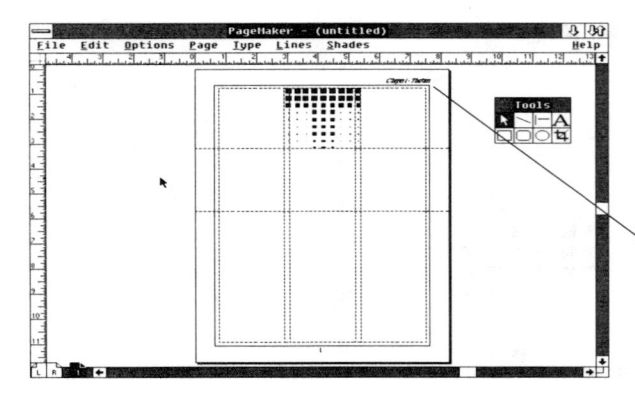

*Figure 9.* Page 1 is now displayed and includes all the master items from the master page—column guides, ruler guides, graphics, headers, and footers. As page 1 is a right-hand page, the header is shown on the right-hand side.

282

*Module 8 - PageMaker Master Pages*

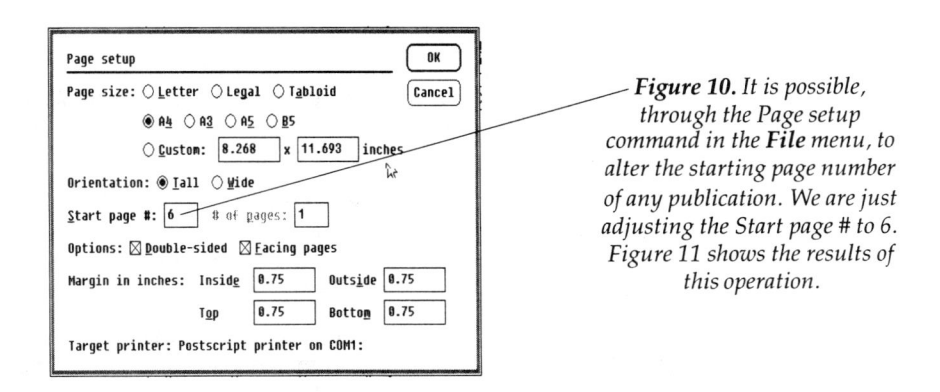

*Figure 10. It is possible, through the Page setup command in the **File** menu, to alter the starting page number of any publication. We are just adjusting the Start page # to 6. Figure 11 shows the results of this operation.*

Composite page numbers are also possible—whereby additional information is included with the basic page number. This can include such items as the word page, or chapter numbering such as 4-1, 8-7, etc. Let's say, for example, we would like to preface all page numbers with the chapter number 8. This is done by typing 8- in front of the Ctrl-Shift-3 (auto page number) combination on the master pages.

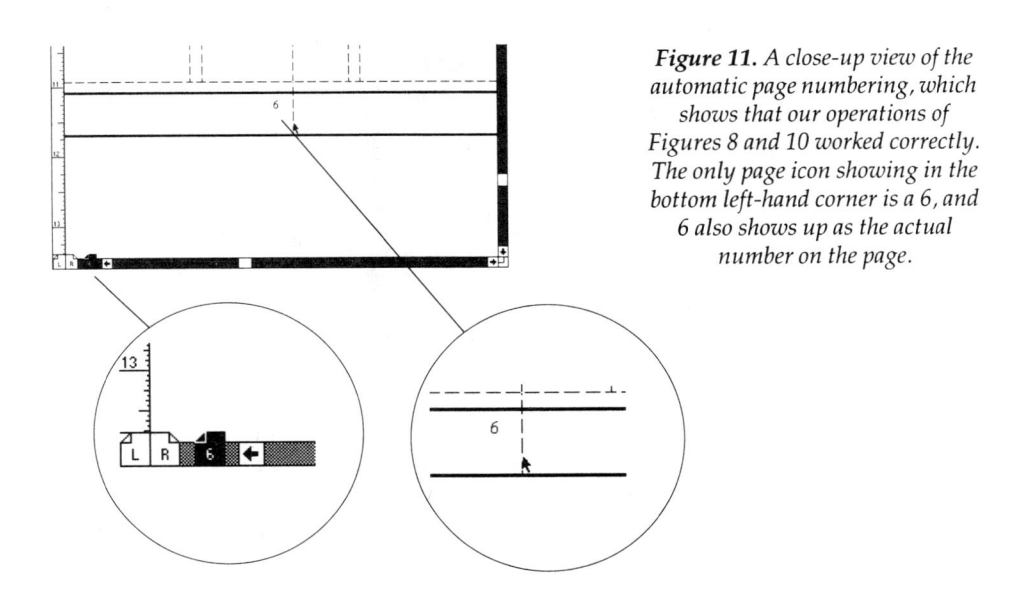

*Figure 11. A close-up view of the automatic page numbering, which shows that our operations of Figures 8 and 10 worked correctly. The only page icon showing in the bottom left-hand corner is a 6, and 6 also shows up as the actual number on the page.*

*Module 8 - PageMaker Master Pages*

## Removing master items

There will, of course, always be pages where master items, such as logos, headers, and footers, will not be needed. The first page in a book, for example, rarely uses a header or footer.

If you move to a normal page that you do not want master items to appear on, you will notice that text or graphic items cannot be deleted simply by selecting and deleting them. As a matter of fact, you will notice they cannot be selected at all.

There are three ways to remove master items from a particular page. Any guides, whether they be column, ruler, or margin guides, can be moved out of the way as if they were created on the page. Unlike text or graphics, these master items can be changed or moved.

One or more master elements can be hidden from view by drawing a white box over them (this is particularly useful when you wish to remove some master elements from a page, but not all). This is illustrated in Figure 12.

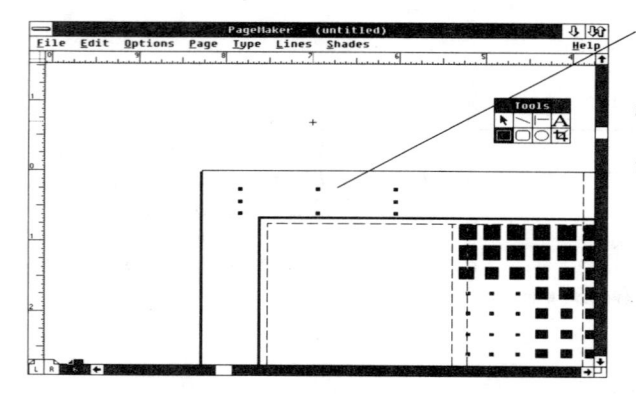

*Figure 12.* This is a white graphics box (only the selection handles are shown) which has been drawn over the master page header. This item is thus removed from the page without upsetting any other master items.
The white box is achieved by choosing None from the **Lines** menu and Paper from the **Shades** menu.
As we are showing page 6 (even page), the the header is on the left.

Finally, if you wish to remove all master items from a particular page, you must deselect the *Display master items* command in the **Page** menu (Figure 13). The result of this is shown in Figure 14.

Any pages that do not use the master items will still be included in the page number count.

284

*Module 8 - PageMaker Master Pages*

As we said above, it is possible to readjust non-printing master guides (column and/or ruler guides) on any actual page. If you wish to revert back to the guides from the master page, select the *Copy master guides* command from the **Page** menu. All relevant non-printing guides will then reappear on your page.

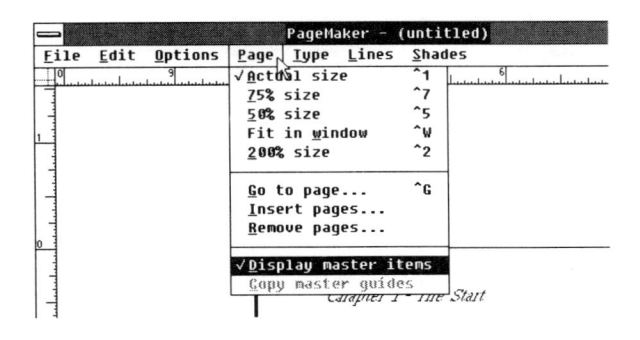

*Figure 13.* The Display master items command removes all master items from your page. The result is shown in Figure 14.

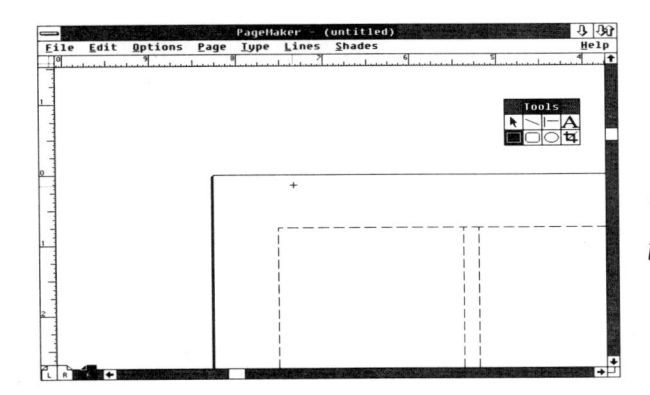

*Figure 14.* The result of using the command of Figure 13. All master items are deleted. They can be brought back by simply reselecting the same command.

285

Module 8 Exercise

# PageMaker Master Pages

# Module 8 Exercise
# PageMaker Master Pages

In this exercise we are going to utilize master pages to set up headers, footers, and column guides. We will then remove master items from selected pages and also change column guides. This is an involved exercise which combines techniques from many of the modules we have already looked at.

This training material is structured so that people of all levels of expertise with PageMaker can use it to gain maximum benefit. In order to do this, we have structured this material so that the bare exercise is listed below this paragraph on just one page, with no hints. The following pages contain the steps needed to complete this exercise for those that need additional prompting. The **PageMaker Master Pages** module should be referenced if you need further help or explanations.

## Module 8 exercise steps

1. Set up a publication with the following specifications: Letter size, Tall, four pages, Double-sided, Facing pages, and 0.75 inch margins all around.

2. Go to master pages to set up left page headers and footers as follows: (a) July 1988, flush left header; (b) DTP Newsletter, flush right header; (c) page number, centered footer. All this text to be Times, 10 point, italic.

3. Set right master pages in mirror image format to that of step 2.

4. Set left and right master pages in two-column format with 1 point intercolumn rules.

5. Go to page 1 and load PHOTO.TIF (GETSTART subdirectory) into the bottom half of the page.

6. Load BROCHURE.DOC (GETSTART subdirectory) using Autoflow method onto pages 1 and 2. Make sure it jumps over the photo.

7. Load BULLETIN.DOC (GETSTART subdirectory) using Autoflow method, starting from top of column 2 on page 2.

8. Remove master item header from page 1 (but not footer).

9. Change column guides on page 3 from two to three columns and adjust text to fit.

10. Remove master items from pages 2 and 3.

11. Change column guides on page 3 back to two columns without using the Column guides command.

The steps for completing this exercise are on the following pages.

*Module 8 Exercise - PageMaker Master Pages*

# The steps in detail.

1. Set up a publication with the following specifications: Letter size, Tall, four pages, Double-sided, Facing pages, and 0.75 inch margins all around.

After choosing *New* from the **File** menu, set up the publication details in the *Page setup* dialog box as shown in Figure 1.

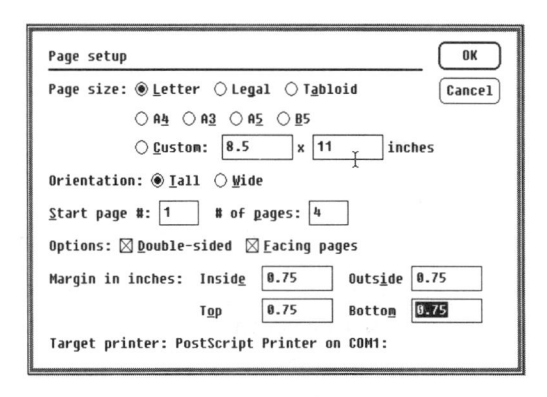

*Figure 1.* The initial Page setup dialog box should be filled in to these exact specifications.

2. Go to master pages to set up left page headers and footers as follows: (a) July 1988, flush left header; (b) DTP Newsletter, flush right header; (c) page number, centered footer. All this text to be Times, 10 point, italic.

Figure 2 shows the left-hand master page with the flush left and flush right headers in place. They were simply created with the text (A) tool and placed 0.5 inches below the top of the page.

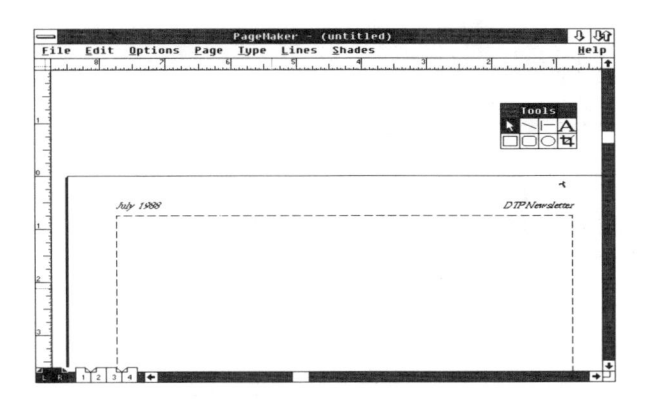

*Figure 2.* The top of the left-hand master page is displayed in 75% view showing the two headers.

289

*Module 8 Exercise - PageMaker Master Pages*

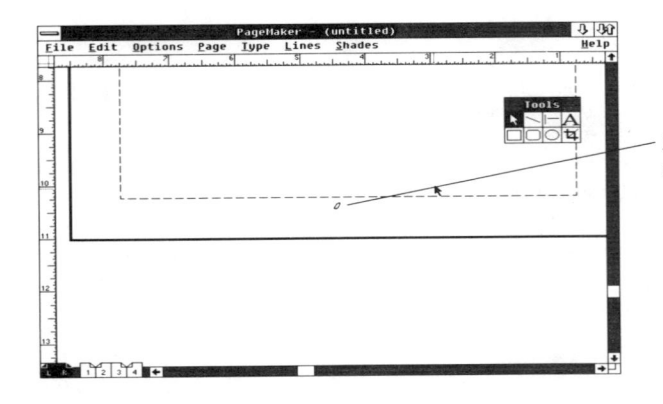

*Figure 3. The Ctrl-Shift-3 automatic page number combination always shows up on the master pages as a zero.*

The page number was then inserted in the middle of the left master page as a footer using the Ctrl-Shift-3 special combination (after the text cursor had been inserted). Figure 3 shows the result in *Actual size* view. This special page number key combination always appears as a zero on the master pages.

Select each block of header and footer text and use the *Type specs* command in the **Type** menu to set these headers and footers in Times, 10 point, italics.

3. *Set right master pages in mirror image format to that of step 2.*

On the right master page, July 1988 should be flush right, and DTP Newsletter flush left. Figure 4 shows the result. The page number footer will still be in the middle of the page, as in Figure 3.

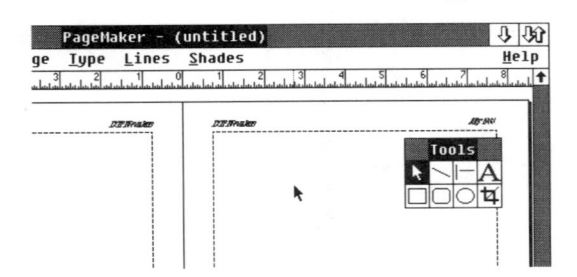

*Figure 4. This is an expanded view of the right master page which is now set up with mirror image headers. Compare this with Figure 2.*

Module 8 Exercise - PageMaker Master Pages

4. Set left and right master pages in two-column format with 1 point intercolumn rules.

To set two columns, we go to the *Column guides* command in the **Options** menu and select two columns. The intercolumn guides are drawn using the perpendicular-line drawing tool selected from the Toolbox. It is wise to turn off the *Snap to guides* option in the **Options** menu when drawing the intercolumn rules (Figure 5). This allows the vertical line to be drawn between the columns without it snapping to either of the column guides. The line thickness of 1 point is chosen from the **Lines** menu. Figure 6 shows the final results for both master pages in *Fit in window* view.

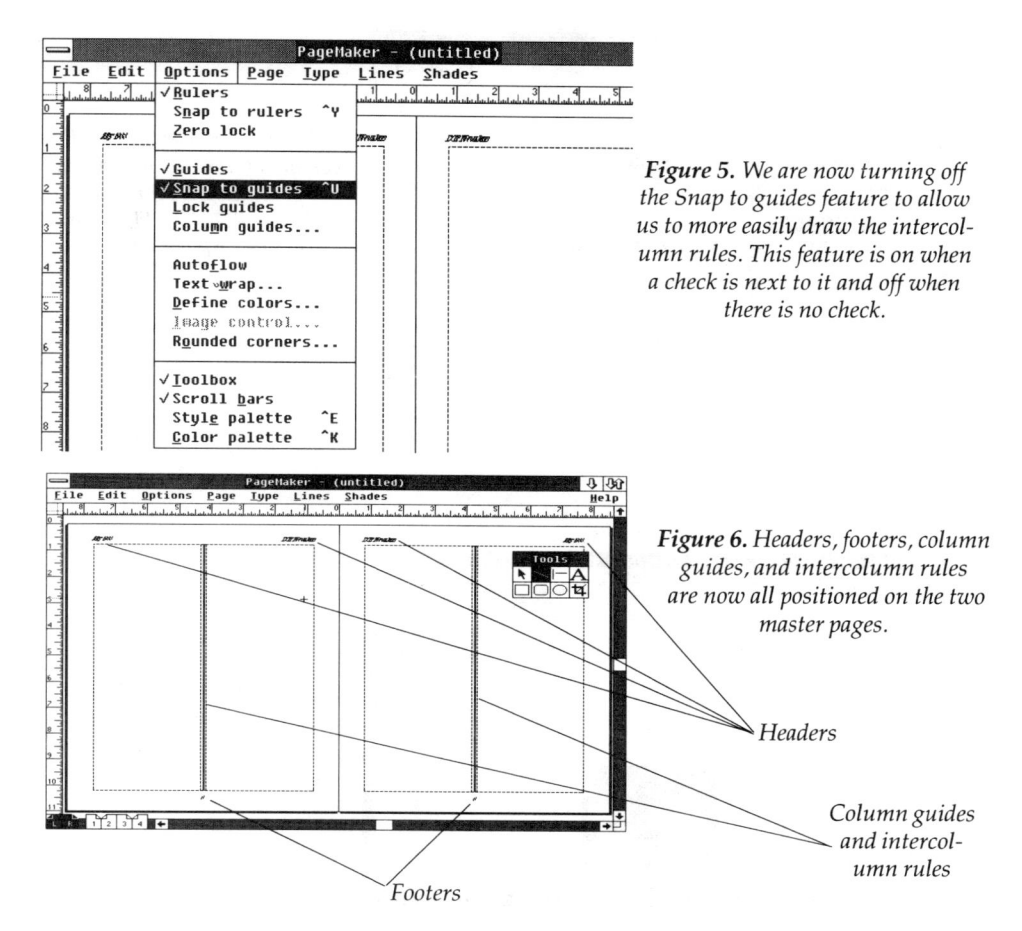

*Figure 5.* We are now turning off the Snap to guides feature to allow us to more easily draw the intercolumn rules. This feature is on when a check is next to it and off when there is no check.

*Figure 6.* Headers, footers, column guides, and intercolumn rules are now all positioned on the two master pages.

Headers

Column guides and intercolumn rules

Footers

291

*Module 8 Exercise - PageMaker Master Pages*

5. *Go to page 1 and load PHOTO.TIF (GETSTART subdirectory) into the bottom half of the page.*

Click on the page 1 icon in the bottom left-hand corner of the screen. Choose the *Place* command from the **File** menu and select PHOTO.TIF from within the GETSTART subdirectory (Figure 7). Paste this picture into page 1 by drawing an imaginary box with your cursor before clicking the mouse button. Position the box at approximately the same position and same size as we have done in Figure 8.

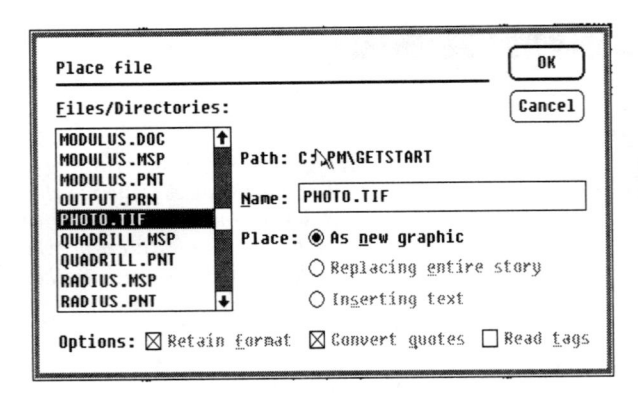

*Figure 7. By selecting the Place command from the **File** menu, we are provided with this dialog box. Choose PHOTO.TIF from the GETSTART subdirectory.*

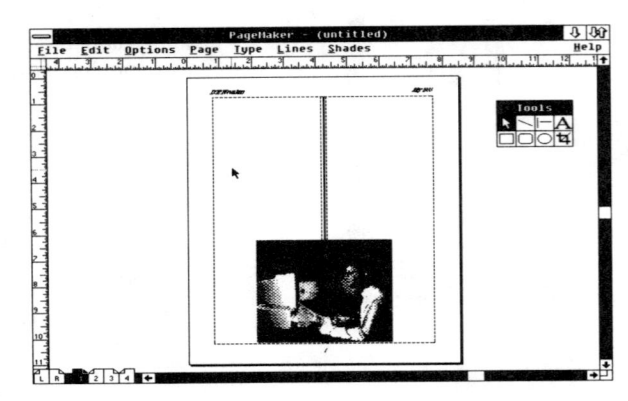

*Figure 8. Put PHOTO.TIF on page 1 at approximately this size and in this position.*

292

*Module 8 Exercise - PageMaker Master Pages*

6. Load BROCHURE.DOC (GETSTART subdirectory) using Autoflow method onto pages 1 and 2. Make sure it jumps over the photo.

Before we select BROCHURE.DOC, we should select the picture on page 1, and specify the correct picture wrap attributes. As we want the text to jump right over the graphic, we should choose the options as shown in Figure 9. This dialog box is accessed through the *Text wrap* command in the **Options** menu.

Now, choose the *Place* command from the **File** menu, and from the associated dialog box (Figure 10), select BROCHURE.DOC from the GETSTART subdirectory. Flow this text onto pages 1 and 2 using the *Autoflow* command (make sure the *Autoflow* command has a check next to it in the **Options** menu). The results of this autoflow are shown in Figures 11 and 12.

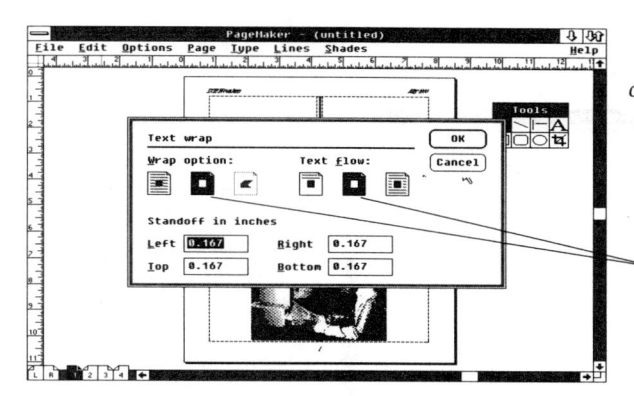

*Figure 9.* To make the text jump over the picture in page 1, we need to choose these two options in the Text wrap dialog box from the **Options** menu.

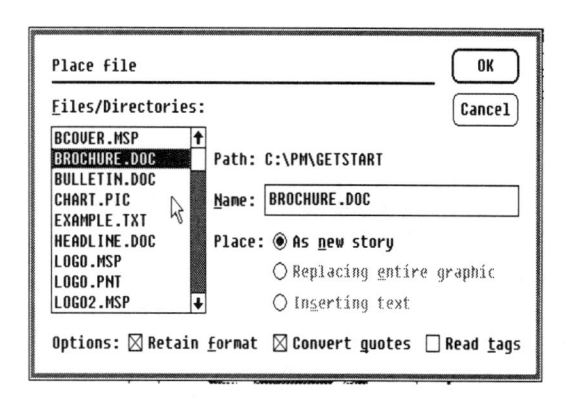

*Figure 10.* This is the Place dialog box again. We are now choosing BROCHURE.DOC from the GETSTART subdirectory.

293

Module 8 Exercise - PageMaker Master Pages

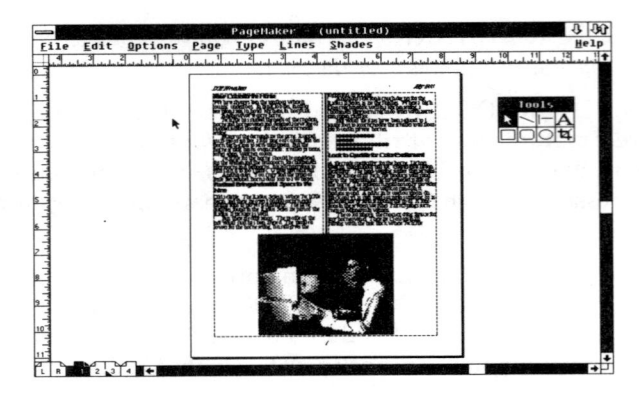

*Figure 11.* BROCHURE.DOC has flowed onto page 1 and has completely jumped over our picture. This is because of our settings of Figure 9.

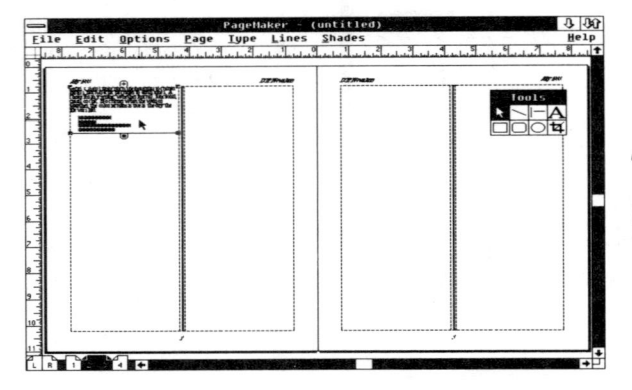

*Figure 12.* As we used the Autoflow method to flow the text, BROCHURE.DOC has flowed automatically onto page 2. Depending on the size of your picture in page 1, your text may take up more or less space than ours. In fact, if your picture size was too small, your text may not even flow onto page 2.

7. Load BULLETIN.DOC (GETSTART subdirectory) using Autoflow method, starting from top of column 2 on page 2.

BULLETIN.DOC is accessed through the *Place* command dialog box. Figure 13 shows its selection. Figure 14 indicates the position at the top of column 2 of page 2 to start flowing this new text file. Note the Autoflow cursor at the top of the column. Figure 15 shows the results of flowing the text.

*Module 8 Exercise - PageMaker Master Pages*

*Figure 13.* BULLETIN.DOC is found in the GETSTART subdirectory accessed through the Place command.

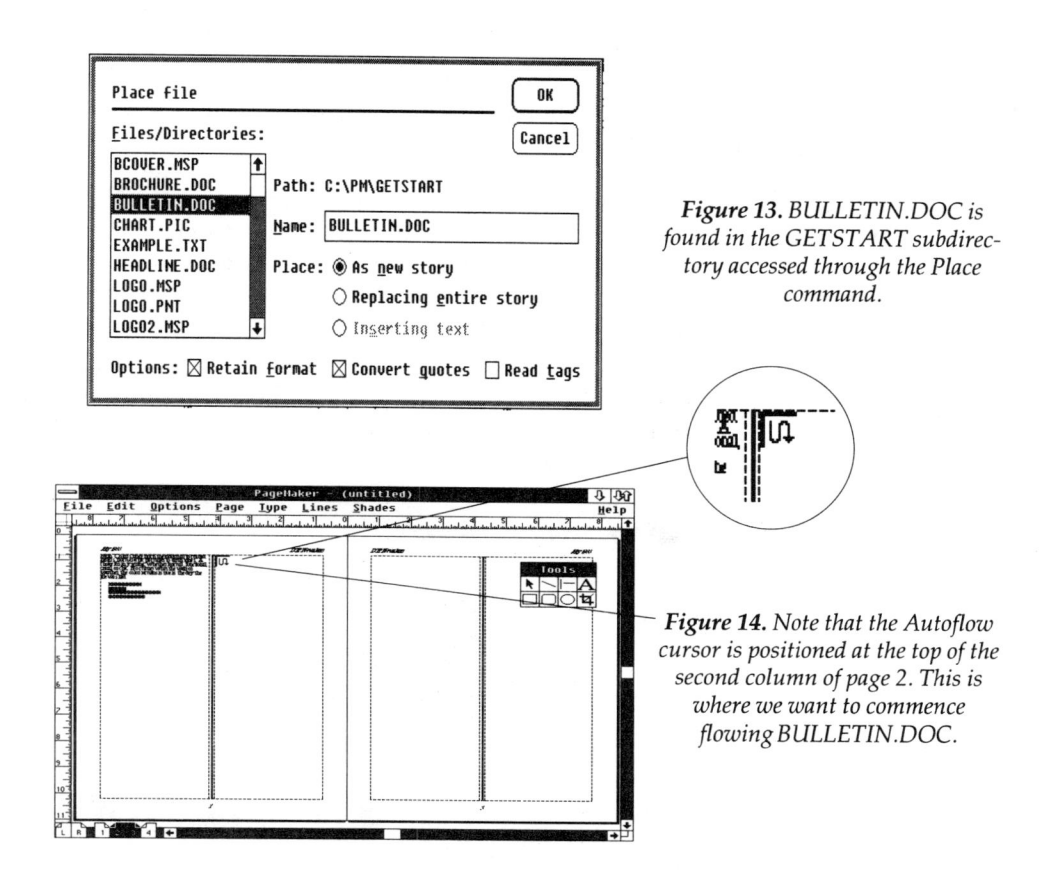

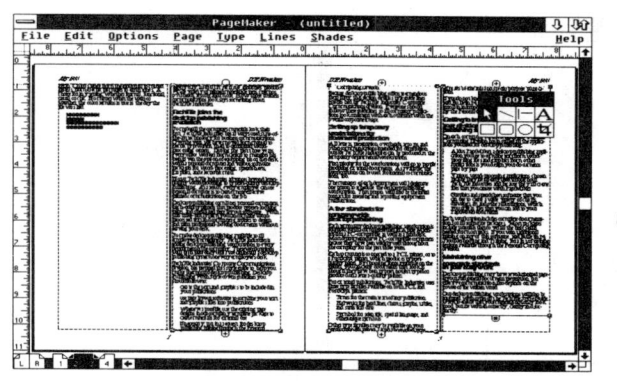

*Figure 14.* Note that the Autoflow cursor is positioned at the top of the second column of page 2. This is where we want to commence flowing BULLETIN.DOC.

*Figure 15.* This is how your pages 2 and 3 should look after flowing BULLETIN.DOC. This text may also flow automatically onto page 4. If it does, just select pages 2 and 3 again through the page icons.

*Module 8 Exercise - PageMaker Master Pages*

*8. Remove master item headers from page 1 (but not footer).*

Under the **Page** menu, we have a command called *Display master items*. When this command is selected (has a check alongside it) all master items are displayed on the page currently being viewed. When it is not selected, no master items are displayed. In this step we have been asked to remove only some of the master items. This command, therefore, cannot be used, as it hides or shows all master items. The simple way to perform this step is to draw boxes around the flush left and right headers, and make the box shade *Paper* (through the **Shades** menu) and the lines *None* (through the **Lines** menu).

This is shown in Figures 16 and 17, where we can see box selection handles, but no box. This *Paper* (white) box completely covers the two headers. As these boxes are white and have no lines, they will not appear on the printout, but will still cover the two headers.

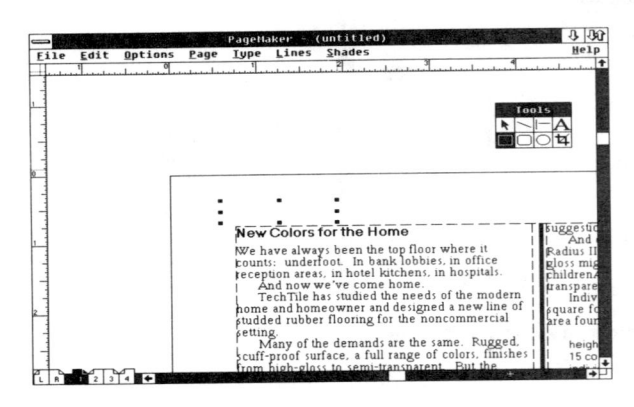

*Figure 16.* We are on page 1 and looking at the top left-hand corner where our flush left header should be. It cannot be seen because we have drawn a box over it, and shaded the box Paper from the **Shades** menu, and made its lines None from the **Lines** menu. The selection handles, however, can still be seen.

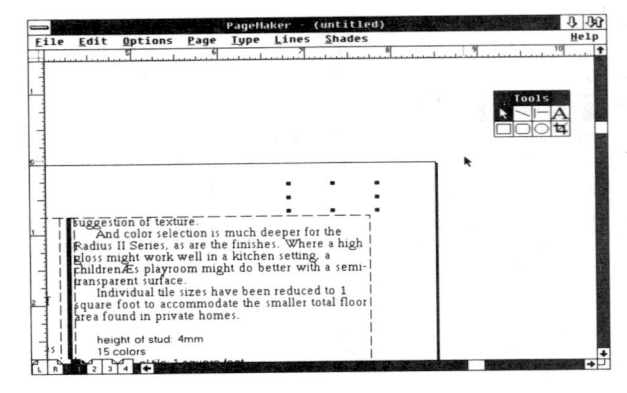

*Figure 17.* Similar to Figure 16, we have drawn the same sort of box around the right header on page 1. The selection handles can be plainly seen.

*Module 8 Exercise - PageMaker Master Pages*

9. *Change column guides on page 3 from two to three columns, and adjust text to fit.*

This step is best explained by pictures. Please read the captions associated with Figures 18 to 24. Remember to move to pages 2 and 3 first.

*Figure 18.* This is the dialog box that results from choosing the Column guides command in the **Options** menu. We are changing the right page figure (page 3) from two to three columns.

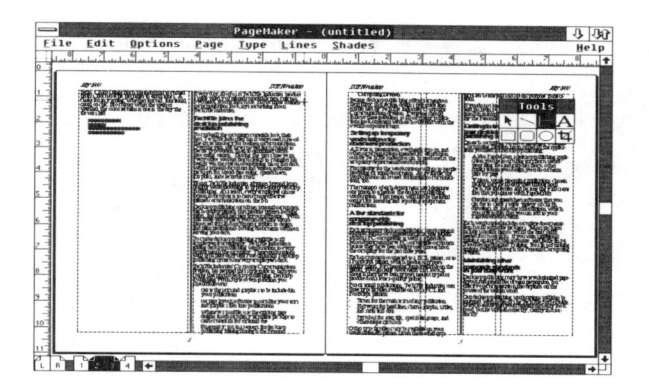

*Figure 19.* Note that page 3 is now showing column guides for three columns in the background of the text. If column guides are changed, as we have just done, the original text still remains in its old format. We need to manually change it, as shown in the following figures.

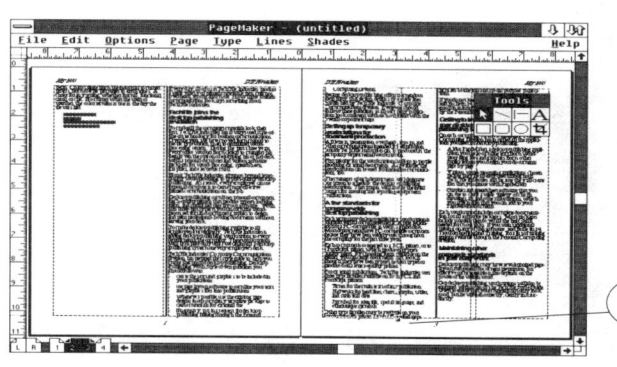

*Figure 20.* We first select the text in column 1 of page 3 with the pointer tool. Next, grab the bottom right-hand corner handle and drag the text to the left to align with the new column guides. The cursor turns into a two-headed diagonal arrow as shown here.

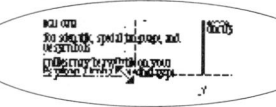

297

*Module 8 Exercise - PageMaker Master Pages*

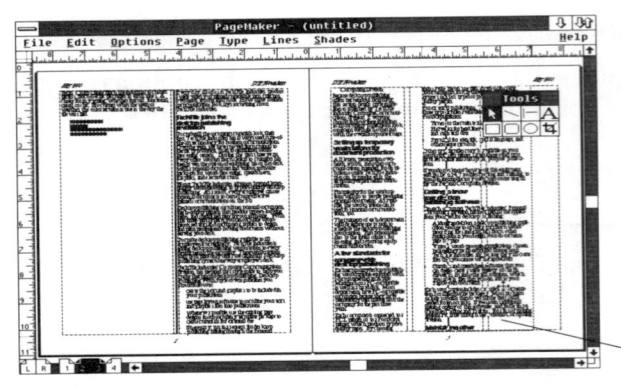

*Figure 21.* The left column of the right-hand page is now aligned. We are in the process of moving the old second column text over to the new middle column to align the text's left-hand boundary with the middle column's left column guide.

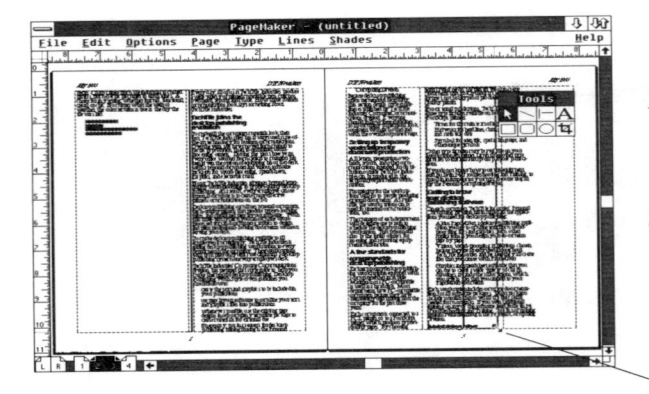

*Figure 22.* The second text column is now aligned with the left-hand margin of the middle column. As this text is too wide, we are in the process of reducing its width using the same procedure as outlined in Figure 20. Note again the two-headed diagonal cursor.

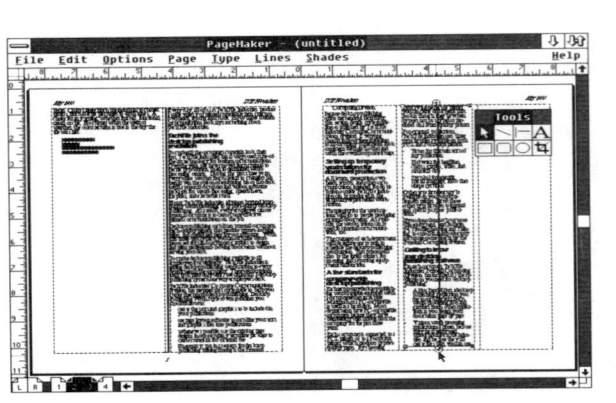

*Figure 23.* The second text column is now adjusted to the same width as the column guides. All we need to do now is select this block with our pointer tool, click on the bottom handle, and reflow more text down the third column. The result is shown in Figure 24.

*Module 8 Exercise - PageMaker Master Pages*

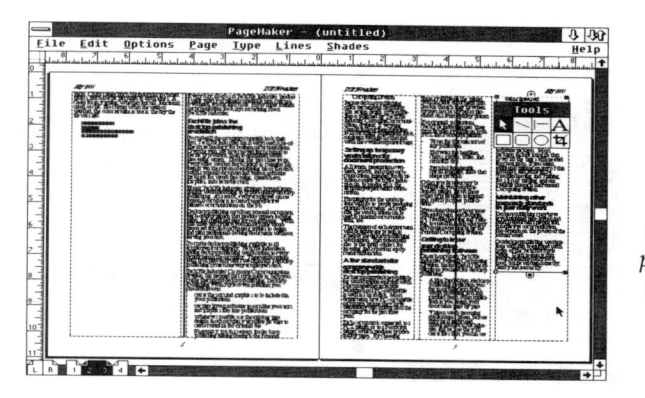

*Figure 24.* *The text now flows correctly down the three new columns on page 3. Note the problem, however—the intercolumn rule drawn for two columns per page on the master page is still showing through the text. This is fixed in the next step.*

10. *Remove master items from pages 2 and 3.*

As we mentioned in step 8 above, the *Display master items* command from the **Page** menu can be used to show or hide (as a group) all master items on any page. We will now select that command (Figure 25). It shows as a check in this figure, indicating that it was already selected. We are currently deselecting it.

The result is indicated in Figure 26. Note that, not only have we removed the intercolumn rule showing in Figure 24, but also have removed the headers and footers on both pages.

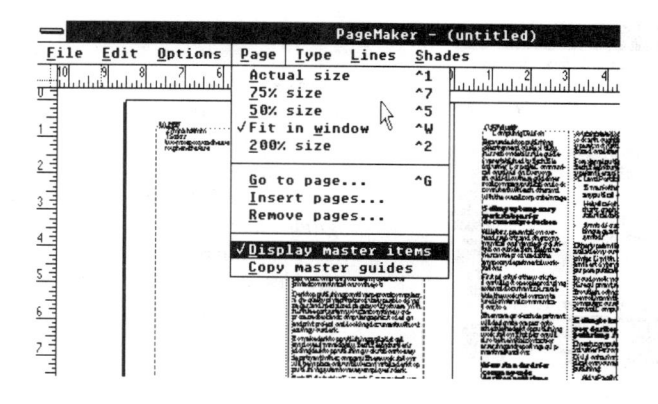

*Figure 25.* *This is the Display master items command which allows us to show or hide items from master pages.*

299

Module 8 Exercise - PageMaker Master Pages

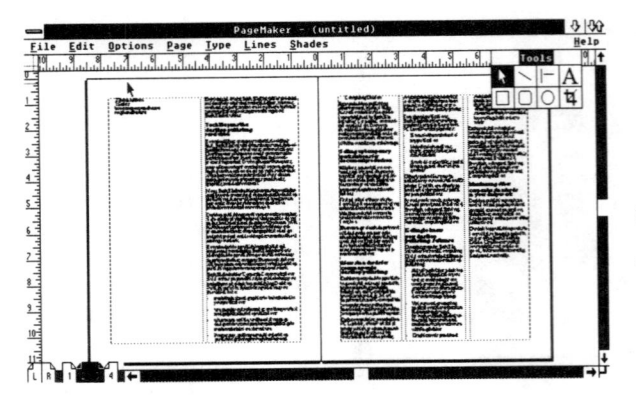

*Figure 26. Here are pages 2 and 3 without master items showing. Note the headers and footers are missing, as well as the intercolumn rules.*
*This figure is the result of choosing the command in Figure 25.*

11. Change column guides on page 3 back to two columns without using the Column guides command.

This step reverses what we were doing in step 9. Again, it is better described in pictures. Please refer to Figures 27 to 31 for details.

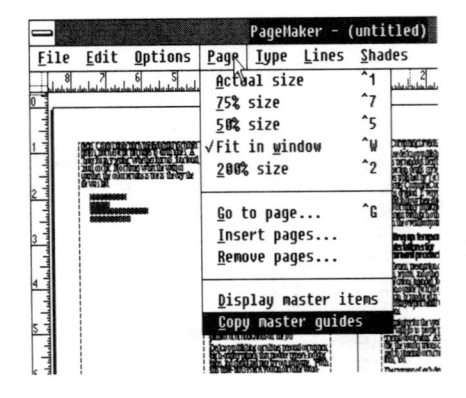

*Figure 27. As our master pages were set up with two columns, it is possible to display those column guides back onto our page 3 without going through the Column guides command. We just choose, as shown here, the Copy master guides command from the **Page** menu.*

300

*Module 8 Exercise - PageMaker Master Pages*

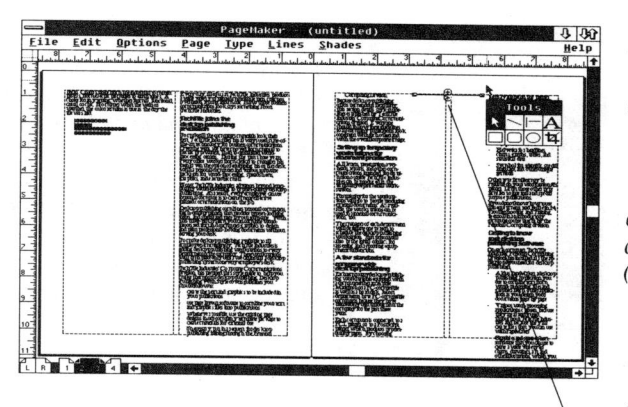

*Figure 28.* Column guides have now changed back to 2 after Figure 27. We then selected the middle column with our pointer tool and dragged it right to the top of the column. By then clicking anywhere on the page, this column disappears (without, however, losing any text).

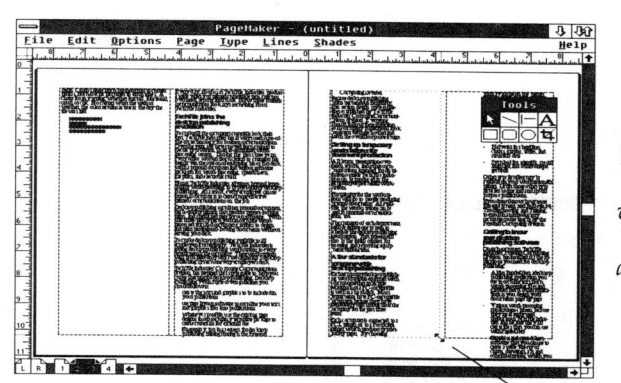

*Figure 29.* Now select the first column of page 3 with the pointer tool. Grab the bottom right-hand handle and pull the text column to the right to widen it to the full width of the two columns. Note the two-arrow diagonal cursor that appears as you are moving the text.

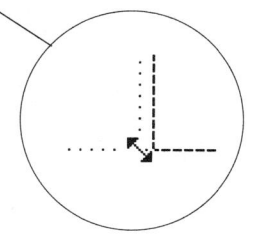

*Module 8 Exercise - PageMaker Master Pages*

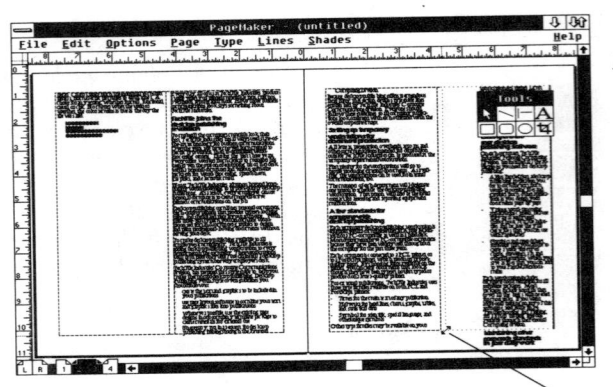

*Figure 30.* The first column on page 3 is now correct. Select the second text column and move it so that its left margin aligns with the left margin of the second column. We are in the process of doing just that in this figure by grabbing the bottom left-hand corner with the mouse, and moving it towards the left margin of the second column.

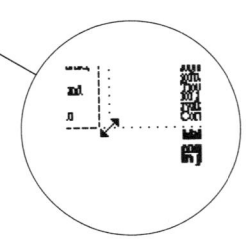

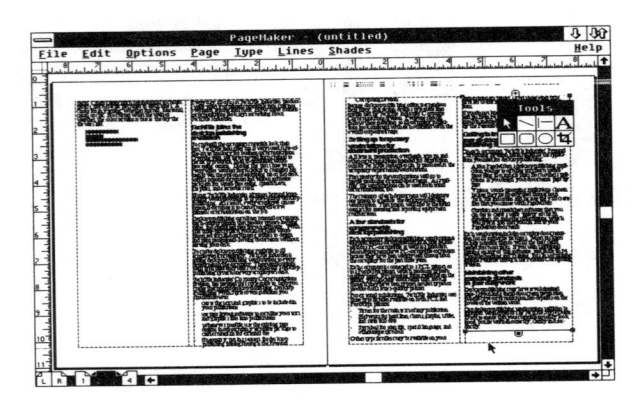

*Figure 31.* The second column is now correctly aligned.

# Module 9

# PageMaker Templates

# PageMaker Templates

The idea of PageMaker templates is to save you time and effort in creating new publications. You do not have to recreate the format of a document if that format exists elsewhere. The way this works is quite simple.

*Templates* are like partially created publications—publications that can be used over and over again without destroying the original. Let's say, for example, that every month you create a company newsletter. The specifications for this newsletter may be: eight pages, A4 page, two columns on pages 1–6, three columns on pages 7 and 8, a border around all pages, vertical rules between all columns, headers and footers, numbered pages, etc.

Initially, this would be set up from scratch in the normal way, and would take a little time. Once done, however, with all these attributes saved as a template, this template could be used as the starting point for the next month's newsletter. By using this approach, you can now spend more time concentrating on the content of the newsletter rather than the format, because the format is already created.

PageMaker 3.0 contains a library of twenty templates, covering a wide range of publication types that can be used as starting points for documents. You can either use these templates as they are, modify them slightly to meet your needs, or simply create your own.

## Creating templates

Initially, creating templates is done in exactly the same way as creating a typical publication. The *New* command is selected, as many pages as you need are added, the margins and columns are defined, and text and graphics added where necessary. This is briefly summarized in Figures 1 to 5. The difference comes when the document is saved.

*Module 9 - PageMaker Templates*

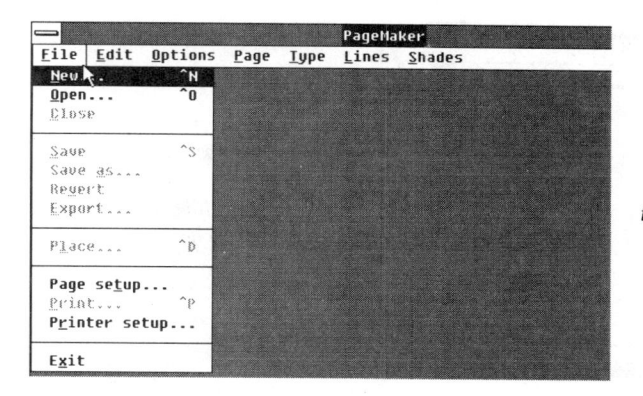

*Figure 1.* We are going to look at the steps in creating a simple template. Start off as you normally would—by selecting the New command from the **File** menu.

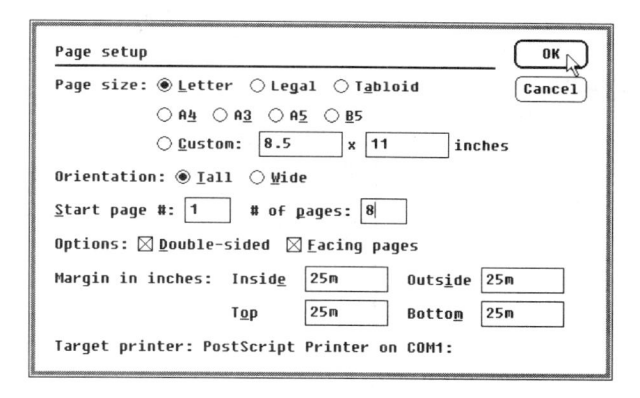

*Figure 2.* Define the page in the Page setup command. In this case we have set the number of pages, new margins, etc.

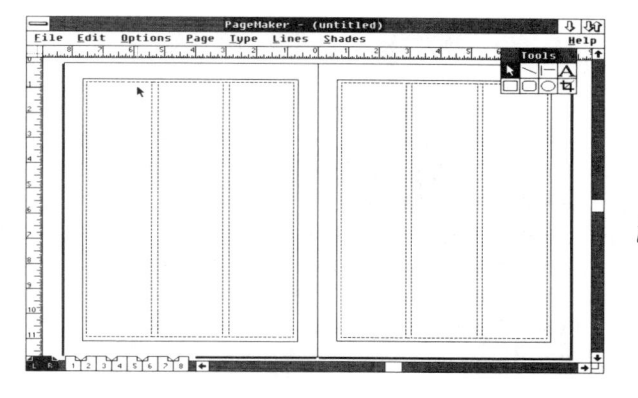

*Figure 3.* Once the document opens, set up all the document formatting—number of columns, borders, intercolumn rules, etc., in the master pages.

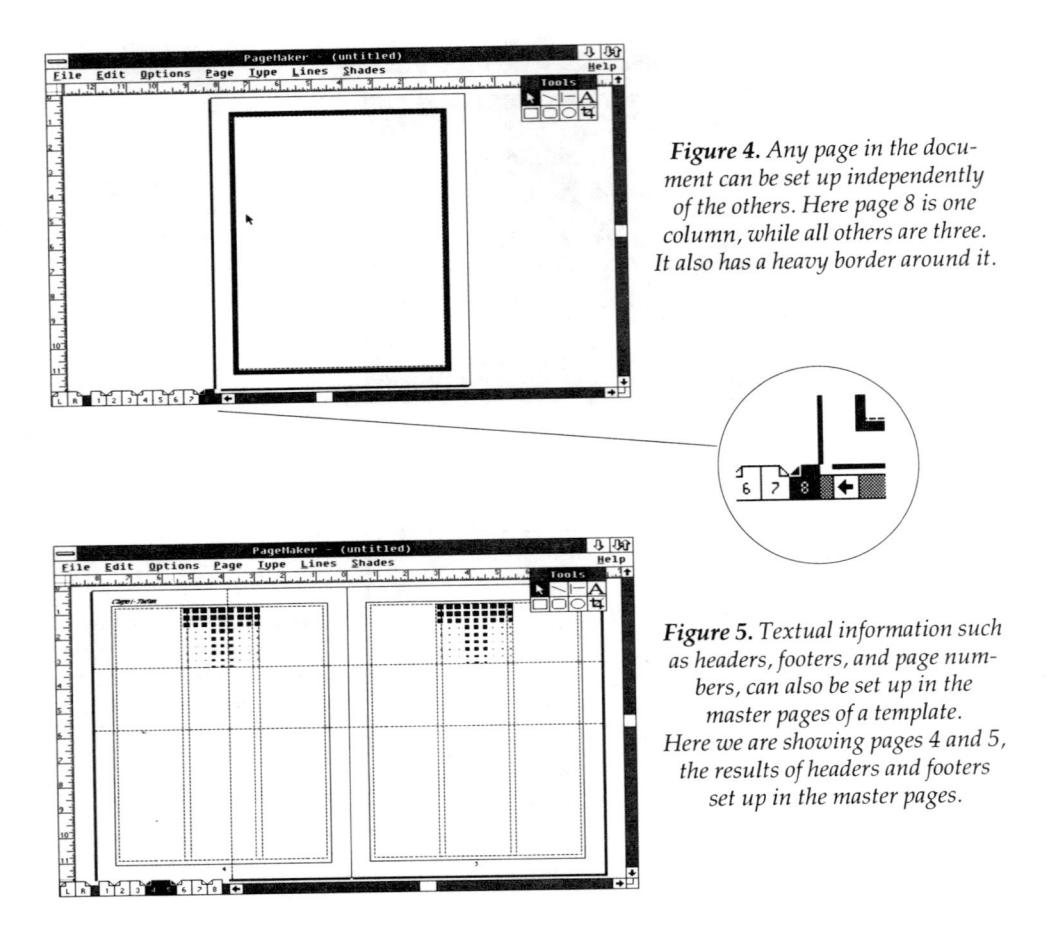

*Module 9 - PageMaker Templates*

**Figure 4.** *Any page in the document can be set up independently of the others. Here page 8 is one column, while all others are three. It also has a heavy border around it.*

**Figure 5.** *Textual information such as headers, footers, and page numbers, can also be set up in the master pages of a template. Here we are showing pages 4 and 5, the results of headers and footers set up in the master pages.*

Whenever you choose the *Save* command for the first time (Figure 6), or the *Save as* command from the **File** menu, you are presented with the dialog box of Figure 7. The name is entered as usual (in our case NEWSLET), but the difference comes in the little option in the bottom right-hand corner of the dialog box. Here you have a choice as to how to save the document—either as a traditional *Publication* (this will be selected by default) or as a *Template*. If you choose Template, this PageMaker file then takes on special qualities.

*Module 9 - PageMaker Templates*

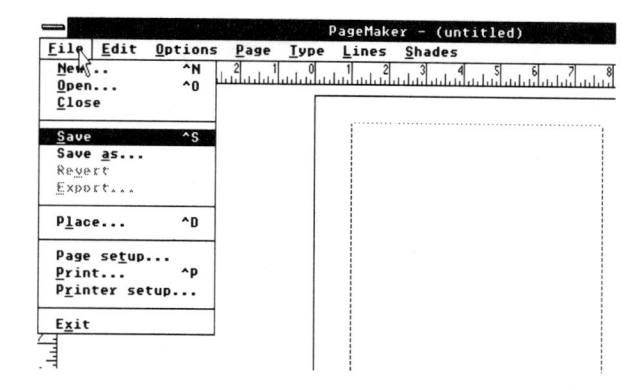

*Figure 6. Up until now, the creation of the template has been exactly the same as the creation of a publication—the difference comes during the Save command.*

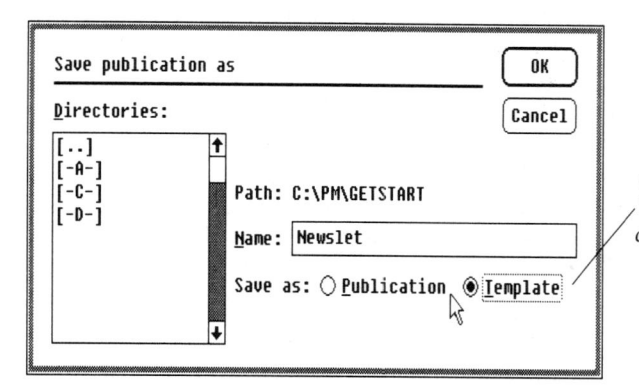

*Figure 7. Give the document a name as you normally would (in our case NEWSLET), but click on Template in the bottom right-hand corner. By default, Publication will be selected. Then click on OK.*

PageMaker publications and PageMaker templates can be distinguished in directory listings quite easily—see the listings below to see the difference between the two files. Publications have a .PM3 extension, while templates have a .PT3 extension.

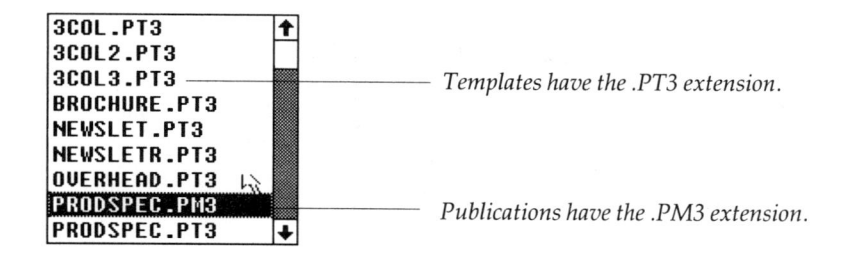

*Templates have the .PT3 extension.*

*Publications have the .PM3 extension.*

307

*Module 9 - PageMaker Templates*

The main difference between publications and templates occurs when the PageMaker file is opened. If a publication is opened, the original file is opened, and any changes saved then alter that file permanently. However, if a template is selected, then by default an unnamed original (a copy) is opened. The named original remains untouched on disk to be used another time. The template copy that was opened can be added to, modified, etc., and saved as a new publication. Because this template opens up without a name, there is no chance of saving over the original template and destroying its contents by mistake.

In Figure 8, the *Open* dialog box shows the options of *Original* or *Copy* in the bottom-right corner. A template always defaults to the Copy option, whereas a publication defaults to Original. Figure 9 gives further examples.

Opening copies or originals of either publications or templates can be manually overridden through the *Open* command in Figure 8. Whenever you select a PageMaker file to be opened from within this dialog box, the default conditions, Original or Copy, will occur as indicated above. As you select a template, however, you can override this and select Original. This is necessary, of course, if you wish to modify the original template. In the same way, you can override the Original default for a publication and open up a copy.

An example of opening up a copy of the NEWSLET.PT3 Template, which we saved in Figure 7 as a template, is shown in Figure 10.

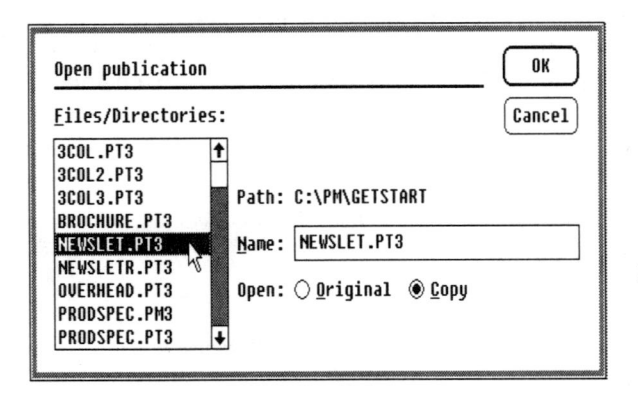

*Figure 8. Here we have used the Open command to gain access to this list of PageMaker files. As we select a template to open (this was the template we just created), note how the option in the bottom right hand switches to Copy, rather than Original.*

*Module 9 - PageMaker Templates*

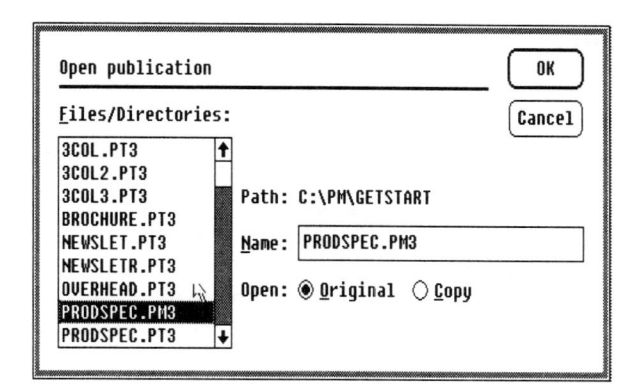

*Figure 9.* However, when we select a normal publication to open, the option now switches back to Original. This can be manually overridden if need be.

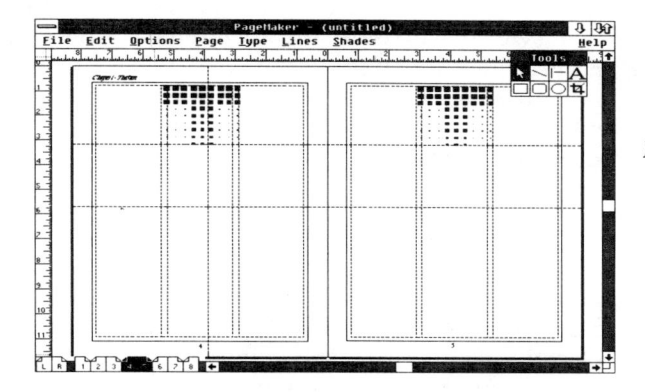

*Figure 10.* Here we have opened up a copy of the template we just created (NEWSLET.PT3). Note how it looks exactly the same as Figure 5, yet is untitled.

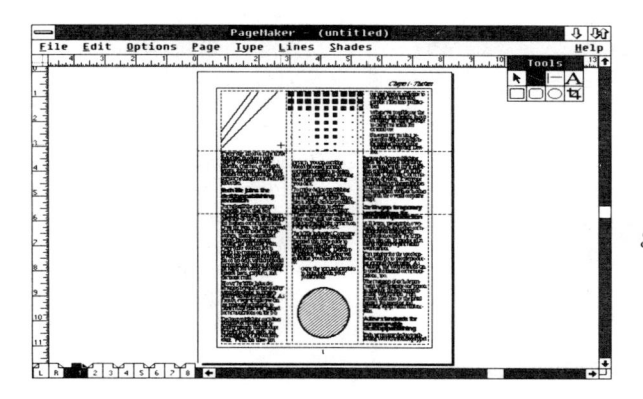

*Figure 11.* Once the copy of the template has been opened, we are free to add this month's text and graphics, withut having to redefine page parameters.

*Module 9 - PageMaker Templates*

## Text and graphic placeholders

We have mentioned that a template can contain any amount of graphics or text. If we consider a monthly newsletter, the actual content of this newsletter will change from month to month. One would think, therefore, we cannot include much text in the template, as it will have to be updated anyway. Using text and graphics as what are called *placeholders,* however, we can include as much text and graphics in our template as we need, without having to worry about this text being removed or updated. Using text and graphics placeholders in templates makes creating a publication much easier.

Let's say that we loaded in one major text file, several graphics files, and several headings throughout our Newsletter Template example. When we open up the template next month, the graphics, text, and headings are all there, but we now have new text, graphics, and headings that are going to replace those of last month. Replacing the old text with the new becomes very easy, and the process of replacing the old text and graphics helps us to precisely format and position the new elements.

## Graphic placeholders

In a simple copy of a newsletter template of Figure 12, let's choose to first replace the old graphics on the first page with a new graphic. Select the old graphic that is going to be replaced immediately before selecting the *Place* command (Figures 13 and 14). When you do choose the *Place* command, locate the new graphic, as in Figure 15, and select it, but do not yet choose OK.

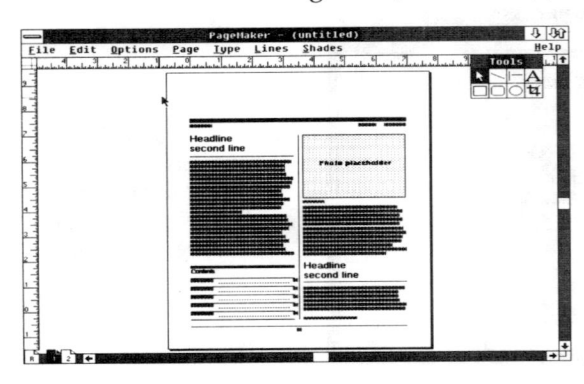

*Figure 12.* To work along with us in this section of the module, load the NEWSLETR.PT3 template contained in the PageMaker TEMPLATE folder. This is provided with PageMaker and should not be confused with the one we just created in Figures 1 to 7. As shown in this figure, it contains various text and graphics placeholders on Page 1. We are about to select the graphic in the top right-hand corner to be replaced.

*Module 9 - PageMaker Templates*

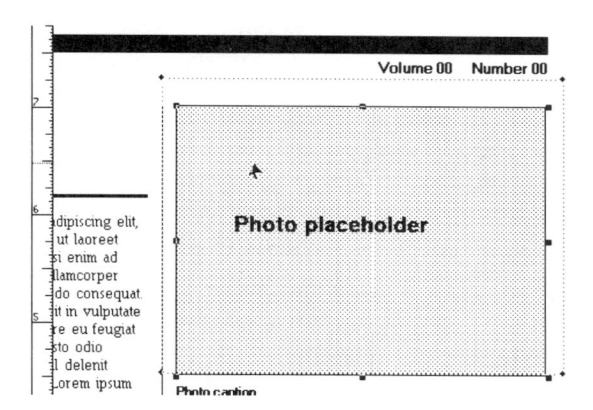

*Figure 13. We have changed to Actual size view so that you can see how the graphic we have selected is going to be replaced.*

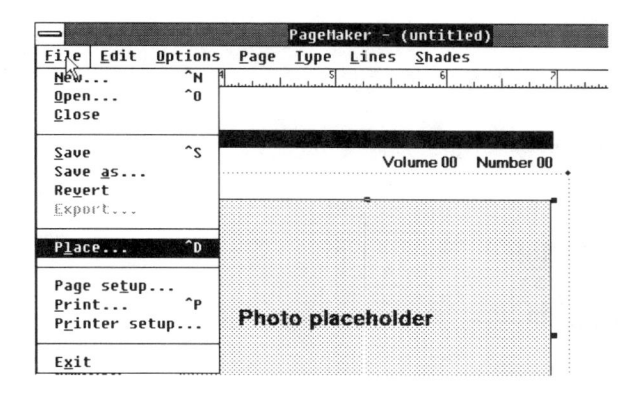

*Figure 14. With the graphic still selected, we choose the Place command from the **File** menu to locate the new graphic.*

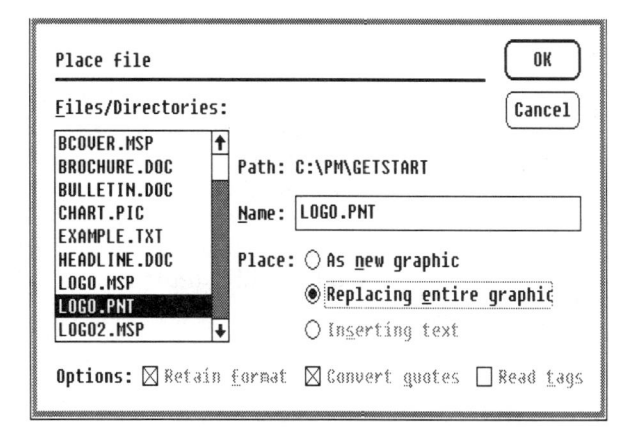

*Figure 15. The graphic we are going to use to replace the old graphic is LOGO.PNT. Note that we also select the option to the right—Replacing entire graphic (see the explanation on the next page).*

*Module 9 - PageMaker Templates*

There are several options within the Figure 15 dialog box that may be active depending on the steps that were taken before choosing this command. The one that should be active now is located to the right of the dialog box, and gives you a choice of two ways to load the graphic—either *As new graphic,* which is selected by default, or *Replacing entire graphic. As new graphic* is a picture loaded in the traditional way—the mouse cursor will change appearance and you may choose where to load the graphic.

*Replacing entire graphic* will insert the new graphic not only in the same area as the existing graphic, but also using the same sizing, cropping, and wraparound attributes as the previous graphic. This can, of course, be modified after the graphic has been replaced. On clicking OK, the new graphic totally replaces the old (Figure 16).

*Figure 16. On choosing OK, the new graphic entirely replaces the old, taking on all of its attributes.*

## Text placeholders

The same theory applies to text replacement as to graphics. Select any part of a text file that you would like to replace with a new file (use the pointer tool, or make an insertion point with the text tool), and choose the *Place* command. Locate the new text file, and note the new option to the right of the list of files. It will read *As new story* and *Replacing entire story.* As with graphics, if you select Replacing entire story, the new text file will completely overlay the previous file—following its exact path. If the files are of different length, this doesn't matter—there will either be a blank space following the file if it is shorter, or more text to flow if it is longer.

See Figures 17 to 19 for examples of this approach.

*Module 9 - PageMaker Templates*

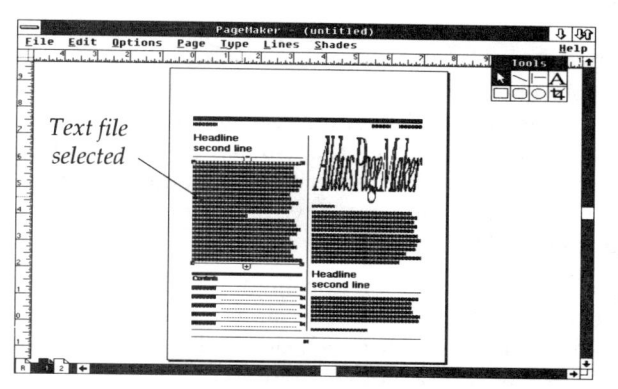

*Figure 17.* The procedure for replacing existing text files with other text files works in the same way as the graphics example. First, select any text block with the pointer tool, or create an insertion point with the text tool within a story. These two options will cause the total text file to be replaced. If you wish to replace only a portion of a text file, then select part of that file using the text tool.

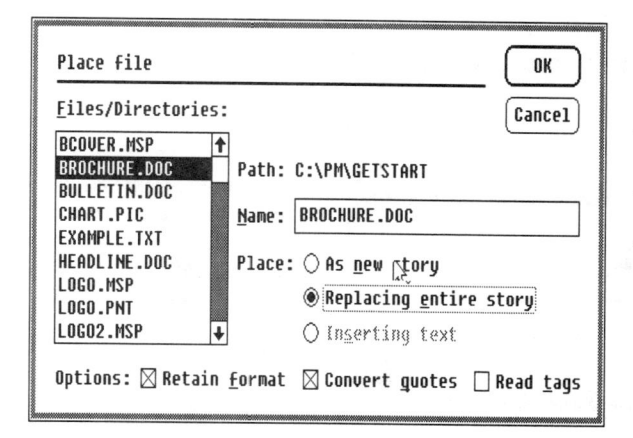

*Figure 18.* After choosing the Place command, we select the new text file, as well as the option Replacing entire story.
If we have selected only a portion of our text, then the Inserting text option would have been available for selection as well.

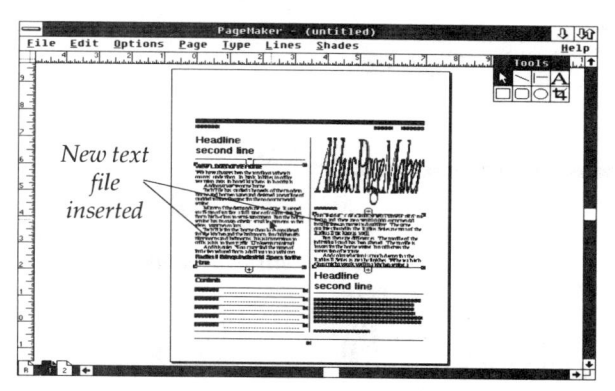

*Figure 19.* On clicking OK, the new text file completely replaces the old—flowing in exactly the same pattern.

313

*Module 9 - PageMaker Templates*

## Heading placeholders

Heading placeholders work in a slightly different way to other text placeholders. Because headings are generally much shorter than text files, three or four words usually, it is much quicker to type them in in PageMaker rather than with a word processor. Let's say, for example, that you have a heading in place in your template as shown in Figure 20.

Simply select the text cursor, and highlight the entire heading "Headline" (Figure 20). Without pressing the Delete key, or using the *Cut* command, type in the new heading. The new heading will completely overwrite the old, yet use exactly the same attributes (Figure 21). The same type style, justification, and spacing will be applied to the new text.

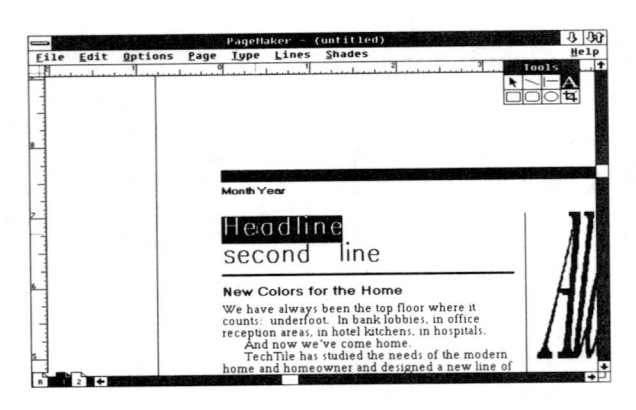

*Figure 20. Replacing headings, yet keeping their formatting, is very simple. Select, using the text cursor, the old heading, but do not cut or delete the text.*

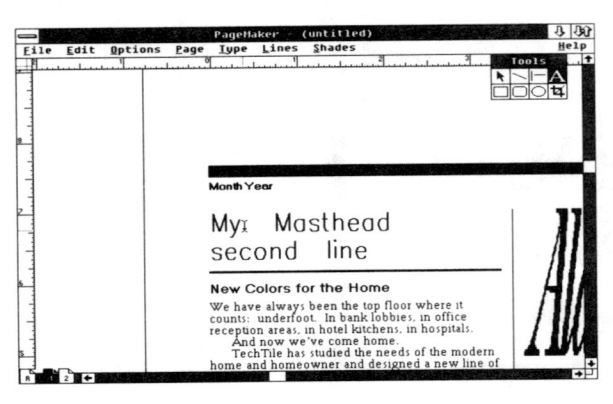

*Figure 21. Simply type in the new heading. The old heading will be deleted, and the new heading will use the exact text and paragraph attributes as did the old heading.*

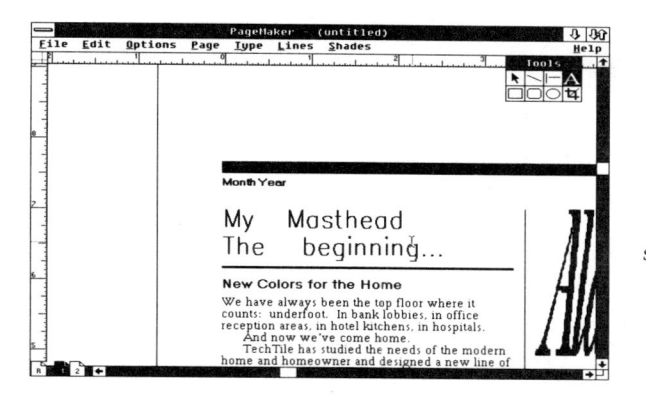

*Figure 22.* The same principles apply to all text files—simply select the text. Here we have just changed the second subhead in column 1.

All text and graphics placeholders can be regular or simulated. Provided with PageMaker are several "dummy" files that can be used to create a template, so that real files do not have to be created and used.

Module 9 Exercise

# PageMaker Templates

# Module 9 Exercise
# PageMaker Templates

In this exercise we are illustrating the use of templates and how to work effectively with them.

This training material is structured so that people of all levels of expertise with PageMaker can use it to gain maximum benefit. In order to do this, we have structured this material so that the bare exercise is listed below this paragraph on just one page, with no hints. The following pages contain the steps needed to complete this exercise for those that need additional prompting. The **PageMaker Templates** module should be referenced if you need further help or explanations.

## Module 9 exercise steps

1. Load the template BULLETIN.PT3 from the TEMPLATE subdirectory.
2. On page 1 of this template we are going to replace four major sections—the logo in the top right-hand corner, the heading, an introduction paragraph (which begins "Lorem ipsum dolor sit amet..."), the major story (which begins "Ut wisi enim ad veniam,..."), and the photo at the bottom left-hand corner of the page. Make sure you understand which parts of page 1 we are talking about when we refer to these sections (see Figure 1 to get a better idea).
3. Replace the current logo with the file LOGO.MSP.
4. Replace the major story with the file BROCHURE.DOC.
5. Replace the introduction paragraph with a paragraph of your own (in other words, delete the existing introduction paragraph and replace it with a few lines typed in on the keyboard).
6. Replace the photo with the file PHOTO.TIF.
7. Replace the headline with a headline of your own choosing.
8. Save the template as a publication called TEMPEX.PM3.

The steps to completing this exercise are on the following pages.

Module 9 Exercise - PageMaker Templates

## The Steps in detail.

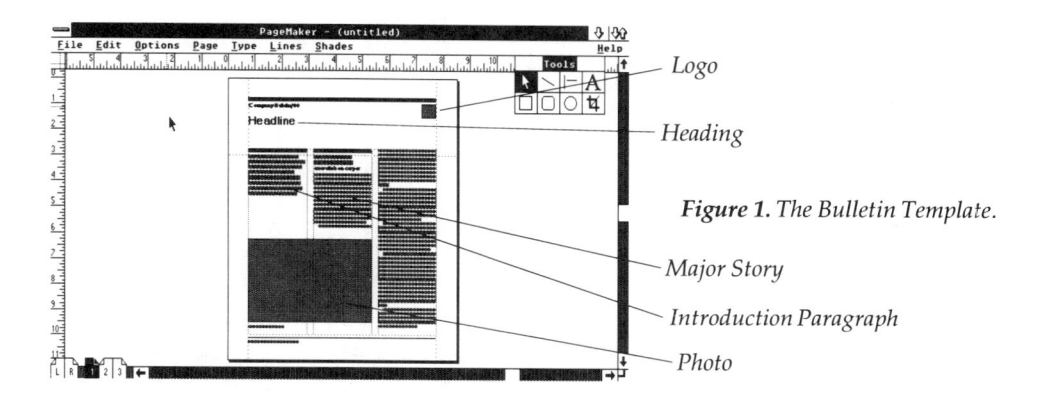

*Figure 1.* The Bulletin Template.

1. Load the template BULLETIN.PT3 *from the* TEMPLATE *subdirectory.*

This step can be achieved using either of two methods—depending on whether or not PageMaker is open at the current time. If it is, then the *Open* command from the **File** menu must be used to access this template from the Templates folder (Figures 2 and 3).

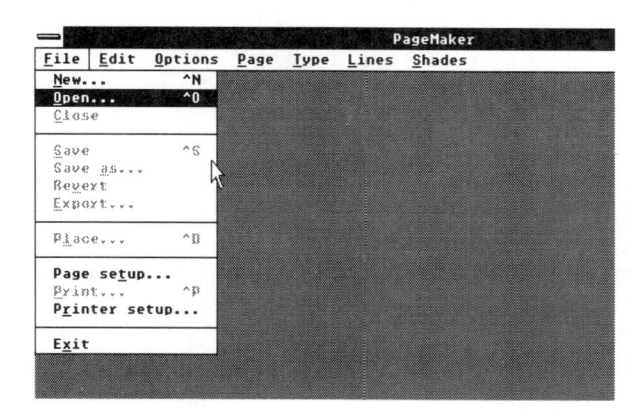

*Figure 2.* The Open command from the **File** menu is the way to get access to both publications and templates.

319

*Module 9 Exercise - PageMaker Templates*

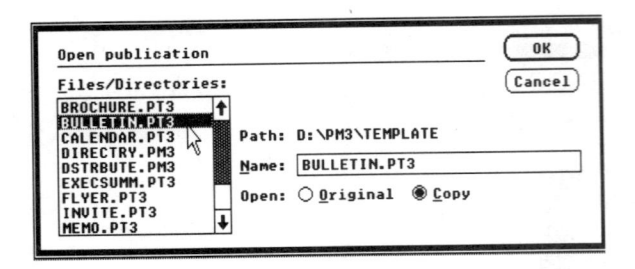

*Figure 3. The BULLETIN.PT3 template is located in the TEMPLATE subdirectory inside the PM3 directory.*

If you are at the Windows desktop, you can open the file from there by locating it and double-clicking on it (Figure 4). In both cases, because the file is a template, a copy will be opened by default. Notice that Copy is automatically selected in Figure 3.

*Figure 4. Alternatively, a template or publication can be opened by locating the file on the Windows desktop and double-clicking on it.*

2. On page 1 of this template we are going to replace four major sections - the logo in the top right-hand corner, the heading, an introduction paragraph (which begins "Lorem ipsum dolor sit amet..."), the major story (which begins "Ut wisi enim ad veniam,..."), and the photo at the bottom left-hand corner of the page. Make sure you understand which parts of page 1 we are talking about when we refer to these sections (see Figure 1 to get a better idea).

See Figure 1 to make sure you understand what we refer to as the logo, the heading, the introduction paragraph, the major story, and the photo.

*Module 9 Exercise - PageMaker Templates*

*3. Replace the current logo with the file LOGO.MSP.*

This step can be completed far more easily than with earlier versions of Page-Maker. Previously, you would have had to delete the existing logo, import the new one, and resize it and place it as necessary. Thankfully the process is now far easier.

If you are not in *Actual size* view, move to this view now through the **Page** menu. Select the existing logo at the top-right of the page simply by clicking on it (Figure 5). Now move to the *Place* command in the **File** menu (Figure 6).

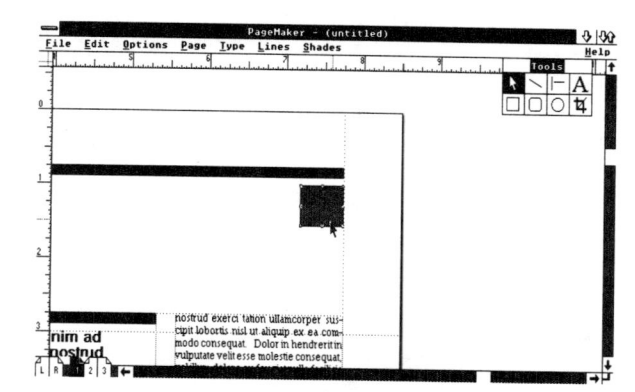

*Figure 5. The first step in replacing a graphic is to select the graphic to replace.*

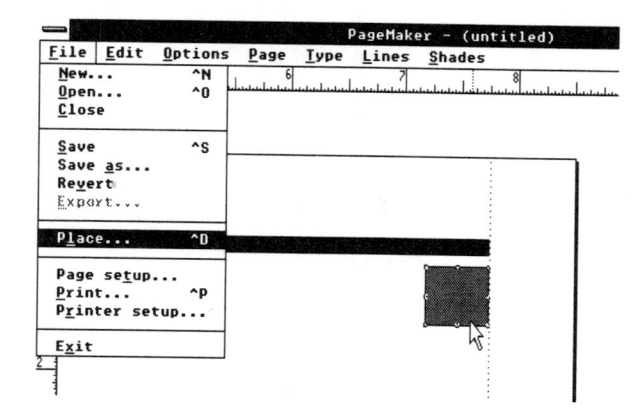

*Figure 6. After Figure 5, move to the Place command in the **File** menu to choose the file to replace the selected one.*

321

*Module 9 Exercise - PageMaker Templates*

Locate the file LOGO.MSP in the GETSTART subdirectory (Figure 7). After selecting it in this dialog box (by clicking on it only once, not twice) check the option to the right of the list of files that reads *Replacing entire graphic*. This will make sure that the current logo is deleted and replaced by this new one at exactly the same place and size. Click on OK. The new graphic then replaces the old (Figure 8).

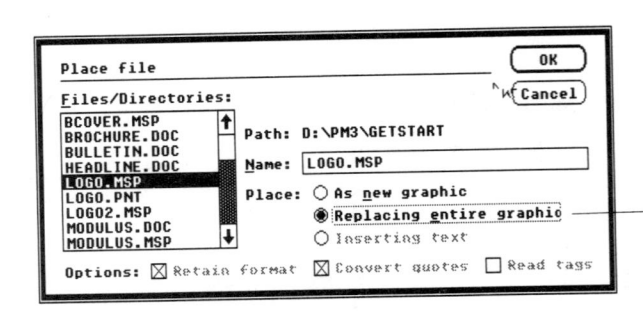

*Figure 7. Select the file LOGO.MSP to replace the graphic we had originally selected on the page in Figure 5. Make sure you also choose Replacing entire graphic.*

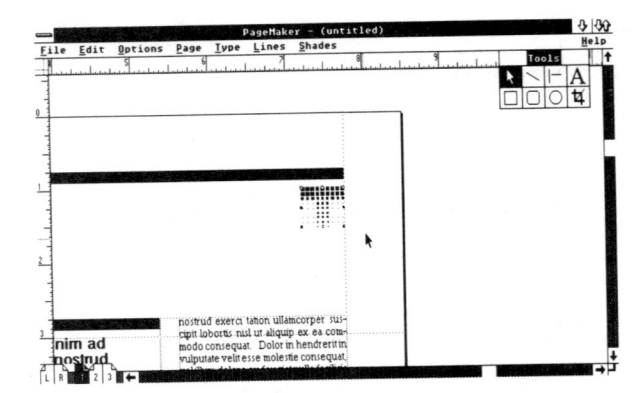

*Figure 8. After clicking on OK in Figure 7, the new graphic will, after a few seconds, replace the old.*

4. Replace the major story with the file BROCHURE.DOC.

The same steps are used to replace one story with another, as are used to replace graphics. However, a text file can stretch over several text blocks, so only the first text block need be selected (Figure 9) before moving to the *Place* command in the **File** menu (Figure 10).

322

*Module 9 Exercise - PageMaker Templates*

*Figure 9. To replace a text file, only the first text block of the file need be selected using the pointer tool. Alternatively, the text tool could have been used to place an insertion point anywhere in the text you want to replace.*

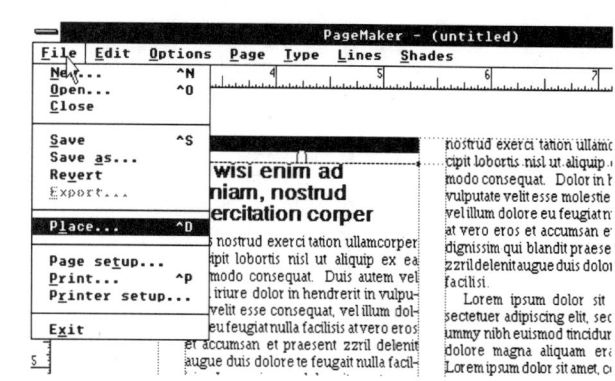

*Figure 10. Once again, after selecting the text block using the pointer tool, move directly to the Place command in the File menu.*

Locate the file BROCHURE.DOC from the GETSTART subdirectory (Figure 11). You will notice that the Replacing entire story option can be selected while the file BROCHURE.DOC is selected in the list of files. Check this replace option (Figure 11) and click on OK.

BROCHURE.DOC will now replace the original text file (Figure 12).

323

Module 9 Exercise - PageMaker Templates

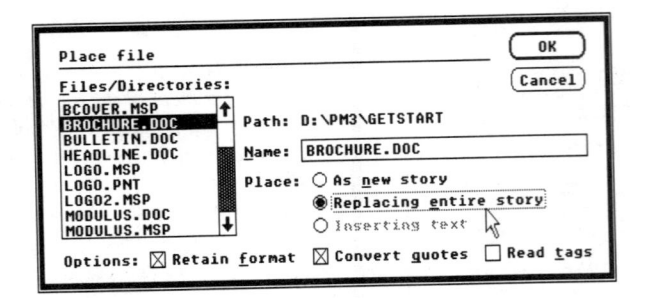

*Figure 11.* Select the file BROCHURE.DOC to replace the text on screen. Make sure you also choose Replacing entire story, and then click on OK.

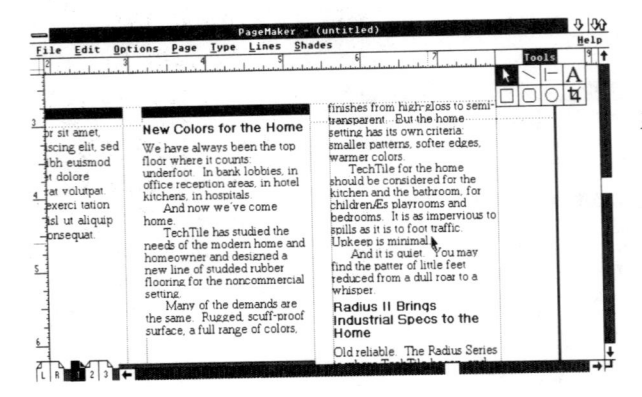

*Figure 12.* The new file will replace the old one entirely. Sometimes, however, this replacement may require a little tidying up—at the bottom of the page, for example, the third column may run a little too close to the bottom of the page.

5. Replace the introduction paragraph with a paragraph of your own (in other words, delete the existing introduction paragraph and replace it with a few lines typed in on the keyboard).

Replacing a few lines of original template text with different lines of text entered directly from the keyboard can be done very simply. Select the text to replace using the text (A) tool (Figure 13).

*Module 9 Exercise - PageMaker Templates*

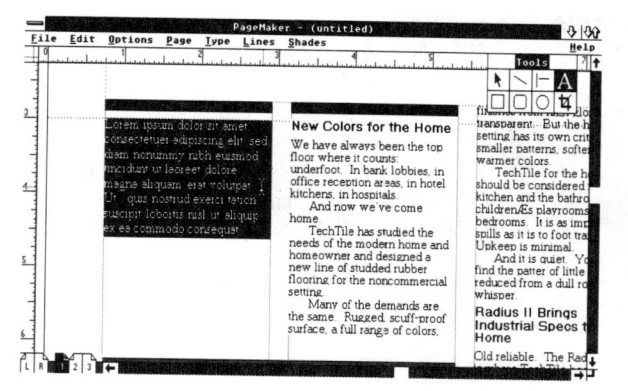

**Figure 13.** Select with the text tool, the text you would like to replace.

After doing this, simply type in the text you would like to add on the keyboard. This typed in text will immediately replace the selected text on screen. It will also have the advantage of using the same type and paragraph specifications (Figure 14).

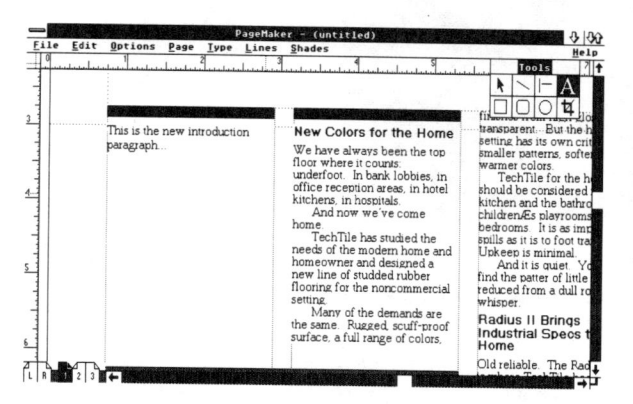

**Figure 14.** Simply type in the new text without doing anything else— the new text you enter will completely replace the selected text, yet keep all of its characteristics.

6. *Replace the photo with the file PHOTO.TIF.*

The photo we refer to here is actually the gray square at the bottom left-hand of the page. See Figure 1 again if in doubt. Move down the page so that you can see this photo (Figure 15).

After selecting the space set aside for a photo, move to the *Place* command (Figure 16), select the file PHOTO.TIF, and check the Replacing entire graphic option (Figure 17).

325

*Module 9 Exercise - PageMaker Templates*

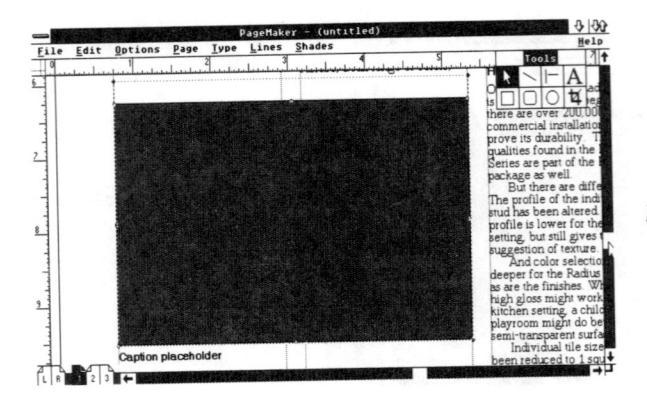

*Figure 15.* Locate the photo placeholder at the bottom left-hand corner of the screen and select it.

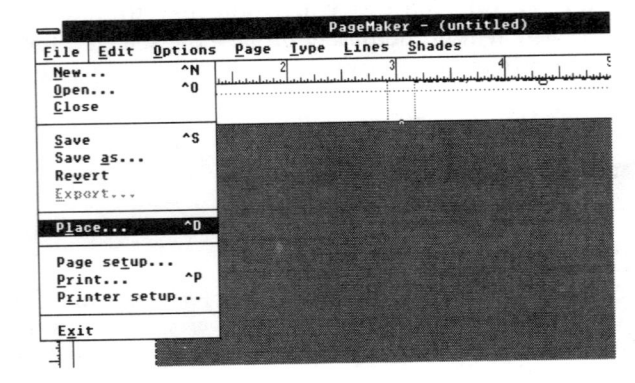

*Figure 16.* After selecting the space set aside for the photo, move directly to the Place command in the *File* menu.

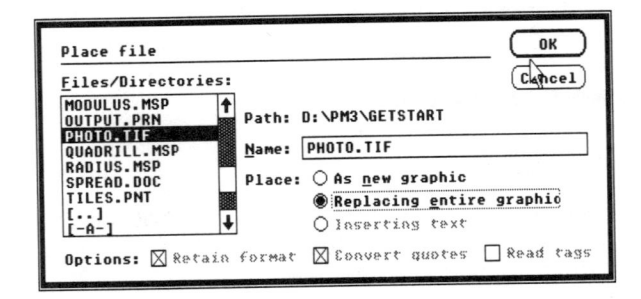

*Figure 17.* Choose the file PHOTO.TIF, and check the Replacing entire graphic option.

The new photo will completely replace the old, shaded placeholder box (Figure 18).

*Module 9 Exercise - PageMaker Templates*

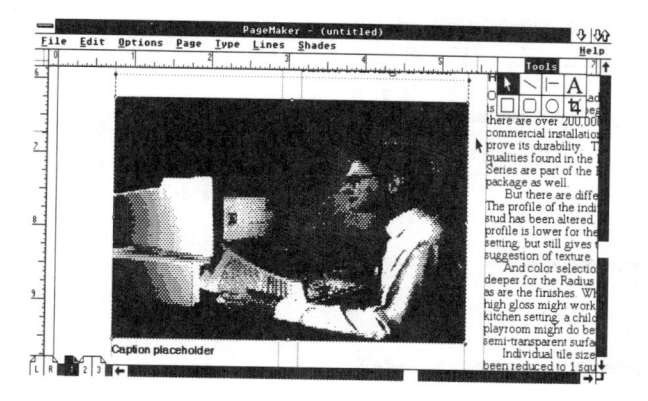

*Figure 18. The file PHOTO.TIF will entirely replace the photo placeholder and take up no extra room.*

7. *Replace the headline with a headline of your own choosing.*

Move up to the top of the page and locate the paragraph that reads "Headline." This is the heading placeholder—it has defined the position, as well as the type specifications, of the headline. In fact, we could replace the headline in either of two ways—by selecting it using the pointer or text tool, and loading a new text file to replace this one; or by selecting the heading with the text tool and simply typing in the new heading. Because the heading is small, the latter method is probably the easier of the two.

Select the heading in text mode and simply type in the new heading—anything you like (Figures 19 and 20).

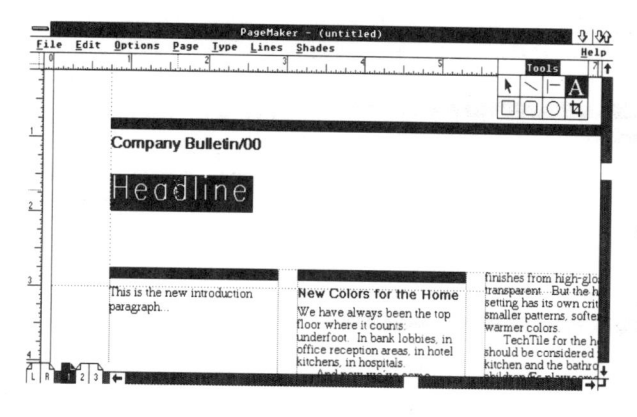

*Figure 19. For this step we have selected the headline using the text editing mode.*

327

## Module 9 Exercise - PageMaker Templates

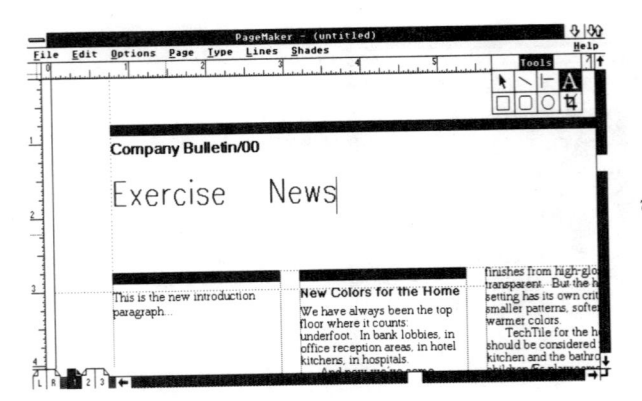

*Figure 20. Type in immediately what you want the new headline to say.*

8. Save the template as a publication called TEMPEX.PM3.

You should note that the template you are working with is actually called *Untitled*—indicating that we are working on a copy of the original. We must now save it as a new publication. Use the *Save* command in the **File** menu (Figure 21), and insert the name TEMPEX.PM3 in the Name rectangle (Figures 22 and 23).

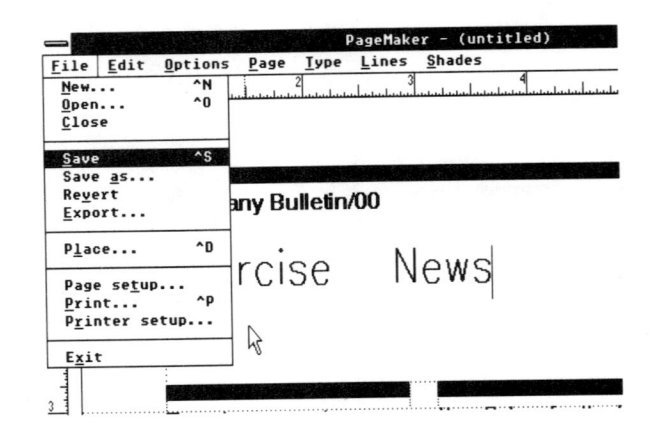

*Figure 21. It is probably a good idea to Save before you finish. You can save your work at any time by choosing the Save command from the **File** menu.*

328

*Module 9 Exercise - PageMaker Templates*

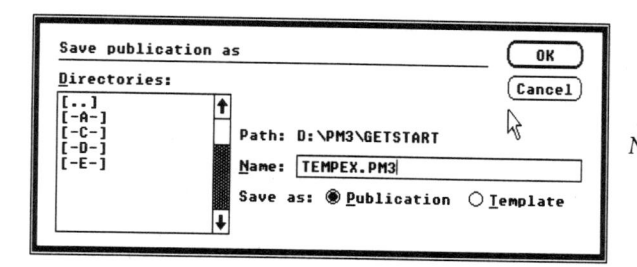

*Figure 22.* Insert the name in the Name rectangle as shown. Here we have called the publication TEMPEX.PM3.

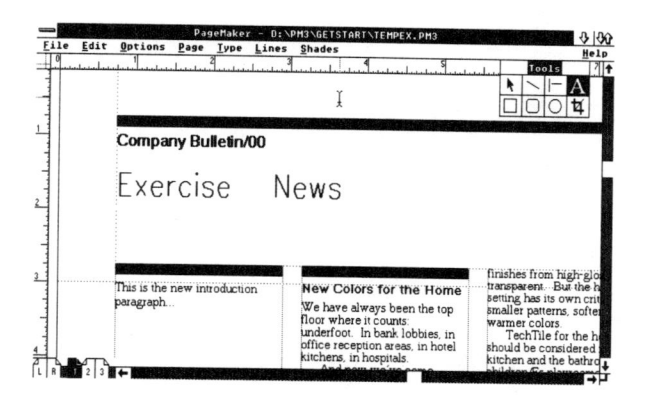

*Figure 23.* The name of the publication replaces Untitled in the menu bar at the top of the screen.

329

# Module 10

# PageMaker Printing

# PageMaker Printing

Your PageMaker job is ready to print at any time. There is no need to save before printing, and certainly no need to have completed your publication. In fact, the more often you get a chance to print your job, the better it will probably turn out. The printer always gives a clearer indication of what the document is going to look like than does the screen, due to the printer's higher resolution.

Several printers are available for use with PageMaker, most either use the printer language PostScript (such as LaserWriters, OmniLasers, AST, QMS, and Dataproducts), or are Hewlett Packard LaserJet Plus compatible. Any printers that are going to be used with PageMaker should have been installed during the actual installation of PageMaker. Printers can, however, be removed and deleted through the *Control Panel*—which we will look at in the next section.

## The Control Panel

If your copy of PageMaker or Windows has been loaded correctly, and you don't often change your printing process (i.e., the printer and printer port you use), you will rarely have to use the Control Panel. However, it is always a good idea to know a little about it, for it can be used in more ways than one (see also Using Windows with PageMaker, in Module 1).

The Control Panel can be accessed directly through Windows as a program, but is best selected through the Windows menu when PageMaker is open. However, make sure that a publication is not open at the same time.

The Control Panel (Figure 2) will occupy a small window near the top left-hand corner of the screen. It has three of its own menus—**Installation**, **Setup**, and **Preferences**. The two menus we will be looking at are **Installation** and **Setup**, as these two menus relate most to printer installing and configuring.

*Module 10- PageMaker Printing*

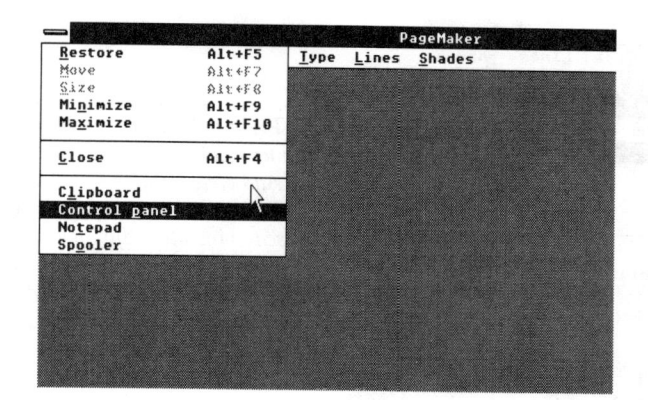

**Figure 1.** *The Control Panel is accessed through the Windows system menu in the top left-hand corner of your PageMaker window, but only when a PageMaker document is not open.*

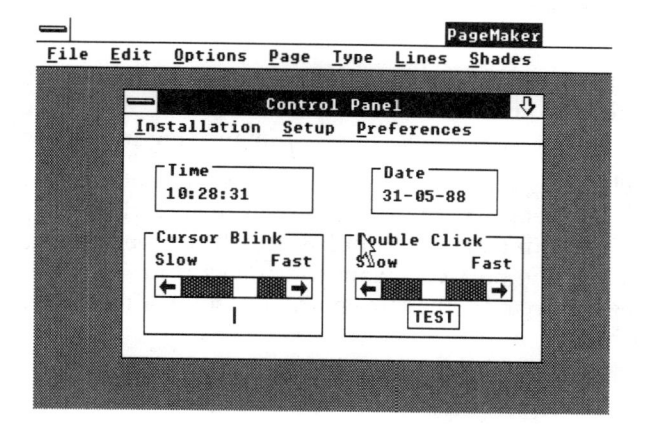

**Figure 2.** *The Control Panel.*

Two commands in the **Installation** menu of interest are *Add New Printer* and *Delete Printer* (Figure 3). These commands allow you, as you might have guessed, to load new printers and/or delete them. If you choose to add a new printer, the Control Panel will ask where you want to load the printers from (normally the A: drive—either the drivers' disk from your copy of PageMaker or Windows, or a special drivers' disk provided by the manufacturer of your printer). After telling the Control Panel where to look for printer drivers, merely select a printer and it will be loaded. Deleting works in a similar way.

Module 10 - PageMaker Printing

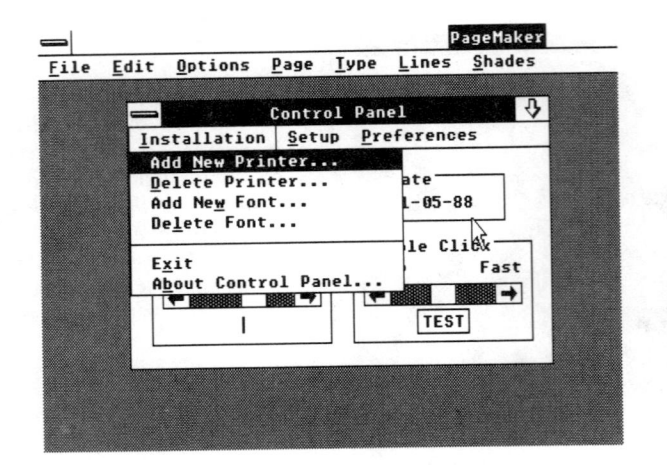

*Figure 3.* The **Installation** menu contains the commands Add New Printer and Delete Printer—these commands are used to install and/or delete new or existing printer drivers in PageMaker. See your PageMaker or Windows manual for more details.

After loading your printer, you must use the commands in the **Setup** menu to customize it and make it usable. The first command to look at is the *Connections* command (Figure 4).

Upon choosing this command you will be presented with a list of all the printers currently loaded (Figure 5), and all the ports available on your machine. Simply select the printer you want to connect, and the port you want to connect it to. Two printers cannot be connected to the same port. Choose OK after connecting your printers.

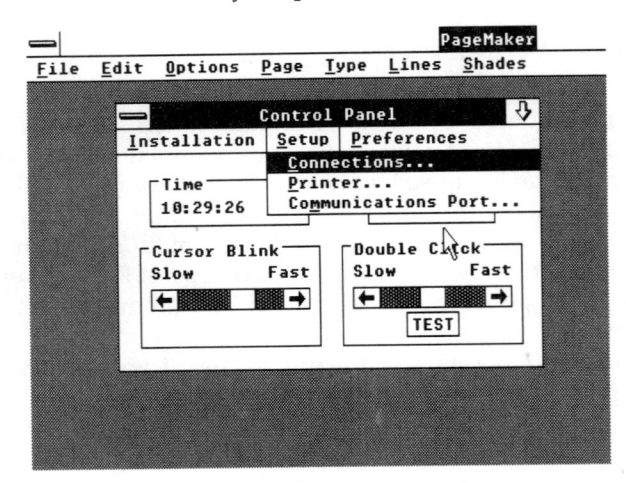

*Figure 4.* The Connections command in the **Setup** menu is used to connect a specific printer to a specific printer or communications port on your PC.

334

*Module 10- PageMaker Printing*

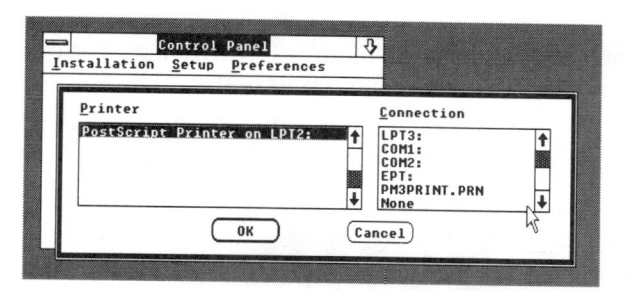

*Figure 5. This dialog box appears after choosing the command in Figure 4. It allows us to choose a printer from the list on the left (in our case there is only one printer) and connect it to a port (or file, as we will see later) on the right.*

Next, you must choose the *Printer* command (Figure 6) underneath *Connections*. With this command, you will be choosing the default printer to be used—when there is more than one to choose from. From the list that appears upon selecting this command (Figure 7), choose the printer that you wish to use. Then click on OK.

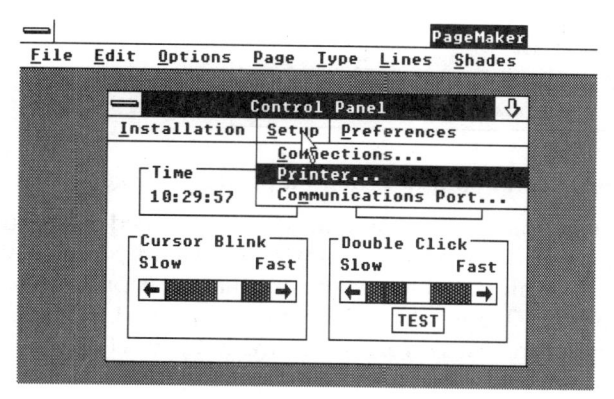

*Figure 6. The Printer command from the **Setup** menu allows you to choose your default printer...*

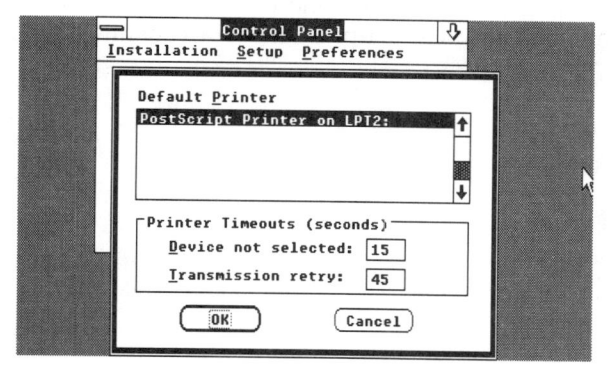

*Figure 7. ... and set that printer up how you like. The dialog box from the command of Figure 6—here again we have only one printer loaded—there may well be a list of printers that you can select from.*

335

*Module 10 - PageMaker Printing*

What appears now is a dialog box (Figure 8) asking for specifications on your printer—the model, the tray it uses, the orientation, and so on. Fill in these options as best you can.

The *Options* button should only really be looked at if you have quite a bit of knowledge about your printer setup.

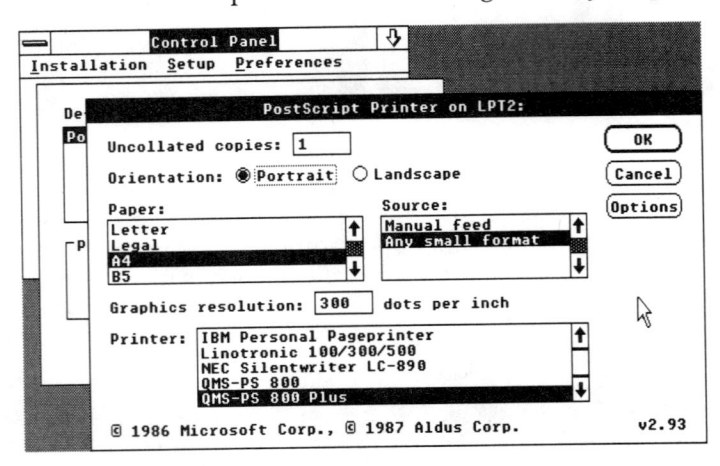

*Figure 8.* *After selecting a printer from the dialog box of Figure 7 and selecting OK, you will be faced with another dialog box that asks you several questions about how your printer is set up.*

Click on OK, and your new default printer has been set up.

The *Communications Port* command (Figure 9) need only be used if your printer is connected to any of the COM ports on your machine. If at all possible, make sure that your printer is connected to an LPT port rather than a COM port—LPT ports are faster for printing. However, make sure that you set up the Communications ports if you are using them for something like we have suggested below. These options will differ depending on your printer and how it is set up—if in doubt, consult your dealer.

*Baud rate*: 9600

*Word Length*: 8

*Parity*: None

*Stop bits*: 1

*Handshake*: Hardware

*Port*: (COM1 or COM2)

336

*Module 10- PageMaker Printing*

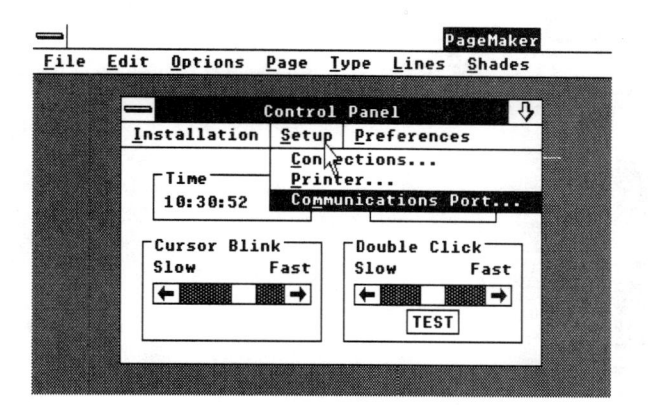

*Figure 9. If you have connected a printer to a communications port (these are the ports that start with COM—always use an LPT port if possible), you may need to use this command to make sure that the port you have connected the printer to is set up correctly for the printer.*

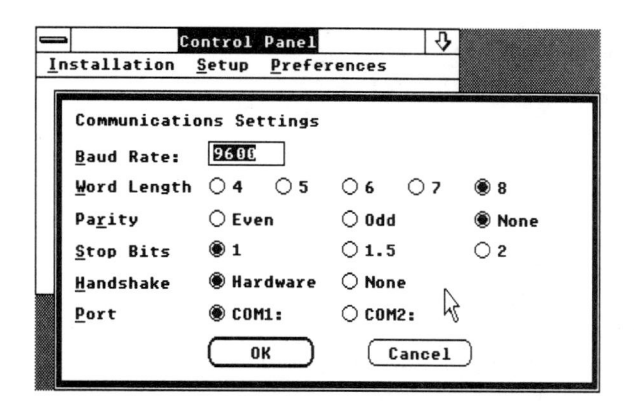

*Figure 10. How exactly the resulting dialog box is set up can depend on your printer. This dialog box represents only a guide—these are the settings we use when printing through a COM port.*

Within PageMaker, you may select a printer to print to (if you do not wish to use the default printer you have loaded, or if the publication or template you opened has been formatted for another printer). If you only have one printer which is always connected, this step is not necessary, as that printer will always be used. However, if you have several printers loaded, you may select the printer you wish to use from the *Printer Setup* command from the **File** menu (Figure 11). On choosing this command, you will be presented with the dialog box of Figure 12.

337

*Module 10 - PageMaker Printing*

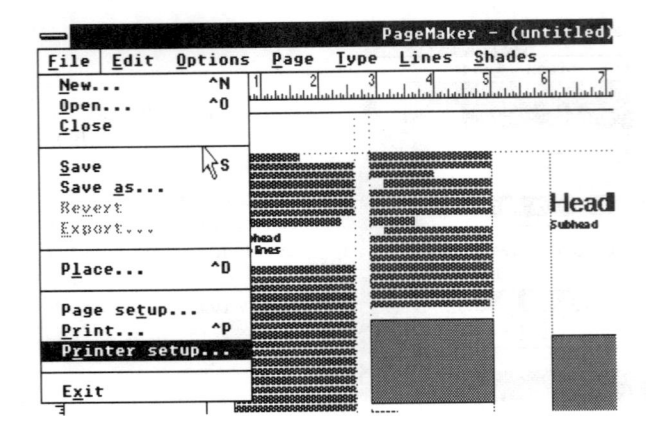

*Figure 11. This command, if used when no publication is open, will set the default printer for all future publications. However, if a publications has already been created using another target printer, or no target printer, you may have to use this command to make sure the currently open publication is formatted correctly for the printer you intend to use.*

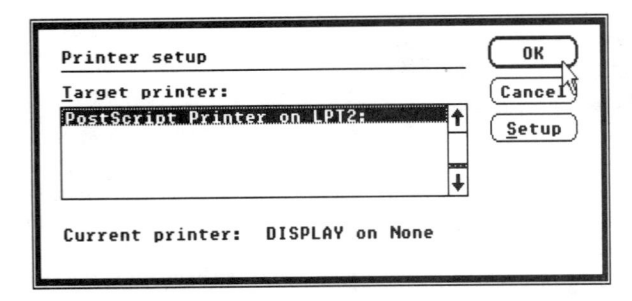

*Figure 12. The Printer Setup command dialog box. Once again, if several printers are loaded, you may select which printer you intend to use.*

All printers that are loaded will be listed in the resulting dialog box. If you only have one printer loaded, it may already be selected. However, select the printer you want from the list, and choose the *Setup* button.

The dialog box that appears upon selecting this button will ask you many questions about the printer you are using: what tray you want to use in the printer, what brand it is, and so on. Make sure that all of these settings are correct—PageMaker may not print unless all settings correspond with the actual printer. If you attempt to print to a printer that the publication was not expecting, and hence was not formatted for, PageMaker will not print to it until you reformat the publication using the Setup command.

PageMaker then gives you the opportunity to recompose your publication for the new printer, as shown in Figure 13.

*Module 10- PageMaker Printing*

*Figure 13. This message will arise whenever you change printers midway through a job. Depending from which printer to which printer you change to, your job may change dramatically. Several fonts that you used, for example, may not be available on the new printer—PageMaker has to substitute them with new ones.*

To print your document, select the *Print* command from the **File** menu (Figure 14). After selecting this command, you will be presented with the dialog box of Figure 15.

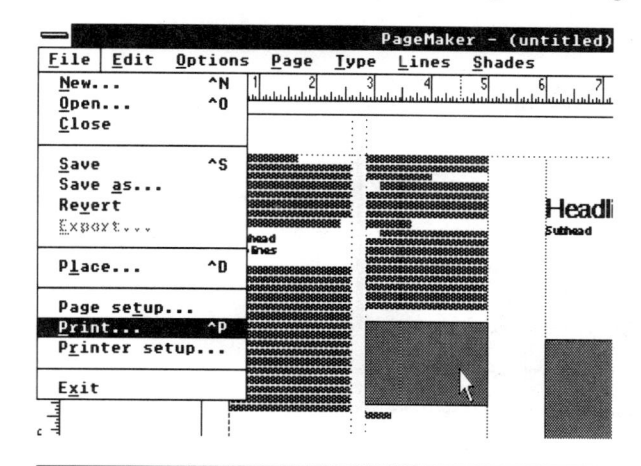

*Figure 14. Printing can be done at any stage of your job—whether it be saved, unfinished, or completed. Simply choose the Print command from the **File** menu.*

*Figure 15. The Print dialog box—quite a bit of control over how to print your work.*

339

## Module 10 - PageMaker Printing

As you can see from Figure 15, printing is not quite as easy as just saying "print." There are a variety of options available to control the print of your publication. We will look at each of these options now in more detail.

At the bottom of the Figure 15 dialog box is listed the name of the currently selected printer. If this is not the printer you wish to use, select Cancel from this dialog box, and look at the *Printer Setup* command from the **File** menu to review the printer choice.

Your first selection is how many copies to print of your publication. This can be any figure up to 99 (Figure 16). (If you have a fairly low throughput printer, don't try to use it as a printing press—a photocopier or instant printer may work far faster and more economically.)

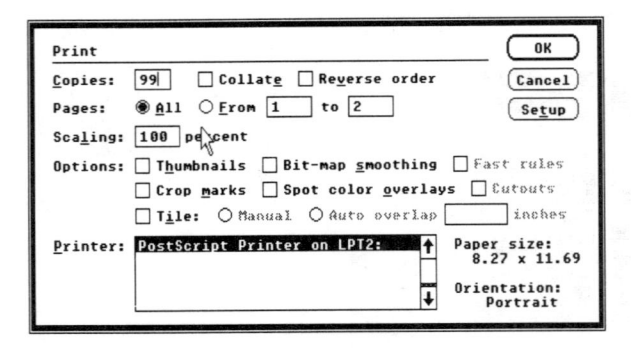

*Figure 16.* Note how we have added the figure 99 in the Copies box. This tells PageMaker to print whatever we specify 99 times.

Next to the number of copies is the *Collate* square. If this square is selected, all copies printed will be collated as they are printed. (This will obviously only work if multiple copies of multiple pages are going to be printed). Although this sounds like an attractive proposition, it will take a lot longer to print when this option is selected, as each page has to be processed individually, rather than just once for multiple copies of the same page.

Alongside the Collate option is the *Reverse order* option. Depending on the output tray of your printer (some flip the pages as they are coming out) you may prefer to print first page to last, or the other way around, so that when the pages are picked up they don't have to be resorted into the correct order. PageMaker will try to determine which way your printer sorts its output, and print so that the pages are in order, not necessarily first to last.

The *Page* line is used to select the actual pages that are to be printed. Choose *All* to print the entire publication, or insert figures into the page range boxes after *From* to print specified pages. If you wish to print just one page, put that same page number in both the *From* and the *to* boxes.

Th *Scaling* option allows you to scale the print of your document, from 25% to 1000%, at full PostScript resolution. This option is only available on PostScript printers. In this way, higher point sizes than can be accessed through the PageMaker dialog boxes can be achieved by scaling the publication as it is printed.

*Thumbnails* are a very useful PageMaker feature that allows you to print a wide range of publication pages shrunken down to fit onto an A4 ot Letter page. This is especially useful to keep on file exactly what is in every publication, rather than spending the time and money to print them out in full. Sixteen thumbnails are printed per page. This feature, too, is only available on PostScript printers.

*Spot color overlays* is a choice that is used when preparing color work to be taken to a printer for finishing. By selecting this option, every new color will be printed on a page by itself, as this is what the printer requires. The option to the right of this, *Cutouts*, is used when several colors overlap each other on one page. Without Cutouts selected, PageMaker will print the overlapped area in each of the overlapping colors. With Cutouts selected, the first page prints the first color with the overlapping area cut out of it, and the second page prints the overlapping area in that color. (Some printers may prefer cutouts, while others may not; check with your print shop before printing.)

*Crop marks* can be added to a printed page, so that a printer can align pages together correctly and see exactly what page size he is working with. They appear as not-quite-joined crosshairs in every corner of the page.

Finally, pages can be *Tiled*, so that you are not limited to the page size supported by your printer (Figures 17 and 18). To print an A3 page size from an A4 printer, tiling can be selected, and it will print out as several A4 pages, all overlapped (to whatever degree you like in manual tiling, or whatever overlap you specify for automatic tiling), and can be pasted back together after printing. This can also be used when scaling A4 or Letter pages higher than normal.

*Automatic tiling* will cause PageMaker to determine the starting point of each tile, based on the specified overlap. PageMaker will start at the upper left-hand corner of a page, and print all of one page's tiles before moving on to another. Automatic tiling should be used when there is no need to control what is printed (i.e., preventing a complex image from printing twice, too many tiles per page, etc.).

Tiling manually is achieved by repositioning the zero point on the ruler to specify where the tile is to start. After the starting point for a tile has been specified, PageMaker prints that tile for every page in the range of pages you are printing. You then set the zero point for the second tile, and PageMaker prints that tile for all pages being printed again. In this way, if your publication consists of ten pages, manual tiling will first cause ten tiles to print (one per page), then another ten (one per page again, and so on).

## Errors

Several errors may occur during the printing process. Nearly all of these are related to the connection between the PC and the printer. Make sure they are connected securely with cables, as well as through the different commands discussed earlier in this module, and that the printer is switched on and selected for the PC.

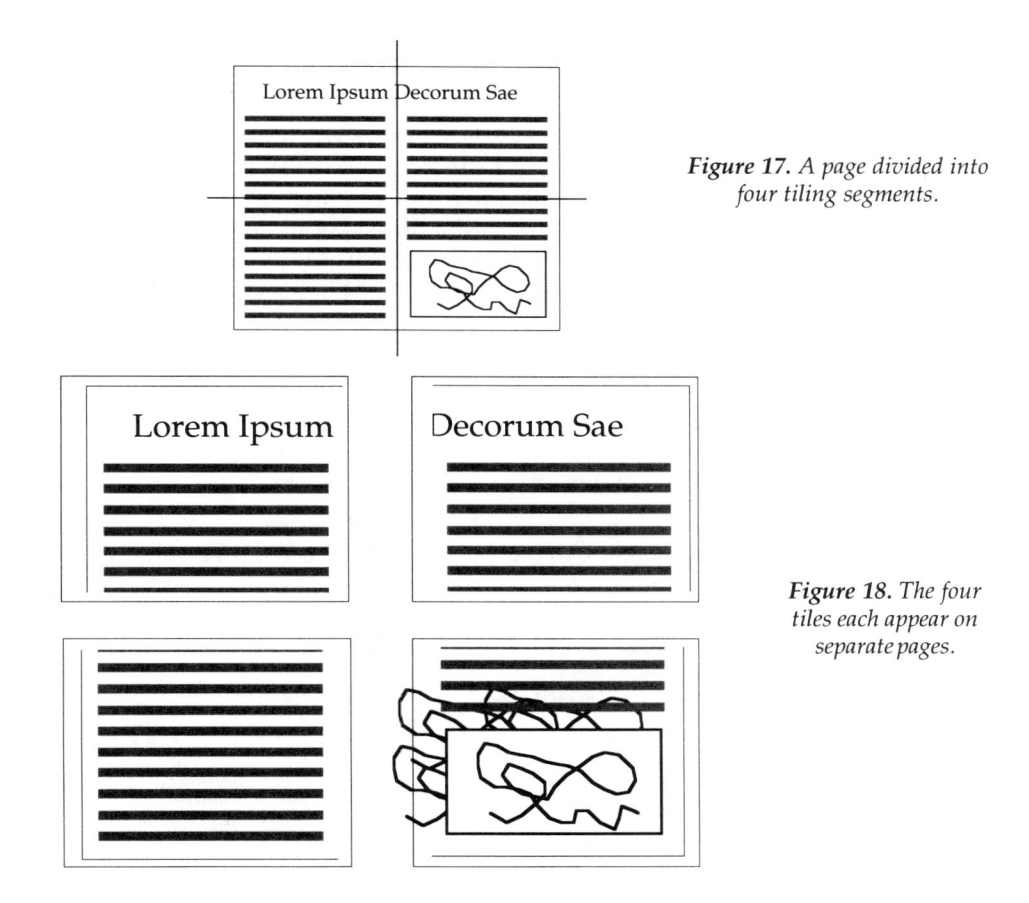

*Figure 17.* A page divided into four tiling segments.

*Figure 18.* The four tiles each appear on separate pages.

*Module 10 - PageMaker Printing*

## Creating print files

Most of the time, when we go to print we print directly to a printer. There exists, however, a way to create a print *file*—one that can be used in a variety of ways. This print file can be used as a way to transmit to a service bureau, but also can be used at a DOS level, utilizing the print spooler found with DOS. PageMaker itself uses the Windows print spooler, so this last option need not be used (although the DOS spooler does have the advantage of working whether or not Windows is open).

In your PM directory (or the Windows directory if you have Windows loaded) you will find a file called WIN.INI. This file contains system information that either Windows or PageMaker looks at every time it is started. It contains information on printers, fonts, memory, and so on.

This file is split up into several different sections—Ports, Fonts, Extensions, Colors, and so on. The section in this file we want to look at is under the heading Ports.

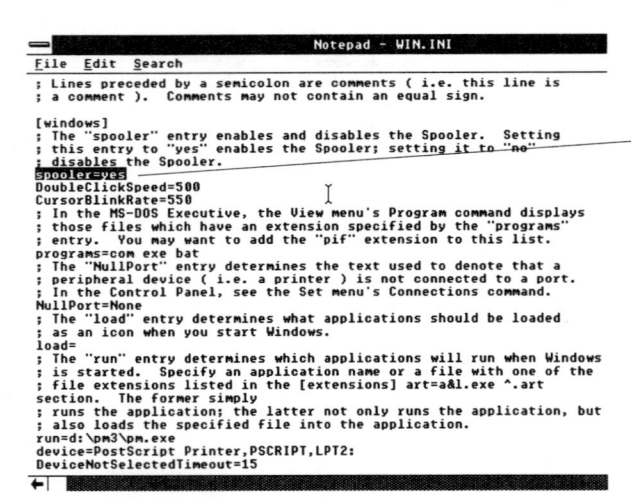

*Figure 19.* The WIN.INI file (shown here using the Windows notepad) controls several defaults for both PageMaker and/or Windows. In this example, if this line is changed to spooler=no, then PageMaker will print directly to the printer rather than to disk first. Using the spooler frees the computer more quickly.

This file will have to be edited using a word processor (even the DOS Edlin, if necessary) if you do not have the full Windows loaded. If you do have the full Windows loaded, you only need to double-click on the filename WIN.INI, and it will be opened up in the notepad, ready for editing (Figure 19).

Within WIN.INI there may be several different lines under the ports heading. However, you should at least have some of the following:

LPT1:=

LPT2:=

COM1:=9600,n,8,1,p

COM2:=1200,n,8,1

EPT:=

Remember, you may have extra lines, or slightly different lines. However, we will be adding a line somewhere in this list. The line we are going to add depends on what the file is going to be called. For instance, let's say that the print file we are going to create will be called PM3PRINT.PRN (they should always have a PRN extension). We would add a line at the end of the Ports section that reads:

PM3PRINT.PRN=

```
                    Notepad - WIN.INI
File  Edit  Search
dialog=yes

[ports]
; A line with [filename].PRN followed by an equal sign causes
; [filename] to appear in the Control Panel's Connections dialog.
; A printer connected to [filename] directs its output into this file.
LPT1:=
LPT2:=
LPT3:=
COM1:=9600,n,8,1,p
COM2:=9600,n,8,1
EPT:=
PM3PRINT.PRN=

[fonts]
Helv 8,10,12,14,18,24 (Set #3)=HELVB
Courier 8,10,12 (Set #3)=COURB
Tms Rmn 8,10,12,14,18,24 (Set #3)=TMSRB
Roman (Set #1)=ROMAN
Script (Set #1)=SCRIPT
Modern (Set #1)=MODERN

[PageMaker]
Defaults=D:\PM\PM.CNF

[devices]
PostScript Printer=PSCRIPT,LPT2:

[PostScript,COM1]
device=Apple LaserWriter Plus
```

*Figure 20.* Under the Ports section in the WIN.INI file, we have added this line—it reads PM3PRINT.PRN=. This file, if we connect a printer to it, will be used to catch the output. This sort of file is often preferred if printing to a bureau or over an Appletalk network.

After doing this, save the changes to the file WIN.INI. If you are using a third-party word processor to do this, make sure that you do not save WIN.INI as a formatted file—merely an ASCII one.

## Module 10 - PageMaker Printing

After making changes to this file and saving them, you must exit and restart PageMaker (or Windows). (If you were using DOS anyway, you can just start Windows.) From here, it is a matter of using the Control Panel to connect a printer to the file PM3PRINT.PRN. As we have added this file to the Ports section in the WIN.INI file, it will appear as a computer port in the Control Panel. See the section earlier in this module on the Control Panel to see how to reconnect a printer to another port.

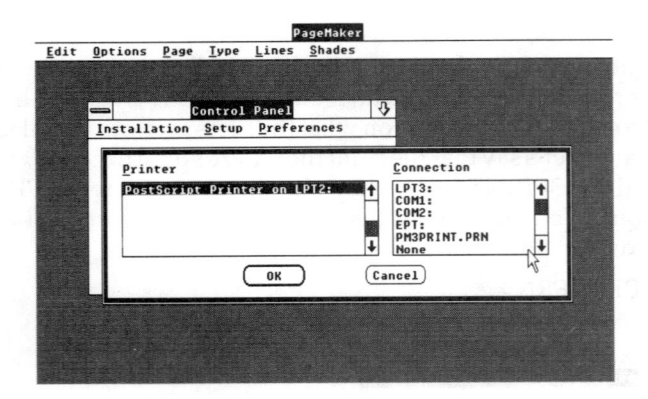

*Figure 21.* As we use the Control Panel next (in particular, the Connections command in the *Setup* menu), we can now see the file is listed in the same list as the ports. Simply choose the file from this list if you wish to print to it.

# Module 10 Exercise

# PageMaker Printing

# Module 10 Exercise
# PageMaker Printing

In this exercise we will look at some of the printing options available with PageMaker—although for this exercise to be completed, a printer is not necessary. Because printing itself is a fairly straightforward exercise (it will either work or it won't, and if it doesn't it is probably a connection problem anyway), we will not be printing directly to a printer in this exercise.

This training material is structured so that people of all levels of expertise with PageMaker can use it to gain maximum benefit. In order to do this, we have structured this material so that the bare exercise is listed below this paragraph on just one page, with no hints. The following pages contain the steps needed to complete this exercise for those that need additional prompting. The **PageMaker Printing** module should be referenced if you need further help or explanations.

## Module 10 exercise steps

1.  Set up the print dialog box to print all of the chapter PRODSPEC.PT3 (located in the GETSTART subdirectory) three times. Tile the print with a 1 inch overlap. Check your dialog box with Figure 5 on page 351. All PostScript printer users should scale the print by 200%.

The details for completing this exercise are on the following pages.

*Module 10 Exercise - Pagemaker Printing*

1. *Set up the print dialog box to print all of the chapter PRODSPEC.PT3 (located in the GETSTART subdirectory) three times. Tile the print with a 1 inch overlap. Check your dialog box with Figure 5 on page 351. All PostScript printer users should scale the print by 200%.*

The first step in this exercise is to open the PageMaker publication PRODSPEC.PT3, located in the GETSTART subdirectory (Figure 1).

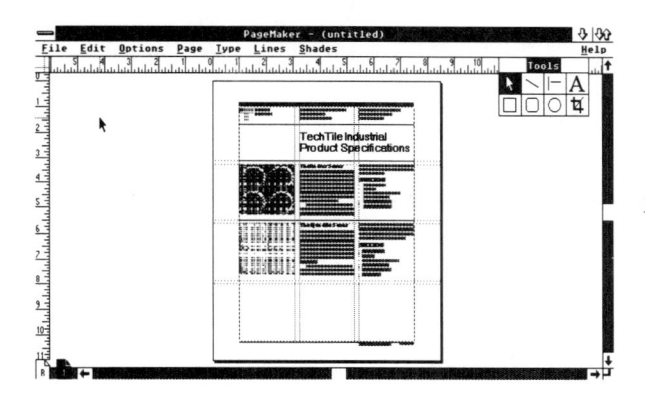

*Figure 1.* Make sure this PRODSPEC.PT3 file is open. As it is a template, an untitled copy is automatically opened.

Upon opening this publication, our next step is to select the *Print* command from the **File** menu (Figure 2).

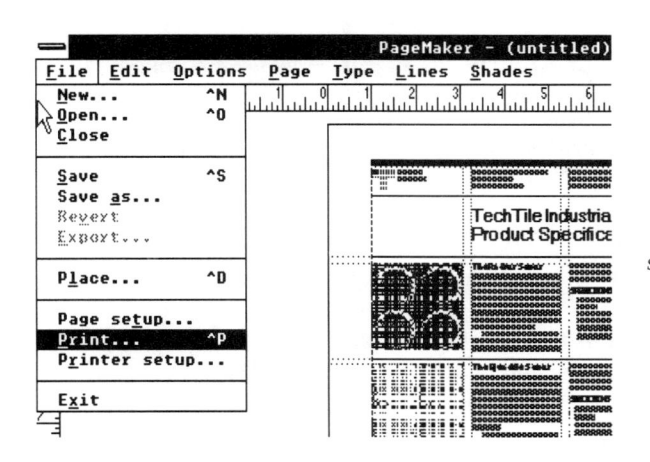

*Figure 2.* After opening the file, select the Print command from the File menu.

349

Module 10 Exercise - PageMaker Printing

To print the publication three times, make sure you alter the number in the Copies box to 3 (Figure 3).

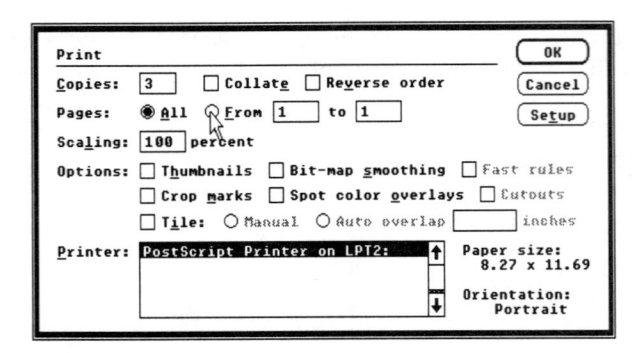

*Figure 3.* Change the figure in the Copies box to 3. This ensures that three copies of the publication are printed.

To scale the print to 200% (PostScript printer users), alter the scale figure to 200 (Figure 4).

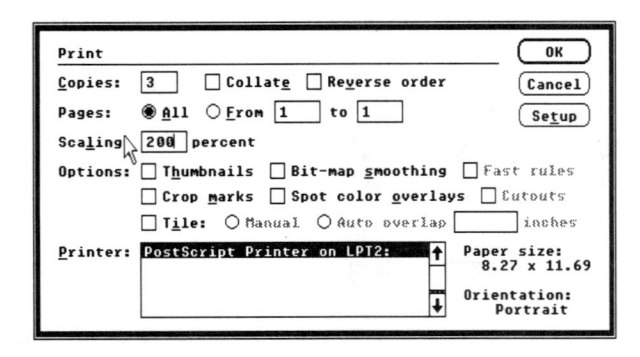

*Figure 4.* Change the figure for Scaling to 200 to double the print size.

Finally, make sure the Tile command has been checked to ensure tiling is used. Select Auto overlap, and change the figure in the overlap box to 1 inch (Figure 5).

350

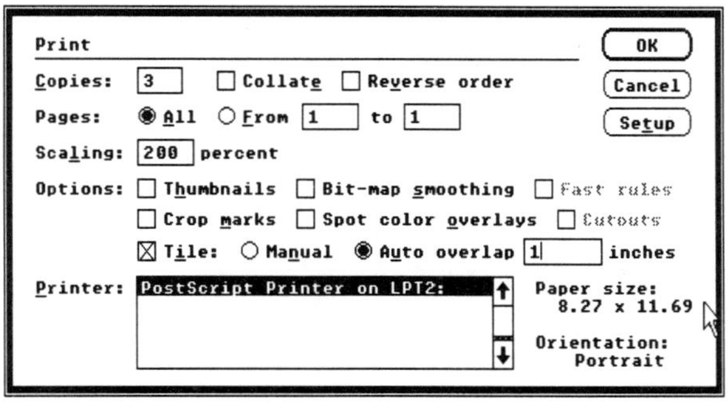

*Module 10 Exercise - Pagemaker Printing*

*Figure 5.* Select the Tile box near the left-bottom of the screen, and set the Auto overlap to 1inch. Choose cancel from here unless you have a printer connected and would like to see the output.

# Module 11

# PageMaker Style Sheets

# PageMaker Style Sheets

A PageMaker *style sheet* comes with every template or publication that you open. A style sheet contains several different groups of text characteristics, identified by *style names*, that can be applied to text. For example, a style sheet may contain four different style types—Heading, Body text, Subheading, and Footnote. (These style names can be anything you want them to be.) Heading may be defined as Bookman, 24 point, Bold, Centered, 1 inch of space below, indented 2 centimeters from the left and right, etc. All other style names are defined differently again. You decide what attributes are saved under what name.

After you have loaded in text and are ready to format, previously you would have had to move through a lot of menus and commands to format such things as headings, footers, etc. However, with style sheets, you can apply the style name Heading to a paragraph on the page, and all attributes defined for this style are applied immediately. This becomes a far quicker way to format text than has been available in earlier versions of PageMaker.

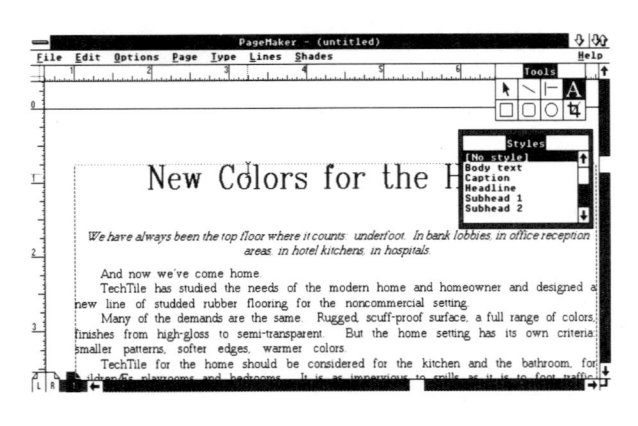

*Figure 1. All these paragraphs on this page were formatted in a matter of seconds using style sheets.*

The benefits of style sheets do not end there. Let's say, for example, that you have applied the style Heading to a hundred or so paragraphs throughout a very large publication. This Heading style may be defined as Palatino, 24 point, bold, yet you decide that it would look better if it were Bookman, 24 point, bold.

Instead of having to find every paragraph and alter its appearance, all you have to do is alter the attributes of the style Heading. Every time this style occurs in the text it will be altered.

Style sheets can be copied from publications and templates to other publications or templates. Style sheets can also link up to word processors, like Microsoft Word, that use style sheets.

Don't get style sheets confused with type styles—which include bold, italic, underline, etc. When we talk about applying a style, we mean applying one of the style names in a style sheet to text.

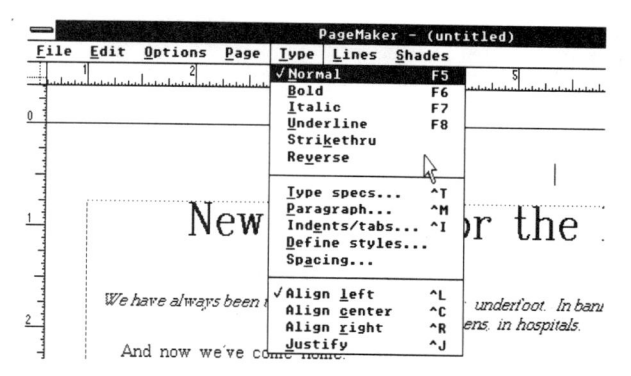

*Figure 2. Don't get the type styles shown here, confused with styles from the style sheet—they are two separate things.*

## Adding new styles to a style sheet

You can add new styles to a publication's style sheet by:

- Defining styles from scratch.
- Basing a new style's definition on one of the current publication's existing styles.
- Copying an existing style sheet from another publication.
- Importing styles with imported word-processed documents.

We will look at each of these methods soon, but first we will look at the default styles in every style sheet.

As already mentioned, every template or publication contains a style sheet, even if you are not really aware of it. To see the styles that are used in your current document, choose the *Style palette* command from the **Options** menu (Figure 3). Just below the Toolbox will appear a small window, as shown in Figure 4.

*Module 11 - PageMaker Style Sheets*

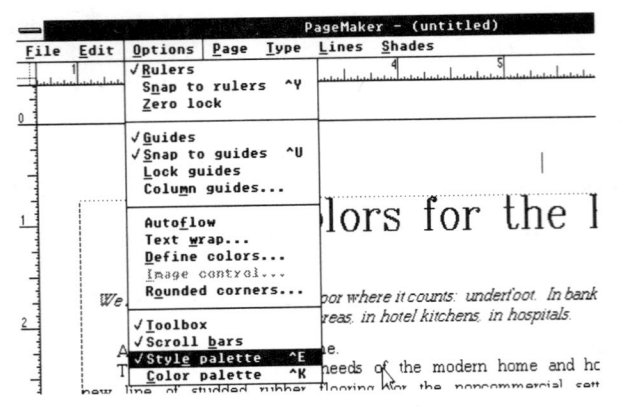

*Figure 3. When using style sheets, make sure that the Style palette is shown by choosing the Style palette command in the **Options** menu.*

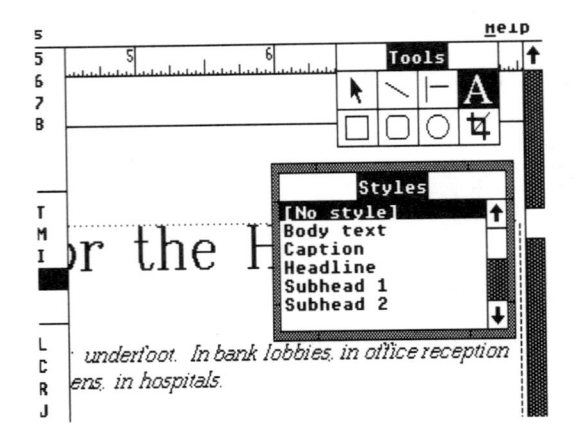

*Figure 4. The Style palette will appear somewhere below the Toolbox, and can be moved around similar to the Toolbox.*

Inside this Style palette there may be listed several different names. However, if this is a new document (i.e., it contains no imported text) it will contain several style names—*No style, Body text, Caption, Headline, Subhead 1,* and *Subhead 2.*

## No style

*No style* is exactly as it sounds—it indicates those paragraphs that do not use a specific style. Consequently, it contains no specific text attributes—it will change all the time.

## Body text and other default styles

Body text is one of the default styles included in all style sheets. Other default styles that may be included in default style sheets include Caption, Headline, Subhead 1, and Subhead 2. Each one of these styles uses different type specifications, providing a good basis for creating attractive publications.

## Defining styles from scratch

Once you become familiar with PageMaker's style sheets, you will continue to add new styles —maybe some to represent headings, others for footnotes, formulas, headers and footers, etc. The alternative (earlier) PageMaker method, that you can also use to format text, involves selecting text, moving through the commands in the **Type** menu, and applying characteristics one at a time. We covered this in detail in Module 4. This latter method can still be used in conjunction with style sheets—so you can phase in the use of style sheets if they are a little confusing at first.

Before we start looking at creating new styles, load some text onto the page to see the effect of creating these new styles. We have used BROCHURE.DOC from the GETSTART subdirectory and loaded it into a single column. If, upon loading the text, new styles appear in the style sheet, ignore them for now. We will look at those a little later on. Don't worry if the formatting of your text file looks different to our Figure 5, we will adjust this later on in Figure 16.

New styles are created using the *Define styles* command in the **Type** menu (Figure 5). Select this command now. The dialog box of Figure 6 appears.

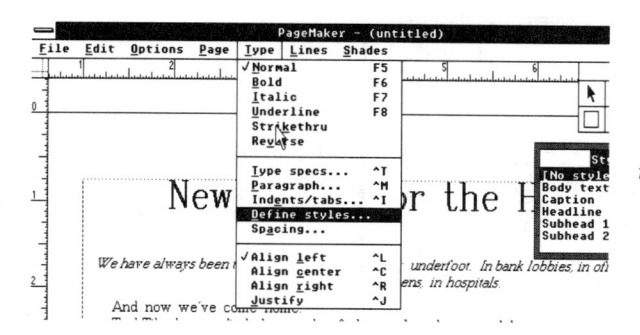

*Figure 5. The Define styles command is used to create new styles to add to the style sheet.*

## Module 11 - PageMaker Style Sheets

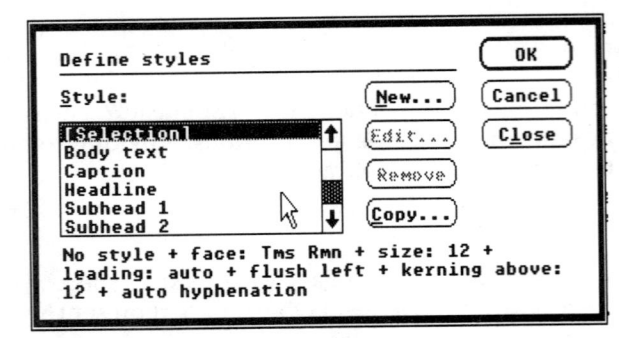

*Figure 6.* The Define styles dialog box. Your dialog box may vary from this. It doesn't really matter for our discussion.

At the left of this dialog box is the list of all the styles in this publication's style sheet. It should read Selection and Body text. Listed below these names may well be the other default styles of Caption, Headline, Subhead 1, and Subhead 2. Next to these styles are several commands we will be using to create and edit new styles.

Click the mouse on *Selection* at the top (Figure 6). A list of type specifications will appear below the list of names. This list reflects the attributes of the selected text (if any is selected). If you click on Body text (Figure 7), the text specifications now reflect exactly how the style Body text is set up. It is possible that Body text and Selection are set up exactly the same.

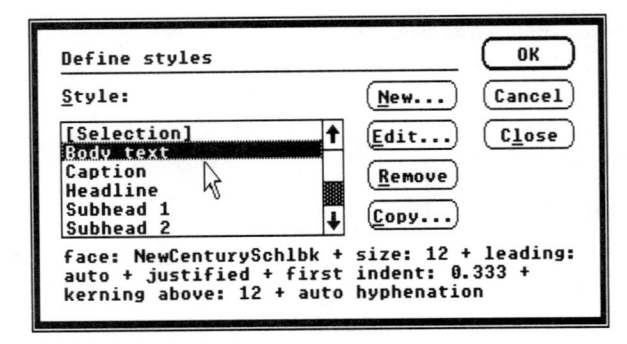

*Figure 7.* Compare Figures 6 and 7 to see the type specifications defined below the list of styles. In this case, the selected text has different type specifications than Body text.

358

*Module 11 - PageMaker Style Sheets*

To create a new style, you must click on the command *New* within the Figures 6 or 7 dialog box. A New dialog box of Figure 8 will appear.

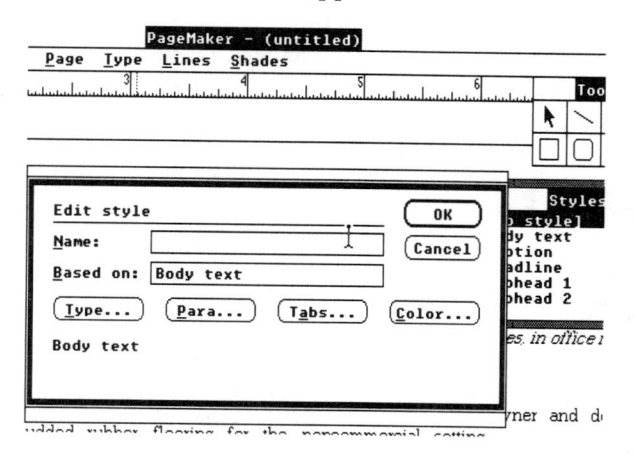

*Figure 8.* Upon selecting the New command from the dialog box in Figures 6 or 7, you will be presented with this dialog box.

The first thing to do in this dialog box is to insert a name for this style. You can call it anything you like, but make it meaningful so that it can be recognized later on. If anything appears in the *Based on* rectangle, delete it now.

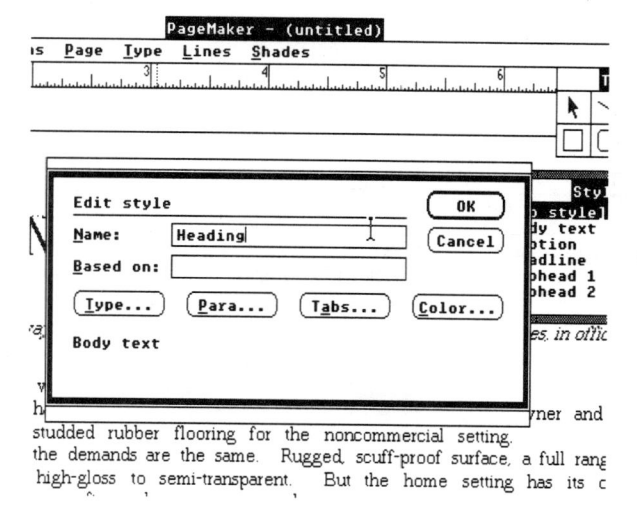

*Figure 9.* Your first step in this dialog box should be to name the style you are about to create. Try to name it something meaningful—it makes things a lot easier later on.

359

*Module 11 - PageMaker Style Sheets*

Below these two rectangles in Figures 8 and 9 are four commands—*Type, Para, Tabs,* and *Color*. As you click on any one of these, the appropriate dialog box relating to these commands will be presented (Figures 10 to 13). In these dialog boxes, adjust this style we have just created so that it is at least a little different from Body text. Every time you use one of these commands in Figures 10 to 13 and click on OK, you are returned back to the dialog box of Figure 9, to choose another command. When you have finished defining the style exactly as you want it, click OK to return to the previous dialog box.

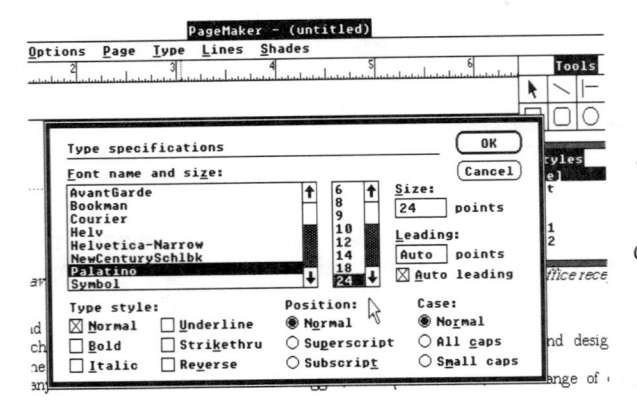

*Figure 10. This dialog box is invoked after clicking once on the Type command in the dialog box of Figure 9. Change your box to reflect these selections. Choose Times font if you don't have Palatino.*

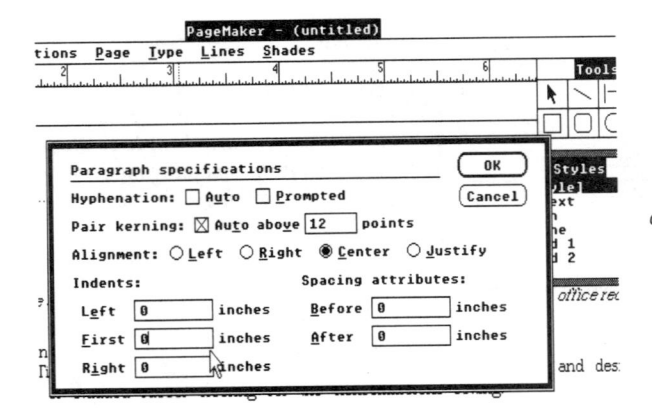

*Figure 11. This dialog box is accessed by clicking on the Para command from the Figure 9 dialog box. Adjust your box the same as this one.*

*Module 11 - PageMaker Style Sheets*

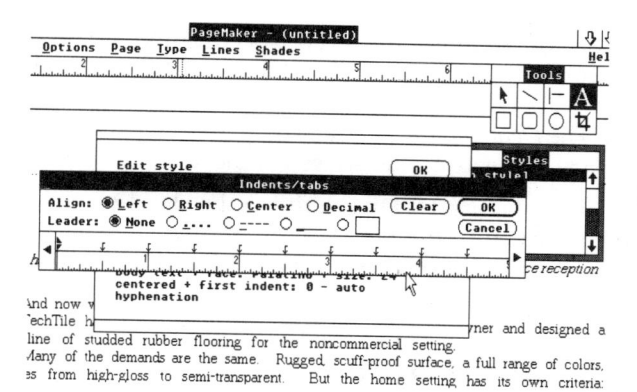

*Figure 12.* This box comes from selecting the Tabs command in Figure 9. Keep as is.

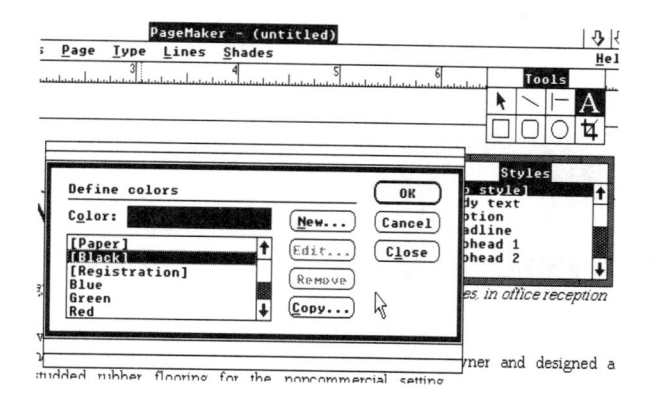

*Figure 13.* And this box from selecting the Color command in Figure 9. Keep as is.

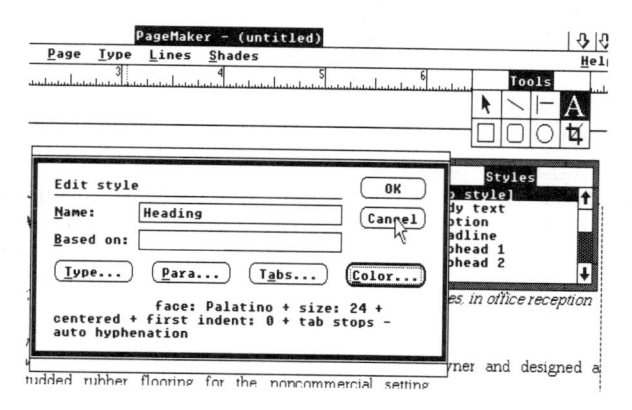

*Figure 14.* Using these commands, we changed the attributes of the style we created. Note at the bottom of the dialog box, the list of new attributes we have assigned to the Heading style.
In your case, Times font may have replaced Palatino.

361

*Module 11 - PageMaker Style Sheets*

In the dialog box of Figure 14, the type specifications for this new Heading style are listed. Click OK twice to return back to the page. Joining the Style palette is the new Heading style we created (Figure 15). The *Define styles* command can be used as many times as is necessary to create all the styles you need.

For example, in Figure 14, after defining the Heading style, we could have returned to the Figure 7 *Define styles* dialog box by clicking on OK once, chosen New again, and created more styles if we wished.

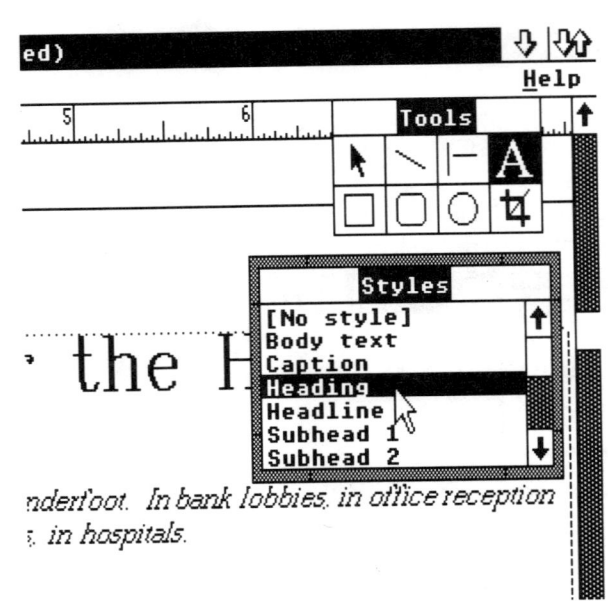

*Figure 15. The style we created has been added to the list of styles in the Style palette. Compare to Figure 4.*

## Applying styles

Styles are very simple to apply to paragraphs on the page. If you want one paragraph alone to use the new style you created, move to the text cursor. Insert this text cursor inside the paragraph, or simply select the entire paragraph if that makes it easier. Now move back to the Style palette, and click on the style you would like to apply to the paragraph. Instantly, any attributes you created with that style are applied to the paragraph on screen (Figure 17). Whatever attributes it had previously have been totally overwritten.

*Module 11 - PageMaker Style Sheets*

Several paragraphs in sequence can be applied a style at once, simply by selecting more than one paragraph before you select the style.

Styles can also be applied via the *Define styles* command, and associated dialog box, from the **Type** menu (Figure 18).

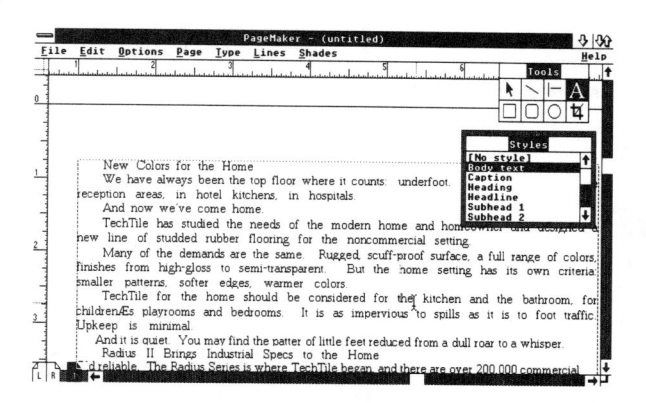

*Figure 16.* To illustrate how we can apply styles to unformatted text, we have changed all the paragraphs of our BROCHURE.DOC file to look the same. We applied the Body text style to everything.

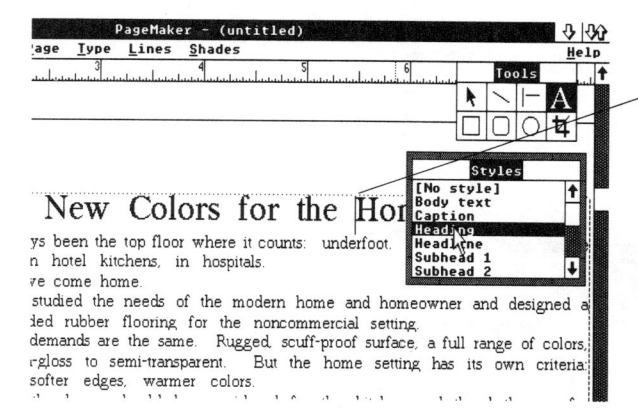

*Figure 17.* To apply styles to text, we insert the text cursor in the first paragraph (or whatever paragraph(s) we like), and click on Heading in the Style palette. The attributes we defined in creating the Heading style are instantly applied to that paragraph.

*Module 11 - PageMaker Style Sheets*

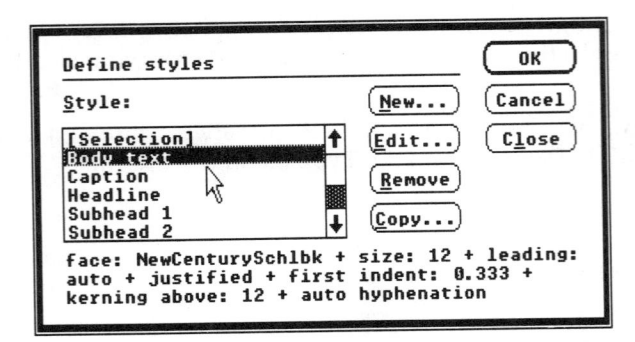

*Figure 18. Apart from clicking on the style name in the Style palette, styles can also be applied via the Define styles dialog box.*

## Editing styles

Let's say you have applied the style Body text to most of your publication, and now decide that it must be changed. As we mentioned, when looking at the benefits of style sheets, there is no need to find all the paragraphs that use the Body text style. Simply edit the Body text style itself, and all paragraphs using this style will change. To perform this example, we first of all change all text back to Body text, as explained in Figure 19.

Select once again the *Define styles* command from the **Type** menu. From the list of styles presented (Figure 20), select the style you would like to edit, and choose the *Edit* command to the right of this box. Alternatively, you can click on the name of the style you would like to edit in the Styles palette, with the Ctrl key depressed, to get the same result. We have chosen to edit Body text.

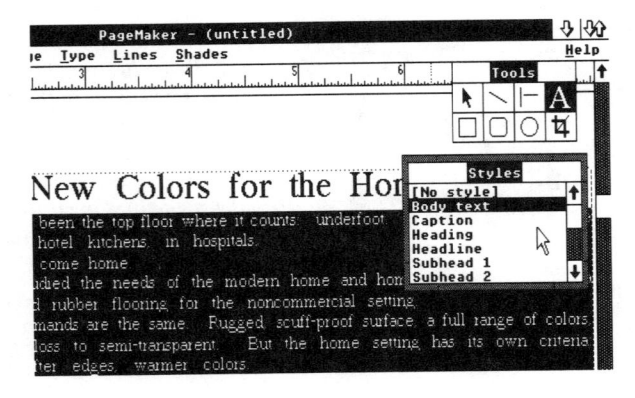

*Figure 19. Every paragraph in this document has been applied the Body text style (apart from the first paragraph). We now want to change the look of Body text, without having to select every paragraph before we do it. Do this to your page now by selecting the whole page (except for the first paragraph) with the text tool, and clicking Body text in the Style palette.*

*Module 11 - PageMaker Style Sheets*

In both cases, you will be presented with the dialog box of Figure 21. You can edit the style in exactly the same way you created a new one. When editing styles, the name comes up automatically in the Name rectangle at the top of the dialog box. Select the four commands—Type, Para, Tabs, and Color—one at a time, and edit the style as you see fit. Choose OK twice when you are happy with the new style.

Figures 20 to 23 provide examples of using the Edit function with the Body text style.

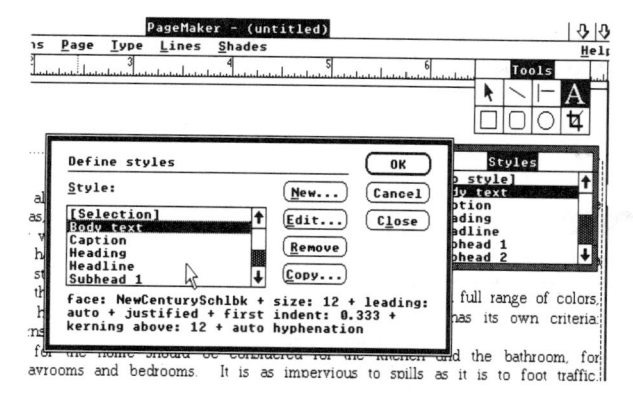

*Figure 20. Our first step in editing Body text is to select the Define styles command again. From the dialog box that then appears, select Body text (or whatever style you would like to edit), and choose the Edit command.*
*The current attributes of Body text are listed at the bottom of this dialog box. Depending upon your printer type, your attributes may be different to ours.*

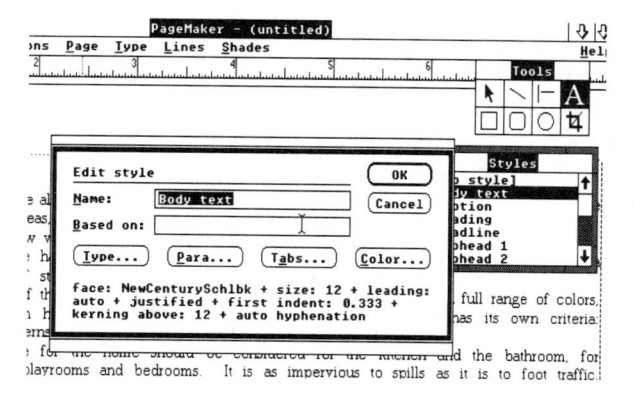

*Figure 21. After selecting Edit from Figure 20, this dialog box will appear. Note how the name Body text already appears next to Name.*

*Module 11 - PageMaker Style Sheets*

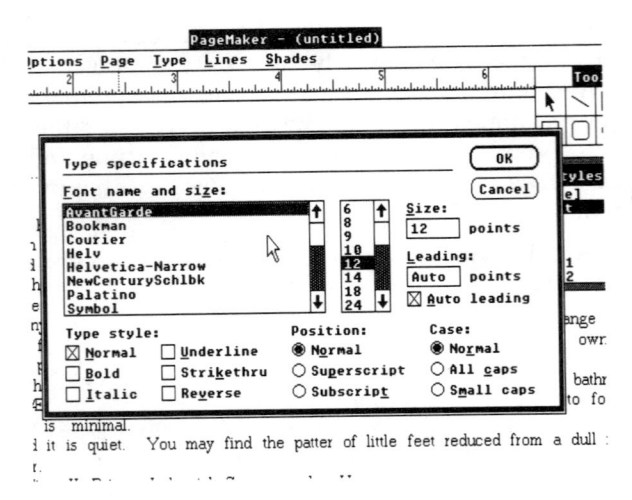

*Figure 22. We chose the Type command from Figure 21, and were presented with this dialog box. We changed the font from New Century Schoolbook to Avant Garde. Choose Helvetica if your system does not include Avant Garde.*

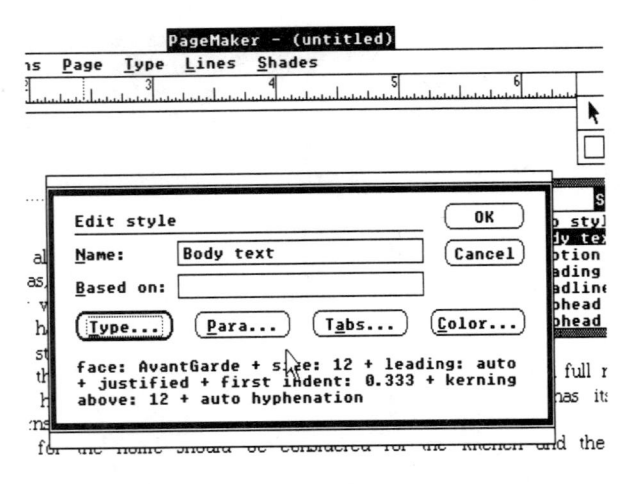

*Figure 23. Note how the definition of Body text has changed to reflect the new attributes.*

In Figures 20 to 23, we have only changed the type specifications to Avant Garde (or Helvetica). Para, Tabs, and Color commands were not changed. The result is shown in Figure 24. All the paragraphs throughout the document that use the Body text style will be updated with its new characteristics.

*Module 11 - PageMaker Style Sheets*

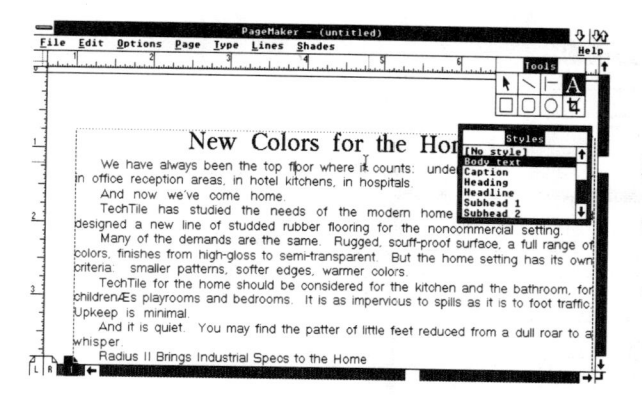

***Figure 24.*** *All paragraphs that use the Body text style have changed, while all paragraphs that use other styles remain as they were. Compare this Body text style with that of Figure 19.*

## Removing styles

Removing a style is even easier than creating or editing a style. Choose *Define styles*, select the style from the list you would like to remove, and choose the *Remove* command (Figures 25 to 27).

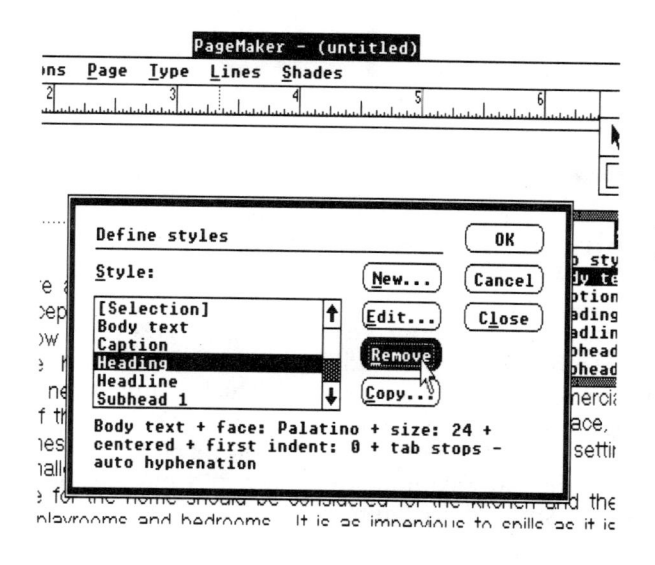

***Figure 25.*** *Removing a style is as simple as selecting it from within the Define styles dialog box and clicking on Remove. We are deleting Heading.*

367

*Module 11 - PageMaker Style Sheets*

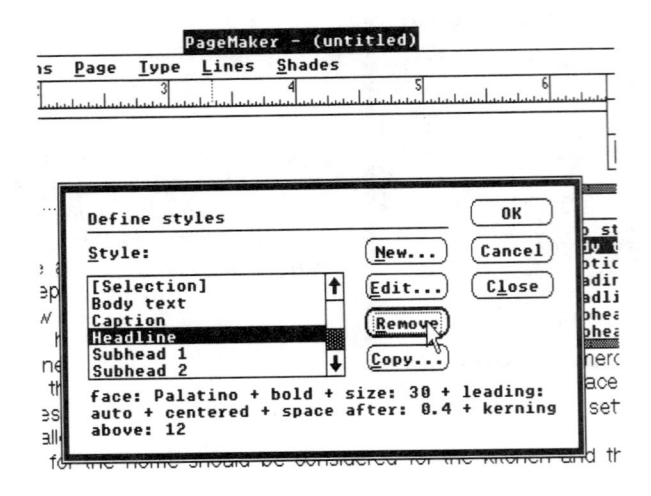

*Figure 26. The style name is immediately dropped from the style sheet.*

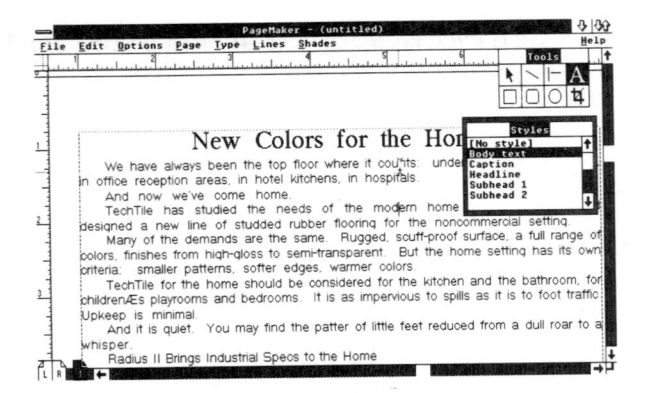

*Figure 27. All paragraphs that use the style we just deleted remain as they were, but they now use the style name No Style.*

# Basing a new style's definition on one of the current publication's existing styles

Let's say that you have now created several styles in this style sheet, one of which may be a Headline style. What you want to do now is to create another Headline style, which is quite similar to the existing Headline style, but with some minor changes. Instead of creating the new style from scratch, it would be nice to be able to start with the old Headline attributes, and modify them to create the new style. This is quite possible.

*Module 11 - PageMaker Style Sheets*

When you choose the *Define styles* command from the **Type** menu, you would normally go straight to the New command to create the new headline style. However, before you do this, click in the list of styles on the original Headline style before you choose New (Figure 28). Upon choosing this command, the name of that style will be in the Based on rectangle in the New dialog box of Figure 29. Insert the name of the new style, and change what you have to. In this way, new styles can be created with a minimum of fuss (Figures 30 to 33).

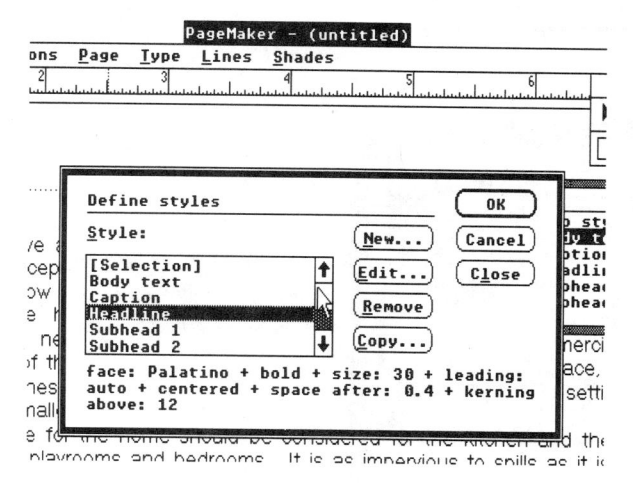

*Figure 28. To create a style similar to another style, select that style in the Define styles dialog box before selecting the New command.*

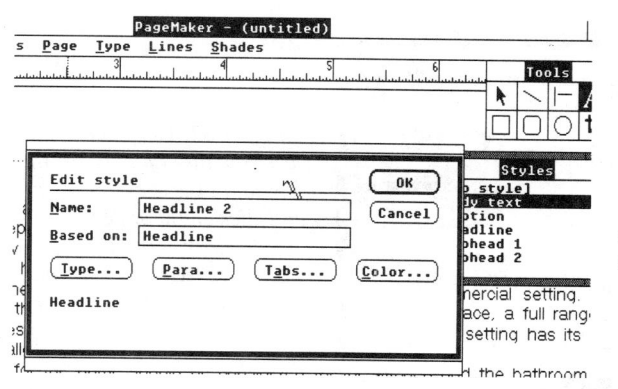

*Figure 29. In the New dialog box that then appears, a name will appear in the Based on box. This will be the name of the style selected before selecting New. Enter the name of the new style above this name.*

369

*Module 11 - PageMaker Style Sheets*

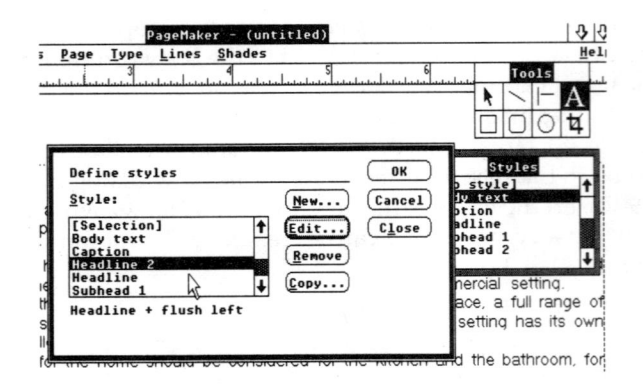

***Figure 30.*** *We used the Para command from the dialog box in Figure 29 to alter slightly the appearance of the new style. Note the description of the new style below the list reads as Headline+ flush left. This tells us that Headline 2 is exactly the same as Headline, except that it is flush left.*

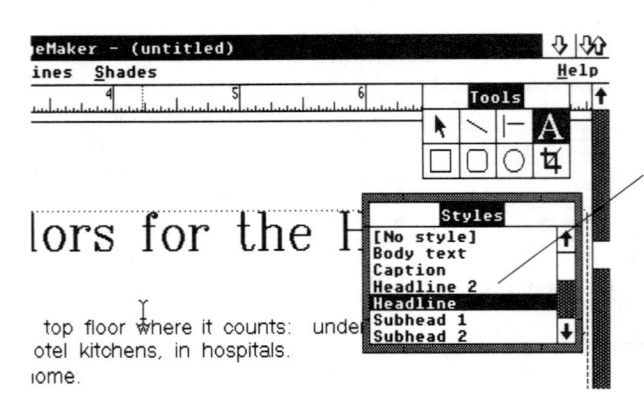

***Figure 31.*** *Note how Headline 2 has been added to the Styles palette.*

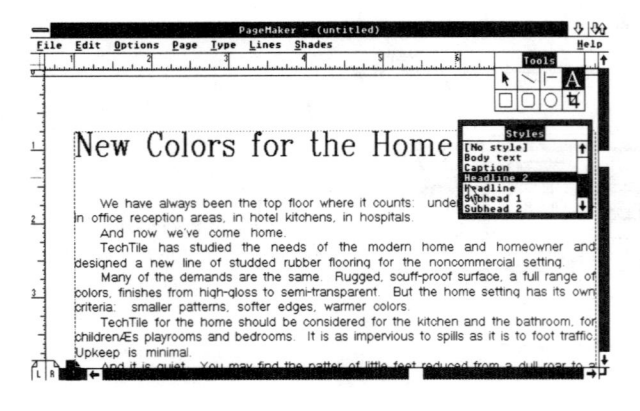

***Figure 32.*** *To see the difference between the styles, insert the text cursor in the very first paragraph and click on the style Headline 2 in the Styles palette. The paragraph now looks basically the same as the Headline style, yet is flush left.*

## Renaming styles

The easiest way to rename a style is to create one exactly the same (using the method described above) with a new name, and then remove the style with the old name. You have effectively renamed the style.

## Copying an existing style sheet from another publication

Copying a style sheet from a separate publication or template into another document will combine the two style sheets together. Once again, to use this function, you must choose the *Define styles* command. This time, however, select the *Copy* command (Figure 33).

You must know which document you want to copy a style sheet from. When the Copy command is chosen, you are presented with a list of publications (you can move to other directories) from which you must select a publication or template (Figure 34). As you select the new document (Figure 35), PageMaker spends a few seconds combining the two style sheets together, and then you are returned to the new *Define styles* dialog box. It now contains a list of styles from both style sheets (Figure 36).

The Style palette will then also reflect the new list of styles that have been added (Figure 37).

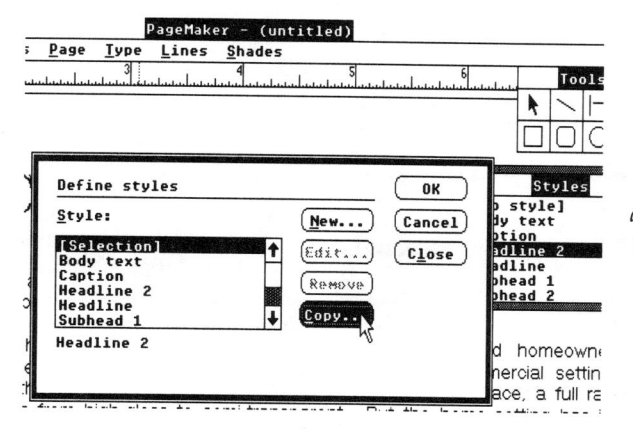

*Figure 33.* To copy the style from an existing style sheet (resident in another publication or template), go to the Define styles dialog box, and then click on the Copy command.

*Module 11 - PageMaker Style Sheets*

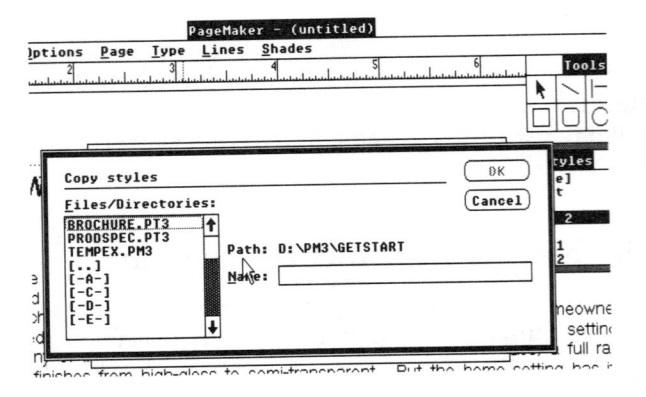

***Figure 34.*** *You will instantly be presented with the list of publications and templates in the currently open folder. Locate the publication or template you know has the other style in it, and click OK.*

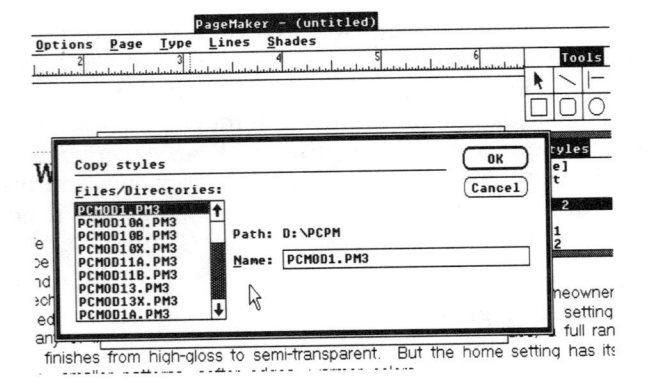

***Figure 35.*** *We have selected a publication of our own—PCMOD1.*

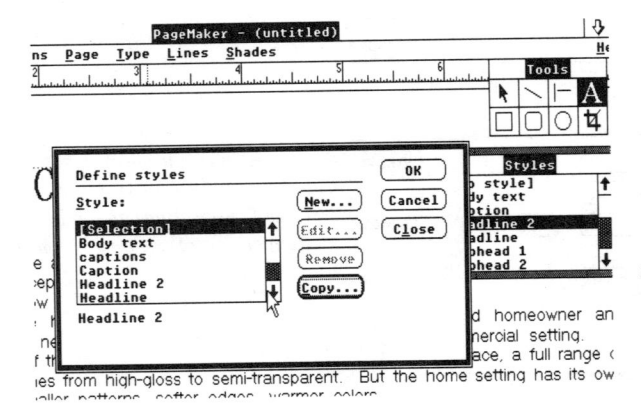

***Figure 36.*** *After a few seconds, the styles from PCMOD1 are combined with the styles already existing in this publication. Note the new Captions style listed in this dialog box, as compared to Figure 33.*

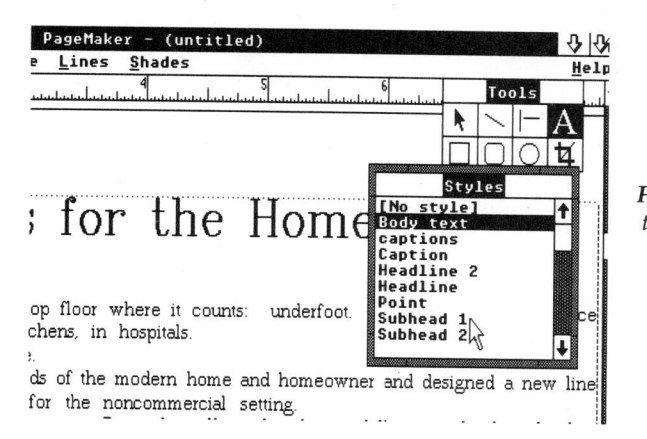

*Figure 37. Here we have extended the Style palette by pulling down on its bottom border to show all the styles now contained in this style sheet. Compare this with Figure 31.*

Any clashing styles (styles with the same name in both style sheets, yet defined differently) take on the attributes of the open publication, rather then the attributes of the publication copied from.

## Importing styles with the imported word-processed document

This can be achieved in two different ways. First, if your word processor uses style sheets, they can be applied and created with all style names being carried through into PageMaker. If the style names already exist in PageMaker, then the imported paragraphs that use that style are applied the attributes of PageMaker's style. Otherwise, the paragraph is still applied that style name, the style name still appears in the style sheet, but initially has the same attributes as the default for that particular file. You must create attributes for all styles imported in this way. This is the reason that you may often see the style name Normal* in your style sheet—it is applied by default to Microsoft Word documents. Any styles added in this way are always named with an asterisk following them.

If your word-processed document does not support style sheets, it is still possible to have the imported text formatted to a predefined PageMaker style. All you need to do is type style name tags in angle brackets (<>) at the beginning of each paragraph, making sure that these tags match the correct style names in your publication's style sheet.

*Module 11 - PageMaker Style Sheets*

Figure 38, which shows the *Place* command dialog box, indicates the different options to choose from in deciding how to import text with styles intact. The *Retain format* option brings in all the style information intact from word processors that support style sheets. The *Read tags* option reads the tag names you have physically typed into your word-processed document using angle brackets.

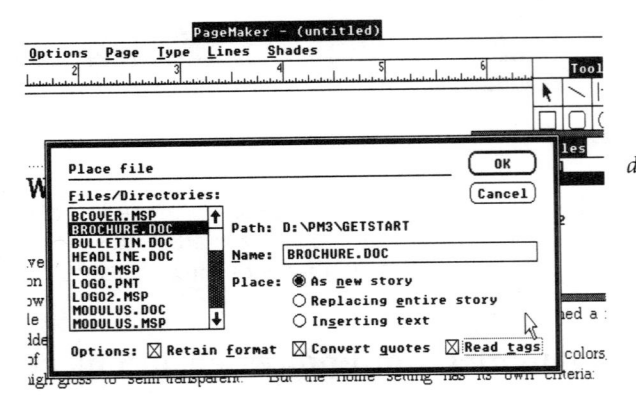

*Figure 38.* The Place command dialog box. Note the Retain format and Read tags options at the bottom of the dialog box.

## Overriding styles

As mentioned earlier, any style can be overridden by selecting the text and applying any type specifications from the **Type** menu. Any paragraph that uses a style which has been overridden with any new type or paragraph specifications, even if it is only part of that paragraph, will be denoted in the Style palette with a + after the style name it uses. If you apply a new style altogether to a paragraph that currently uses an overridden style, only type style changes will survive the style change.

374

## Module 11 Exercise

# PageMaker Style Sheets

# Module 11 Exercise
# PageMaker Style Sheets

In this exercise we are working with style sheets and seeing how quickly we can format text using this method.

This training material is structured so that people of all levels of expertise with PageMaker can use it to gain maximum benefit. In order to do this, we have structured this material so that the bare exercise is listed below this paragraph on just one page, with no hints. The following pages contain the steps needed to complete this exercise for those that need additional prompting. The **PageMaker Style Sheets** module should be referenced if you need further help or explanations.

## Module 11 exercise steps

1. *Create a document using one A4 or Letter vertical page, with margins of your choice.*
2. *Create and/or modify three style sheets using these names and parameters:*

   **(a) Body text**
   10 point Helvetica
   Left justified
   Automatic leading
   2 mm paragraph spacing
   2 mm first line indent
   50 mm left indent

   **(b) Heading**
   24 point Times Bold
   Centered
   Automatic leading
   5 mm above and below para spacing

   **(c) Introduction**
   14 point Times Italic
   Centered
   15 point line spacing
   3 mm above and below para spacing

3. *Load the file BROCHURE.DOC, making sure that it comes in totally unformatted.*
4. *Apply the **Heading** style to the first paragraph of the text file, the style **Introduction** to the second paragraph, and make sure that the rest of the paragraphs in the text file use the style **Body text**.*
5. *Change the **Body text** style so that it uses the font Times Roman, and is 12 point.*

The steps to completing this exercise are found on the following pages.

## The steps in detail.

1. *Create a document using one A4 or Letter vertical page, with margins of your choice.*

This is achieved by starting PageMaker and using the *New* command from the **File** menu. In the *New* dialog box, choose an A4 or Letter page and select a single page publication.

See Figures 1 and 2 for this first step.

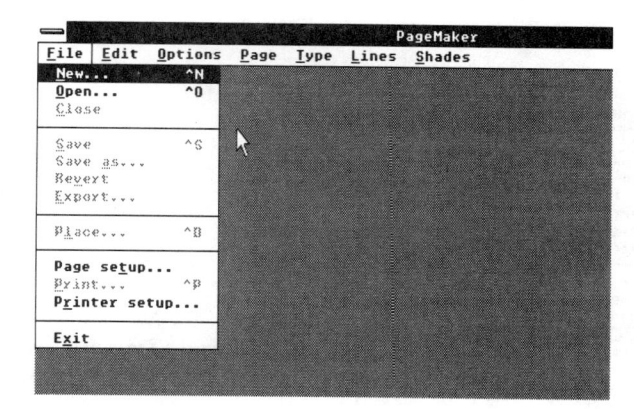

*Figure 1. Select the New command from the **File** menu to create a new publication.*

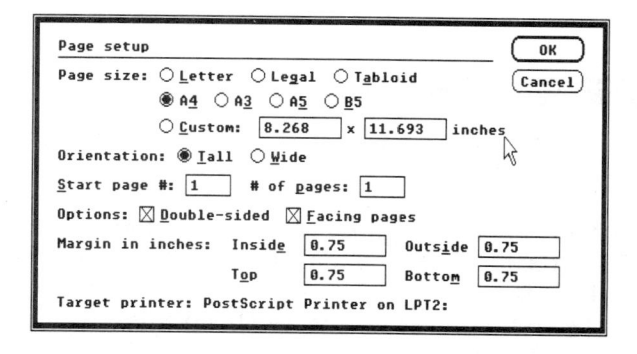

*Figure 2. Set up a single, vertical A4 (or Letter) page (the other settings do not matter for this exercise).*

377

*Module 11 Exercise - PageMaker Style Sheets*

2. *Create and/or modify three styles using these names and parameters:*

**(a) Body text**
*10 point Helvetica
Left justified
Automatic leading
2 mm paragraph spacing
2 mm first line indent
50 mm left indent*

**Body text** is a style that will have to be modified rather than created, as it always exists by default in every publication. In order to modify how it is set, first choose the *Define styles* command in the **Type** menu (Figure 3).

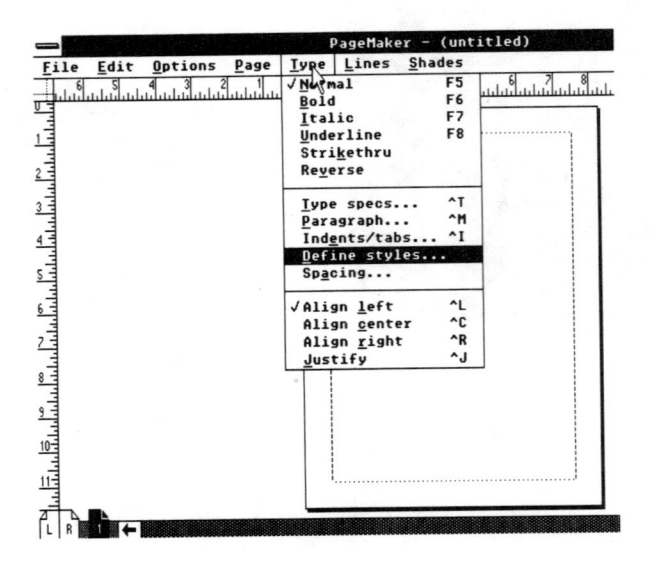

*Figure 3.* The Define styles command from the **Type** menu is used to alter and create styles.

In the dialog box that then appears (Figure 4), you must click on the line that reads Body text. When you do this, the bottom of this dialog box will list all the attributes currently assigned to Body text—these are the ones we will be changing. Some may be set up correctly already—it depends on how Body text is currently set for your publication.

*Module 11 Exercise - PageMaker Style Sheets*

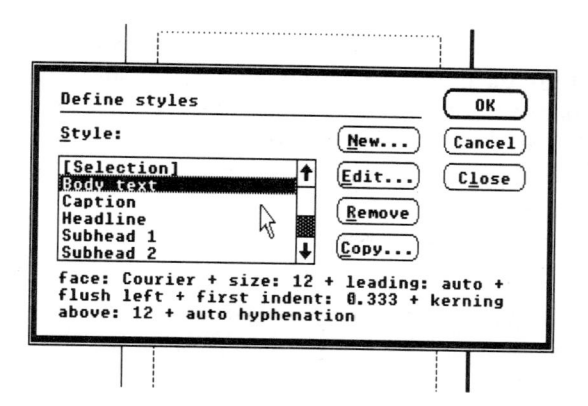

```
Define styles                          OK
Style:                        New...   Cancel
[Selection]
Body text                     Edit...  Close
Caption
Headline                      Remove
Subhead 1
Subhead 2                     Copy...

face: Courier + size: 12 + leading: auto +
flush left + first indent: 0.333 + kerning
above: 12 + auto hyphenation
```

*Figure 4.* The Define styles dialog box—note how we have clicked on Body text to select it. The current attributes for Body text are then shown in the bottom of this dialog box. Your settings may differ—it really doesn't matter at this moment.

To alter the settings for Body text we must click on the *Edit* command within the Figure 4 dialog box. Upon doing this, you will be presented with the additional dialog box of Figure 5.

```
Edit style                             OK
Name:    Body text                     Cancel
Based on:

Type...   Para...   Tabs...   Color...

face: Courier + size: 12 + leading: auto +
flush left + first indent: 0.333 + kerning
above: 12 + auto hyphenation
```

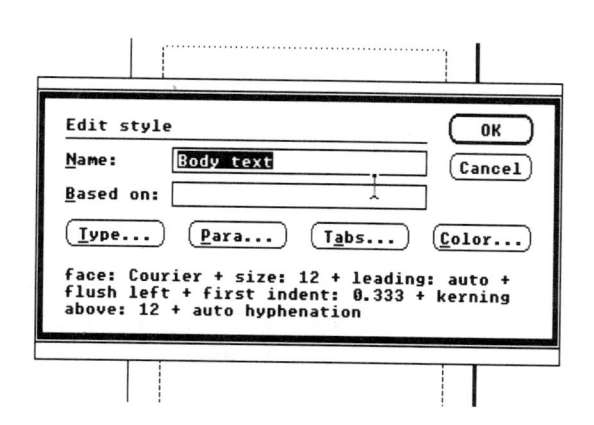

*Figure 5.* After clicking on the Edit command in Figure 4, you will be presented with this new dialog box.

This *Edit style* dialog box will have the name of the style we are editing (in our case Body text) at the top of its dialog box, as well as the current attributes of this style listed at the bottom of the box. In between the name of the style and its attributes are four commands—Type, Para, Tabs, and Color. Each one of these commands allows us to alter a different part of the style. The two commands we will have to look at to change the style according to our step 2 (a) specifications for Body text are the Type and Para commands. Click first on the Type command.

379

*Module 11 Exercise - PageMaker Style Sheets*

Yet another dialog box will appear (Figure 6)—this one is concerned with the type specifications of the style Body text. Part of our specifications for step 2 tell us that we must change Body text to 10 point Helvetica. Just change the *Font* and *Size* commands in the normal way to those shown in Figure 7.

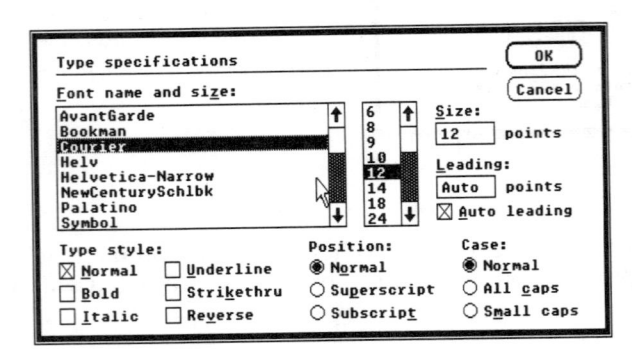

*Figure 6.* After selecting the Type command from Figure 5, you will be presented with this dialog box—don't worry if it contains different values than this—the values depend on the defaults currently set for your copy of PageMaker.

*Figure 7.* Simply change your settings to match these—as defined in the specifications for this step.

All we have adjusted is Helvetica for Font and 10 points for Size. Also make sure that Leading is set to Auto.

The *Leading* must also be set to *Auto*. When you have set the text attributes correctly, click on OK to return you to the Figure 8 Edit style dialog box (same as Figure 5).

You will notice in the dialog box of Figure 8 that the current settings for Body text have been altered. Compare Figure 8 with the earlier settings of Figure 5.

Module 11 Exercise - PageMaker Style Sheets

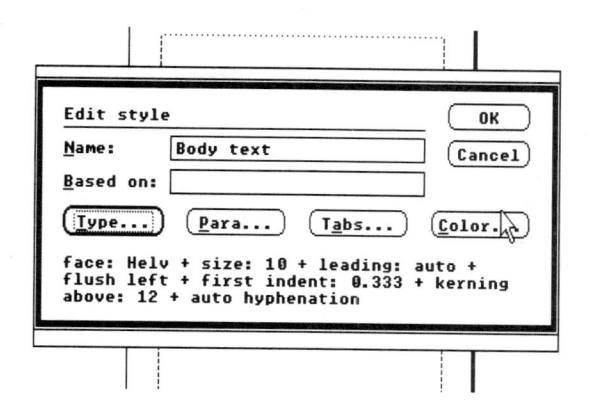

*Figure 8.* Read the attributes for Body text now in this dialog box—they have changed to reflect the changes we just made. Compare with Figure 5.

We must now click on the Para command in the Figure 8 dialog box to alter the other settings for Body text. Once again, you will be greeted with a new dialog box, this time that of Figure 9.

*Figure 9.* The Para dialog box is identical to the Paragraph command in the **Type** menu—although this time it applies to a style, rather than simply selected text.

Here we must set a 2 mm paragraph spacing, a 2 mm first line indent, and a 50 mm global left indent. If you find that you are working in inches, don't panic or try to change to millimeters using the *Preferences* command from the **Edit** menu. Remember, we can still set measures in millimeters even if inches are selected.

To set the paragraph spacing, we have chosen to put 2m in the After rectangle (Figure 10). We could have put it in the Before rectangle if we wished. It is entirely up to you. The 2 refers to the 2 mm, and the m overrides the current

381

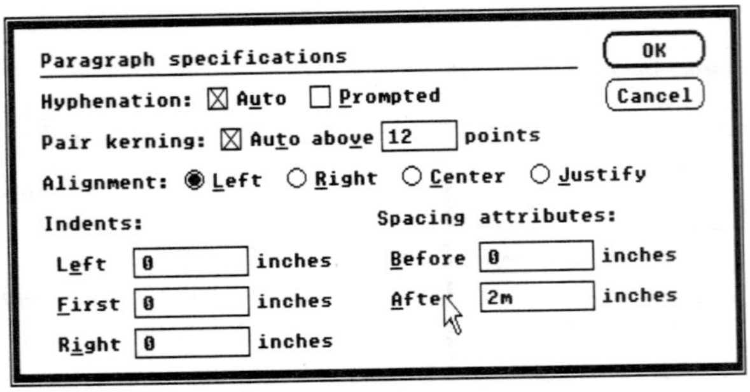

## Module 11 Exercise - PageMaker Style Sheets

*Figure 10. Even though we are working in inches in this dialog box, we can override the inches by inserting the letter m after a measure (or p for picas, and so on). The figure we have inserted here forces 2 mm of space after every Body text paragraph.*

measure in use and uses millimeters. In Figure 10, even though we are using inches as you can see, we can still insert measurements in millimeters.

The first line indent is set using the First rectangle—type in 2m (Figure 11). To set a global left indent of 50 mm, you must use the Left rectangle. Insert 50m (Figure 11).

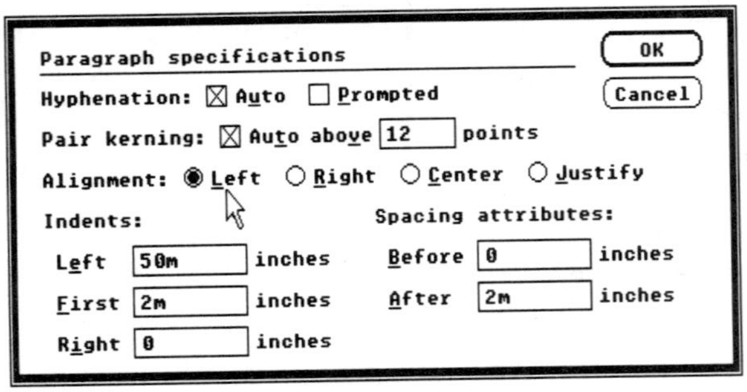

*Figure 11. Here we have set a global left indent of 50 mm and a first line indent of 2 mm, all while using inches as our unit of preference.
Also, we have checked Left as our preferred alignment.
(If you wish to work in inches, note the approximate equivalents—50mm = 2i; 2mm = 0.08i.)*

Finally, make sure that the setting for Alignment is Left, as per our specifications of Left justified.

After making these settings, click OK in Figure 11 to return you to the Edit styles dialog box of Figure 12. There you can see all the settings we have altered for Body text.

*Module 11 Exercise - PageMaker Style Sheets*

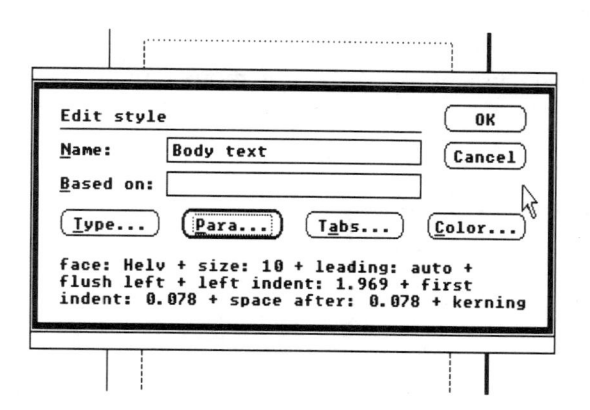

*Figure 12.* After clicking OK from the dialog box in Figure 11, we are returned to the Edit style dialog box. Note all the new settings for Body text (note also how all measurements have been converted to inches).

From here we can go about creating the other styles we were asked to create.

**(b) Heading**
24 point Times Bold
Centered
Automatic leading
5 mm above and below para spacing

To create any new style, click on the New command from the *Define styles* dialog box of Figure 4. The Edit style dialog box will be presented yet again (Figure 13), although this time it will be slightly different. Initially, it has no name in the Name box.

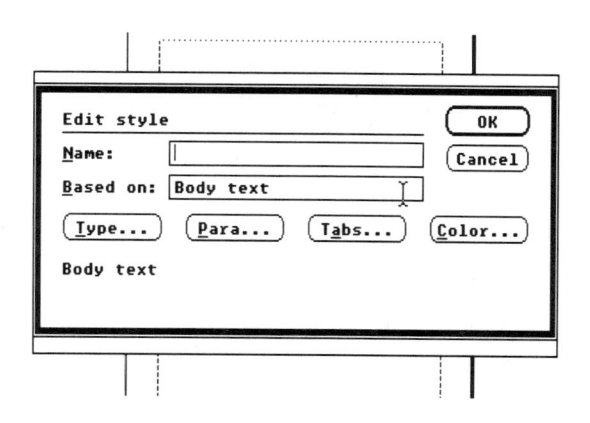

*Figure 13.* The New dialog box is very similar to the Edit style dialog box—but this time we must insert a name for the new style (Figure 14).

383

Module 11 Exercise - PageMaker Style Sheets

This time, as we are creating a new style, we must name the style before we create it. Simply type the name of this style—the mouse cursor is correctly positioned to receive the name—which in this case is Heading (Figure 14).

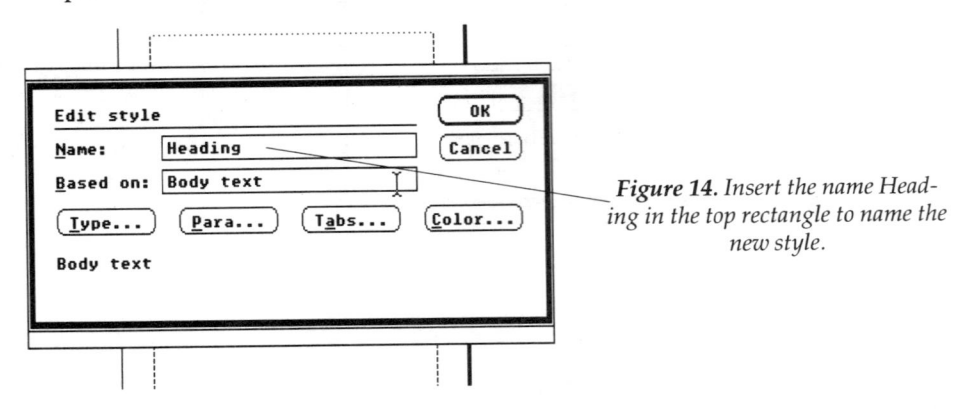

*Figure 14. Insert the name Heading in the top rectangle to name the new style.*

After naming the new style it is once again a case of using the four commands in this dialog box to alter the settings for the Heading style, although once again the Type and Para commands are the main commands used. Select Type first of all to get to Figure 15.

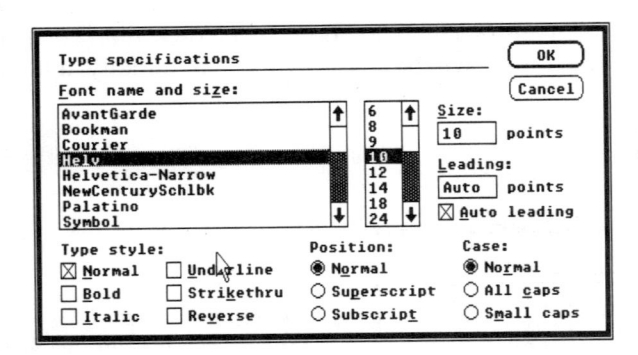

*Figure 15. This is the dialog box we get after selecting the Type command from Figure 14. This needs to be altered to match that of Figure 16.*

Within this command we must make the size 24 point, the font Times, and the type style Bold. We must also make sure the leading is set at Automatic. Perform these steps as you would normally do, as shown in Figure 16, then click OK. You will then be returned to the Figure 14 dialog box. Click then on the Para command to get to Figure 17.

384

*Module 11 Exercise - PageMaker Style Sheets*

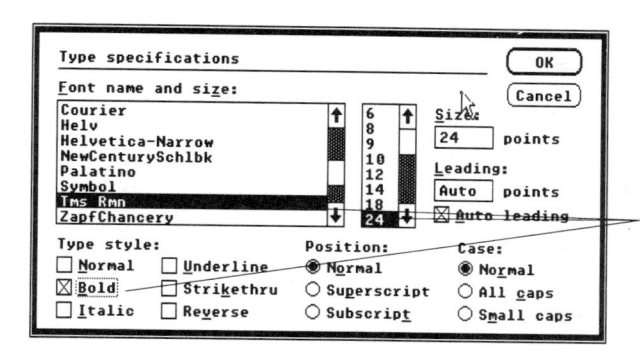

*Figure 16.* Change the settings to those defined in this step—Times, 24 point, and Bold. Then click on OK.

Use the Figure 17 dialog box to center the paragraph, and also to put 5 mm (0.2") of space above and below it (Figure 18). Click OK twice to return to the *Define styles* dialog box of Figure 19.

*Figure 17.* The dialog box for the Para command may initially look like this—all measures once again converted to inches. However, all we want for Heading is space before and after—not left, first, or right.

*Figure 18.* We must change to zero all the Indents rectangles on the left, and insert 5 mm (0.2") of space in the Before and After Spacing attributes rectangles. We have also changed the Alignment to Center and turned Hyphenation off.

385

*Module 11 Exercise - PageMaker Style Sheets*

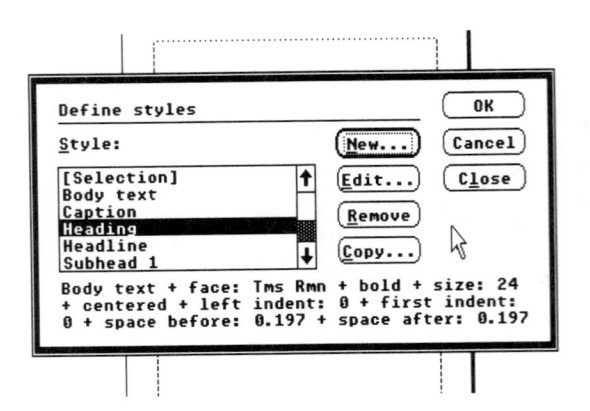

*Figure 19. After returning once again to the Define styles dialog box, you will find Heading has been added to the list of styles. If selected, its attributes will then be listed at the bottom of the dialog box, as shown here.*

Within the Figure 19 dialog box you will now find the Heading style we just created added to the list, as well as its attributes at the bottom of the screen. Click on Body text in the list, and the attributes will change again as indicated in Figure 20.

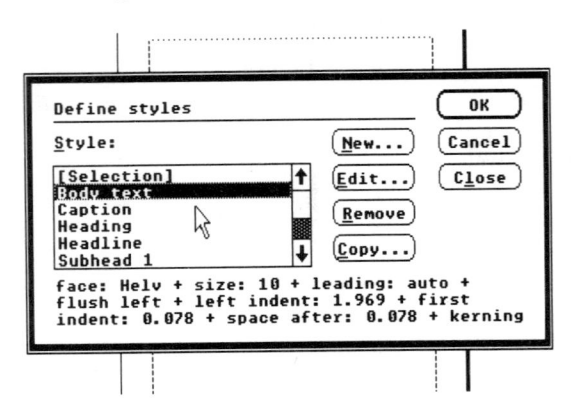

*Figure 20. If Body text is selected within this dialog box then its settings are immediately reflected beneath the list of styles.*

We must create one more tag from within this dialog box.

### (c) Introduction
14 point Times Italic
Centered
15 point line spacing
3 mm above and below para spacing

Following the steps we used above for Heading, try to create this style on your own.

*Module 11 Exercise - PageMaker Style Sheets*

*3. Load the file BROCHURE.DOC, making sure that it comes in totally unformatted.*

This file is loaded via the *Place* command in the **File** Menu, and exists in the GETSTART subdirectory. However, as you choose the file to load in, remember that we want the file to come in totally unformatted. To ensure that this occurs, click on the *Retain format* option in the bottom left-hand corner of the *Place file* dialog box to uncheck it as shown in Figure 21. This makes sure that the formatting of the text file is lost.

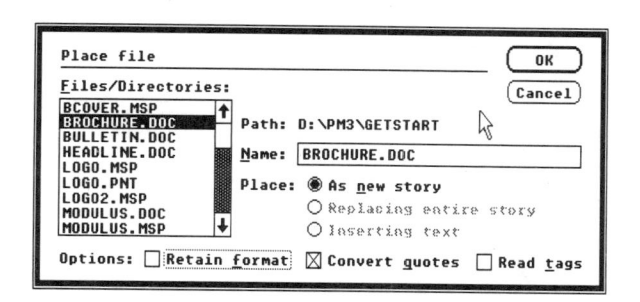

*Figure 21. Here we are loading in the file BROCHURE.DOC. Note, however, that the Retain format option in the bottom left-hand corner of the dialog box has been unchecked—so that the selected file come in totally unformatted.*

Once loaded, flow the file onto the first page as indicated in Figure 22 (this page should only have one column).

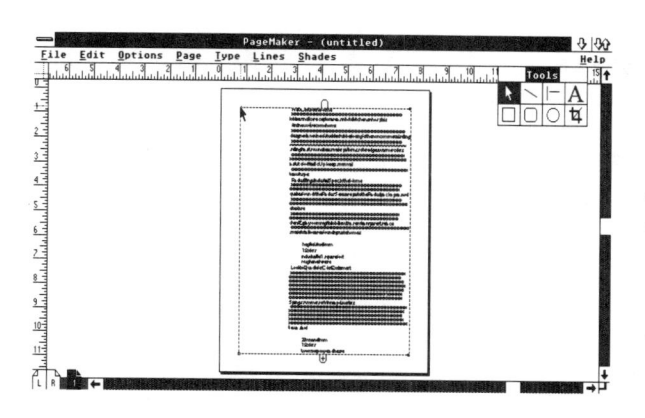

*Figure 22. How your text appears as it flows in depends entirely on which style was selected last in the Define styles dialog box or style palette. Here we had Body Text selected, but don't worry if you didn't—we will be changing the look of the text as we apply styles anyway.*

387

## Module 11 Exercise - PageMaker Style Sheets

4. Apply the **Heading** style to the first paragraph of the text file, the style **Introduction** to the second paragraph, and make sure that the rest of the paragraphs in the text file use the style **Body text**.

After the text has been loaded onto the page, applying styles is simple. You must, however, first make sure that the Style palette is visible—through the *Style palette* command in the **Options** menu (Figures 23 and 24).

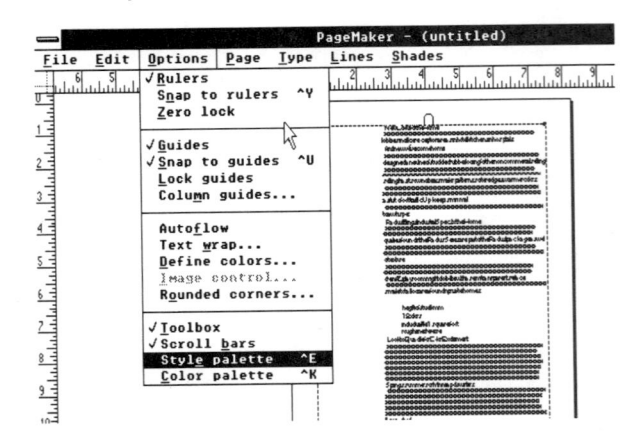

*Figure 23.* The Style palette is accessed via the command of the same name in the **Options** menu.

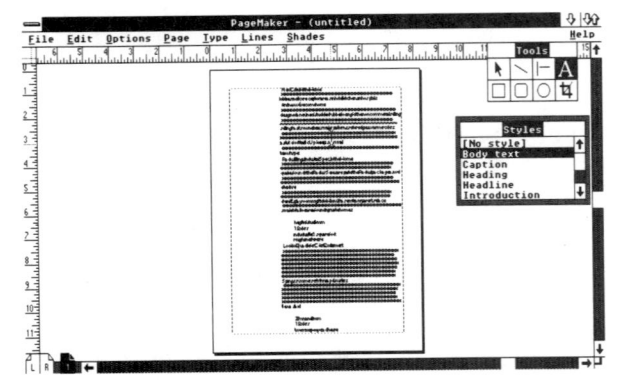

*Figure 24.* The Style palette is now visible, complete with default styles, the styles we created, and any styles that may have been carried through from the word processor that created the text.

We have been asked to apply the style Heading to the first paragraph in the text file. This is achieved by simply inserting the text cursor (make sure this is selected in the Toolbox) somewhere in this first paragraph. The whole paragraph need not be selected. From here, move to the Style palette and click on the style Heading (Figures 25 and 26). All the attributes we gave to Heading will be instantly applied to this paragraph.

*Module 11 Exercise - PageMaker Style Sheets*

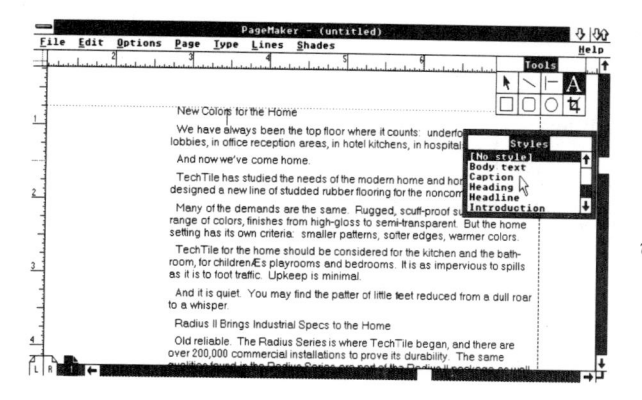

*Figure 25.* Insert the cursor in, or select the paragraph that you would like to apply a new style to...

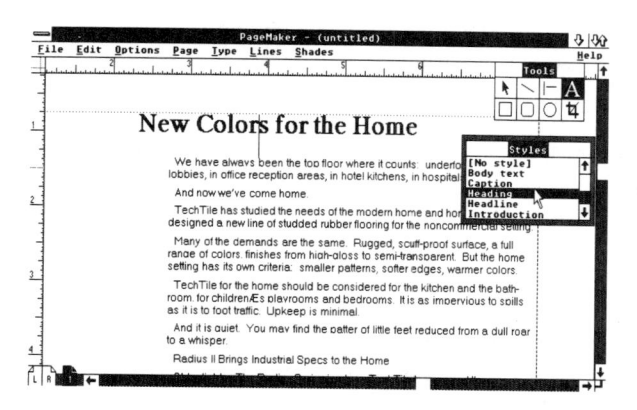

*Figure 26.* ...and click on the name of the style in the Style palette. The paragraph instantly takes on the attributes as described by the Heading style.

To apply the style Introduction to the second paragraph the steps are exactly the same—insert the text cursor in this paragraph, and click on the style Introduction in the Style palette. Once again, everything that was set up for Introduction is applied to the paragraph with the text cursor in it.

Figure 27 illustrates the result.

## Module 11 Exercise - PageMaker Style Sheets

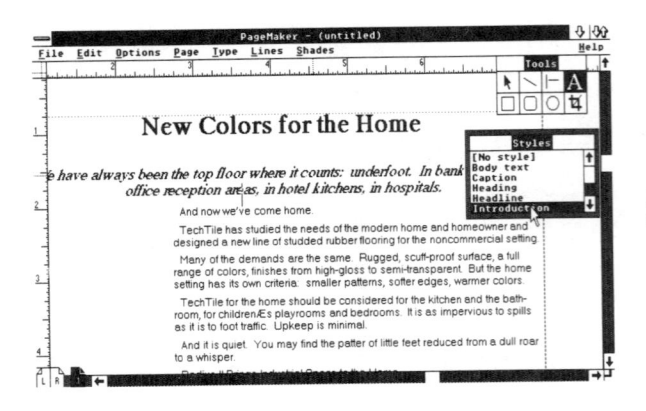

*Figure 27.* Here we have inserted the text cursor in the second paragraph on the page and clicked on the style Introduction. Immediately the text has been altered to reflect this.

Finally, to make sure that all other paragraphs are using the style Body text, select the rest of the page using the text tool and click on the style Body text in the Style palette (Figure 28). All the text will change to Body text if it was not already using it. Don't worry about the extra styles that may have entered the Style palette—these are merely carried through from the word processor—we will not use them.

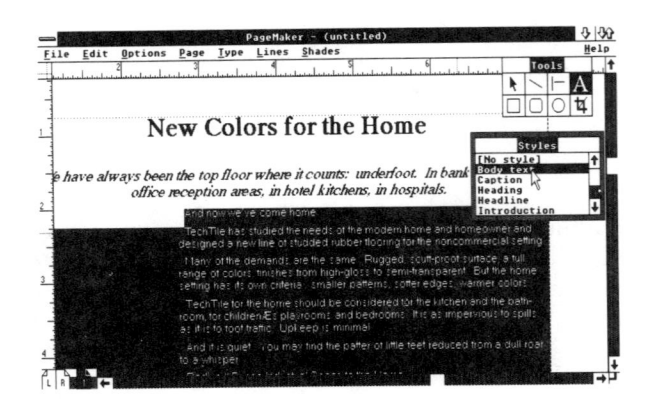

*Figure 28.* All other paragraphs were selected and applied the style Body text in one operation. Remember, when applying a style to more than one paragraph, select these paragraphs in the normal fashion before clicking on the style in the Style palette.

Module 11 Exercise - PageMaker Style Sheets

5. Change the **Body text** style so that it uses the font Times Roman, and is 12 point.

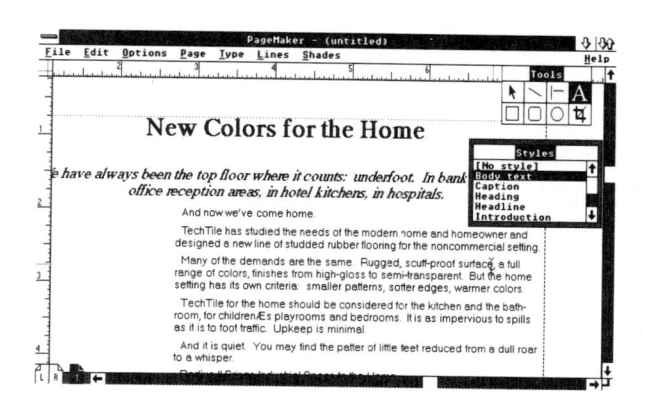

*Figure 29.* Here we see in Actual size view, the look of Body text at 10 point Helvetica. We will now change all Body text to 12 point Times by making one simple change.

The style Body text can be altered without having to select any text. Merely move to the *Define styles* command in the **Type** menu and select the style Body text from the list (Figures 30 and 31).

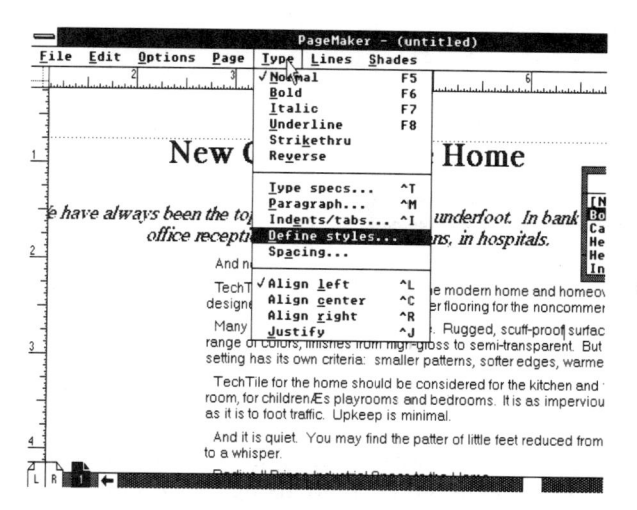

*Figure 30.* Move to the Define styles command in the **Type** menu to change the attributes of Body text style.

From here, choose the *Edit* command (Figure 31), and from within the Edit style dialog box, choose the Type command (Figure 32).

391

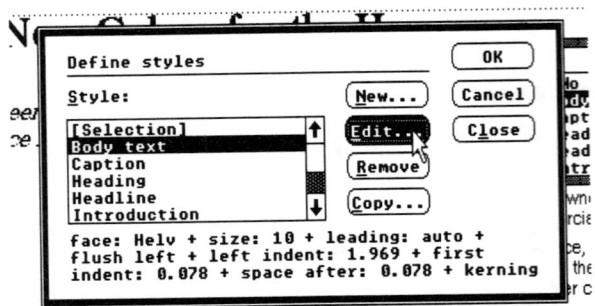

*Module 11 Exercise - PageMaker Style Sheets*

*Figure 31. From the Define styles dialog box select the style Body text and choose the Edit command.*

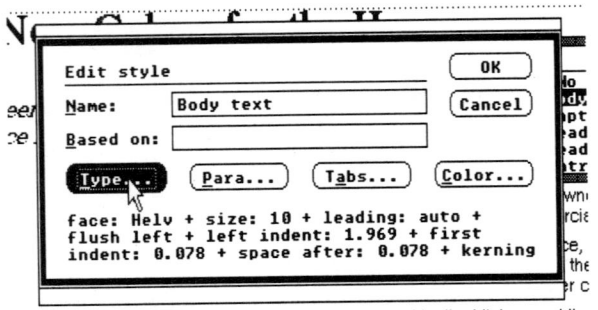

*Figure 32. Once in the Edit style dialog box, choose the Type command. Note that the Body text name is already included, as we had selected it in Figure 31. Now move to Figure 33.*

    From within the Type dialog box of Figure 33, alter Body text to use the font Times at 12 points size. Once you return to the page from here, all paragraphs using the style Body text will have been altered, using the new attributes just set (Figures 34 and 35).

    Compare Figure 35 to that of Figure 29.

Module 11 Exercise - PageMaker Style Sheets

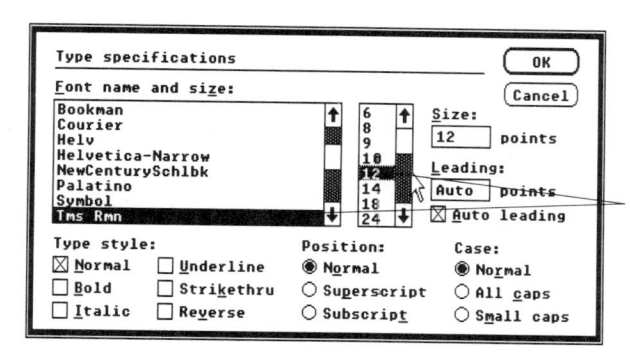

*Figure 33.* Change the settings for the Type specifications of Body text to reflect this dialog box, i.e., Times at 12 points.

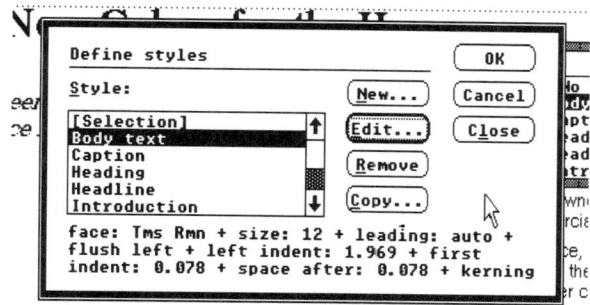

*Figure 34.* When you return back to the Define styles dialog box, the attributes for Body text listed along the bottom of this box have changed to reflect the new settings.

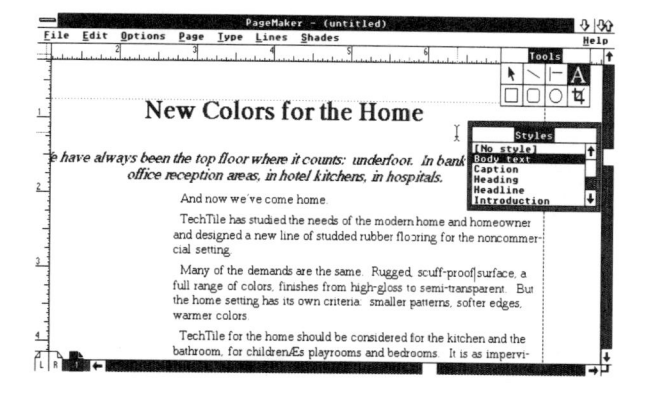

*Figure 35.* Back on the page, all Body text paragraphs have been altered to reflect the new settings for Body text.
Compare to Figure 29.

393

# Module 12

# Setting PageMaker Defaults

# Setting PageMaker Defaults

## Introduction

At times it is useful to be able to utilize certain preset options within PageMaker, without having to readjust them each time PageMaker is opened or used to create new publications. Of course, you could set up a template to do this (one that used all the settings you want to), but there are times when we just don't need to use a template.

So far, we have looked at many options that can be invoked within PageMaker. Rulers, column guides, and the Style palette are but a few of the things that can be invoked when entering PageMaker. Suppose, however, that you always wanted the Style and Color palettes, you always wanted rulers, and you always wanted to use an A3 page with predefined margins all around (Figure 1). Setting this up each time you opened PageMaker would not be very productive.

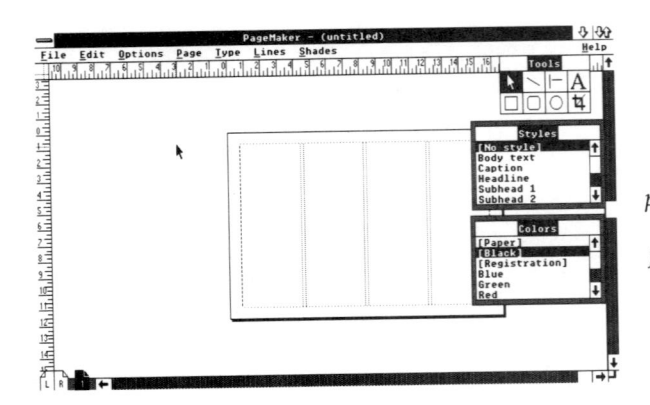

*Figure 1. If all of your documents start off like this (Rulers, Style palette, Color palette, four columns, A3 page size), you would spend a fair amount of time setting up each one.*

PageMaker is normally shipped with predefined options for many of its settings. These are referred to as the *default settings* and may differ for the US and non-US versions. The settings for these standard defaults are listed in the PageMaker User Manual in Part 1, PageMaker Basics.

*Module 12 - Setting PageMaker Defaults*

What we would like to do, for ease of operation, is to sometimes change these defaults to those of our own choosing. This can be done in two ways—through what are called *Application defaults* or *Publication defaults*.

## Application defaults

To customize the use of PageMaker with Application defaults, you must have no publication currently open. This will involve either using the *Close* command to get rid of the current document, or simply restarting PageMaker (it always opens at the PageMaker desktop without a publication).

You may have noticed that, even with no publication open, all the menus appear at the top of the screen, and all can be invoked (Figures 2 and 3). Further, many of the commands within these menus can be selected.

The long and short of it is—any command that can be selected while no publication is open can be set up as a default. For example, we could now select the *Rulers* command, and although no rulers would show now, whenever a new publication was opened, it would use rulers. In this way, you can set up defaults in the following areas:

*Page Size and Margins*

*Rulers command*

*Text flow*

*All guide commands*

*Lines and Shades*

*Preferences*

*Palettes*

*Colors, and so on*

Remember that any of these commands, if altered while no publication is opened, will become the new default. Any time a new publication is opened, it will use these settings. These defaults can be changed, if wished, for a single publication. This method is described next.

*Module 12 - Setting PageMaker Defaults*

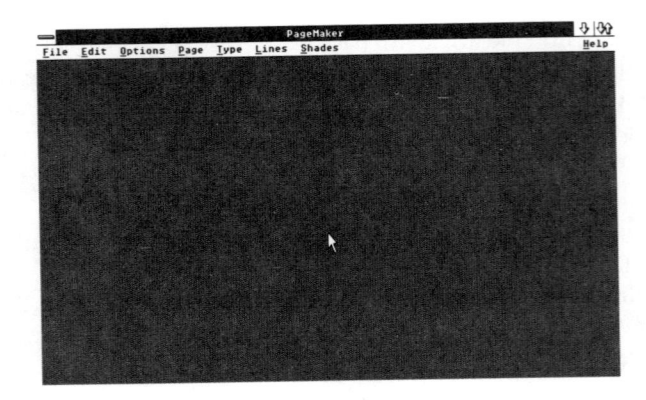

*Figure 2. PageMaker opened without a publication will look exactly like this.*

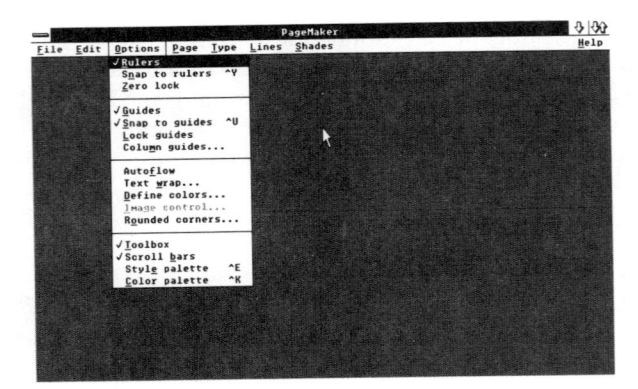

*Figure 3. All menus and many commands can be used, even though no publication has been opened.*

## Publication defaults

Publication defaults differ from Application defaults in that Publication defaults are set up inside a publication and are only defaults for that particular document. For instance, you may decide that in one publication you wish to draw lines of 8 point thickness. Before you draw any lines, you would move to the lines menu, and select an 8 point thickness line (Figure 4). Any line now drawn within this publication will automatically be of 8 point thickness (Figure 5).

*Module 12 - Setting PageMaker Defaults*

To create these Publication defaults, it is important that the pointer tool is used, and no text or graphics is selected.

As another example, if you want to use rulers for a particular publication, turn them on and they will remain on every time this publication is opened and used (unless, of course, you turn them off).

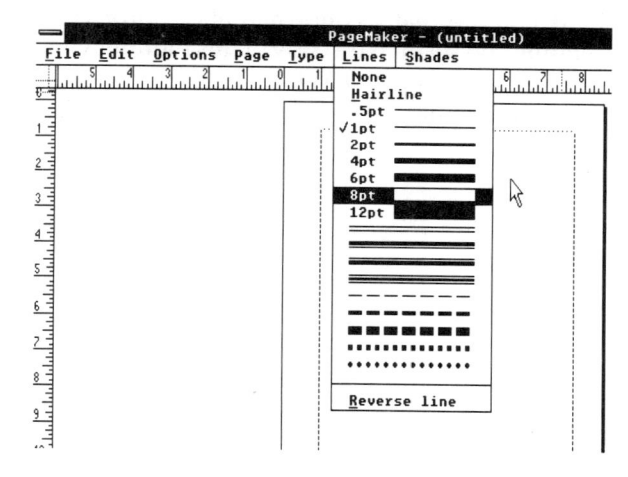

*Figure 4. Publication defaults are set up within a publication. In this case, because a line is not selected as we set a line thickness, all future lines will be of 8 point thickness.*

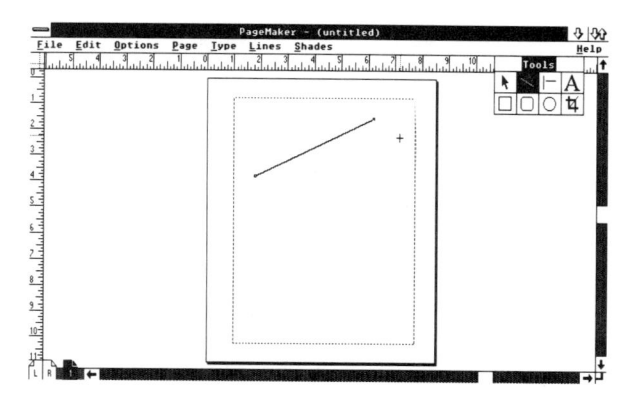

*Figure 5. Any line drawn now is of 8 point thickness.*

399

## Protecting defaults

If several people use your copy of PageMaker, the idea of defaults may become a little confusing, as each person may prefer to set his or her own defaults oriented to a particular type of publication. In other words, how do we get two or more sets of application defaults?

In your PageMaker directory you will find a file called PM.CNF. This file controls exactly what defaults are used when you create publications. If you are really concerned about protecting the particular defaults you set, make a copy of this file after you have set your defaults, and rename it PM.CNF before you start PageMaker again. Your defaults will be used and protected.

# Module 12 Exercise

# Setting PageMaker Defaults

# Module 12 Exercise
# Setting PageMaker Defaults

In this exercise we are going to set different defaults, both Application and Publication, to illustrate how easy this is to do within PageMaker.

This training material is structured so that people of all levels of expertise with PageMaker can use it to gain maximum benefit. In order to do this, we have structured this material so that the bare exercise is listed below this paragraph on just one page, with no hints. The following pages contain the steps needed to complete this exercise for those that need additional prompting. The **Setting PageMaker Defaults** module should be referenced if you need further help or explanations.

## Module 12 exercise steps

1. Set the Application default for PageMaker as follows:
   *Letter size page*
   *2 columns*
   *20 mm margins top, bottom, left, and right*
   *Style and Color palettes showing*
2. Start a new publication to check if the set defaults have worked.
3. Once you have started the new publication, set Publication defaults as follows:
   *Lines at 2 point thickness*
   *Shades at 10 percent black*
   *Text must be 14 point, Helvetica, bold, and left justified*
4. Test both graphics and text to determine if you were successful.

The steps to completing this exercise are found on the following pages.

*Module 12 Exercise - Setting PageMaker Defaults*

# The steps in detail

*1. Set the Application default for PageMaker as follows:*
    **Letter size page**
    **2 columns**
    **20 mm margins top, bottom, left, and right**
    **Style and Color palettes showing**

Application defaults are the defaults that are set when no publication is open, yet will apply to all publications that are created subsequently. So to set these defaults, make sure that only PageMaker (and not a publication or template) is open. Upon starting PageMaker 3, the screen will appear as shown in Figure 1.

Alternatively, if you are in an existing PageMaker publication, even with a blank page, you must choose *Close* from the **File** menu (not the *Windows* system menu). Your screen will then look like Figure 2.

*Figure 1.* PageMaker without a publication open will look like this or the figure below.

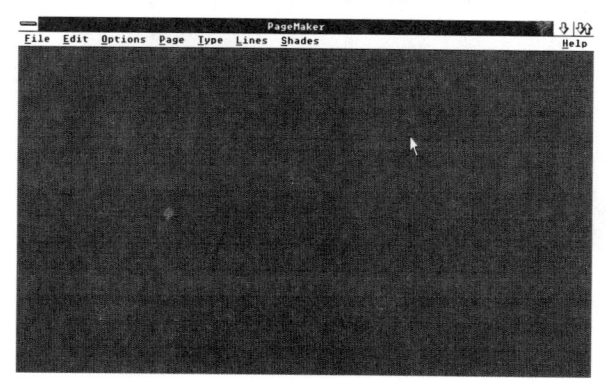

*Figure 2.* The above window will disappear whenever the mouse is clicked or a menu is used.

403

## Module 12 Exercise - Setting PageMaker Defaults

To set the page size and margin defaults, we must choose the *Page setup* command in the **File** menu as shown in Figure 3 (remember, do not open or create a new publication). In the dialog box that appears (Figure 4), set up Letter page size, and change all four margins to 20 mm (or 0.78").

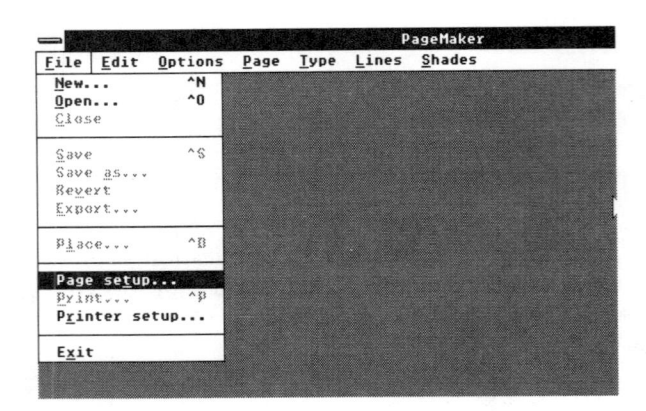

*Figure 3.* Select the Page setup command in the **File** menu.

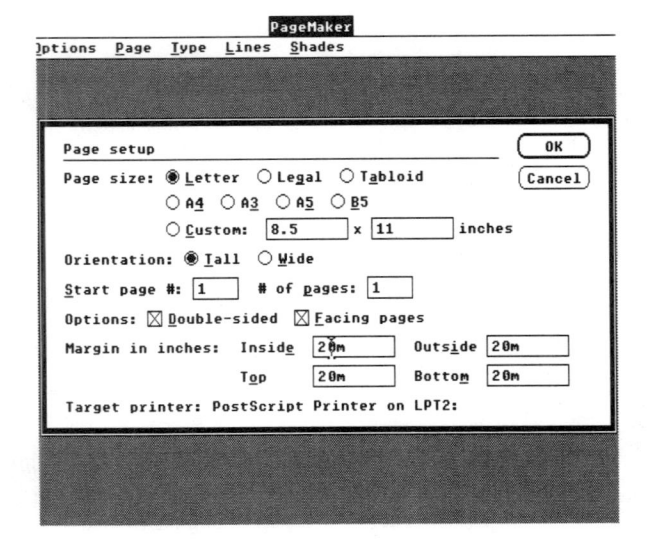

*Figure 4.* Change the page size to Letter, and change all margins to 20 mm (or 0.78"). Click on OK.

The columns default figure must be set using the *Column guides* command in the **Options** menu (Figure 5). Set the number to 2 in the ensuing dialog box (Figure 6).

404

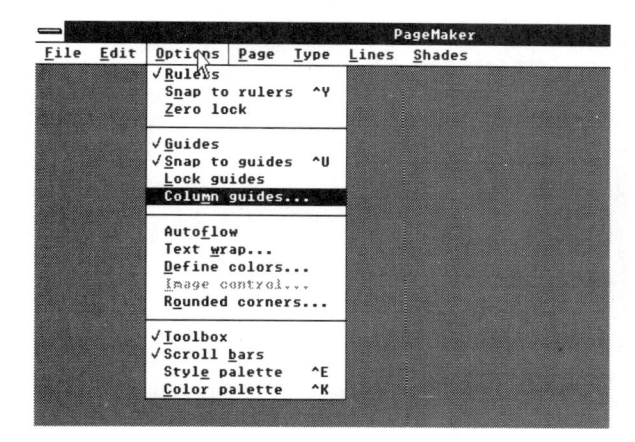

*Module 12 Exercise - Setting PageMaker Defaults*

*Figure 5.* Select the Column guides from the **Options** menu.

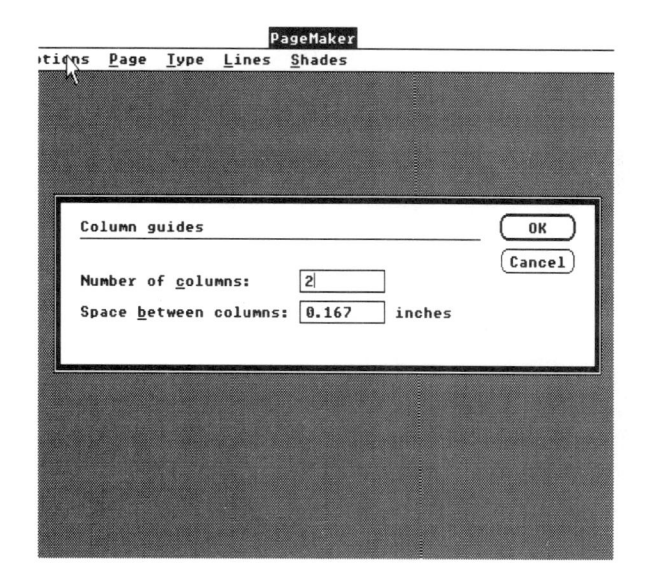

*Figure 6.* In the dialog box that ensues, insert 2 for the number of columns. Once again, this number of columns will become the default.

Finally, to make sure that the Style and Color palettes are showing, select these options from the **Options** menu (Figures 7 and 8). Although once again you will not see anything happen, you know these palettes will show if the options are checked in this menu.

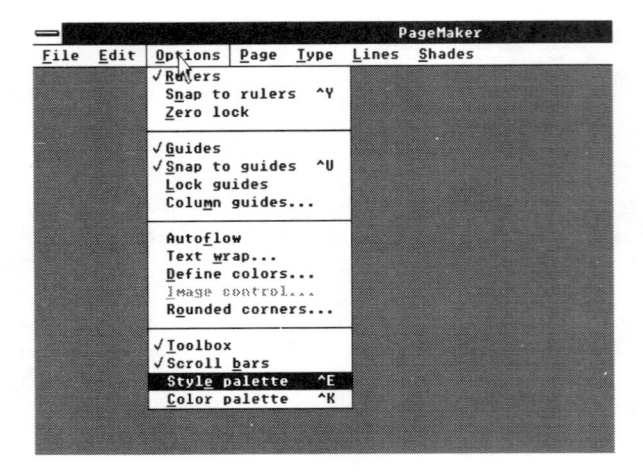

*Module 12 Exercise - Setting PageMaker Defaults*

*Figure 7.* Select the Style palette command from the **Options** menu.

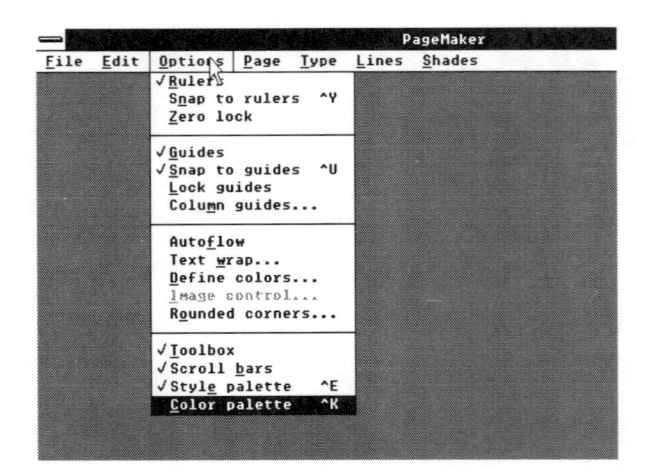

*Figure 8.* Also select the Color palette command from the same menu.

2. Start a new publication to check if the set defaults have worked.

Select *New* from the **File** menu—all the options we set in step 1 should be visible on the page. See Figure 9 for what to expect.

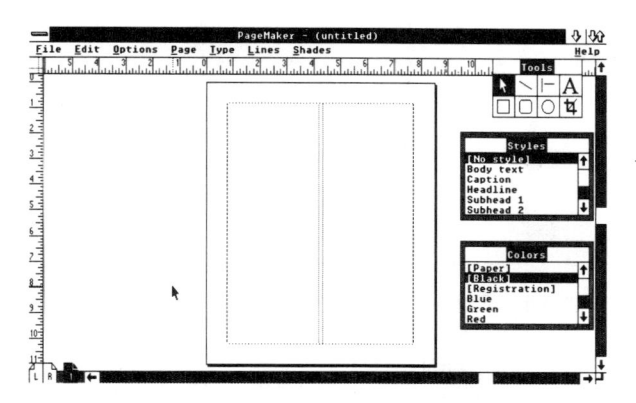

# Module 12 Exercise - Setting PageMaker Defaults

*Figure 9.* Your PageMaker publication, opened using the New command from the **File** menu, now shows the options displayed in this figure—including the palettes and two columns.

3. Once you have started the new publication, set Publication defaults as follows:
   **Lines at 2 point thickness**
   **Shades at 10 percent black**
   **Text must be 14 point, Helvetica, bold, and left justified**

Publication defaults are set when a publication is opened. These defaults will not affect any other publications, but will affect the future operation of this publication.

To set the line thickness default, make sure that there are no selected lines on the page, and the pointer tool is highlighted. To make sure, do not even draw any lines or even select a line drawing tool. Move to the **Lines** menu and select the 2 points thickness line (Figure 10). As with Application defaults, you will not see anything happen as yet.

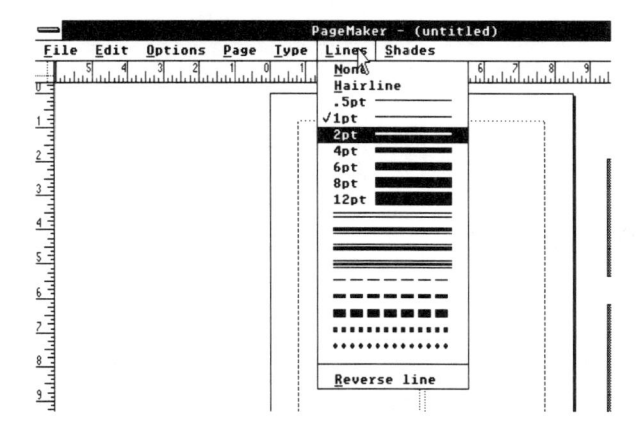

*Figure 10.* Select the 2 pt option in the **Lines** menu to ensure the default for all lines drawn in this publication is 2 points. Make sure before you do this that NO lines are selected on the page, because if they are, only these lines are affected by this command.

407

## Module 12 Exercise - Setting PageMaker Defaults

The same procedure is followed to set the graphic fill pattern—make sure there are no selected graphics on the page, your pointer tool is selected, and move to the **Shades** menu. Within this menu, select 10% as the fill pattern (Figure 11).

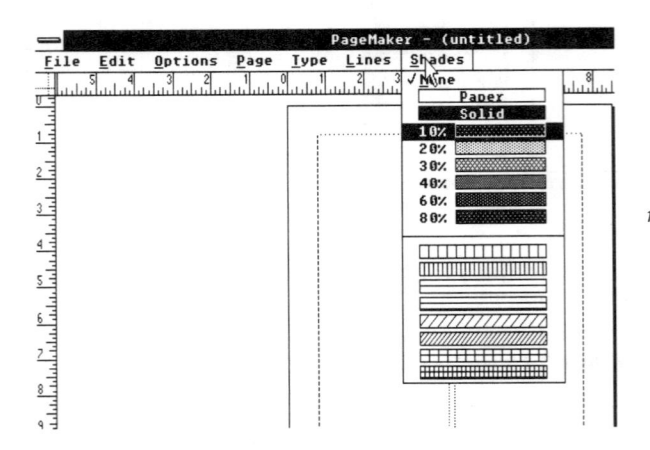

*Figure 11.* Select the 10% command from the **Shades** menu to set this graphic default.

The text default setting also works in a similar way. Make sure the pointer tool is selected, move to the **Type** menu, and select the *Type Specs* command. Select Helvetica from the list of fonts (Figure 12).

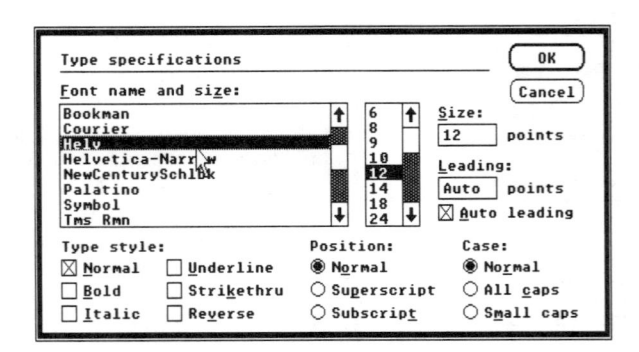

*Figure 12.* Here we set the Font default to Helvetica.

408

*Module 12 Exercise - Setting PageMaker Defaults*

Change the Size from the *Type Specs* command to 14 point (Figure 13).

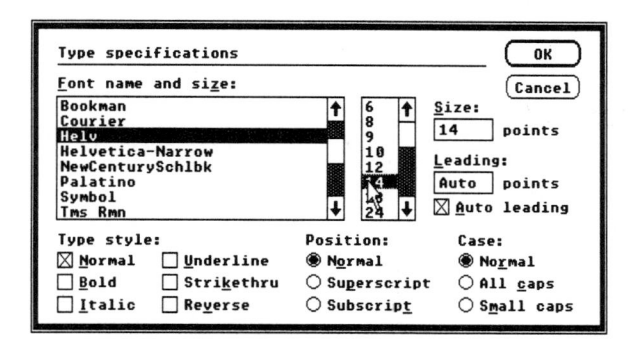

**Figure 13.** *The size default is set to 14 point.*

Select Bold from the style options in the Type Specs dialog box (Figure 14).

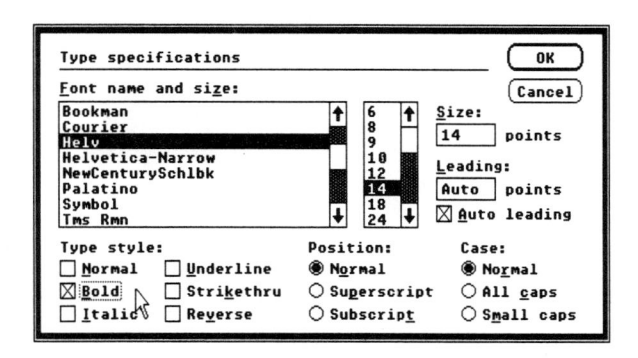

**Figure 14.** *The type style default is set to Bold.*

Finally, select left justified by choosing *Align left* towards the bottom of the **Type** menu.

409

## Module 12 Exercise - Setting PageMaker Defaults

**4. Test both graphics and text to determine if you were successful.**

To test whether the Publication defaults we set were successful, the first step would be to draw a rectangle on the page. It should look like it has a 2 point outline and a 10% shade. Compare your graphic to Figures 15 and 16. Test both line thickness and fill shade settings through the **Lines** and **Shades** menus.

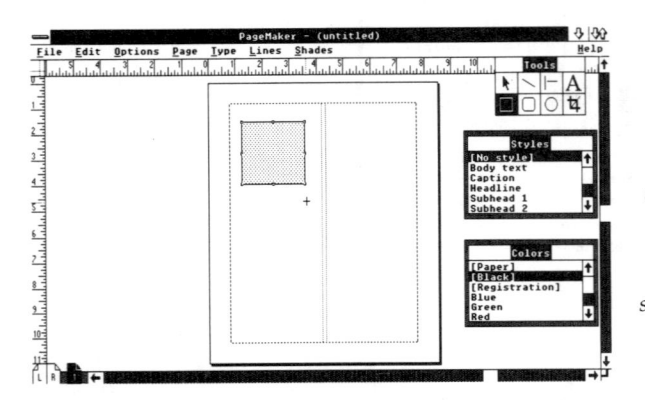

*Figure 15. Here we have selected the rectangle tool and drawn a rectangle on the page to test the default settings. Go to the **Lines** and **Shades** menus to check that 2 point thickness and 10% shade actually apply to this box. Unless you have made an error in step 3 (Figures 10 and 11), this will be the case.*

To test the type specification defaults, we must type some text onto the screen. Make sure you are in a view that allows you to read the text, select the text tool, click on the page, and tap on the keyboard. Although you may not immediately be able to tell how the text is set up (Figure 16), select the text and move through the **Type** menu to see exactly what its attributes are.

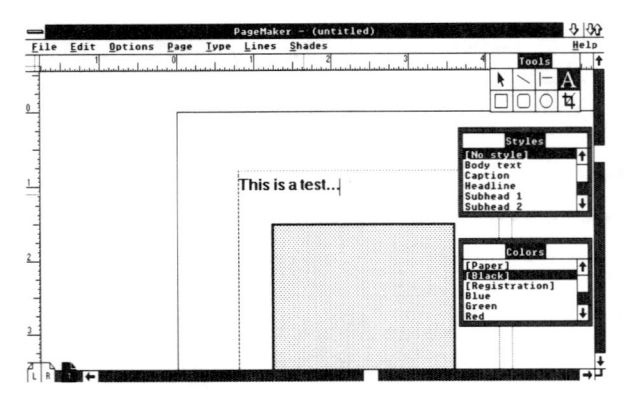

*Figure 16. Now we select the text tool and type some text on the page. Once again, it appears as though the default settings we created have worked. However, to make sure, select the text and check its attributes through the **Type** menu.*

410

# Module 13

# PageMaker Color

# PageMaker Color

PageMaker 3 now supports color operation on both the screen and output devices (printers). To see PageMaker in color you need a PC with the appropriate color monitor. PC monitors can display up to 16 million colors, with 256 showing at any one time. All the features of PageMaker involving color can also be run on monochrome monitors, although obviously it becomes a little more difficult to follow, define, and apply colors.

On a monochrome monitor, the PageMaker page appears as a black outline, with a dotted line representing the margin inside that page. On a color monitor, all guides appear as solid colors, making them easy to see, and also making it easy to quickly see which are printing guides and which are non-printing.

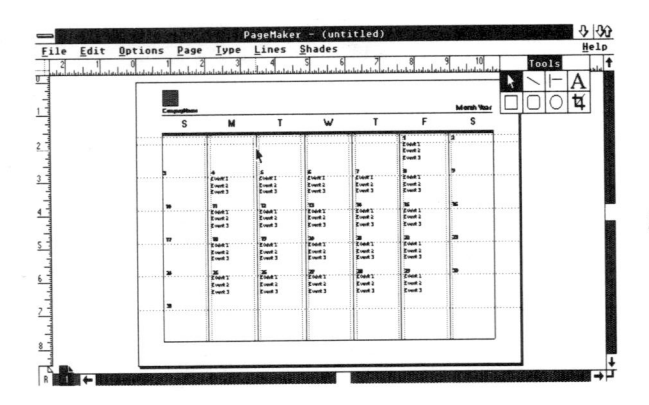

*Figure 1.* PageMaker color still works on monochrome monitors. This page, with the appropriate printer, will print in full color. On all printers, color separations can be made of any publication.

*Module 13 - PageMaker Color*

# Using color

Two commands in the **Options** menu, *Define colors* and *Color palette*, both need to be invoked to see how color works within PageMaker. Select first the *Color palette* command as shown in Figure 2.

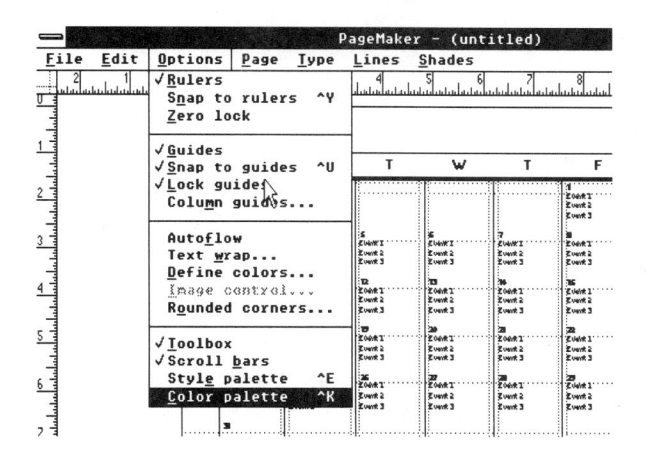

*Figure 2.* The Color palette command in the **Options** menu will make visible the Color palette as shown in Figure 3 (assuming that it is not already visible).

The *Color palette* which then appears (Figure 3), looks very similar to the Style palette, and in fact, works in a very similar way. Colors can be defined much as styles are, and can be applied to any selected portion of the page simply by clicking on the color you want from the palette. This is virtually identical to the process of applying styles as discussed in Module 11.

Three colors are defined by default within the Color palette (Figure 3). These are *Paper*, *Black*, and *Registration*. Other default colors may also be included. We will look quickly at what each of these mean before we start creating and applying other colors.

# Paper

The *Paper* color is set to white by default—you can change it, however, to any color you wish.

413

Module 13 - PageMaker Color

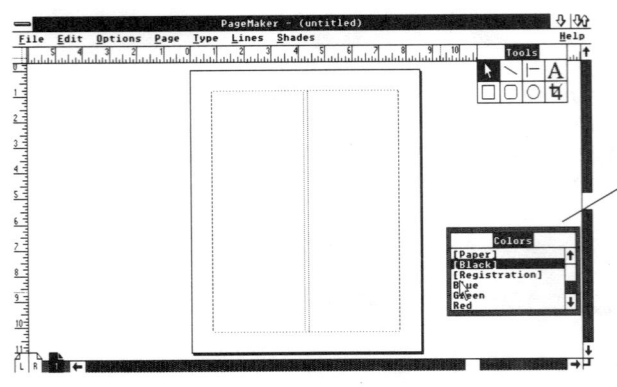

*Figure 3.* The Color palette looks very similar to the Style palette used by PageMaker. Your Color palette may also include Red, Blue, and Green colors by default.

## Black

*Black* is the tone black and cannot be altered. It is more or less the normal color—the color you apply to an element on the page in the absence of any other color. Black initially applies to all text.

## Registration

*Registration* is not really a color—but it can be applied to any element of the page. It is used when color separations are to be created directly from PageMaker. (This is also discussed in Module 10, PageMaker Printing). Normally for separations, every new color is printed on a page by itself. Any page element that uses the color Registration, however, will be printed on every page in the document.

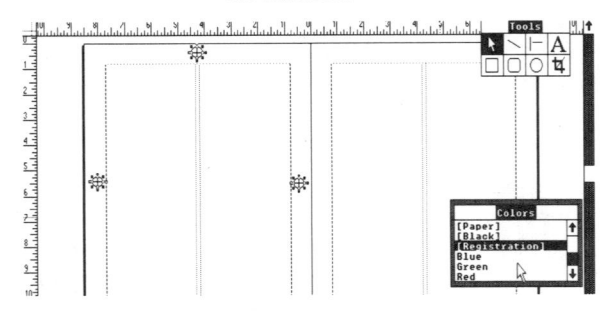

*Figure 4.* The color Registration is applied to Registration marks placed on the master pages of your document. These Registration-colored markers help a printer align color separations much more accurately. These Registration markers print on every page when using color separations.

## Other default colors

*Red*, *Blue*, and *Green* are the other default colors that may be defined and may appear in your Color palette.

*Module 13 - PageMaker Color*

Registration marks can be added manually to a publication when that publication occupies an entire page. You produce them in any blank area on the master pages (Figure 4), and they will then be replicated throughout the document. The color Registration is then assigned to these marks allowing them to print on every page irrespective of the overlay's color. Registration marks are created so that the page can be aligned perfectly when the color printing is done.

If your publication's page is smaller than the printed page, PageMaker can then automatically add the Registration marks. This is done by checking *Spot color overlays* and *Crop marks* in the *Print* dialog box.

## Creating new colors

Theoretically, you can create up to 64,000 new colors in PageMaker, although memory constraints will probably mean that you will run into memory problems by creating this many colors.

To create a new color to use, you must select the *Define colors* command in the **Options** menu (Figure 5). The dialog box of Figure 6 then appears.

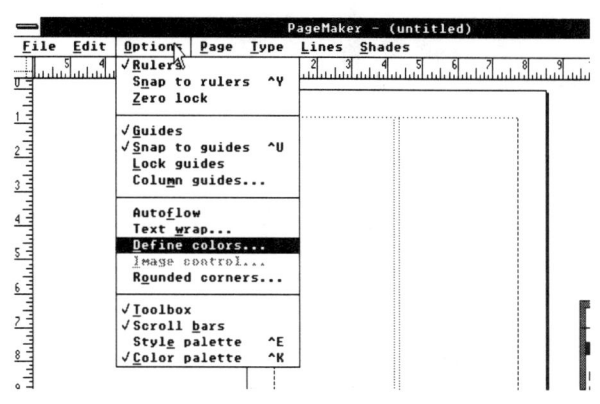

*Figure 5. The Define colors command is used to create your own colors. It causes the dialog box of Figure 6 to occur.*

As you can see, the process of creating new colors is almost identical to creating new styles, up to this point at least. Select *New* in the dialog box of Figure 6 to define a new color.

After selecting New, you will be presented with the additional dialog box of Figure 7.

Module 13 - PageMaker Color

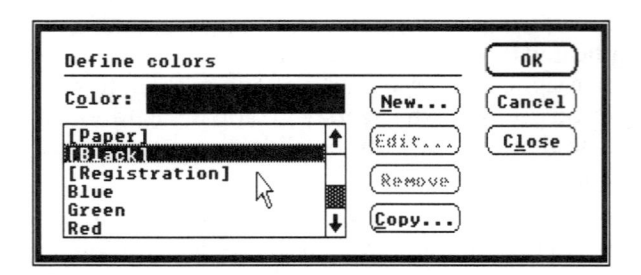

*Figure 6.* The Define colors dialog box looks like this—much like the Define styles dialog box.

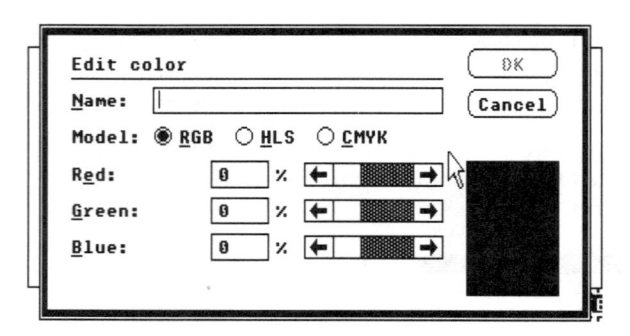

*Figure 7.* After selecting New from the dialog box in Figure 6, this additional dialog box appears.

*Figure 8.* Enter a name for your color in the rectangle at the top of the dialog box—in exactly the same way as you would name a new style.

This box is actually in two parts. The top half reflects the color as it is edited. On a color monitor, it constantly changes to reflect any changes made to the percentages to the left.
The bottom half of the box will reflect the current color as it is defined.

*Module 13 - PageMaker Color*

There are several ways from here to create the new color. The first step you must take is to give the color its name, in much the same way in which we gave the style its name. In Figure 8, we have chosen Martian Blue.

Your next choice is the *Model* to be used to create the color. The reason that you can select between three models, *RGB*, *HLS*, and *CMYK*, is because traditionally these are the three ways in which colors can be defined. Depending on your background, your available information, and the output device you are using, you can opt for any one of the three.

## RGB

The *Red*, *Green*, and *Blue* method is perhaps the easiest and most common of the three methods for defining colors. It relies on the defining of a percentage of each of the three colors (Figures 8 and 9)—which gives an incredible range of possibilities as to actual colors, although not quite as many as the other methods. Use the horizontal scroll bars to the right of the colors (Figure 9) to adjust the percentage of each color.

This is much like mixing red, green, and blue paint in different proportions to create a new color.

```
Model:  ● RGB   ○ HLS   ○ CMYK
Red:      48  %
Green:    27  %
Blue:     88  %
```

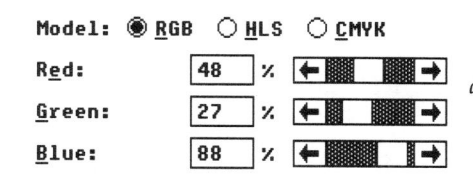

*Figure 9. Here we have defined a color using different values for Red, Green, and Blue using the RGB method.*

On the right side of the Figure 8 dialog box, a small rectangle showing the current color will constantly update, giving you some idea of what color you have created (this is assuming that you have a color screen—you are working blind with a monochrome monitor). With a monochrome monitor, you must have some idea beforehand as to what percentages makeup the color that you are trying to create.

Module 13 - PageMaker Color

## HLS

The *Hue, Lightness,* and *Saturation* method of changing existing colors (Figure 10) works in a similar way to the RGB method. Hue, however, is defined from zero to 360 degrees, while Lightness and Saturation are defined as percentages. Once again the color being created will be constantly updated next to the percentage bars on color monitors.

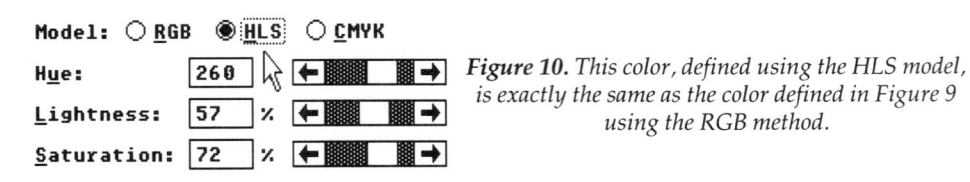

Model: ○ RGB  ● HLS  ○ CMYK
Hue:        [260]
Lightness:  [57] %
Saturation: [72] %

*Figure 10. This color, defined using the HLS model, is exactly the same as the color defined in Figure 9 using the RGB method.*

The HLS model cannot be used to create new colors—only to edit or change existing ones.

## CMYK

The *Cyan, Magenta, Yellow,* and *Black* method is the most precise —each of these four colors and tones can be defined in percentages. Otherwise, it works in exactly the same way as the two methods described above. The CMYK model is commonly used in four-color printing.

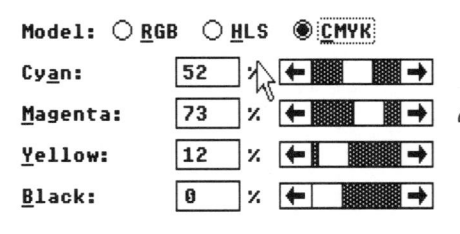

Model: ○ RGB  ○ HLS  ● CMYK
Cyan:    [52] %
Magenta: [73] %
Yellow:  [12] %
Black:   [0]  %

*Figure 11. Once again we have the same color defined as in the last two figures, yet this time using the CMYK model.*

Note that with any method you use to describe a color, selecting a new method will cause the percentage bars to display that color in the new method (see examples in Figures 9 to 11).

After selecting OK from here (Figure 12), the new color has been created, and will appear in the *Define colors* dialog box of Figure 13, and the Color palette of Figure 14. It is then available for selection when required.

*Module 13 - PageMaker Color*

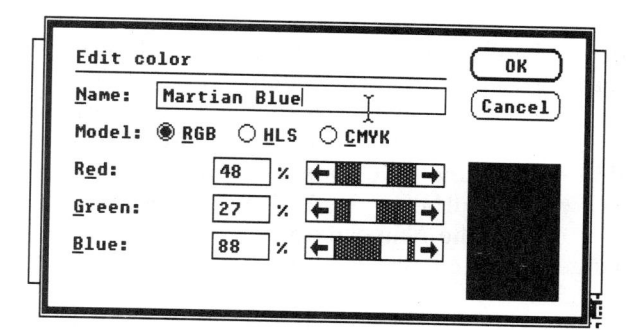

*Figure 12.* After having gone this far—naming the color, and defining the color using any of the three models in this dialog box, you are ready to click on OK.

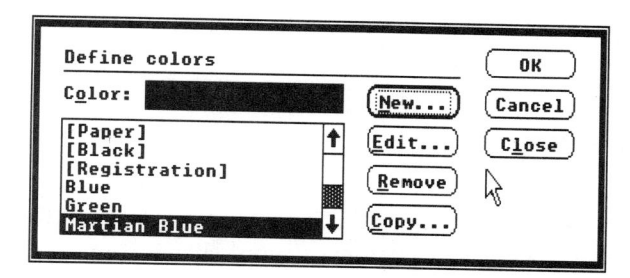

*Figure 13.* After clicking OK in the previous dialog box of Figure 12, you will be returned to this dialog box. The new color is now listed with the default colors, and on a color monitor, will be displayed in the rectangle next to the word Color.

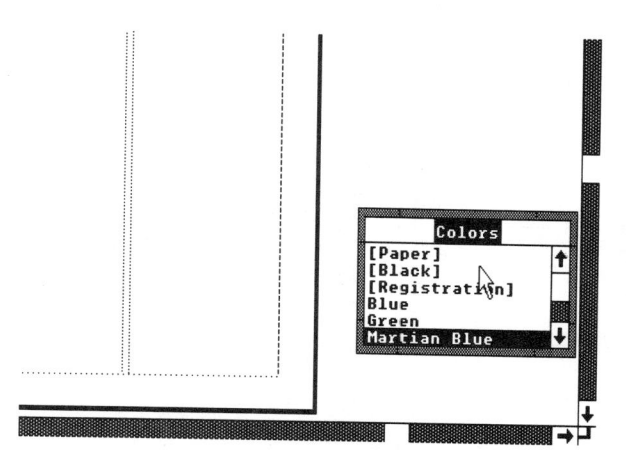

*Figure 14.* After exiting the Figure 13 dialog box, the new color will be listed in the Color palette.

419

Module 13 - PageMaker Color

## Editing colors

Any color besides Black and Registration can be edited using the *Edit* command in the Figures 6 or 13 dialog box. Select the color you would like to edit—note that the defined color is displayed above the list of colors for color monitors. Now select the Edit command from this same dialog box. The same dialog box as for creating a new color will be displayed (Figure 7), but with a name already included in the Name rectangle—from here you can simply change the percentages for the color using any of the three models, and click OK.

The only difference in editing versus creating a color is that with editing we do not have to type in a new name as we did in Figure 8 for color creation. The name of the color to edit will already appear in the Name section of the dialog box.

## Removing colors

Colors are also removed using the *Define colors* dialog box shown again in Figure 15. Select the color you would like to remove from this list, and choose the *Remove* command. The color is then permanently removed from the Color palette. See further notes in this regard in the Figure 15 caption.

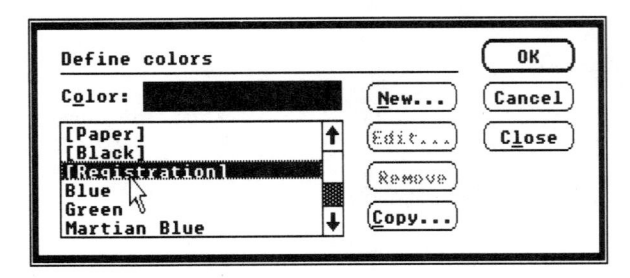

*Figure 15.* The colors Paper, Black, and Registration cannot be removed. Black and Registration cannot be edited either. Note in this figure that the Edit and Remove commands are grayed and not available when Registration is selected.

*Module 13 - PageMaker Color*

## Copying colors

Copying colors into your publication is also a simple process. After choosing *Define colors* from the **Options** menu to get the Figure 15 dialog box, you choose the *Copy* command at the bottom of the box. The *Copy colors* dialog box (Figure 16) then appears. This provides a list of publications from which it is possible to copy color descriptions.

Select the publication (or even template) whose colors you wish to copy into your current publication, and click on OK in Figure 16. Any new colors will now be added to your Color palette as shown in Figure 17.

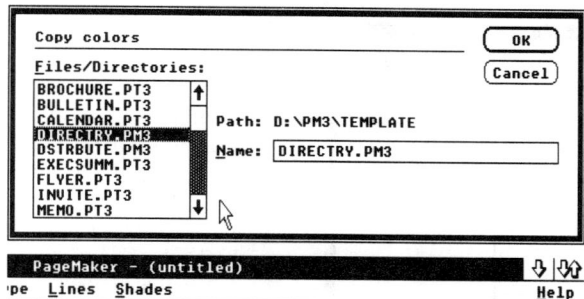

*Figure 16. The Copy colors dialog box lists publications and templates that can be used to copy color descriptions into your currently opened document.*

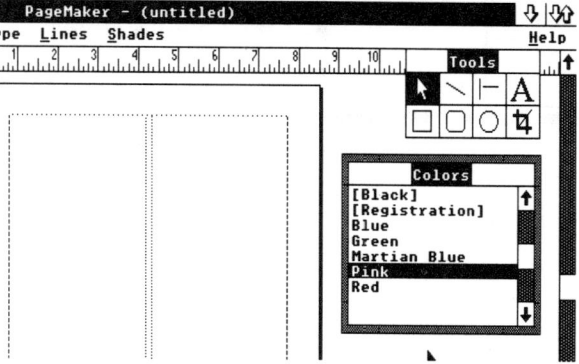

*Figure 17. The color Pink in this example was added to the list of colors after copying from another publication. By default, the DIRECTRY.PM3 publication—the one we copied from in Figure 16—will not contain the color Pink. We had added this color previously.*

## Applying colors

Colors are applied exactly as are styles. If a dialog box is still showing, click OK to remove it from the screen. Any printing element on the screen can be applied a color—whether it be text, created graphics, or imported graphics. Simply select the element you would like to color—text using the text cursor, other elements using the pointer tool (Figure 18).

421

## Module 13 - PageMaker Color

As the object is selected, one option is to move to the Color palette (if this is not showing, choose the command *Color palette* from the **Options** menu), and click on the color you want to use. On color monitors this becomes apparent immediately, and on color output devices the color will be matched as closely as the output device can make it.

The other option of applying color is to use the *Define colors* command from the **Options** menu. Again select the object, move to this command and then, in the resulting dialog box (same as Figure 13), select the required color from the list shown.

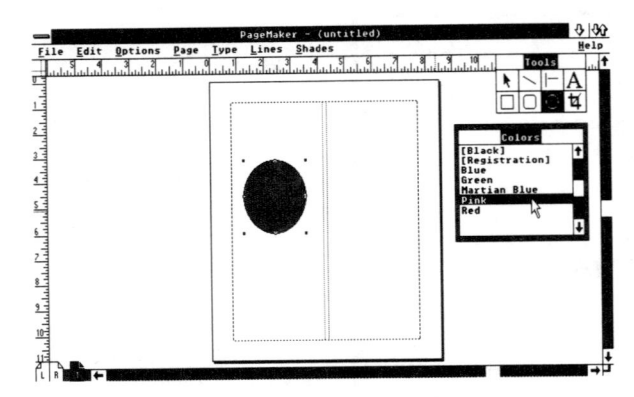

*Figure 18.* To apply a color to any element on the page, select the element, and select a color from the Color palette. Although not visible on a monochrome monitor, the Color has been applied to that graphic or text.

## Module 13 Exercise

# PageMaker Color

# Module 13 Exercise
# PageMaker Color

In this exercise we will be working with color within PageMaker. A color screen or printer is not necessary to complete this exercise—it would only make it a little easier.

This training material is structured so that people of all levels of expertise with PageMaker can use it to gain maximum benefit. In order to do this, we have structured this material so that the bare exercise is listed below this paragraph on just one page, with no hints. The following pages contain the steps needed to complete this exercise for those that need additional prompting. The **PageMaker Color** module should be referenced if you need further help or explanations.

## Module 13 exercise steps

1. Open up the template SPKRNOTE.PT3 from the TEMPLATE subdirectory.
2. Define three new colors—*orange*, **purple,** and **aqua**. Use the RGB method to do this. Orange will be 100% red, 40% green; purple will be 100% blue, 75% red; and aqua will be 100% green and 100% blue.
3. Show the Color palette.
4. All Headlines must be purple, and all Bulletpoints orange. The two boxes on the left-hand side of the page must be aqua.
5. The company logo must also be aqua (you will have to move to the master page to do this).
6. Create registration marks on the master pages at the top and bottom of the page, and make sure they are correctly colored for registration.

The steps to completing this exercise are on the following pages.

Module 13 Exercise - PageMaker Color

## The steps in detail.

*1. Open up the template SPKRNOTE.PT3 from the TEMPLATE subdirectory.*

This template is located in the TEMPLATE subdirectory—it can be accessed either from the Windows desktop, or from the *Open* command in the **File** menu if you are already in PageMaker.

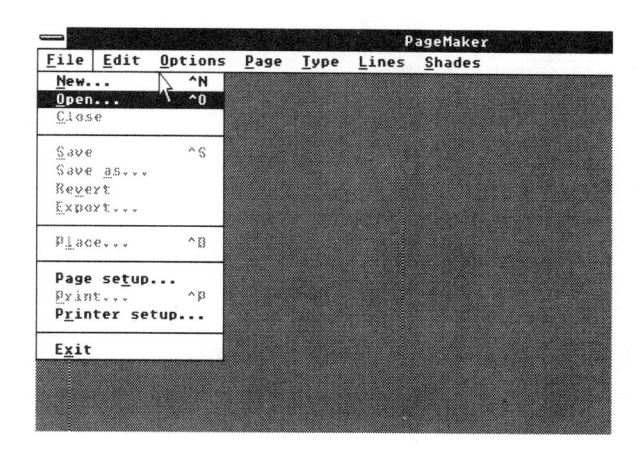

*Figure 1.* Use either the PageMaker Open command (as shown here), or open directly from the Windows desktop.

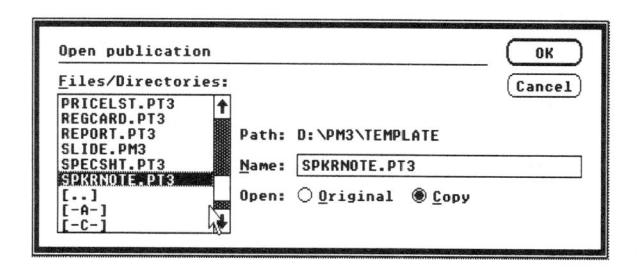

*Figure 2.* This follows on from Figure 1. SPKRNOTE.PT3 in the TEMPLATE subdirectory is the template we wish to open. Notice that with templates, a Copy of the document is always chosen by default in the Open dialog box.

425

*Module 13 Exercise - PageMaker Color*

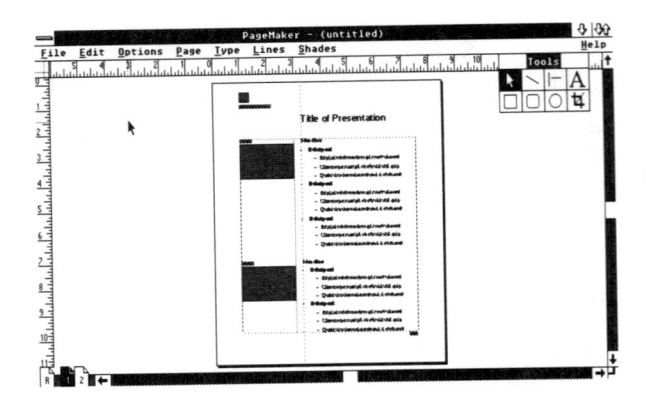

*Figure 3. A copy of the template SPKRNOTE.PT3 will look like this on your screen in Fit in window view. Notice that templates always open as untitled copies.*

2. *Define three new colors—orange, purple, and aqua. Use the RGB method to do this. Orange will be 100% red, 40% green; purple will be 100% blue, 75% red; and aqua will be 100% green and 100% blue.*

Defining colors is done through the *Define colors* command in the **Options** menu (Figure 4). You will be greeted with the dialog box of Figure 5.

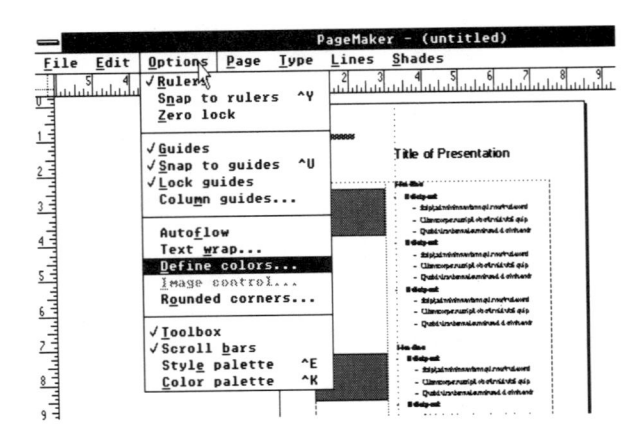

*Figure 4. Choose the Define colors command from the **Options** menu to create and use new colors.*

426

*Module 13 Exercise - PageMaker Color*

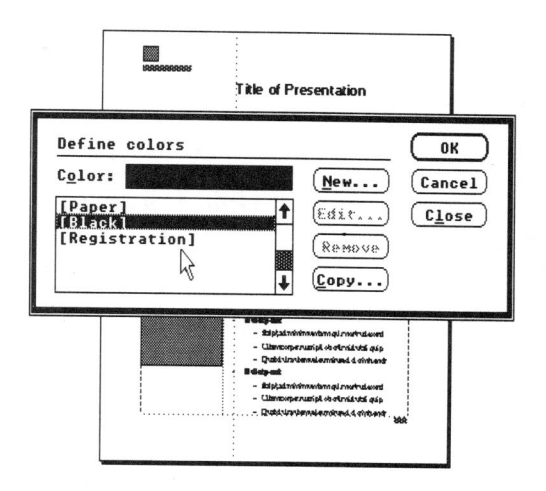

*Figure 5.* The Define colors dialog box. Red, Blue, and Green may also be included in this box as default colors.

The Figure 5 dialog box will have three colors defined by default—Paper, Black, and Registration. It may also include Red, Blue, and Green. To create new colors, click on the New option. You will then be greeted with the Figure 6 dialog box.

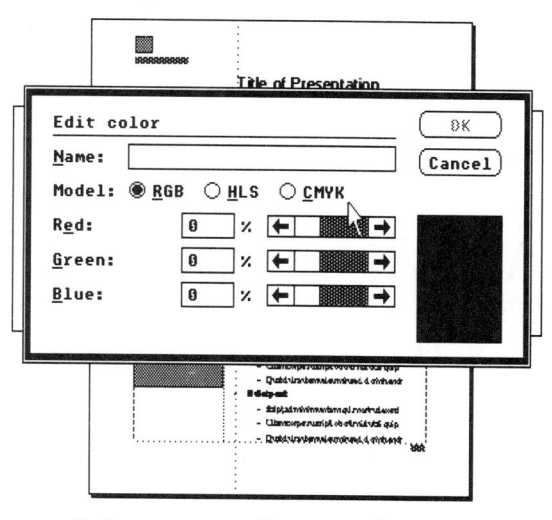

*Figure 6.* The Define colors New dialog box is actually the same as the Define colors Edit dialog box. The only difference is that with clicking on New in Figure 5, you need to type in a new name in the Name rectangle.

Before we actually create this new color we must name it. Type in the name of the new color in the rectangle at the top of the dialog box. First, orange (Figure 7), although to be imaginative you may wish to call it sunset orange or something like that.

427

*Module 13 Exercise - PageMaker Color*

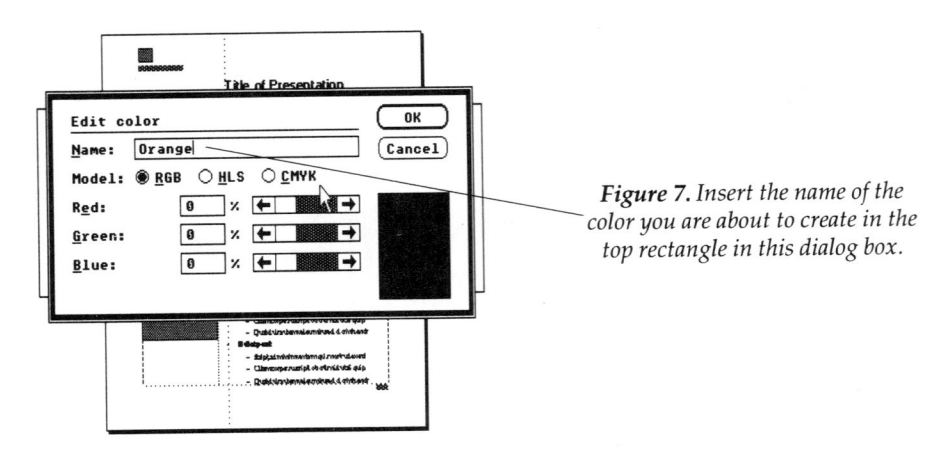

*Figure 7. Insert the name of the color you are about to create in the top rectangle in this dialog box.*

We have been asked to create three colors using the RGB method—the method which will be selected by default. Using this method, you will see sliding scale bars—one representing Red, one Green, and one Blue. To create orange, move Red to 100%, Green to 40%, and make sure that the Blue sliding scale is at 0% (Figure 8). Although it is not noticeable on monochrome screens, the color orange has been created and represented in the bar to the right of these sliding scales. Now click on OK.

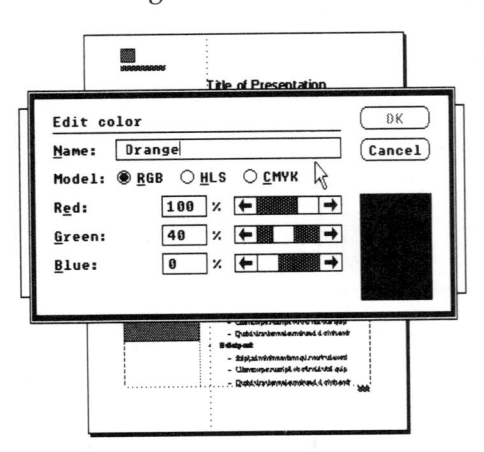

*Figure 8. To create the color orange, use the scroll bars on the sliding scales to set the Red bar at 100%, the Green at 40%, and the Blue at 0%.*

You will then be returned to the previous dialog box (Figure 9), to which the color orange will have been added. From here, you may click on New again to create the next two colors. Creating purple is shown in Figures 10 to 12, while aqua is shown in Figure 13.

428

*Module 13 Exercise - PageMaker Color*

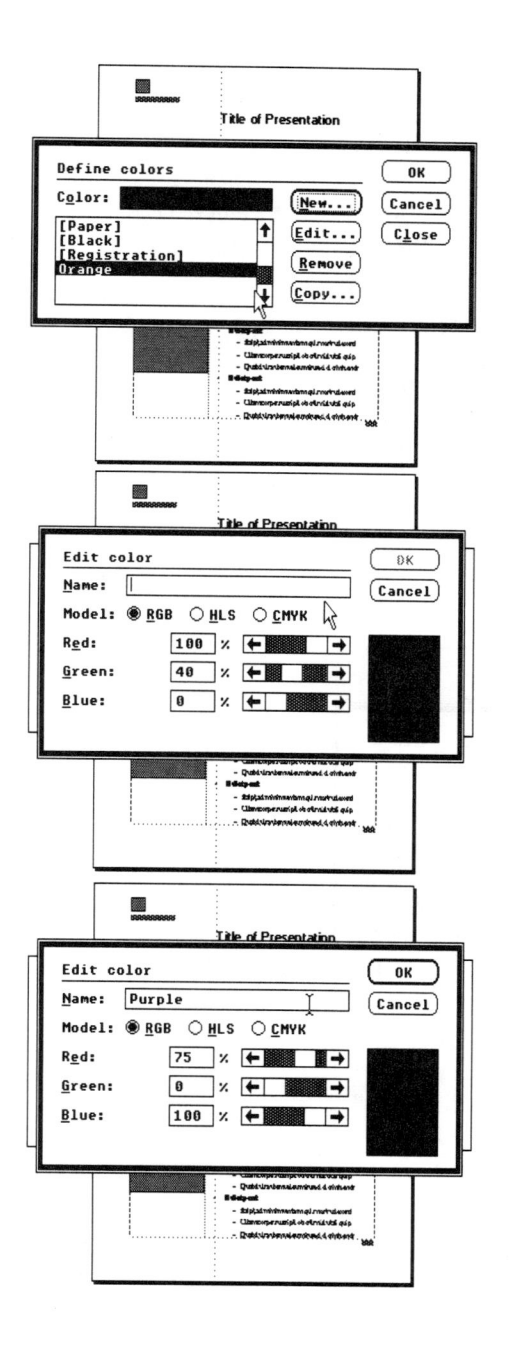

***Figure 9.*** *After clicking OK from the box in Figure 8, you will be returned to this dialog box, and the Orange color you just created will be included in the list of colors.*

***Figure 10.*** *You must click on New again from the dialog box in Figure 9, and once again you will be presented with this dialog box.*

***Figure 11.*** *For the color purple, insert the name at the top, and set the Blue scale at 100%, the Red at 75%, and the Green at 0%.*

429

*Module 13 Exercise - PageMaker Color*

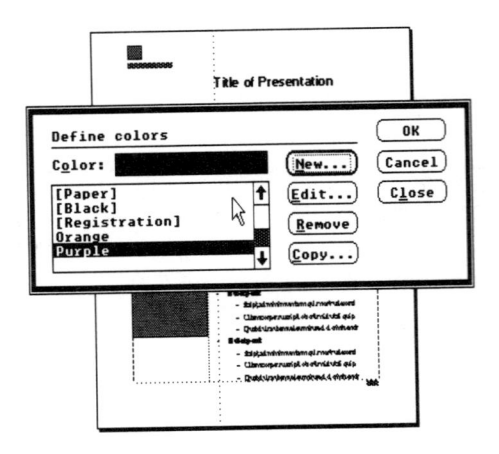

***Figure 12****. After clicking OK from Figure 11, you will once again be returned to this dialog box, with the color Purple added to it.*

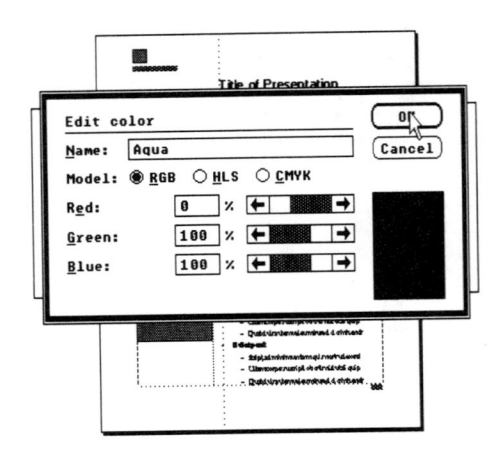

***Figure 13****. Match your dialog box with this one (after choosing New again from Figure 12) to create the color Aqua.*

After getting this far, click on OK twice to get back past the two dialog boxes and onto the PageMaker page.

*Module 13 Exercise - PageMaker Color*

3. *Show the Color palette.*

The Color palette can be accessed via the *Color palette* option in the **Options** menu (Figure 14). In this Color palette will be listed all the colors we have just created. You may want to resize the Color palette so that you can see all the colors (Figure 15).

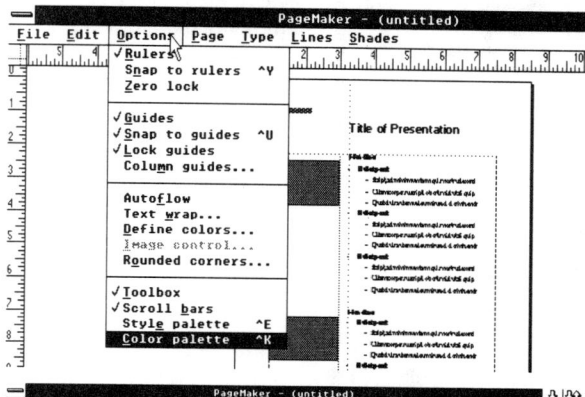

*Figure 14.* Choose the Color palette command from the **Options** menu to display the Color palette on screen.

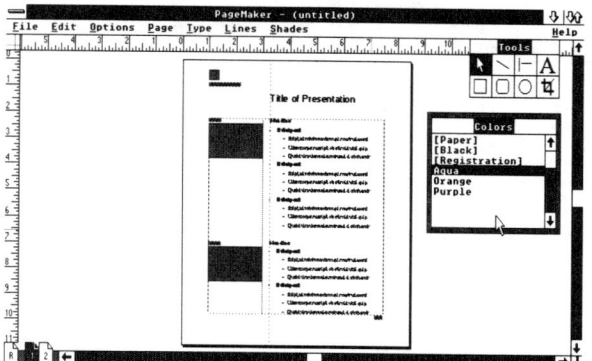

*Figure 15.* Here the Color palette has not only been displayed, but we have moved it up slightly and increased it in size a little so we can see all the colors listed.

4. *All Headlines must be purple, and all Bulletpoints orange. The two boxes on the left-hand side of the page must be aqua.*

To make any text a certain color is a simple procedure. Select that text using the text tool, and click on the color that you want to turn the text to in the Color palette. The selected text will then be registered as that color. Although these colors can be applied with style sheets, none have been defined for this template, so we will apply colors manually. This means selecting all the occurrences of Headlines and Bulletpoints separately, and assigning them colors. See the next series of figures (16 to 19) as examples.

431

*Module 13 Exercise - PageMaker Color*

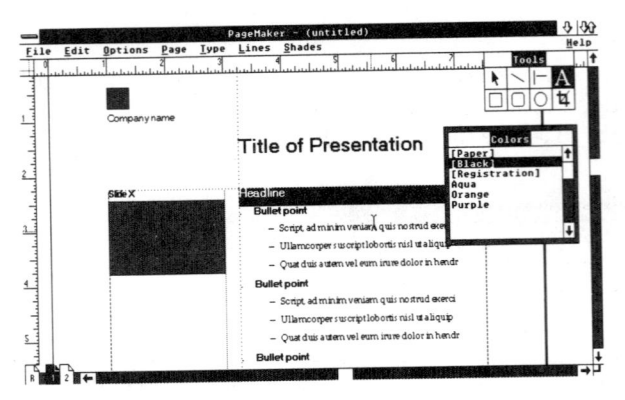

*Figure 16.* 75% view has been used here to allow us to read the text, yet see a good deal of the page. To turn the Headlines purple, select the first one using the text tool (they must be selected and colored one at a time), as shown here.

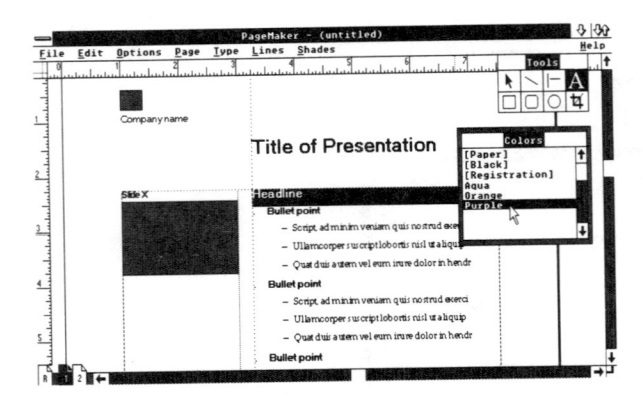

*Figure 17.* Click on the color Purple in the Color palette—all that will happen on a monochrome screen is perhaps the text will appear slightly spaced. This step will have to be repeated on each Headline.

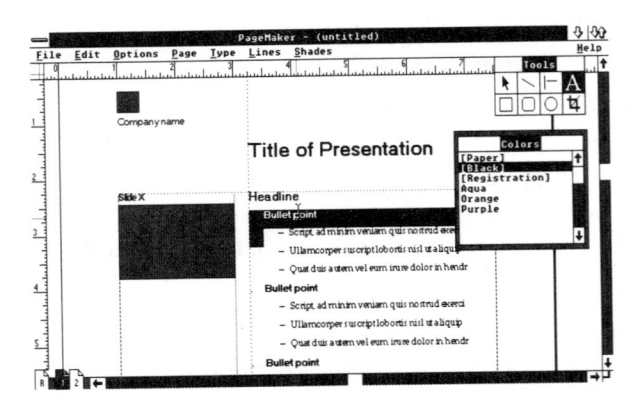

*Figure 18.* Select the first Bullet-point in text mode as shown ...

432

Module 13 Exercise - PageMaker Color

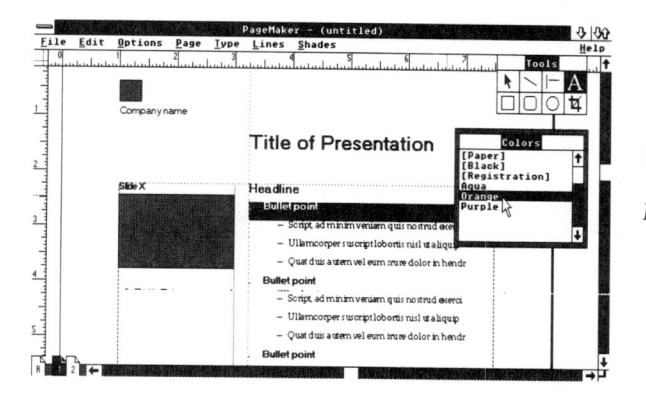

*Figure 19.* ...and click on the color Orange from the Color palette. Repeat this step for every Bulletpoint encountered.

Graphics must be selected using the pointer tool, but are applied colors in exactly the same way as text is. Once the graphic is selected, click on the correct color in the Color palette and the graphic will then assume that color. Do this for both boxes on the page.

Figures 20 and 21 show the procedure for the top box.

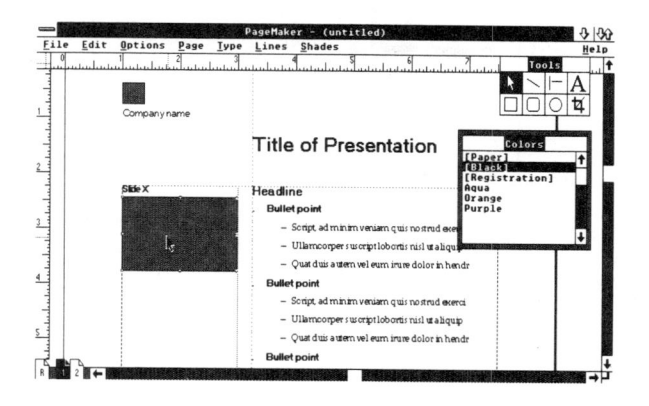

*Figure 20.* Select the first box on the page using the pointer tool.

433

*Module 13 Exercise - PageMaker Color*

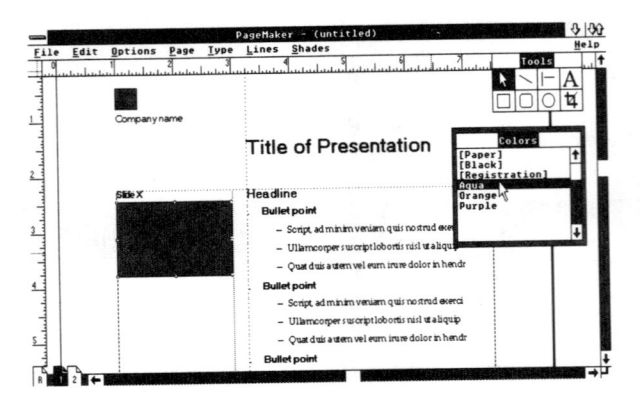

*Figure 21.* Click on the color Aqua in the Color palette to turn the box this color.

5. The company logo must also be aqua (you will have to move to the master page to do this).

Because the company logo is on the master page, you will not be able to select it from page 1. Click on the R icon in the bottom left-hand corner of the page to move to the master page (Figure 22).

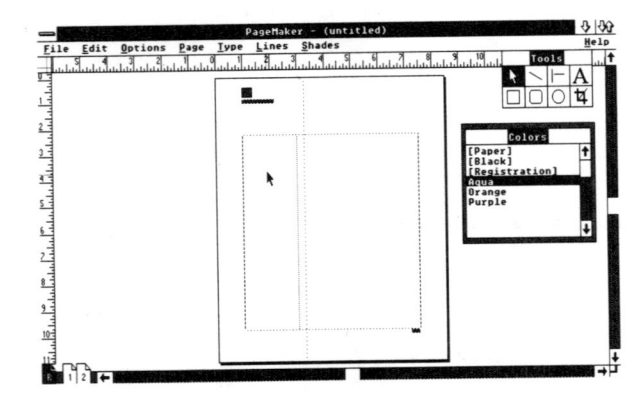

*Figure 22.* Note how the R icon in the bottom left-hand corner of the page has been selected—we are looking here at the master page. Note the company logo and name near the top left-hand corner of the page.

At the top of the page is the company logo. Select the logo using the pointer tool and click on the color Aqua from the Color palette (Figure 23). This logo is now treated as aqua, although once again only color monitors will be able to see this.

434

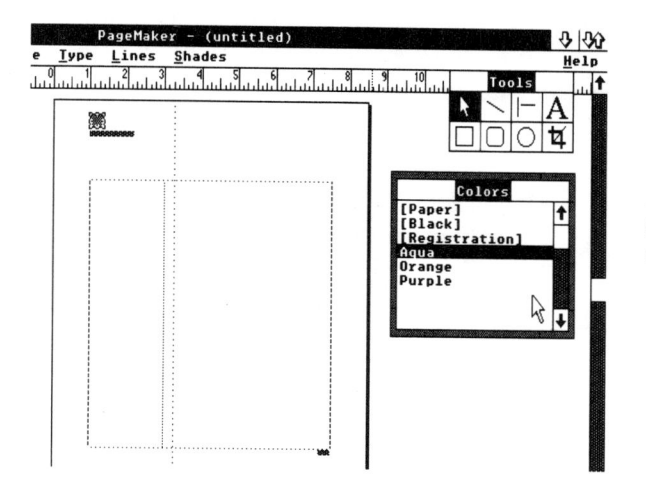

*Figure 23. Here we have selected the graphic and turned it aqua by selecting the color Aqua from the Color palette.*

6. *Create registration marks on the master pages at the top and bottom of the page, and make sure they are correctly colored for registration.*

These registration marks are only created as a guide to the printer—they help align color separations. They are also very simple to do, and are created on the master page.

Create, at the top of the master page, a fairly small symbol (Figure 24), and repeat it at the bottom of the page (Figure 25). Although it does not matter exactly what you create, a common symbol is shown in Figure 24.

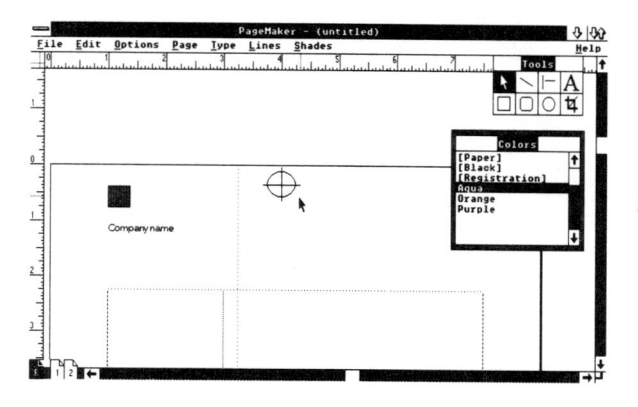

*Figure 24. This symbol has been created using the graphic drawing tools within PageMaker—two lines drawn through a circle. Copy this graphic and paste it at the bottom of the page as well.*

## Module 13 Exercise - PageMaker Color

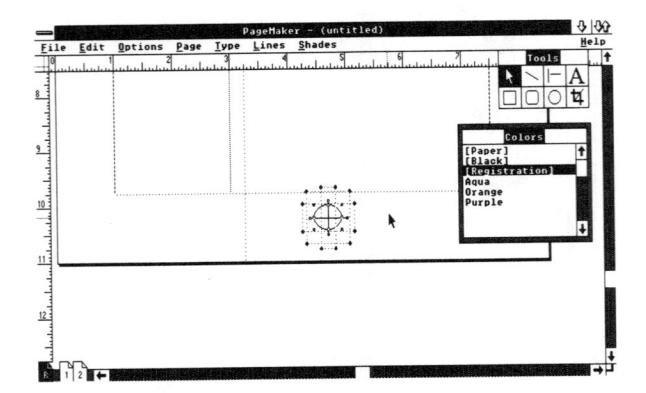

*Figure 25.* The graphic has been copied and pasted at the bottom of the page.

After creating a symbol and placing it at the top and bottom of the page, make sure that all parts of both symbols are colored Registration by using the Registration color from the Color palette (Figure 26). This ensures that these registration marks will print on every page, if color separations are created at print time.

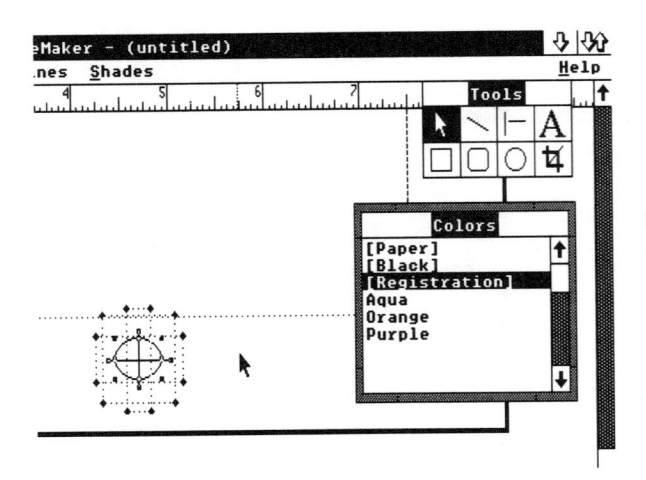

*Figure 26.* Assign the color Registration to the special symbol marks. This ensures that these registration marks will print on every page of color separations.

# Appendix A—Keyboard Shortcuts

Many shortcut key commands have been explained throughout this book and are also listed in detail in the PageMaker documentation.

We have listed below some of the more useful shortcut commands for your information.

## Pages

| | |
|---|---|
| Move to next page | Command + Tab |
| Move to previous page | Command + Shift + Tab |
| Move publication window in any direction | Alt+ drag |
| Move publication window constrained | Alt+ Shift + drag |
| Change to Actual size (from any view) | Right mouse button |
| Change to Fit in window (from Actual size) | Right mouse button |
| Change to 200% (from any view) | Shift + right mouse button |

## Text

| | |
|---|---|
| Normal | F5 |
| Bold | F6 |
| Italic | F7 |
| Underline | F8 |
| Remove space between letters | Control +Backspace |
| Add space between letters | Control +Shift + Backspace |
| Discretionary hyphen | Control + - |
| Em dash — | Control + Shift + + |
| En dash (non-breaking hyphen) – | Control + + |
| Opening double quote " | Control + Shift + { |
| Closing double quote " | Control + Shift + } |
| Opening single quote ' | Control + { |
| Closing single quote ' | Control + } |
| Page number marker 0 | Control + Shift + 3 |
| Em space | Control + Shift + M |
| En space | Control + Shift + N |
| Thin space | Control + Shift + T |
| Fixed space | Control + spacebar |
| Bullet | Control + Shift + 8 |
| Center text | Control + C |

*Appendix A - Keyboard Shortcuts*

Left align text ..................................................... Control + l
Right align text ................................................... Control + r
Justify text ......................................................... Control + j

## Adjusting Text Selection

Move to beginning of line .............................. 7 (home)
Move to end of line .......................................... 1 (end)
Move to beginning of sentence ..................... Control + 7 (home)
Move to end of sentence ................................ Control + 1 (end)
Move left a character ...................................... 4 (left arrow)
Move right a character ................................... 6 (right arrow)
Move left a word .............................................. Control + 4 (left arrow)
Move right a word ........................................... Control + 6 (right arrow)
Move up a line .................................................. 8 (up arrow)
Move down a line ............................................ 2 (down arrow)
Move up a paragraph ...................................... Control + 8 (up arrow)
Move down a paragraph ................................ Control + 2 (down arrow)

# About the Authors

**Tony Webster**               **David Webster**

**Tony Webster** has worked in the computer industry for over twenty years, and in the publishing industry for over ten. He is the author of the popular book *Microcomputer Buyer's Guide* and was the winner of the 1986 McGraw-Hill award for Distinguished Achievement in New Product Development for his work in publishing.

**David Webster** is currently the Training Manager at Webster & Associates. His experience and enthusiasm is one of the factors behind the success of the company. He is very involved in the training and development of desktop publishing materials and is also a contributing editor to the *Australian Desktop Publishing* Magazine.

# Index

## A
actual size command   36
alignment   135, 137–8
Arts & Letters   50, 221
AutoCAD   221
autoflow command   58, 94

## B
bit-map graphics   220
bring to front command   187

## C
cancel button   19
clear command   98
close command   38
color
  applying   421
  creating   415
  CMYK   418
  editing   420
  HLS   418
  palette—see color
    palette
  printing—see printing
  RGB   417
color palette   26–7, 413–414
column guides command   84, 86, 279
command shortcuts   17, Appendix A
control panel   48, 332

copy command   124, 184
copy master guides command   285
Corel Headline   50–1, 58, 221–2
cut command   124, 184, 314

## D
defaults
  application   397
  graphics   399, 196
  publication   398
define colors command   413, 415, 421
define styles command   357, 364, 367, 369, 371
delete key   118, 121, 314
dialog box   18
display master items command   284

## E
edit menu   15, 38, 98, 184, 195
EPSF   51, 58, 221, 223, 259
exit command   39
export command   151

## F
file menu   15–7
fit in window view   34
fifty percent size view   36
fonts   128, 131

441

full Windows   41

## G

grabber hand   34
graphics
  creating   176, 220
  cropping   234
  editing   184
  image control—see image
     control
  importing   222
  keeping aspect ratio   197
  moving   182, 226
  multiple   195
  resizing   183, 230
  wraparounds   197, 227, 252
  tools—see toolbox
gray levels   260
guides
  column—see column guides
  commands—see lock guides,
     guides command, snap to
     guides
  margin—see margins
  ruler—see ruler guides
guides command   88

## H

headers and footers   281
hyphenation   134

## I

image control command   259
indents/tabs command   138

## K

kerning   134

## L

leading   129
lines menu   15, 180, 189, 196, 399
loading files   52
lock guides command   89
Lotus 1-2-3   221

## M

margins   22, 29, 87
master page
  guides   279
  headers and footers—see
     headers and footers
  page number icons   278
  page numbering   281–3
measurement units   37
menu commands   16
menus   15
Microsoft Word   50, 355, 373
mouse cursor   58, 223

## N

new command   20, 304

## O

open command   308
options menu   15, 60, 84, 90, 189

## P

page menu   15, 35
page number icons   28, 278
page numbering   281
page orientation   21, 336

page setup command   23, 278, 282
page size   21
page views   34
paragraph command   135, 143
paste command   124, 184
pasteboard   29, 150
place command   52, 223, 310, 374
preferences command   37, 90, 190
print command   339
printing
  color separations   341
  crop marks   342
  number of copies   340
  scaling   341
  tiling   342
  to a file   344
Publisher's Paintbrush   220

# R

rounded corners command   189
ruler guides   193
rulers command   30, 190
run-time Windows   43

# S

save command   306
save as command   306
scroll bars   31
select all command   124
send to back command   187
seventy-five percent size   36
shades menu   15, 179, 181, 196
snap to guides command   88
spacing command   142
style palette   26, 355
style
  applying   362
  copying   371
  creating   357
  editing   365
  palette—see style palette
  removing   367
system menu—see Windows menu

# T

templates
  creating   304
  editing   310
  opening   308
  placeholders   310
  using—see Module 9
text blocks
  moving   79
  multiple   92
  removing   98
  resizing   81
text editing
  changing alignment   135–141
  changing font   127
  creating text files   146
  editing files   116
  exporting text   151
text wrap command   227, 252
TIFF   59, 222
title bar   23
toolbox   24, 177
two hundred percent size   37
type menu   15, 125, 127
type specs command   127

# U

undo command   38

## W

Windows   40
windowshade handle   78–9, 81
Windows Draw   50, 221
Windows Menu   39, 47–8
Windows Paint   50, 220
Windows Write   42
word processors   80, 117, 373

## Z

zero lock command   192

# More Management and Business Resources from M&T Books

## Public-Domain Software and Shareware, Second Edition

by Rusel DeMaria and George R. Fontaine

Why pay $150 or $300 for software when you can buy a comparable package for only $15 or $30? This book critically reviews the public-domain and Shareware gems that are available, and provides all the information you'll need on how and where to find them. The new 498-page second edition contains twice as many program reviews with expanded software categories. You'll find accounting, database, graphics, and entertainment software, as well as editors, utilities, DOS shells, desk managers, menu programs, and much more. Sample public-domain programs are available on disk.

*Book & Disk (MS-DOS)*  *Item #014-1*  *$34.95*
*Book only*  *Item #011-7*  *$19.95*

## Building Local Area Networks with Novell's Netware

by Patrick H. Corrigan and Aisling Guy

***Building Local Area Networks*** is a practical guide to selecting and installing PC local area networks (LANS). The specifics of building and maintaining PC LANs, including selection criteria, cabling, installation, and on-going management are described in a clear, concise, step-by-step manner. This book is designed to help you make effective and informed LAN planning, purchasing, and operating decisions.

*Book & Disk (MS-DOS)*  *Item #025-7*  *$39.95*
*Book only*  *Item #010-9*  *$24.95*

# More Resources ...

## PC Accounting Solutions

by the Editors of *PC Accounting* (formerly *Business Software*)

*PC Accounting Solutions* is a well-rounded collection of articles written by accounting experts and is an excellent source of information for managers who want to implement a PC-based accounting system or gain better control of their existing system. From choosing and maximizing your accounting systems and software to building better spreadsheets and budgets, you'll find that *PC Accounting Solutions* is an immensely valuable source that will improve your ability to analyze the information that is critical to the success of your business.

Additional topics include choosing and maximizing PC-based accounting systems, generating and using management accounting reports, developing vertical applications and accounting solutions, forecasting with regression analysis, and more.

| | | |
|---|---|---|
| *Book & Disk (MS-DOS)* | *Item #008-7* | *$37.95* |
| *Book only* | *Item #009-5* | *$22.95* |

## SQL for dBASE Programmers

by Edward Dowgiallo

*SQL for dBASE Programmers* provides a detailed introduction to the Structured Query Language (SQL) world. Written specifically for the dBASE programmer, this 450-page book is an invaluable resource that serves as a bridge between dBASE and SQL. Chapter topics discussed in detail include the anatomy of the SQL language, facilities for constructing database structures, an advanced discussion of database views, set manipulation aspects, overview of SQL implementations, SQL kernels, application generators, multiple-user environments, SQL and SAA, and more!

*SQL for dBASE Programmers* is the reference you need to make design decisions. It will provide the information required to make your next project a success.

| | | |
|---|---|---|
| *Book & Disk (MS-DOS)* | *Item #035-4* | *$39.95* |
| *Book only* | *Item #034-6* | *$24.95* |

# More Resources ...

### PageMaker 3 by Example

by Tony Webster and David Webster

*PageMaker 3 by Example* is an excellent, hands-on tutorial designed to make this versatile program easy to understand and use. Its contents and approach are based on over 1,000 hours of training users on desktop publishing.

The book is broken up into modules, with each progressive module covering more detailed operations of PageMaker. Each module contains an information section designed to introduce and outline the associated concepts. Provided are numerous examples of how different concepts are utilized. By making use of these exercises and screen illustrations, the learning process is reinforced. Topics include loading files, manipulating PageMaker text blocks, text editing, internal graphics, advanced picture formatting, templates, setting defaults, printing, and much more. *PageMaker 3 by Example* is available for both the Macintosh and IBM PC compatibles.

| | | |
|---|---|---|
| **Book  (PC version)** | Item #050-8 | $22.95 |
| **Book  (Macintosh version)** | Item #049-4 | $22.95 |

---

**To Order:** Return this form with your payment to: **M&T Books**, 501 Galveston Drive, Redwood City, CA 94063 or **CALL TOLL-FREE 1-800-533-4372** Mon-Fri 8AM-5PM Pacific Standard Time (in California, call 1-800-356-2002).

❏ **YES!** Please send me the following:      ❏ Check enclosed, payable to **M&T Books**.

| Item# | Description | Disk | Price |
|---|---|---|---|
| | | | |
| | | | |
| | | | |
| | | | |

Charge my  ❏ Visa  ❏ MC  ❏ AmEx
Card No. _____
Exp. Date _____
Signature _____

Name _____
Address _____
City _____

Subtotal _____
CA residents add sales tax ___ % _____
Add $2.99 per item for shipping and handling _____
TOTAL _____

State _____ Zip _____

7030

**M&T BOOKS**